Affective Artificial Intelligence

Scrivener Publishing
100 Cummings Center, Suite 541J
Beverly, MA 01915-6106

Leading-Edge Breakthroughs in Artificial Intelligence

Series Editor: Dr. S. Balamurugan (sbnbala@gmail)

The world is on the cusp of several breakthroughs in artificial intelligence (AI), rapidly transforming industries and the research field. The "Leading-Edge Breakthroughs in Artificial Intelligence" book series is dedicated to exploring the most pioneering developments in artificial intelligence. The series aims to highlight both theoretical and practical advancements, offering insights into several cutting-edge advancements in AI and how the same could be deployed to solve complex problems in fields such as healthcare, finance, manufacturing, robotics, marketing, energy management, agriculture, autonomous systems, and many more. It also addresses critical issues like AI governance, ethics, trust, security, transparency, and societal impacts, making it an essential resource for researchers, engineers, and industry leaders looking to leverage AI for future breakthroughs.

Publishers at Scrivener
Martin Scrivener (martin@scrivenerpublishing.com)
Phillip Carmical (pcarmical@scrivenerpublishing.com)

Affective Artificial Intelligence

Fundamentals, Challenges, and Applications

Edited by

N. Thillaiarasu

School of Computing and Information Technology, REVA University, Bengaluru, India

G. Revathy

Department of CSE, Srinivasa Ramanujan Centre, SASTRA Deemed to be University, Kumbakonam, Tamil Nadu, India

T. Saravanan

GITAM School of Technology, GITAM (Deemed to be University), Bengaluru, India

V. Muthukumaran

Dept. of Mathematics, College of Engineering and Technology, SRM Institute of Science and Technology, Kattankulathur Campus, Tamil Nadu, India

and

S. Balamurugan

Intelligent Research Consultancy Services, Coimbatore, Tamil Nadu, India

Scrivener Publishing

WILEY

This edition first published 2026 by John Wiley & Sons, Inc., 111 River Street, Hoboken, NJ 07030, USA and Scrivener Publishing LLC, 100 Cummings Center, Suite 541J, Beverly, MA 01915, USA

For more information about Scrivener publications please visit www.scrivenerpublishing.com.

Wiley Global Headquarters
111 River Street, Hoboken, NJ 07030, USA

For details of our global editorial offices, customer services, and more information about Wiley products visit us at www.wiley.com.

The manufacturer's authorized representative according to the EU General Product Safety Regulation is Wiley-VCH GmbH, Boschstr. 12, 69469 Weinheim, Germany, e-mail: Product_Safety@wiley.com.

Library of Congress Cataloging-in-Publication Data

ISBN 978-1-394-42272-2

Cover image: Generated by Adobe Firefly
Cover design by Russell Richardson

Set in size of 11pt and Minion Pro by Manila Typesetting Company, Makati, Philippines

Printed in the USA

10 9 8 7 6 5 4 3 2 1

Dedicated to

The Almighty, our parents, our spouses, and our children

Contents

Series Preface

This book explores the principles, technological foundations, and practical applications of AI systems that can comprehend, interpret, and respond to human emotions, while highlighting the significant challenges and emerging opportunities. The material within addresses one of the most transformative frontiers of AI, where machines utilize human emotion in communicative contexts to bridge the chasm between people and technology. The content encompasses the scientific foundations, technological apparatus, ethical considerations, and broad applications in sectors such as healthcare, education, marketing, and human–robot interaction, and offers predictions for this emergent phase. This book belongs in the *Leading Edge Breakthroughs in Artificial Intelligence* series because it focuses on cutting-edge advancements that push AI beyond logic and computation toward emotional intelligence, which is essential to creating empathetic, adaptive, and human-centric AI systems for complex social environments.

Dr. S. Balamurugan
Director, Intelligent Research Consultancy Services, Coimbatore, Tamil Nadu, India
Series Editor - Leading Edge Breakthroughs in Artificial Intelligence

Preface

This book explores the emerging field of AI systems that not only recognize emotions but also understand, process, and respond to them in meaningful ways. It begins by introducing Affective AI, showing how it goes beyond traditional logic-based systems to those attuned to human emotions, interactions, and psychological states, and emphasizing its potential to create more natural, empathetic, and intuitive human-AI interactions.

Next the book examines the technological foundations of Affective AI, including facial expression analysis, speech emotion recognition, and physiological signal processing. These methods enable AI to interpret emotional cues, anticipate needs, and integrate multimodal data for a richer understanding of human states. It also highlights how machine learning and deep learning approaches strengthen emotional intelligence through continuous improvement.

The central chapters focus on real-world applications, from healthcare to customer service, where Affective AI enhances experiences by adapting to emotional contexts. In healthcare, it supports mental health detection, while in entertainment it drives more immersive, personalized content. Case studies demonstrate its ability to transform industries through empathetic, human-centered technologies.

Finally, the book addresses the ethical challenges posed by Affective AI, including emotional manipulation, bias, privacy, and the impact of AI-driven emotional decisions on behavior. Ensuring transparency, fairness, and trust is essential as these systems advance. By the end, readers will understand how Affective AI is reshaping the relationship between humans and machines, offering new opportunities while raising critical ethical questions for the future.

Chapter 1 introduces the fundamental techniques of emotion recognition, covering facial expressions, speech, physiological signals, and multimodal approaches. Chapter 2 explains how Natural Language Processing methods are used to detect emotions in text, with applications in chatbots and social media. Chapter 3 turns to healthcare, showing how edge-based computing supports real-time emotion detection for patient care.

Chapter 4 explores deep learning approaches, including CNNs, RNNs, transformers, and self-supervised learning, and their role in emotion recognition.

Chapter 5 examines how Affective AI can identify early signs of mental health disorders through social media analysis. Chapter 6 presents multimodal systems that combine facial, voice, and physiological data to enhance emotional understanding. Chapter 7 discusses the use of Affective AI with ensemble learning techniques to predict cardiac disease risks, while Chapter 8 highlights its role in diagnosing depression, anxiety, and autism spectrum disorders.

Chapter 9 applies emotionally aware machine learning to medical imaging, demonstrating its use in X-ray fracture classification with interpretable methods. Chapter 10 provides a broad review of computational foundations and real-world applications of Affective AI across industries. Chapter 11 illustrates its use in education, where facial recognition and analytics tools enhance attendance tracking and engagement. Chapter 12 explores neurosymbolic perspectives that combine logic and emotion understanding.

Chapter 13 considers transfer learning, emphasizing both challenges and opportunities for improving emotion recognition models. Chapter 14 addresses explainability and interpretability, focusing on the importance of transparency and trust in Affective AI. Chapter 15 explores the use of EEG signals and spatio-temporal deep learning for real-time recognition of affective states.

N. Thillaiarasu
School of Computing and Information Technology, REVA University, Bengaluru, India
G. Revathy
Department of Computer Science and Engineering, Srinivasa Ramanujan Centre, SASTRA Deemed University, Kumbakonam, Tamil Nadu, India
T. Saravanan
GITAM School of Technology, GITAM (Deemed to be University), Bengaluru, India
V. Muthukumaran
Department of Mathematics, College of Engineering and Technology, SRM Institute of Science and Technology, Kattankulathur Campus, Tamil Nadu, India
S. Balamurugan
Intelligent Research Consultancy Services, Coimbatore, Tamil Nadu, India

Acknowledgement

First, we thank our **Almighty** for enabling use to complete this challenging task.

The preparation of this book was a journey that lasted several months. We wish to express our heartfelt gratitude to our respective organizations, our families, friends, colleagues, and well-wishers for their constant support throughout this endeavor. We extend our gratitude to all the chapter contributors, who allowed us to quote their remarks and work in this book. We also acknowledge the hard work of the authors and their cooperation during the revisions of their chapters. Furthermore, we gratefully recognize the valuable comments of the reviewers, which enabled us to select these chapters from the many we received and to improve their quality. We acknowledge and appreciate the Scrivener Publishing team, especially Martin Scrivener, for their continuous support throughout the entire publication process. Finally, our gratitude goes to the readers, who have given us their trust, and we hope this work guides and inspires them.

N. Thillaiarasu
G. Revathy
T. Saravanan
V. Muthukumaran
S. Balamurugan

Part I

FUNDAMENTALS OF AFFECTIVE AI

1

Emotion Recognition Techniques: Facial Expression Analysis, Speech Emotion Recognition, Physiological Signal Processing, and Multimodal Approaches

Monish L.[1], Shaila S.G.[1], Ramesh Chundi[2]*, Sumana S.G.[2], Shivamma D.[1] and Manjula M.[1]

[1]*School of Engineering, Dayananda Sagar University, Bangalore, India*
[2]*School of Computer Applications, Dayananda Sagar University, Bangalore, India*

Abstract
The field of emotion recognition is progressing very fast and it has great potential in the area of human-computer interaction, affective computing, and psychological assessment. The rapid advances in Artificial Intelligence (AI) have seen minor but continual steps of development in Emotion recognition. The chapter gives a comprehensive look at various techniques of emotion recognition that are majorly concentrated on the four key methods: face expression analysis, speech emotion recognition, physiological signal processing, and multimodal fusion algorithms. The readers will be able to relate to the pioneering technologies that have been leveraged to achieve emotion awareness. A way technology has been used in digital learning to recognize emotions is by using a webcam to track facial expressions through machine learning, deep learning, and computer vision complimented with emotions tagging through facial muscle movements. Whereas the Speech emotion recognition is the second technique which employs acoustic and linguistic features such as tone, pitch, speech rate, and spectral values to make inferences about emotional states. This model relies on the AI and deep architecture to improve the accuracy of the model. The study is also extended to third technique on Physiological signal-based emotion recognition. This is achieved using the signals such as electrocardiogram (ECG), electroencephalograms (EEG), and galvanic skin responses (GSR). An unconscious emotional response is achieved

**Corresponding author*: rameshreddy-bca@dsu.edu.in

N. Thillaiarasu, G. Revathy, T. Saravanan, V. Muthukumaran and S. Balamurugan (eds.) Affective Artificial Intelligence: Fundamentals, Challenges, and Applications, (3–24) © 2026 Scrivener Publishing LLC

using this technique. Advanced AI models such as deep neural networks and hybrid deep learning architectures are used in physiological signal processing and emotion recognition to provide high accuracy. Towards the end the chapter also discusses the multimodal fusion of features extracted from various sources of facial features, vocal speech, and physiological signals to enhance classification accuracy as well as to compensate for all the shortcomings inherent with unimodal systems. This integration enables the multimodal fusion system to be more robust and accurate. Multimodal fusion approaches like early, late, and hybrid methods enhance emotion detection accuracy by leveraging the important information available across various sources. This chapter also discusses the advantages and disadvantages of every technique and problems associated with data acquisition, feature extraction, and optimization processes. It further discusses the revolutionary trends in deep learning methods, real-time emotion recognition models, in the domains like health care, education, and human-computer interaction systems. Case studies demonstrate the influence of AI-driven emotion recognition systems in assisting the mental health monitoring, learning environments to facilitate the design of emotionally intelligent virtual assistants.

Keywords: Facial expression analysis, speech emotion recognition, physiological signal processing, multimodal emotion recognition, affective computing

1.1 Introduction

A basic component of human behavior, emotion influences perception, communication, and decision-making. Understanding and interpreting human emotions is becoming as a major objective in the domains of artificial intelligence (AI), affective computing, and human-computer interaction (HCI) as technology develops toward more intelligent and personalized systems. The machine-learning identification of emotional states from a variety of human signals, including voice patterns, facial expressions, physiological signals, and behavioral cues, is known as Emotion Recognition (ER). The need for emotion recognition in machines has increased in a number of fields. Emotion-aware systems in education can modify the way content is delivered according to how engaged students are. Emotion recognition aids in the diagnosis and tracking of mental health issues in the medical field. Safety in the automotive industry can be improved by identifying driver fatigue or distress. Other domains like advertisement, entertainment, robotics, and virtual assistant are also seizing the capability of ER to foster a more human-like and more responsive experience. This paper investigates four common emotion recognition methods:

- Facial Expression Analysis (FEA) which is the interpretation of visible muscle movements in the face to show the mouth emotional facial expressions of emotions such as happiness, sadness, anger, and surprise.
- Speech Emotion Recognition (SEA) involves the extraction of voice features e.g. tone, pitch, and rhythm for emotional status classification.
- Physiological Signal Processing (PEA) includes the analysis of bio signals (such as EEG, ECG and GSR) to recognize the user's internal emotional state (the internal emotional response).

Multimodal Emotion Recognition, where face and voice must be used together for more accurate and robust recognition. Any of these techniques have strengths and weaknesses, specific to implementation, datasets used, real-time performance, and ethical issues. This paper provides a detailed description of those approaches, the tools and datasets used, examples of real-world applications, limitations and future research directions to overcome these challenges.

1.2 Related Study

The study of emotion recognition has matured and grown in the past several decades by borrowing knowledge from psychology, neuroscience, signal processing and machine learning. In the first stage studies were mostly theoretical, however, with advancements in technology, work in this field has moved on and expanded to practical applications for different modalities. Zeng *et al.* [1] includes a holistic review of affect recognition from audio, visual, and spontaneous expressions, incorporating methodologies such as facial expression analysis, speech features, and multimodal fusion. Advances in feature extraction and temporal modeling in naturalistic settings are highlighted with an emphasis on the need for spontaneous data and adaptability to real-world scenarios. Performance improves significantly for constrained settings but shows pitfalls towards a holistic but natural environment-the lack of robustness in such scenarios-and in modality-specific input integration. El Ayadi *et al.* [2] surveyed speech emotion recognition (SER), covering acoustic feature types (prosodic, spectral, and voice quality), classification techniques (HMMs, SVMs, GMMs), and databases. It finds that fusion of features and hybrid classifiers yield better emotion recognition performance. However, results vary significantly across databases due to speaker dependency and mismatched recording conditions, making generalization a key limitation. Picard [3] exemplary book opens up the area of affective computing that poses a new class of systems to be able to recognize, interpret, and simulate human emotions. The book establishes basic concepts for emotional modeling in human-computer interaction and puts forth the possibility of wearable and physiological sensing. Though visionary, the work is conceptual and restricted by experimental validation at that time. Zhao & Pietikäinen [4] proposed the use of Local Binary Patterns from Three Orthogonal Planes (LBP-TOP) for dynamic texture recognition, applied to facial expression analysis. It shows high accuracy in recognizing micro-expressions in video sequences. However, its performance drops in low-light or occluded conditions, and its dependency on controlled datasets limits real-world usability. Calvo & D'Mello [5] categorized affect detection models, techniques, and applications into education, health, and intelligent systems. The model synthesizes psychological theories with computational methods like Bayesian networks and affective state modeling. Although the authors frame a good theoretical framework, there are some limitations regarding model scalability and the lack of standard evaluation metrics. Jafari *et al.* [6] investigated the influence of fine-grained emotions on detecting implicit hate speech, using emotion-enhanced NLP models. Their deep learning model outperforms traditional models in nuanced hate detection. However, interpretability of fine-grained emotion contribution remains a limitation, along with cultural variability in emotion expression. Shaila *et al.* [7] discussed face emotion recognition through attention to nose features based on a pyramid-structured geometry variation extraction. The technique holds promise in recognizing basic emotions with less-studied facial regions and moderate accuracy. The limitation of only using the nose area for holistic analysis and inability to deal with occlusion or dynamic expressions makes the model weak. Shaila *et al.* [8] proposed a deep learning-based MobileNet model for recognizing compound emotions—emotions consisting of two or more basic emotions—through facial expression analysis. The light-weight model facilitates real-time implementation with reasonable performance on compound emotion datasets. Nevertheless, the main drawback is the absence of large-scale, labeled compound emotion datasets, influencing model robustness and generalizability. Shaila *et al.* [9] proposed a deep learning model based on EEG signals for emotion detection, recording brainwave patterns to classify user emotion. The model detects emotional states with satisfactory performance and has potential applications in HCI and mental health monitoring. The limitation lies in its reliance on EEG devices that are not always portable or user-friendly, nor do they perform consistently over individual differences. Monish *et al.* [10] proposed a real-time emotion prediction model based on crowd images or video using a deep neural network. It is designed to capture collective crowd emotions for use in public safety and event management. Results indicate efficient group emotion prediction in controlled environments. The performance of the system decreases with occlusions, non-uniform camera angles, and absence of individual-level granularity.

Hulipalled *et al.* [11] reviewed current automated models of stock market forecasting that range from conventional statistical models to contemporary AI approaches such as neural networks and reinforcement learning. This paper presents comparative performances and categorizes deep learning-based models to have improved adjustability in highly unpredictable market environments. The paper, however, admits that most models are still hampered by unpredictability and practical use in real-life because they are prone to overfitting and are not explainable. Revathy, *et al.* [12] proposed a secure e-voting framework that integrates CNN-based face recognition for voter authentication to prevent impersonation and electoral fraud. The system demonstrates reliable performance in accurately verifying voters under real-world conditions. Tang *et al.* [13] examined cross-modal semantic emotion equivalence across visual and auditory modalities using Chinese emotion-label words. The results reveal perceptual mismatches between modalities, challenging the assumption of shared semantic affect. While insightful for cross-modal research, it's limited by language specificity and stimulus complexity. Sweeney-Fanelli & Imtiaz [14] presented a temporal convolutional neural network (TCN) model for machine-based emotion identification from ECG signals. The TCN model excels over conventional ML approaches in terms of temporal modeling performance and emotion classification accuracy. ECG signal sensitivity and absence of large, labeled datasets limit its wider applicability. Tokmak *et al.* [15] discussed AI-based techniques for emotion recognition based on ECG, concentrating on feature extraction, neural networks, and hybrid models. The authors establish feasibility in health monitoring scenarios. Model overfitting, data imbalance, and absence of cross-subject validation are some of the limitations. Turchet *et al.* [16] analyzed emotions of musicians using a multimodal setup involving EEG, ECG, and acoustic features during live performance. Results show that combining physiological and acoustic data enhances emotion classification. Limitations include synchronization challenges and the complexity of real-time data acquisition during performance. Govarthan *et al.* [17] explored emotion classification using ECG and ML, comparing different windowing techniques on classification accuracy. The study finds that optimal windowing significantly impacts feature quality and model performance. Its main limitation lies in generalizing results across individuals and emotion types due to physiological variability. Chundi *et al.* [18] offered a systematic overview of artificial intelligence (AI) and computer vision technology applications in diabetes detection and management. It discusses image-based diagnostics, wearable monitors, and predictive analytics with enhanced early detection accuracy. The research finds promising deep learning models but highlights limitations such as inadequate clinical validation, issues of generalization between populations, and the necessity of extensive, diversified databases to prevent bias

- **Cross-Cultural and Context-Aware Emotion Recognition:** Although initial theories such as Ekman's one had the universality of facial expressions as their main idea, some comparative studies have proved that the context and the culture have an influence on the emotional judgment. As a matter of fact, it has been observed that cultural norms determine the way in which people show and read emotions. As a result, it is essential that the databases and the related models reflect the ethnic and socio-cultural diversity. On the other hand, context-aware systems that are the systems, which are capable of utilizing situation-based cues or are rich in semantics, can be used to enhance the accuracy of the emotion prediction, especially in cases of ambivalent or slight emotional states. The research work where datasets with context-based information and attentional mechanisms were applied revealed the increasing efficiency of recognition, particularly in real-life environments characterized by emotional cues that are typically heterogeneous.
- **Emotion Recognition Systems that are Real-Time and Edge-Based:** Before, people mainly focus on ubiquitous computing but the most recent research has moved into real-time emotion recognition in small devices where the resources are limited such as smartphones, wearables and edge AI hardware. These systems have to be able to do the requested job quickly and with the manipulation of models they operate in

a smart way on cloud infrastructure too. Then, there are certain techniques, like model pruning, quantization, etc., that are quite useful in running deep learning models on edge devices with a little, or sometimes no decrease in accuracy. The said applications are easy of reach with the help of a few samples to track emotions, detect the sleep of the driver, and make the virtual alike intelligent. Datasets like EmotiW and DAiSEE are empowering this aspect of the research that is all about the deployment of the least demanding real-time inference on very unlikely environments.

1.3 Facial Expression Analysis for Emotion Recognition

Facial Expression Analysis (FEA) is one of the most spontaneous and robust approaches to recognize human expressions. Our faces are the tools for expression, capable of expressing happiness, anger, surprise, and an infinite range of emotions without our having to say a word. We already knew that we can learn emotions from facial expressions. In the age of advanced technology, the ability to decode them using machines also grew. In the beginning, computers used manually shaped rules and features, to recognize emotions. With technology came the possibility to decode these expressions using machines. In the beginning, computers had used manual strategies to detect emotions like rule development and feature crafting. And in the end, the real breakthrough was the emergence of machine learning, and specifically deep learning. Today, 'Convolutional Neural Networks (CNNs)- powered' algorithms can look through thousands of face images and observe complex patterns which correlate with emotions — without the need for any manual coding. These models have been trained to recognize on datasets such as FER2013, CK+, and Affect Net which is a wide range of emotions across diverse populations. For the task of interpreting facial expressions, facial emotion recognition is achieved through facial landmark tracking tools such as Open Face, Dlib, and Media Pipe, and commercial analysis platforms like Face Reader and emotions. Custom model training is also supported by deep learning frameworks such as TensorFlow and PyTorch for experimental purposes. These are being applied across the board — health systems use them to identify signs of depression or pain, automobile companies embed them in car seats to monitor whether the driver is falling asleep, and e-learning platforms customize lessons based on students' attention ERRR levels. Popular projects such as Affective acquired (MIT Media Lab spinoff), [19] Microsoft's Emotion API and Apple acquiring Emotion have helped popularize facial expression recognition. Even with its success, the technology has some limitations. It can have a hard time in low light, with covered faces (think masks or glasses) or subtle and culturally complex expressions. There are also the big ethical questions — of protecting users' privacy, and avoiding algorithmic bias, particularly when those models are trained on skewed data sets. FEA has tremendously improved the accuracy, response time and flexibility of emotion recognition techniques in diverse application domains. It is based on earlier research such as Paul Ekman's Facial Action Coding System (FACS), and uses advanced deep learning technology, including Convolutional Neural Networks (CNNs), to analyze facial expressions in both static images and live video. Adversarial training has recently been extended to semi-supervised learning with unlabeled data to improve generalization and lightweight models such as MobileNetV3 make it possible to perform in-device real-time emotion Recognition. Encrypt and encrypt and encrypt and encrypt on mobile devices. Notably, projects like Affective and Microsoft's Emotion API have demonstrated the practical use of emotion detection in the wild. Additionally, emerging areas such as micro-expression recognition and few-shot learning are helping address the challenges of subtle emotion detection and data scarcity. Meanwhile, real-world applications are expanding—from monitoring driver alertness to analyzing public figures' expressions during economic announcements. But scholars have also raised ethical questions regarding bias, privacy, and the vagueness of emotional signals, calling for more balanced data sets, transparent algorithms, and strong privacy protections. These advances represent a twin aim of advancing technology's capabilities while ensuring responsible and inclusive use of facial emotion recognition systems. In the future, researchers will develop solutions such as 3D face modeling and lightweight real-time models, as well as cross-cultural training data sets, to achieve robust and fair systems. Given the expansion that emotion-aware technology is making, FEA will be a big contributor to making machines more responsive, more empathetic and more human-like in how interact with us.

Figure 1.1 illustrates an architecture for emotion recognition using facial expressions [20]. In the pre-processing step, facial regions are detected and lighting effects are reduced. The feature extraction module then converts the face into a symbol sequence. During the training stage, these sequences along with labels are used to train Hidden Markov Models (HMMs). In the recognition stage, the extracted features from a new input are compared

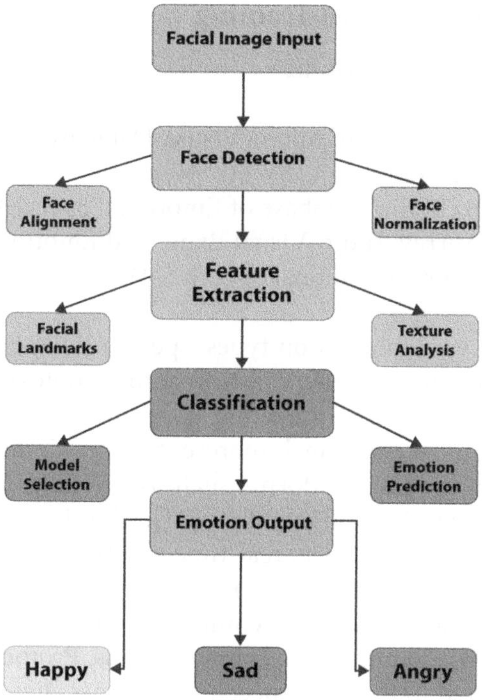

Figure 1.1 Facial expression analysis architecture.

against the trained HMMs to output the corresponding emotion labels. This architecture emphasizes sequential modeling of facial expressions over time.

1.4 Speech Emotion Recognition (SER) for Emotion Recognition

Speech Emotion Recognition (SER) is a vital component of affective computing that focuses on identifying human emotions using vocal characteristics. Human speech carries both linguistic and paralinguistic information. While the former conveys literal meaning, the latter—comprising tone, pitch, speed, and intensity—reveals the speaker's emotional state. SER systems analyze these features to classify emotions such as happiness, sadness, anger, fear, disgust, and neutrality, enabling machines to interpret and respond to users more naturally.

1.4.1 Datasets and Model Training

Commonly used datasets include:

- RAVDESS (Ryerson Audio-Visual Database of Emotional Speech and Song)
- EMO-DB (Berlin Database of Emotional Speech)
- SAVEE (Surrey Audio-Visual Expressed Emotion)
- TESS (Toronto Emotional Speech Set)

These datasets vary in emotion types, speaker demographics, and language, allowing for broad generalization across contexts. Data augmentation and transfer learning are often applied to compensate for class imbalance or limited emotional representation. Modern SER systems leverage cloud computing platforms such as AWS, Microsoft Azure, or Google Cloud for training and inference [21]. Cloud services offer scalable resources for model deployment, real-time emotion detection, and secure data storage. For latency-sensitive applications—such as in-car voice assistants or mobile health tools—edge computing enables on-device processing, reducing delay and improving responsiveness. Protocols like WebRTC and MQTT are used to transmit speech data across client-cloud networks efficiently and reliably.

1.4.2 Challenges and Future Directions

Challenges in SER include speaker variability, ambient noise, cultural diversity in emotional expression, and the lack of context-aware modeling. Additionally, real-world speech is often spontaneous and unbalanced across emotions, complicating model training. Emerging trends such as self-supervised learning, cross-lingual SER, and multimodal fusion (combining speech, facial expressions, and physiological data) are being explored to overcome these limitations. Figure 1.2 depicts the speech emotion recognition process. It starts with preprocessing the speech signal (e.g., noise reduction), then extracts features like MFCC, pitch, and energy, and finally classifies emotions using models like SVM or CNN. The output identifies emotions such as Happy, Surprised, or Sad [22].

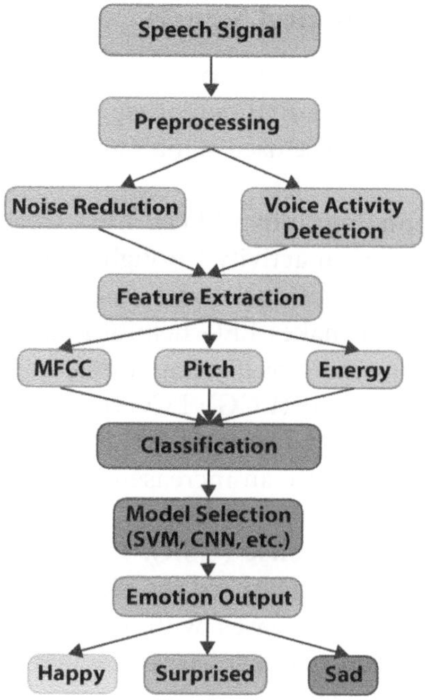

Figure 1.2 Speech emotion recognition architecture.

1.5 Physiological Signal Processing for Emotion Recognition

Emotions are observed through facial expressions or speech; they also cause internal changes in the body that are not always visible. These internal responses are heart rate, skin conductivity, and brain activity which can be captured using physiological signals. Physiological signal processing involves analyzing these signals to detect emotional states such as stress, calmness, excitement, or anxiety. This method is useful because these signals are usually harder to fake, making them more reliable. Sensors in wearable devices are used to collect the data, and there are various algorithms which help in identifying patterns that link to specific emotions [23]. This approach enhances emotion recognition systems and is most helpful in areas like mental health tracking, human-computer interaction, and smart environments.

1.5.1 Types of Physiological Signals

Physiological signal processing relies on many types of bio-signals for emotion recognition; each reflects on different aspects of the body's response to emotional stimuli. Some of the used signals are:

- **Electroencephalography (EEG):** EEG works by detecting the brain's electrical activity through sensors placed on the head. Different emotional states cause unique patterns in brain waves that makes EEG helpful and useful signals for understanding emotions like happiness, fear, sadness.
- **Electrocardiography (ECG):** ECG tracks the heart's electrical signals. Emotional states affect heart rate and rhythm, like anxiety may cause an increased heart rate, while calmness is related to a steady pattern.
- **Galvanic Skin Response (GSR):** It is also known as skin conductance. GSR measures the skin's ability to conduct electricity which increases with increase in sweat gland activity. Emotions like fear, stress, excitement cause higher skin conductance levels.
- **Respiration Rate:** Breathing patterns change with emotions. Deep, slow breathing suggest relaxation while rapid, shallow breaths point to stress or panic.
- **Electromyography (EMG):** EMG measures muscle activity and it is used to observe slight muscle movements or tension that happens in facial muscles during emotional responses.

Before any emotional analysis to be performed, it's necessary to first collect and clean the physiological signals. This first step is known as signal acquisition and plays a major role in how accurate the final results are. If the data picked up by sensors is unclear, then it becomes much harder for the system to identify what emotions are being felt. Different sensors are used to gather data depending on signal type. For example, EEG sensors are placed on top of the head using a headset, while ECG sensors are attached to the chest or the wrists to monitor heart function. GSR sensors are attached on the fingers or palms. But the raw data includes unwanted noise from body movements, external interference, or hardware limitations. To handle this, preprocessing is used. It works by cleaning signals through filtering out noise, removing artifacts, normalizing the data, and breaking the data into meaningful time segments. This step ensures that the next phases, like feature extraction and emotion detection can run smoothly and give reliable results.

1.5.2 Feature Extraction and Emotion Mapping

After cleaning and preprocessing of signals, the next step is to know which parts of the data are useful for detecting emotions. This step is called feature extraction and it focuses on identifying patterns in the physiological signals that show different emotional states. These patterns are then used as inputs for machine learning models to classify emotions. For example, EEG signals come from the brain and show how active certain regions are during emotional states. Different brainwave frequencies like alpha, beta and gamma waves are observed, while more alpha waves might suggest a calm or relaxed state. EEG is mainly useful because its features like power spectral density or wavelet coefficients help to identify these brain activities. If someone is stressed, beta waves become more prominent. But a relaxed person shows more alpha wave activity. EEG is powerful because it directly reflects how the brain responds to different emotional factors. In ECG signals, the main focus is on the heart's activity. Emotions can affect how fast or regular the heart beats. Some useful things include heart rate variability (HRV), the time between heartbeats (RR intervals), and the shape of the heart's electrical signals. Example, if someone is stressed, HRV gets decreased, while in a calm state, the heartbeat is regular. These changes are small and hard to see without tools but machines can easily find and use them to know what emotion a person is feeling. After all features are extracted, they are sent to classification algorithms. These algorithms include machine learning techniques like Support Vector Machines (SVM), Random Forests, or K-Nearest Neighbors (KNN) and deep learning techniques like Convolutional Neural Networks (CNNs). The model to be chosen depends on how much data is there and how accurate or fast the system is needed. The advantages of using physiological signals for emotion recognition are that they do not rely on controllable actions. While facial expressions or speech can be controlled consciously or faked, signals from the brain and heart happen automatically. This makes physiological signals a dependable source of emotional data and mainly when visual or audio signals are missing or misleading. As these signals can be collected continuously, so they are great for real-time tracking in long-term monitoring setups.

1.5.3 Challenges and Future Directions

The method is useful but it also has some problems. It is not easy to understand what the signals are trying to point to, and same signal can point to different emotions for different people or in different situations. Wearing too many sensors can be uncomfortable, especially for long periods. Things like how the sensors are placed or small movements can disturb the data. Because of this, the signals have to be cleaned well before being used. It also helps a lot if we have a big set of examples to train the system properly. Even with these issues, using body signals to understand emotions can be very helpful. It can be used in mental health care, smart devices, or games. Example, if someone is feeling stressed, the system can try to help to calm down by changing the lights or music. In hospitals, it can help doctors to know how a patient is feeling, if the patient cannot say it. Figure 1.3 shows how emotions are recognized using signals from the body like ECG (heart) and EEG (brain). First, the signals are collected by using sensors. Then, the signals go through a cleaning process (preprocessing) to remove noise. Next, important details are extracted (feature extraction), like changes in

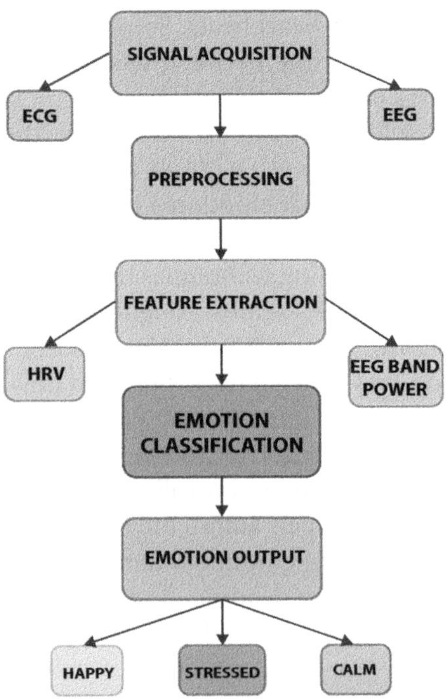

Figure 1.3 Physiological signal-based emotion recognition architecture.

heart rate or brain wave patterns. These features are then sent to a system (emotion classification) that determines what emotion the person is feeling. At last, the system gives the result — for example, whether the person is happy, stressed, or calm.

1.6 Multimodal Emotion Recognition

The use of emotional identification techniques has sparked great interest due to its ability to improve interactions between humans and computers. This technology has a variety of signals that can distinguish emotions. However, the implementation of such techniques in the real world is associated with many complications that need to be evaluated. Facial analysis records and evaluates movements to recognize underlying emotions using a computer. This is one of the most popular methods. This method works in a laboratory environment, but it turns out to be less accurate in this area as it doesn't take into account culture, lighting, or unique adjustments that are personal. In some cultures, smiles can be seen as a sign of happiness, while others show polite expressions. Furthermore, the use of poor lighting and headgear and make-up makes it difficult to analyze clarity due to the filling. This is the sound, pitch, and rhythm. However, understanding background noise, accents and speech poses a variety of challenges. For example, an increase in tone may mean anger in a given context, but it can reflect excitement in other contexts. These subtleties in context can make emotion detection very complicated. It provides a wider range of information, but often requires special devices, but is susceptible to non-emotional factors and is complicated to interpret. To illustrate, an increase in heart rate may be the result of physical exercise rather than emotional stimulation. Multimodal emotion detection is a combination with several data records such as facial expressions, voices, and even body language to provide an entire overview of an individual's emotional state. However, addressing the unification and potential conflicts of these various data records is a problem. For example, different signals can correlate with the same emotions, while different modalities can contradict each other. In addition to the expected benefits, the widespread adoption of emotional identification techniques poses serious problems. Data protection questions have priorities. Continuous observation of an individual's emotional state can infringe their rights. The hidden film material case draws great attention to permission and uses collected data. Cultural sensitivity is essential as emotional expressions of cultures are very different and can be interpreted slightly incorrectly. Related measures should be implemented related to ethical considerations such as stopping discrimination and creating and monitoring police profiles. Additionally, data distortions need to be handled. This is due to the non-representative data records used to train these systems. After all, the general reliability of performance technology is controversial and is debated in real life situations.

1.7 Real-Time Issues in Emotion Recognition Systems

Regardless of the progress made, a multitude of obstacles still hinder the simple adoption of systems aiming at recognizing emotions in real-time. Below are five fundamental problems faced during real-time implementation.

1. **Data and Environmental Noise Quality:** One of the most persistent issues in real-time evoked emotion recognition, specifically within speech and physiological signal processing, is advanced noise interference. The uncontrolled environment of streets, offices, and other public places offers background sounds that disturb accurate speech feature extraction. Movement, improper sensor contact, or electromagnetic interference also result in useless artifacts being picked up by physiological sensors. Noisy input invariably reduces model performance and emotion classification inaccuracies arise.
2. **Fluctuations in Occlusion and Lighting:** Analysis of facial expressions is heavily dependent on observing straightforward and direct visual features of the face. During real-time video capture, there can be occlusion (people hiding their faces with hands, the wearing of glasses and masks) along with poor lighting resulting in distortion of facial landmarks. Surveillance cameras or low-resolution webcams, in addition to varying levels of daylight, lead to feature loss and misinterpretation by a computer vision model.
3. **Perceptual Processing Constraints:** For a typical chat-bot or vehicle infotainment system, interaction in real-time is of paramount importance. As such, features need to be extracted and classified in milliseconds, or else their entire interactive flow fails. Such tasks require task-specific and

complicated deep learning models such as CNNs, RNNs or Transformers. These algorithms are notoriously expensive computationally. It is, therefore, impractical to run these models on edge devices and smartphones because they lead to increased latency, diminished battery, thermal throttling, and other usability constraints.

4. **Subject Variability and Generalization:** The cross-cultural, age, gender, and individual psychological differences all cause diverse forms of human emotional expression. Emotion recognition systems require universal adaptability in real-time to avoid bias or emotion labeling mistakes, yet one trained model is unlikely to perform optimally across demographics. Some culturally Anger might be expressed in very minimal ways while other cultures tend to be very expressive. The same applies for physiological responses to fear, where a certain body is excited while another is fearful. These make it extremely difficult for real-time systems to function without deep personal customization.
5. **Fusion Complexity and Failure of Modality:** In systems that recognize emotions through various modes, streams of multi-modal data decomposition into sub-components may induce failures in one or more modalities, causing system breakdown. For example, during a phone call, a speech signal could be missing or a camera could be frozen, leading to incomplete input stream.

Moreover, the real-time synchrony and integration of multi-modal data streams (e.g., video and audio integration with physiologic signals) is a complicated engineering problem. Blending several methods requires exceedingly careful timing; otherwise alignment will cause the system to output predictions of competing emotions which misleads the system causing reduction in confidence.

1.7.1 Solution to the Issues Using Robust Approach

A promising solution to the limitations of individual emotion recognition techniques is the implementation of a multimodal emotion recognition system that integrates facial expression analysis, speech emotion recognition (SER), and physiological signal processing into a unified framework. This approach leverages the complementary strengths of each modality while mitigating their individual weaknesses. The core idea is to extract emotion-relevant features from each modality—such as facial muscle movements *via* Convolutional Neural Networks (CNNs), speech features like pitch and MFCCs *via* Long Short-Term Memory (LSTM) networks, and temporal patterns in physiological signals through 1D-CNNs or BiLSTMs. These extracted features are then fused at the feature level to create a rich, multidimensional representation of the user's emotional state. To handle varying reliability of modalities due to noise, occlusion, or sensor failure, an attention mechanism is employed to dynamically assign importance weights to each modality based on their current quality or relevance. This allows the system to adaptively rely more on speech when the face is partially occluded, or on physiological data when audio is noisy. The fused representation is then passed through a fully connected deep neural classifier to predict the final emotional state. Such a multimodal architecture not only increases robustness and accuracy but also enhances emotion recognition in real-time and uncontrolled environments. Furthermore, deploying this system using a hybrid of edge computing (for initial processing on devices) and cloud computing (for model inference and analytics) ensures both low latency and scalability. This integrated solution creates a more reliable, context-aware, and human-like emotion recognition system suitable for applications in healthcare, education, virtual assistants, and human-robot interaction.

1.8 Future Directions

Emotion recognition is evolving at a fast pace, and the future looks bright and significant. For Facial Expression Analysis, future breakthroughs will be on real-time 3D facial tracking and micro-expression recognition, which can identify even slight, unconscious facial movements indicating true emotions. Enhanced generalizability across cultures and environments, facilitated by AI learning from high-quality, international datasets, will make such systems more accurate and equitable. In the field of Speech Emotion Recognition, there is a well-defined path that will lead to the creation of virtual assistants with higher human emotion awareness and the ability to perform context-rich analysis. With the progress in technology, these systems are expected to become even better at understanding emotions by not just hearing the subtleties of tone and pitch but also by taking into account the semantic meaning of the words, the context in the background, and the prior knowledge about the speaker. In addition, the integration of emotion-aware voice interfaces is expected to greatly improve communication quality in various fields such as healthcare, education, and customer support, resulting in more effective and empathetic communication. In Physiological Signal Processing, we can expect the wearable technology and artificial intelligence to become more and more integrated and seamless in the user experience.

The future devices will be able to monitor and evaluate emotional states in a fully non-intrusive way, offering helpful assistance in stress management, mental health therapy, and the development of personalized experiences based on individual requirements. The trend is also towards the development of multi-sensor fusion, where multiple measures like heart rate, skin conductance, and brain signals are combined to give a more detailed and comprehensive insight into emotional well-being. The most exciting and promising developments in the realm of technology are taking place in the domain called Multimodal Emotion Recognition. Future systems that are created will have the incredible ability to merge different forms of data seamlessly, such as visual inputs, audio signals, text information, and physiological data, in order to read human emotions with much greater precision—much like the way humans naturally read and perceive emotions in other humans. Additionally, these new systems will have the capacity to learn and recognize each user's personal emotional patterns and reactions as they use the system over time. Notably, as this technology continues to advance, privacy and ethics concerns will remain a top priority; thus, it is safe to assume the use of more robust on-device processing power in conjunction with privacy-preserving models to keep user data safe and secure. Generally, the science of emotion recognition is going to be a kind that is more contextual, empathetic, and more personalized. It will change profoundly and take forward the manner in which we will interact and communicate with various technologies—enabling machines to be much more effective at actually being able to know our emotions and sentiments, rather than simply providing us with a response to what we've given them.

1.9 Conclusion

Emotion recognition has become a cornerstone of human-computer interaction, enabling machines to understand and respond to users more naturally. Techniques such as facial expression analysis, speech emotion recognition (SER), and physiological signal processing each offer valuable insights into a user's emotional state. However, each modality faces its own set of challenges—ranging from environmental noise and occlusions to variability in individual physiological responses. While unimodal systems often struggle with real-world inconsistencies, multimodal emotion recognition approaches overcome these limitations by combining the strengths of multiple modalities. By fusing facial, speech, and physiological signals through advanced machine learning architectures—such as hybrid deep learning with attention mechanisms—systems can achieve more accurate, context-aware, and resilient emotion detection. These robust models can dynamically adjust their reliance on different inputs depending on data quality, enhancing performance even in complex environments. As the field progresses, the integration of these techniques into real-time applications across healthcare, education, and affective computing holds transformative potential. Moreover, future advancements must also consider ethical implications, such as privacy and consent, to ensure responsible deployment of emotion-aware systems.

AI disclosure statement: The author acknowledges the use of AI-based tools for minor language editing or grammatical correction. However, all intellectual contributions, analyses, and conclusions presented in this chapter are entirely the author's own.

References

1. Zeng, Z., Pantic, M., Roisman, G.I., Huang, T.S., A Survey of Affect Recognition Methods: Audio, Visual, and Spontaneous Expressions. *IEEE Trans. Pattern Anal. Mach. Intell.*, 126–133, 2009.
2. El Ayadi, M., Kamel, M.S., Karray, F., Survey on Speech Emotion Recognition: Features, Classification Schemes, and Databases. *Pattern Recognit.*, 44, 3, 572–587, 2011.
3. Picard, R.W., *Affective Computing*, MIT Press, 1997.
4. Zhao, G. and Pietikäinen, M., Dynamic Texture Recognition Using Local Binary Patterns with an Application to Facial Expressions. *IEEE Trans. Pattern Anal. Mach. Intell.*, 29, 6, 915–928, 2007.
5. Calvo, R.A. and D'Mello, S., Affect Detection: An Interdisciplinary Review of Models, Methods, and Their Applications. *IEEE Trans. Affective Comput.*, 1, 1, 18–37, 2010.
6. Jafari, A.R., Li, G., Rajapaksha, P., Farahbakhsh, R., Crespi, N., Fine-grained emotions influence on implicit hate speech detection. *IEEE Access, 11*, 105330–105343, 2023.
7. Shaila, S.G., Vadivel, A., Avani, S., Emotion estimation from nose feature using pyramid structure. *Multimed. Tools Appl.*, 82, 27, 42569–42591, 2023. https://doi.org/10.1007/s11042-023-14789-w.

8. Shaila, S.G., Shivamma, D., Monica, U.S., *et al.*, Facial expression recognition for compound emotions using mobile net architecture, in: *International Conference on Artificial Intelligence and Data Engineering*, IEEE, 2022.
9. Shaila, S.G., Sindhu, A., Shivamma, D., *et al.*, Human Emotion Recognition Based on EEG Signal Using Deep Learning Approach, in: *International Conference on Recent Trends in Communication and Intelligent Systems*, Springer, 2023.
10. Monish, L., Shaila, S.G., Sumana, S.G., Uppin, A., *et al.*, Emotion Prediction Based on Real-Time Crowd Analysis Using Deep Network, in: *International Conference on Recent Trends in Communication and Intelligent Systems*, Springer, 2023.
11. Hulipalled, V.R., Simha, J.B., Chundi, R., Intelligent automation in stock market prediction: A survey of automated models, in: *Proceedings of the Fourth International Conference on Smart Technologies in Computing and Communication*, IEEE, 2023.
12. Revathy, G., Raj, K.B., Kumar, A., Adibatti, S., Dahiya, P., Latha, T.M., Investigation of E-voting system using face recognition using convolutional neural network (CNN). *Theor. Comput. Sci.*, *925*, 61–67, 2022.
13. Tang, E., Fan, X., Fang, R., Zhang, Y., Gong, J., Guan, J., Ding, H., Not perceptually equivalent in semantic emotion across visual and auditory modalities: Cross-modal affective norms of two-character Chinese emotion-label words. *Curr. Psychol.*, *43*, 17, 15308–15327, 2024.
14. Sweeney-Fanelli, T.C. and Imtiaz, M.H., ECG-based automated emotion recognition using temporal convolution neural networks. *IEEE Sens. J.*, 24, 18, 29039–29046, 2024.
15. Tokmak, F., Subasi, A., Qaisar, S.M., Artificial intelligence-based emotion recognition using ECG signals, in: *Applications of Artificial Intelligence Healthcare and Biomedicine*, pp. 37–67, Academic Press, 2024, ISBN 9780443223082, https://doi.org/10.1016/B978-0-443-22308-2.00002-0.
16. Turchet, L., O'Sullivan, B., Ortner, R., Guger, C., Emotion recognition of playing musicians from EEG, ECG, and acoustic signals. *IEEE Trans. Hum.-Mach. Syst.*, 54, 5, 619–629, 2024.
17. Govarthan, P.K., Peddapalli, S.K., Ganapathy, N., Ronickom, J.F.A., Emotion classification using electrocardiogram and machine learning: A study on the effect of windowing techniques. *Expert Syst. Appl.*, *254*, 124371, 2024.
18. Chundi, R., Sasikala, G., Basivi, P.K., Tippana, A., Hulipalled, V.R., *et al.*, Exploring diabetes through the lens of AI and computer vision: Methods and future prospects. *Comput. Biol. Med.*, *185*, 109537, 2025. https://doi.org/10.xxxx/j.compbiomed.2025.109537.
19. Chen, K., Gou, Y., Huang, R., Liu, Z., Tan, D., Xu, J., Xu, H., Emova: Empowering language models to see, hear and speak with vivid emotions, in: *Proceedings of the Computer Vision and Pattern Recognition Conference*, pp. 5455–5466, 2025.

20. Alessandro, G., Dimitri, O., Cristina, B., Anna, M., The emotional impact of generative AI: negative emotions and perception of threat. *Behav. Inf. Technol.*, *44*, 4, 676–693, 2025.
21. Ma, S., Wang, Y., Chen, M., Ma, T., Li, W., Chen, Y., Public emotions and the built environment in hazards: A case study of the Shenzhen catastrophic landslide. *Cities*, *160*, 105814, 2025.
22. Dümen, A.S. and Rasmussen, B., Emotions elicited by neighbour noise and coping process: a social media research based on two newspaper articles. *Build. Environ.*, *269*, 112432, 2025.
23. Erbe, R.G., Emotional Integration and Spiritual Formation: Integrating Emotion Into Formation of the Spirit. *J. Spiritual Form. Soul Care*, 19397909241309290, 18, 1, 110–123, 2025.

2

Natural Language Processing for Sentiment and Emotion Analysis – AI-Driven Methods for Detecting the Emotions in Text, Chatbots, and Social Media

Shaila S.G.[1], Monish L.[1], Sumana S.G.[2] and Ramesh Chundi[2]*

[1]School of Engineering, Dayananda Sagar University, Bangalore, India
[2]School of Computer Applications, Dayananda Sagar University, Bangalore, India

Abstract

NLP became a strong subfield of artificial intelligence through the offering of extraction and understanding of human sentiment and emotion through text inputs. As internet communications increased exponentially, emotion and sentiment analysis emerged as an important need in the vast majority of all AI-powered chatbot applications, social media surveillance, and sentiment analysis of consumers in reviews. The capacity to quantify human emotion in an effective manner from text data improves computer–humans communication, customer practices interaction, and offers valuable counsel on the evolution of public opinion. The description of NLP methods applied to emotion detection and text data sentiment orientation determination is completely explained in this chapter. It discusses the contributions of the transformer models like BERT, RoBERTa, and GPT, which have greatly enhanced the accuracy and context awareness of sentiment analysis. Apart from this, traditional machine learning methods and the hybrid methods which combine deep learning with lexicon-based and neuro-fuzzy techniques are also reviewed. These hybrid methods have proven efficient in improving sentiment categorization, especially where there are blended or conflicting sentiments where context relationship becomes crucial. Emotion recognition in NLP involves many problems such as failure to identify sarcasm, uncertainty of context, and cultural difference affecting the expression of sentiment. Better modeling methods and utilization of external sources of information are needed to solve such issues

**Corresponding author*: rameshreddy-bca@dsu.edu.in

N. Thillaiarasu, G. Revathy, T. Saravanan, V. Muthukumaran and S. Balamurugan (eds.) Affective Artificial Intelligence: Fundamentals, Challenges, and Applications, (25–44) © 2026 Scrivener Publishing LLC

to improve interpretability. The chapter also discusses real-world applications in which emotion analysis using NLP is ground-breaking. Virtual assistants using artificial intelligence use sentiment analysis to provide emotionally intelligent answers and enhance the user experience. Sentiment monitoring on social media helps companies monitor public attitudes and stay ahead of reputational risk. In medicine, sentiment analysis assists in diagnosing mental illness by looking for early indications of emotional suffering according to text patterns in patient words. Sentiment analysis and emotion detection are ethical issues that should be examined. Bias in AI models is also a threat because biased training data will result in biased sentiment interpretation and therefore discriminatory or incorrect judgments. Privacy issues also apply in the evaluation of sensitive user-generated content, where robust data privacy controls and ethical AI benchmarks must be implemented. Transparency and equity must be guaranteed within AI-based sentiment analysis systems such that trust and proper deployment to real-world use can be facilitated. Experimental trials and comparison trials on benchmark corpora decide the efficacy of AI-based sentiment and emotion analysis strategies. Experimental verification attests to the superior performance of deep learning models versus conventional methods in detecting subtle sentiments and perceiving delicate linguistic cues. Findings confirm the prospects of sentiment analysis using AI for improving human-computer interactions, decision-making support, and facilitating applications across such broad domains ranging from customer experience management to assessing psychological well-being. The purpose of this chapter is to provide researchers and practitioners with a comprehensive grasp of AI-based sentiment and emotion analysis as the foundation for the construction of more powerful, interpretable, and ethical NLP models. With the progress in NLP and AI, the construction of more advanced sentiment analysis methods will be crucial in an effort to allow more precise and context-sensitive emotion recognition, providing improved insights into human communication and behavior.

Keywords: Natural language processing, sentiment analysis, emotion detection, AI-powered chatbots, transformer models, deep learning, social media, contextual analysis

2.1 Introduction

Natural Language Processing (NLP) is mainly concerned with the automatic identification and classification of tones and opinions within textual data. One area of importance in NLP is sentiment analysis, which has gained much attention due to the meteoric rise of digital communication. Text-based forms of interaction—like posts on social media, reviews submitted to e-commerce websites, or conversations held with chatbots—have become a part of everyday life. AI-based emotion and sentiment analysis relies on an array of deep learning and machine learning methods. While new methods employ deep models capable of discerning context and nuance, traditional methods like Naïve Bayes and Support Vector Machines (SVMs) continue to be applied [1]. Accuracy of emotion detection has been significantly enhanced by transformer-based models like BERT (Bidirectional Encoder Representations from Transformers) and GPT (Generative Pretrained Transformer). These are pre-trained on massive corpora and tuned for tasks so that they can recognize sophisticated emotional expressions even from casual or vague speech. Sentiment analysis usually tags texts as positive, negative, or neutral. Emotion analysis is superior in that it shows actual emotions of surprise, fury, joy, sorrow, or fear. These methods enable companies to track public sentiment, react to customer feedback, and create emotionally intelligent systems. Sentiment and emotion analysis with artificial intelligence is based on a range of deep learning and machine learning techniques. While newer ones employ deep learning models that can understand context and nuance, older methods such as Naïve Bayes and Support Vector Machines (SVMs) remain common. Significantly enhanced emotion detection precision is provided by transformer models like GPT (Generative Pretrained Transform) and BERT (Bidirectional Encoder Representation from Transform). They are pre-trained on enormous corpora and further fine-tuned for tasks so that they can recognize complex emotional expressions even from loose or ambiguous language. Emotion analysis allows chatbots to have more human-like and empathetic conversations. Based on an emotional state of a user, emotionally intelligent chatbots can alter the tone, lift the discussion, or maybe even offer guidance. Emotion analysis software aids businesses on social media in tracking brand sentiment, identifying early crises, and measuring audience response to advertisements or campaigns [2].

In real-time marketing and public relations campaigns, these observations are vital. Most cloud-based systems offer sentiment and emotion analysis *via* their natural language processing (NLP) tools. Businesses typically use Google Cloud Natural Language API, IBM Watson NLU, and Microsoft Azure Text Analytics. Such applications offer emotion scores, sentiment polarity, and even entity-level sentiment analysis. Open-source frameworks like Hugging Face Transformers give developers and researchers further scalability and adaptability by allowing them to build unique models for sentiment and emotion detection. Additionally, increasingly being used in mental health applications is sentiment and emotion analysis. Supporting early intervention programs, AI systems can find signs of emotional suffering in messages or social media posts. In business, emotion detection aids in customer experience management, product feedback analysis, and market research, therefore allowing brands to more accurately meet consumer expectations. Though its development is impeded by sarcasm detection, cultural background variations, and language variations, emotion analysis is also affected. Multilingual and contextual approaches help researchers continue to past obstacles. As artificial intelligence develops, so too becomes the integration of emotion recognition into human-computer interaction increasingly seamless [3]. This shift is causing artificial intelligence systems to be emotionally sensitive as well as intellectually brilliant. Finally, sentiment and emotion analysis driven by NLP is transforming our understanding of human emotion in digital communication. From social media monitoring to chatbots, these machine learning-driven techniques are enabling better, more empathetic interactions at scale. Emotion analysis lets chatbots have more natural and sympathetic interactions. On social media, emotion analysis software assists businesses with tracking brand sentiment, identifying early crises, and determining audience responses to events or campaigns. These insights are crucial in real-time marketing and public relations efforts. Most cloud-based platforms provide sentiment and emotion analysis through their NLP offerings. Google Cloud Natural Language API, IBM Watson NLU, and Microsoft Azure Text Analytics are commonly used in business environments. These instruments offer sentiment polarity, emotional scores, even entity-level analysis of sentiment. Hugging Face Transformers and other open-source models also provide scalability and flexibility so that researchers and developers may create custom models for sentiment and emotional detection. Sentiment and emotion analysis is also being applied more and more in mental health uses [4]. AI platforms can identify indicators of emotional distress in messages or social media posts, supporting early intervention initiatives. In business, emotion detection helps customer experience management, product feedback analysis, and market research, enabling brands to better match consumer expectations. Though its progress, emotion analysis is challenged by sarcasm detection, differences in cultural context, and linguistic variations. Studies persist in overcoming the challenges through multilingual and contextual models. The Figure 2.1 depicts a deep learning–based NLP pipeline wherein raw text documents go through pre-processing to be converted into numerical embeddings. These embeddings are fed through several hidden neural network layers that learn semantic patterns and contextual relations. The model finally produces task-specific outputs like sentiment analysis, classification, entity extraction, translation, or topic modeling, which facilitates sophisticated applications such as emotion detection in digital communication [5].

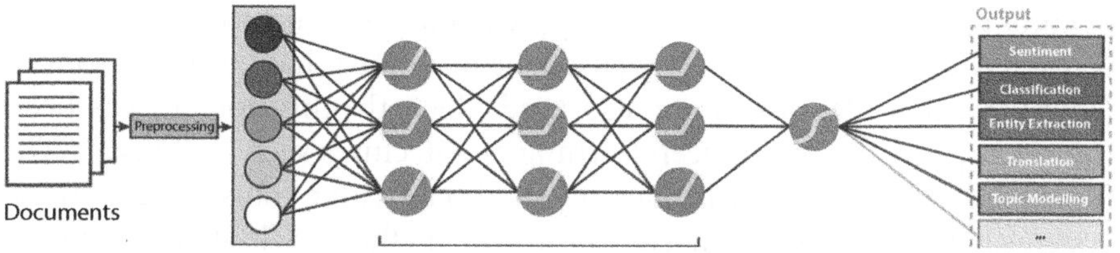

Figure 2.1 Deep learning based NLP for emotion analysis.

2.2 Convergence of Technologies

2.2.1 Natural Language Processing (NLP)-Based Sentiment Analysis

Artificial intelligence utilizes Natural Language Processing (NLP) to facilitate the processing, analysis, and creation of human language by computers through computational algorithms. In order to identify subjective information and emotional tone, natural language processing (NLP) can be used to analyze sentiment and emotion in text. Emotion analysis looks at particular emotions like joy, anger, fear, sadness, and surprise, whereas sentimental analysis of text is usually classified as positive, negative, or neutral. Customer service, mental health, social media monitoring, marketing, and human–computer interaction are all examples of why these methods are important. By breaking down sentences and analyzing grammar, syntax, semantics, context, and context using NLP, computers can mimic human language [6]. This approach is known as machine learning. Tokenization, stemming and lemmatization (restoring word structure), part-of-speech tagging, and dependency parsing are among the core techniques employed in this work. These aid in the conversion of unstructured text into a structured representation that machines can interpret. In addition to other functions, NLP involves acknowledging named entities and determining the names, organizations, locations, and other relevant terms in the text that could impact emotional connections. Two primary methods for analyzing sentiment and emotions are lexicon-based and machine learning–derived.edu. The use of pre-defined lists of words with sentiment or emotion labels is the foundation of lexicon-based approaches. While this approach is straightforward and easy to grasp, it frequently lacks a comprehensive understanding of the context. Words in dictionaries can be inadequate in distinguishing between intended and actual meaning, such as sarcophagus or irony. Supervised learning and other machine learning-based techniques involve training models on extensive labeled datasets. Patterns are learned by models from text information and they can predict the sentiment or emotion of new, unseen data. The implementation of algorithms like SVM, Naive Bayes, Decision Trees, and ensemble techniques has been widespread. However, other algorithms are also used. Recently, this domain has been transformed by the use of deep learning architectures such as RNN, LSTM networks, and BERT models that are based on existing transformers. These systems have also revolutionized data storage methods. Self-attention mechanisms in models like BERT, RoBERTa, and GPT allow for a self-conceptualization of context that is both left-directed and right-direction [7]. These aid in capturing the true essence of words, regardless of their meaning. Training these models involves examining large corpora and fine-tuning them for specific uses, such as emotion recognition or sentiment analysis. A sentence such as "I cannot believe this is amazing" would obviously be positive, while "you did that" could be a case of either disappointment or anger. Context is all, and contemporary NLP models have more and more capacity to catch it. Affective analysis, as opposed to simple sentiment analysis, is targeted at detecting emotion states, in many cases invoking psychological models such as Ekman's six elementary emotions or Plutchik's wheel of emotions. NLP systems also need to be able to deal with issues like negations (e.g., "not happy"), intensifiers (e.g., "very sad"), slang, emojis, and multilingual text, particularly in social media environments. This renders pre-processing and normalization of text essential steps. In real-world applications, NLP for sentiment and emotion analysis is extensively used in chatbots and virtual assistants, enabling them to respond more empathetically to users by being able to sense the mood behind messages. In psychiatry, such systems can identify initial warning signs of emotional suffering or depression based on text-based communication analysis [8].

In social media websites such as Twitter or Facebook, sentiment analysis can be used to track public opinion regarding brands, political activities, or products. Firms use this to modify marketing plans or counteract crises. Software such as VADER (Valence Aware Dictionary and sentiment Reasoner), Text Blob, and proprietary APIs from IBM Watson, Google Cloud NLP, or Microsoft Azure offer sentiment analysis as an out-of-the-box feature. They employ both rule-based and machine learning algorithms to analyze language. Furthermore, the emergence of multi-modal sentiment analysis, where text, speech, and visual signals are blended together, makes emotion detection even more powerful. For instance, together with voice tone and content of the message, facial expression analysis produces a fuller emotional sense, although this generally falls under affective computing. Practically applied, NLP-based emotion analysis is used on customer service interfaces in order to route emotionally negative messages to human staff, but those that are neutral or positive may be managed by AI bots. In educational technology, NLP programs measure student enthusiasm or frustration using written responses or conversational history and respond back based on it. In law and compliance environments, tone-of-expression analysis may enable the detection of potentially hostile, biased, or inappropriate text content. For political analysis, academics employ NLP to monitor over time the manner in which politicians or citizens state emotions for some issues, and this offers richer sentiment tracking compared to mere polling. Even with its progress, NLP for emotion and sentiment analysis has problems. Sarcasm and metaphor are still hard for computers to understand correctly. For instance, "Great, another delay" is negative and sarcastic, but older models could misread it as positive because of the word "great." Emotional display is also culturally subtle; the same words could have other meanings in other places or among other groups. Furthermore, long-text context is challenging to maintain, particularly in discourse or narratives. But new models such as GPT-4 and more scale-language models display better functionality for the purpose of retaining long-contextual memory and generating affect-relevant response. Another development area is few-shot or zero-shot learning, when a model is able to comprehend and classify new emotions using fewer training examples. This eliminates the necessity for large, labeled datasets, which are costly and time-consuming to create. In addition, multilingual sentiment and emotion analysis are becoming increasingly vital since international communication occurs across languages. Pretrained multilingual models like mBERT or XLM-Roberta enable emotion detection in a number of languages simultaneously, avoiding the hurdles linguistic diversity presents [9]. Besides classification, NLP applies to emotion intensity scoring—scoring how strong an emotion is being expressed—and emotion cause detection, which finds out what produced a particular emotional state. Finally, natural language processing (NLP) of sentiment and emotions is a solid and fast-emerging discipline that requires the marriage of psychology, artificial intelligence, and computational linguistics. In making machines decipher human emotions from text, it allows humans to interact more emotionally intelligent and human-like with AI [10]. Apart from enhancing user experience for platforms like chatbots, virtual assistants, and customer support platforms, it also brings opportunities in mental health diagnostics, education, politics, and business intelligence. With better NLP models that are contextually aware, their ability to understand human emotions and respond appropriately will become even better, leading eventually to more empathetic, smart, and useful AI systems [11]. The Figure 2.2 depicts the NLP workflow for sentiment analysis, beginning with data gathering followed by preprocessing to identify useful textual features. Data pattern understanding and model training are facilitated through exploratory and predictive

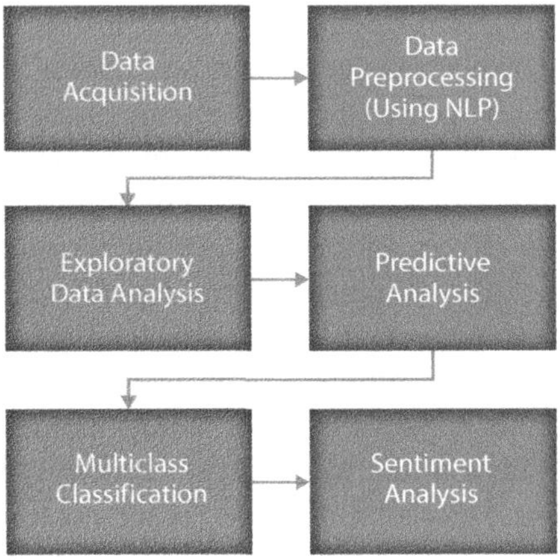

Figure 2.2 NLP workflow for sentiment analysis.

analysis. At the end, the system conducts multiclass classification and sentiment analysis, thus allowing automatic text categorization into sentiment labels like positive, negative, or neutral.

2.3 AI-Based Techniques for Emotion Detection in Text, Chatbots, and Social Media

Emotion detection by artificial intelligence (AI) has come to the forefront of enhancing human-computer interaction, user experience, and identifying psychological states from text content. With the advent of e-conversations through messaging, virtual assistants, and social networks, emotion detection is crucial in analyzing human sentiment and intent. This paper delves into how AI-based approaches are utilized in three significant domains: text-based emotion analysis, emotion-sensitive chatbots, and sentiment mining on social networks.

a. **AI-Based Emotion Detection in Text:** AI systems examine text data to detect the underlying emotions using natural language processing (NLP), sentiment analysis, and deep learning. Traditional methods apply lexicon-based models such as WordNet-Affect and SentiWordNet, whereas contemporary methods employ machine learning classifiers (e.g., SVM, Random Forest) and deep structures such as RNNs, LSTMs, and transformers (e.g., BERT, RoBERTa).

These models learn on tagged corpora with emotional labels (e.g., anger, sadness, joy) to understand contextual subtleties and emotional polarity. Despite excellent performance, difficulties remain in identifying sarcasm, cultural sentiments, and implicit emotions.

b. **Emotion-Aware Chatbots:** Chatbots have shifted from rule-based scripting to emotionally conscious agents with the help of AI. Emotion recognition allows them to provide empathetic responses, improving user satisfaction across areas such as healthcare, customer service, and mental health. Emotionally intelligent chatbots tend to incorporate sentiment classifiers and affect-aware dialog management systems trained on affective corpora. For instance, GPT-fine-tuned models with emotional awareness can adjust tone, suggest empathy, or tone down negative user sentiment. Nonetheless, these come with the constraints of training data bias and emotional inconsistency across multi-turn conversational flows.

c. **Emotion Mining on Social Media Platforms:** Social media is an abundance of real-time, emotional expression. Large-scale sentiment and emotion mining methods are used by AI models on social media platforms such as Twitter, Reddit, and YouTube comments. NLP is typically integrated with network-based analysis and geotagging for understanding public sentiment, crisis prediction, or brand sentiment analysis. Multimodal fusion (text + image/video) and emotion graphs are additional methods used to improve accuracy. However, the noisy nature of language (slang, emoji), multilingual text, and dynamic online conversation pose challenges.

2.4 Facial Expression Recognition (FER) for Emotion Analysis

In order to help machines identify and comprehend human emotions from facial expressions, the multidisciplinary field of computer vision for facial expression recognition (FER) combines artificial intelligence (AI), image processing, and psychology. The main objective of FER is to bridge the emotional communication gap between humans and machines in order to improve the responsiveness, empathy, and intuition of human-computer interaction. Facial expressions are one of the most accurate and immediate ways to assess someone's emotional state. Because expressions like joy, sadness, anger, surprise, fear, and disgust are universally recognized, facial cues are a powerful input modality for emotion recognition structures. Face detection, facial landmark localization, feature extraction, and emotion classification are the usual steps in the FER process. The initial step by step is face being identified, where techniques. The face is localized after which facial landmarks—individual points such as the edges of the eyes, mouth, eyebrows, and nose—are identified to examine facial geometry. They are used to obtain shape-based or appearance-based features. Handcrafted feature extraction methods are Local Binary Patterns (LBP), Histogram of Oriented Gradients (HOG), and Gabor filters, which measure texture and shape details from facial areas. Still, with the advent of deep learning, convolutional neural networks (CNNs) have deposed handcrafted feature extraction almost entirely, learning discriminating features directly from raw pixels [12]. CNNs naturally identify subtle spatial hierarchies in face images, and they are very effective at identifying nuanced expressions. For facial expression tasks, cutting-edge architectures like VGGNet, ResNet, and Inception have been adjusted and refined. Recurrent neural networks (RNNs) and Long Short-Term Memory (LSTM) networks are used in video-based FER in addition to CNNs to detect temporal dependencies and changes in facial movements. Datasets like FER2013, CK+, JAFFE, and Affect Net can be used to train and evaluate facial expression recognition models. These datasets provide thousands of labeled facial images with different emotions in different occlusion, pose, and lighting conditions. Variations in head posture, illumination, occlusions (e.g., glasses, beards), and inter-subject variation (how different people display the same emotion) make real-world expression recognition difficult. Data augmentation techniques such as rotation, flipping, cropping, and the creation of synthetic images using GANs (Generative Adversarial Networks) are widely employed for improved generalization. Along with static image classification, real-time FER usage is dependent on fast models capable of handling video streams at low latency. Methods such as lightweight CNNs and model compression (pruning and quantization) enable reduction of computational complexity without loss of accuracy.

Emotion classification is usually carried out either by a categorical approach—placing expressions into discrete classes such as the six Ekman emotions—or through a dimensional model, in which expressions are plotted against continuous dimensions such as valence (pleasantness) and arousal (intensity). More advanced models also consider Action Units (AUs) as labeled in the Facial Action Coding System (FACS), which specify specific facial muscle movements, e.g., raising the eyebrows or pursing the lips. AU-based FER systems are more specific and can infer complex emotions based on facial muscle activation patterns. For instance, a robot nurse detecting grief in a patient can respond with calming talk, music, or alert a human nurse. In marketing and retail, FER can be used to gauge consumers' reactions to products or ads by analyzing facial expressions in real-time. Though these possible uses are intriguing, ethical concerns such as privacy, consent, and bias are on everyone's minds. FER systems are invasive, especially if employed in public areas without a clear articulation of informed user consent. Additionally, facial expression and recognition models tend to be biased—doing well on some demographics, but not others, most notably under-represented demographics in training datasets. These issues require rectification through data use transparency, diverse training sets, and following ethical AI practices. Multi-modal emotion recognition, incorporating facial expression information along with voice tone, body posture, and physiological measures like heart rate or skin conductance, is yet another newer area of research to yield stronger emotion inference. The other field that is being advanced in FER is the use of transformers and vision-language models such as Vision Transformers (ViTs) [13] and CLIP to combine visual data with semantic knowledge to more effectively draw out emotion context. With developing technology, FER is now advancing not only to detect evident emotions, but also to predict subtle or hidden emotions and understanding complex affective states like empathy, frustration, or deception. The Figure 2.3 illustrates the intersection of artificial intelligence, machine

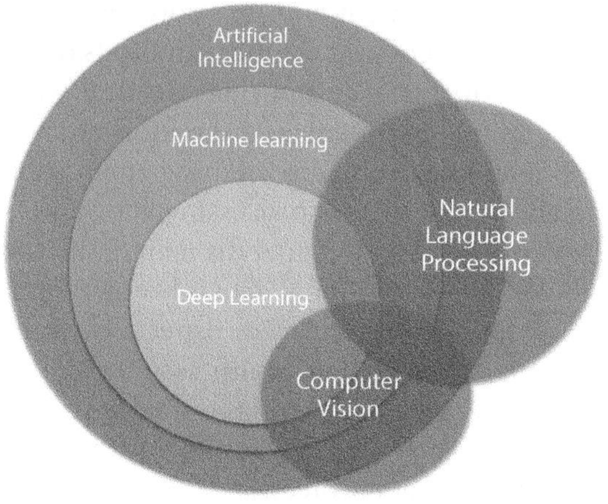

Figure 2.3 Relationship between computer vision and NLP.

learning, deep learning, NLP, and computer vision, indicating their common areas. NLP and computer vision intersect in deep learning, which allows multimodal tasks to combine text and image processing. Such an integration facilitates applications like facial expression recognition, image captioning, and visual question answering, thus improving human–computer interaction with natural, adaptive, and affect-sensitive systems.

2.5 Real-Time Issues in the Convergence

2.5.1 NLP Convergence Issues for Sentiment Analysis

Most multifaceted challenges regarding the blend of sentiment and emotion analysis with the help of Natural Language Processing (NLP) already hinder the maximum capability of AI-based emotional comprehension of text. The lack of standardized methods for combining sentiment analysis with deep emotion detection represents one of the primary issues. While emotion analysis seeks a broader set of richer emotions such as joy, anger, fear, or sadness, sentiment analysis is generally more reductionist, classifying texts into positive, negative, or neutral categories. It is contradictory and difficult to build coherent models that seamlessly combine both abilities due to the disparity in scope and approach. In addition, contextual comprehension, or the ability to accurately interpret language-based sentiments and emotions, is another weakness shared by today's NLP models [14]. Such rhetorical devices conceal or manipulate the actual sentiments of the speaker, in turn misleading literal translations of language. The reliability of the issue of data quality and intrinsic biases makes it even more difficult to design sentiment and emotion analysis systems that are accurate and reliable. Also required are huge amounts of processing power and a sophisticated algorithmic design that can deal with the additional complexity of integrating sentiment and emotion analyses into existing applications. Chabot and social media listening applications are instances of real-time applications that require processing enormous streams of data. In addition, sentiment and emotion analysis using NLP tools have significant ethical concerns. Users' emotional data is brought into concern where it is collected, processed, and interpreted. Especially in sensitive contexts such as customer support or mental health assistance, users are required to be well informed and give their permission before their emotional data are analyzed. To maintain user trust and prevent the abuse of emotional information, transparency, data protection, and legal compliance are vital. Overall, there are compelling ethical, methodological, and technical issues, despite the huge potential in combining sentiment analysis with NLP-driven sentiment for more empathetic and responsive AI systems. This will require advancements in contextual language understanding, figurative language processing, emotional modeling, and high-quality data.

2.5.2 Multilingual and Code-Mixed Inputs

Natural Language Processing (NLP) has many complications when it comes to sentiment and emotion detection analysis in real-time as it relates to multilingual and code-mixed data. In a world of globalization and digital communities, users now put together various perspectives and formats in their language, whether it is through code-switching or code mixing, which allows for terminology from various language sets to be used interchangeably in a single line. The informality of online platforms presents the largest source of such language combination. For example, on online forums, WhatsApp, social media, and YouTube comments, code mixing will be prevalent. In expressing, "*Yeh movie was lit bro, full paisa vasool*", a user combined Hindi and English. Using unusual language combinations or regional vernacular makes tokenization, part-of-speech tagging, and words embedding that much more difficult to accurately mark. Moreover, the portrayal of emotion differs by culture languages, but the meaning of emotion components of a phrase may change even when translated. When multilingual aspects are included it's even more difficult to determine emotions as well. In many cases, you might use pre-trained models and if they have multilingual capabilities, such as mBERT or XLM-R, [15] you still find that the language-specific system that are pre-trained, like BERT, underperform on applicability in real-time code-mixed use case scenarios. In addition, there are system issues and delays to consider when trying to measure context adaptation in real-time because the system is still running through its processes of translation, language detection and appropriating its context adaptation before it can show you any results. In order to create a functional system a proper understanding of nonstop linguistic diversity must appropriately consider cross-lingual embedding's, proper domain adaptations, and creation of training data across a variety of code-mixed and ill-defined domains.

2.5.3 Continual Learning and Model Drift

Artificial Learning and Natural Language Processing (NLP)-driven real-time sentiment and emotion analysis systems face two significant challenges: Continuous Learning, and Model Drift. On Twitter, TikTouch or

Reddit -- all dynamic platforms -- language is changing in real life with the introduction of new slang, memes and cultural references to use patterns and other usage patterns. Within weeks or months, a model's knowledge may become outdated and insufficient. When the distribution of real-world data changes over time and doesn't reflect new linguistic or emotional patterns, model drift causes it to perform slower, as seen in the recent shift in meaning for emojis like or phrases such as "it's giving " (from literal to sarcastic or humorous use). It is possible that a model trained on older data may not accurately capture the intended sentiment or misunderstand it. The semantics of politically charged words, brands, and current events can be context-sensitive and could affect sentiment. Continuous learning is the gradual updating of models as new data is received while taking the approach of building rather than rebuilding [16]. Continuous learning is simple in theory. Executing this is more difficult. To execute this effectively and maintain performance, it is important to reduce catastrophic forgetting, this is where learning the historical knowledge is lost, and also to simply ensure the updated model is objective and not overfitting with new data. Work is ongoing to determine how to achieve stability, adaptability, and fairness in real-time NLP.

2.5.4 Ethical Dilemmas

There are serious ethical challenges tied to real-time sentiment and emotion analyses utilizing AI and NLP. This is especially true since we continue to see these technologies integrated directly into our public discourse, behavior tracking, and human decision making. The data privacy surrounding user sentiment and emotions is a considerable ethical aspect. However, emotions and sentiment analysis frequently involve collecting and interpreting private data (typically without user agreement), such as political interests, preference, or emotional states; including mental health markers. This generates serious surveillance, ownership of obtained data, and informed consent issues in particular, across open platforms such as Facebook or Twitter, where users may not even acknowledge their emotional expressions are mined algorithmically. Emotional profiling, which includes forming categories of people or targeting people based on their emotional state, presents another problem. On the one hand perhaps, this can be positive in some scenarios, such as offer a personalized user experience or supporting mental health concerns; however, it can also be utilized to affect political propaganda, targeted advertising streams, or designed content that takes advantage of emotional aspects [17]. Also, if certain emotion recognition models produce poor performance with representative groups across culture, language, gender, or age-related groups, it could be devilishly implemented leading to discrimination or misclassification.

2.5.5 Handling Streamed Data

The capability to process large volumes of data from streams requires proper management so that the system can handle multiple events/messages/posts. Events create scale-back challenges (e.g. live sporting events/political debate) that result in increased use of data which could overwhelm the processing ability of the time it parallel processes. The throughput of the infrastructure is especially important. Large volumes of data streams are processed in live mode using services such as Apache Kafka, Google's cloud streaming service, API Labs, Apache Flink, and Spark. Streaming, to name a few. They are setup and run by technical people. The goal is to provide immediate output using low-latency processing that has shorter processing times. If a chatbot is processing data for customer support, or a crisis management/monitoring system, waiting for each processing time in support of insights in sentiment and emotion analysis, the processing time may result in rendering even the insight useless. Shortening the processing time is crucial in determining one's sentiment or emotion from text.

2.5.6 Sarcasm and Irony Detection

Depending on the context, irony and sarcophagus are highly dependent on their use. An opportune line may be devoid of humor and have a sarcastic or ironic quality, depending on the speaker's perspective, the topic, or the circumstances. While it may seem like a genuine expression, saying "I enjoy standing in long queues!" is likely sarcastic considering the circumstances. The challenge for real-time systems is to make correct decisions by considering the historical discourse and the surrounding context. Unlike other emotional cues, irony and spitting out emotions are not always identified with clear language indicators [18]. In some instances, emojis, exclamation points, and additional punctuation might provide a cue, but sarcasm largely depends on facial expressions or vocal tone in spoken language, making it a challenge to identify this type of textual content.

2.5.7 Low Latency Requirements

Low latency needs are critical for fast and accurate responses in dynamic settings such as live interactions, social media monitoring, or customer service chatbots. This is particularly the case for real-time sentiment and emotion analysis. Text processing and analysis are critical for real-time systems to deliver relevant insights or actions, such as customer frustration detection or public sentiment. The large amount of data from different sources is the cause of this. With the use of complex deep learning models such as BERT or GPT, it may be difficult to maintain low latency at the expense of accuracy due to computational complexity and latency. For this, optimizations like the use of lighter versions of the model, edge computing and techniques such as parallel processing and model compression are needed. The management of sarcasm or irony is made more complicated by the intricacies of contextual knowledge. The scalability of the infrastructure and functionality of heavy traffic without clogging requires great attention to speed. Not only does this enhance the user experience but also facilitates quicker decision making through low latency, something that is essential in domains such as brand management or content moderation, and crisis management.

2.5.8 Inconsistent or Missing Labels

The training of sentiment and emotion models is severely compromised by the presence or absence of inconsistent or missing labels. Models in supervised learning have to be taught to identify particular emotions or sentiments in text using labeled datasets. Real-world data can nevertheless have flaws including inconsistent labeling across several data sets, erroneous annotations, or missing labels. A positive and negative sarcasm on the same dataset could lead to variations in the model's understanding. During inference, the model's encounter with similar vague statements during inferential processing can cause problems and lead to incorrect sentiment classification. Additionally, models can be unreliable due to inadequate labels in data, particularly when particular feelings or emotional states are not captured. Due to the absence of emotions like fear, disgust and surprise in training datasets that are not readily available for use in real-world scenarios, the model remains ill-prepared. In datasets with multiple languages or dialects, annotators tend to interpret the same text differently due to cultural, regional, or personal biases. This problem is worse in many cases. Discordant labeling can also occur as a result of this. The difficulties lead to models that are less dependable and generalizable, particularly when dealing with real-time data, which may contain subtleties and expression variations [19].

2.5.9 Scalability Issues

Large volumes of data produced by social media, customer support portals, and IoT-enabled environments requiring real-time sentiment and emotion analysis systems call especially significant scalability issues. These systems must grow in scale as data volume rises, velocity rises, or variety increases if we are to keep great accuracy and low latency. While the computational complexity of scaling NLP models—especially those in BERT, GPT, or LSTM-based architectures—can be noteworthy, in practical settings it can also be costly and difficult to manage [20]. The great resource demands of model inference compromise scalability. Deep learning models' high memory and processing power needs can create a bottleneck in real-time analysis of hundreds of thousands of messages per second. One also has to keep contextual awareness across several languages and threads. Moreover, organizational issues sometimes prevent sentiment analysis tools from being included into current systems. More and more solutions including distributed computing, model parallelism, cloud-native architectures, and edge processing help to overcome scalability restrictions so guaranteeing dependable and effective performance at scale.

2.6 Resolving the Issues

We can employ sophisticated modeling techniques, system-level optimizations, and sound design choices to facilitate real-time sentiment or emotion analysis. Models, such as mBERT and XLM-R, that are pre-trained on many languages and fine-tuned to the domain of interest, can deal with multilingual, code-mixed inputs, and methods of normalization. We can also use transliteration and translation pipelines which integrate language detection modules, allowing us to normalize mixed-language inputs before running the model. We can employ regular model updates or online learning techniques to maintain the relevance of the analyses without having to retrain the model from scratch. On the other hand, while not identical, we can use transfer learning methods and Elastic Weight Consolidation (EWC) to mathematically retain the previously learned information while incorporating those from recent inputs that can be reliably added to the model. In a micro services architecture both the processing and storage of model input or inference are stand-alone processes capable of rapid scaling in order to accommodate potential internal organizational needs more effectively while increasing external consumer satisfaction across multiple markets. Scalability may include but is not limited to cloud-native, model pruning and hastily distributed computing approaches. Using Distil BERT or Mobile BERTH models retain relevance without extensive computational time and resources. It is also important to audit ethical issues in any AI pipeline that may also include user consent, and bias. Although sentiment/emotion analysis systems, obviously use a foray of integrated procedures that facilitate responsiveness, flexibility, and scalability paired with high-throughput multilingual concurrent real-time content analysis.

2.7 Conclusion

The way that machines understand human language or emotions is changing as a result of the convergence of sentiment analysis, emotion detection, and natural language processing. Customer service, content moderation, public sentiment tracking, and mental health monitoring are just a few of the many possible applications; however, the development of fully functional, real-time emotion-aware systems is hampered by a number of ethical and technological issues. Low latency, handling multilingual and streamed data, detecting irony and sarcasm, model drift, elasticity, and ethical deployment are among the requirements. A multi-layered solution is required to meet these demands. Model optimization techniques must be used in conjunction with sophisticated transformer-based models, distributed processing frameworks, continuous learning pipelines, and multilingual capabilities in order to achieve real-time performance at scale. With AI continuing to evolve, these capabilities such as emotional intelligence, contextual discernment, and real-time responsiveness allowed to merge will eventually bring machines closer to communicating like humans. If we study sentiments and emotions a truly more intelligent and empathetic digital systems can emerge with even better study coordination and moral vision. Contextual awareness, emotional intelligence, and real-time responsiveness will all blend together more smoothly as AI develops, bringing machines closer to communicating like humans. Sentiment and emotion analysis will be essential in creating more intelligent and sympathetic digital systems with further study, cooperation, and moral vision.

AI disclosure statement: The author acknowledges the use of AI-based tools for minor language editing or grammatical correction. However, all intellectual contributions, analyses, and conclusions presented in this chapter are entirely the author's own.

References

1. Calefato, F., Lanubile, F., Novielli, N., EmoTxt: A toolkit for emotion recognition from text. *Empirical Softw. Eng.*, *23*, 3, 1350–1382, 2018.
2. Chundi, R., Sasikala, G., Basivi, P.K., Tippana, A., Hulipalled, V.R., *et al.*, Exploring diabetes through the lens of AI and computer vision: Methods and future prospects. *Comput. Biol. Med.*, *185*, 109537, 2025. https://doi.org/10.xxxx/j.compbiomed.2025.109537.
3. Chundi, R., Hulipalled, V.R., Simha, J.B., Identification of monolingual and code-switch information from English-Kannada code-switch data. *Int. J. Electr. Comput. Eng.*, *13*, 5, xx–xx, 2023.
4. Mohammad, S.M. and Turney, P.D., Crowdsourcing a word–emotion association lexicon. *Comput. Intell.*, *29*, 3, 436–465, 2013. https://doi.org/10.1111/j.1467-8640.2012.00460.x.
5. Felbo, B., Mislove, A., Søgaard, A., Rahwan, I., Lehmann, S., Using millions of emoji occurrences to learn any-domain representations for detecting sentiment, emotion and sarcasm, in: *Proceedings of the 2017 Conference on Empirical Methods in Natural Language Processing*, pp. 1615–1625, 2017.
6. Kim, Y. and Kim, H., BERT-based contextualized embedding for emotion recognition in text. *IEEE Access*, *9*, 80606–80613, 2021. https://doi.org/10.1109/ACCESS.2021.3085152.
7. Zhou, H., Huang, M., Zhang, T., Zhu, X., Liu, B., Emotional chatting machine: Emotional conversation generation with internal and external memory. *Proc. AAAI Conf. Artif. Intell.*, *32*, 1, 730–739, 2016.
8. Revathy, G., Raj, K.B., Kumar, A., Adibatti, S., Dahiya, P., Latha, T.M., Investigation of E-voting system using face recognition using convolutional neural network (CNN). *Theor. Comput. Sci.*, *925*, 61–67, 2022.
9. Parveen, H. and Pandey, P., Deep learning-based sentiment analysis and emotion detection in text: A review. *Int. J. Adv. Comput. Sci. Appl.*, *12*, 4, 135–143, 2021. https://doi.org/10.14569/IJACSA.2021.0120418.
10. Shaila, S.G., Sindhu, A., Shivamma, D., *et al.*, Human Emotion Recognition Based on EEG Signal Using Deep Learning Approach, in: *International Conference on Recent Trends in Communication and Intelligent Systems*, Springer, 2023.
11. Monish, L., Shaila, S.G., Sumana, S.G., Uppin, A., *et al.*, Emotion Prediction Based on Real-Time Crowd Analysis Using Deep Network, in: *International Conference on Recent Trends in Communication and Intelligent Systems*, Springer, 2023.
12. Shaila, S.G., Anirudh, B.M., Nair, A.S., Monish, L., *et al.*, EEG signal-based human emotion recognition using power spectrum density and discrete wavelet transform, in: *Conference on Emerging Research in Computing, Information, Communication and Applications*, Springer, 2023.
13. Yu, J.H. and Chauhan, D., Trends in NLP for personalized learning: LDA and sentiment analysis insights. *Educ. Inf. Technol.*, *30*, 4, 4307–4348, 2025.

14. Bandarupalli, G., *Enhancing Sentiment Analysis in Multilingual Social Media Data Using Transformer-Based NLP Models A Synthetic Computational Study*, Authorea Preprints, 2025.
15. Badawi, S., Kazemi, A., Rezaie, V., KurdiSent: a corpus for kurdish sentiment analysis. *Lang. Resour. Eval.*, *59*, 1, 601–620, 2025.
16. Rana, M.R.R., Nawaz, A., Rehman, S.U., Abid, M.A., Garayevi, M., Kajanová, J., BERT-BiGRU-Senti-GCN: An Advanced NLP Framework for Analyzing Customer Sentiments in E-Commerce. *Int. J. Comput. Intell. Syst.*, *18*, 1, 21, 2025.
17. Dubey, P., Dubey, P., Gehani, H., Enhancing sentiment analysis through deep layer integration with long short-term memory networks. *Int. J. Electr. Comput. Eng. (2088-8708)*, *15*, 1, 949–957, 2025.
18. Zainal, N.H., Eckhardt, R., Rackoff, G.N., Fitzsimmons-Craft, E.E., Rojas-Ashe, E., Taylor, C.B., Newman, M.G., Capitalizing on natural language processing (NLP) to automate the evaluation of coach implementation fidelity in guided digital cognitive-behavioral therapy (GdCBT). *Psychol. Med.*, *55*, e106, 2025.
19. Babu, M.S.S., Suryanarayana, S.V., Sruthi, M., Lakshmi, P.B., Sravanthi, T., Spandana, M., Enhancing Sentiment Analysis With Emotion And Sarcasm Detection: A Transformer-Based Approach. *Metall. Mater. Eng.*, 31, 5, 794–803, 2025.
20. Hong, X., Gong, Y., Sethu, V., Dang, T., AER-LLM: Ambiguity-aware emotion recognition leveraging large language models, in: *ICASSP 2025-2025 IEEE International Conference on Acoustics, Speech and Signal Processing (ICASSP)*, IEEE, pp. 1–5, 2025, April.

3

Affective Computing in Edge-Based Healthcare Systems

Dhamarai Selvi K.V.[1], G. Revathy[2*], Raja Rajeswari Balaji[3] and M. Shyamalagowri[4]

[1]Department of Electrical and Electronics Engineering, Sri Sairam College of Engineering, Bangalore, India
[2]Department of CSE, Srinivasa Ramanujan Centre, SASTRA Deemed to be University, Kumbakonam, Tamil Nadu, India
[3]Department of CSE (Cyber Security), Nandha Engineering College, Erode, Tamil Nadu, India
[4]Department of EEE, K.S. Rangasamy College of Technology, Tiruchengode, Tamil Nadu, India

Abstract

The combination of Affective Computing (AC) combined with Edge-Oriented Health Systems is an emerging paradigm in patient treatment where instantaneous emotional state is monitored right at the point of care. Traditional cloud-driven AC deployment in healthcare have inherent drawbacks such as the latency in emergency, network bandwidth constraints of constant dataflow from wearables/IoT devices, and severe privacy implications as intimate emotional and physiological data is being transmitted to remote servers. This chapter presents how edge computing, facilitating the offloading of computation from remote or cloud based servers to edge devices, can address these issues to enable real time processing, analytics and reflection on emotional cues in clinical and remote patient monitoring applications. We discuss the architecture and operating mechanism of edge-based AC and discuss its applications including early prediction of mental decline, personalize intervention, pain management, and doctor-patient communication. In addition, the chapter discusses the specific challenges formed at the intersection of AC and edge computing in healthcare, such as maintaining data integrity and security on distributed devices, managing computational resources

**Corresponding author*: revathyjayabaskar@gmail.com

N. Thillaiarasu, G. Revathy, T. Saravanan, V. Muthukumaran and S. Balamurugan (eds.) Affective Artificial Intelligence: Fundamentals, Challenges, and Applications, (45–76) © 2026 Scrivener Publishing LLC

on devices near the edge, providing interoperability with the already deployed healthcare infrastructure, and learning robust, unbiased emotion models that can generalize across different patient populations and settings. Lastly, we address the critical ethical issues of privacy, consent, and algorithmic fairness in this quickly developing field while highlighting the enormous opportunities for innovation, highlighting the potential for proactive healthcare, lower operating costs, and the development of more responsive and sympathetic AI-driven health solutions.

***Keywords*:** Affective computing, edge computing, healthcare systems, real-time emotion recognition, wearable sensors, patient monitoring, data privacy, low latency

3.1 Introduction

A proactive, patient-centric paradigm is replacing the largely reactive, disease-centric model that has dominated the modern healthcare landscape. Some of the factors driving this evolution are the aging of the global population, the increasing prevalence of chronic diseases, the escalation of healthcare costs, and the widespread use of digital technology. Preventive options, personalized interventions, and continuous monitoring are increasingly relevant, expanding the horizon of health from clinics to the everyday life of people. Given this paradigm shift, new technologically-enabled solutions that can deliver timely, relevant, and actionable information about a person's health state—including those elements not typically considered within the realm of the objectively medical— are needed. Cross-disciplinary areas such as Edge AI and AC are converging in this dynamic environment to offer ground-breaking opportunities, particularly when it comes to empowering healthcare systems with an indispensable, but not limited to it, dimension of proactive care and emotional support.

At its core, the discipline of affective computing is being developed to enable computers to detect, understand, and respond to human emotions. With this technology's ability to understand and respond to users' emotions, brought into the mainstream by Rosalind Picard in the mid-1990s, AC ultimately seeks to bridge that gap in order to make communication between humans and machines more natural. This goes beyond sentiment analysis to be a broader range of human affect, presumably including continuous emotional dimensions (e.g., valence, arousal), discrete emotions (e.g., joy, sadness, anger, fear), and cognitive states (e.g., engagement, stress, exhaustion). AC has inhomogeneous and unavoidable effects in medicine.

Human emotions considerably influence the state of health, the course of disease, the adherence to therapy and in general the well-being.

And particularly in the case of already-existing conditions, stress, anxiety, and depression are known risk factors that can exacerbate many chronic conditions. Positive emotions, however, can help people recover more quickly and lead better lives. By correctly identifying and analyzing these emotional states, AC systems can provide clinicians, caregivers and even the patients themselves with invaluable information to deliver more caring and effective care. For instance, early identification of signs of emotional distress may facilitate timely psychological interventions; assessment of pain levels may permit tailored pain management programs; and identification of frustration with a treatment plan emphasizes the need for changes therein. Instantaneous understanding of how a patient is feeling opens up possibilities for proactive health care never before thought possible, fosters higher empathy levels in human-computer interaction in a health context, and, in the end, better patient results.

The gathering and evaluation of various emotional data modalities makes up the complex Affective Computing process. Each of these modalities provides distinct insights into an individual's emotional state and is used as the raw input for AC systems. Physiological signals stand as the most immediate physiological indicators which directly show how emotions affect the body. The physiological measurement methods include Electrocardiography (ECG) to track heart rate alongside heart rate variability and Electrodermal Activity (EDA) or Galvanic Skin Response (GSR) to detect sweat gland activity through skin conductivity measurements and Electroencephalography (EEG) for brainwave patterns and Electromyography (EMG) to monitor muscle activity including facial muscle tension along with respiration rate and skin temperature. Signals provide an uninterrupted and hidden glimpse of one's emotional state, even when expressions are deliberately masked. Facial expressions, which stem from culture yet transcend it, represent another rich dimension. AC systems apply techniques such as Action Unit (AU) detection based on the FACS to identify particular muscle movements associated with different emotions. With advances in computer vision and deep learning, facial images and video streams can now be analyzed to accurately detect emotions such as joy, sorrow, rage, surprise, disgust, and fear. In the context of speech, vocal characteristics offer critical additional emotion-related information—especially prosody: intonation, rhythm, stress level variations and pitch changes. The spoken content does not need to carry any meaning; rather the tone used can express a significant amount of emotional intent coupled with volume and speaking pace.

AC models analyze pitch, jitter, shimmer as well as speaking rate and voice quality to determine basic emotional states like joy, boredom, or distress. Additionally, linguistic and textual cues articulate with clarity the insights of the writer's emotional world. Emotion recognition from text is more advanced than sentiment analysis which simply classifies text into positive, negative or neutral. It classifies text using advanced techniques of Natural Language Processing (NLP) alongside emotion lexicons to pinpoint particular emotions embedded in written documents, social media content, patient testimonials, or chat transcripts. The synergy born out of combining and fusing these different modalities enhances precision within model frameworks when dealing with multifaceted complex emotions that are difficult to interpret accelerates automation in robust and coherent systems for emotion recognition.

The numerous emotional data modalities present unique logistical and computational challenges when processing and extracting them for real-time healthcare applications, particularly at scale. This is where Edge Computing transforms the situation for the better. By definition, edge computing relocates the required processing, storage, and networking resources closer to the data sources rather than relying on a single cloud-based infrastructure. Edge devices process information locally at or near the "edge" of the network, which eliminates the need to send all raw sensor data from wearables and Internet of Things devices to remote data centers for processing. This localized processing fundamentally alters the data flow and operational dynamics.

The advantages of Edge Computing are particularly pronounced in sensitive and time-critical domains like healthcare. First and foremost is **low latency**. In scenarios where immediate emotional insights are vital—such as detecting a sudden panic attack, assessing real-time pain levels during a procedure, or identifying distress in an elderly patient—the delay introduced by transmitting data to the cloud, processing it, and sending back a response can be detrimental. Edge computing eliminates this round-trip delay, enabling near-instantaneous analysis and response. Secondly, **bandwidth efficiency** is a significant benefit. Healthcare environments, especially remote clinics or home settings, may have limited or intermittent internet connectivity. Continuous streaming of high-fidelity multimodal data (e.g., continuous video, high-resolution physiological signals) to the cloud can quickly exhaust available bandwidth and incur substantial costs. Edge processing allows for local aggregation, filtering, and pre-processing of raw data, sending only crucial insights or compressed data to the cloud, thereby significantly reducing bandwidth consumption. Thirdly, and perhaps most critically in healthcare, Edge Computing offers enhanced **privacy and security**. By processing sensitive patient data locally on the device or a nearby edge gateway, the need to transmit raw, personally identifiable emotional and physiological data over public networks to remote cloud servers is minimized. This significantly reduces the attack surface for cyber threats and helps in complying with stringent healthcare data privacy regulations like HIPAA in the US or GDPR in Europe, fostering greater trust among patients and healthcare providers. In addition to these fundamental benefits, edge computing lowers operating costs by reducing data transmission and cloud computing resources and improves reliability by functioning even with sporadic cloud connectivity.

The aforementioned drawbacks of cloud-centric methods make it essential to incorporate Edge-Based Affective Computing into healthcare systems. Cloud computing's traditional architecture is not well-suited to the particular requirements of real-time, privacy-sensitive healthcare applications involving emotional data, despite the fact that it offers enormous scalability and computational power. In active clinical settings, latency due to data transmission to remote cloud servers can render AC insights stale. It is not simply possible to wait around for seconds or minutes for cloud-processed feedback when a patient in an intensive care unit is showing faint emotional distress that may signal a deteriorating condition. Along similar lines, cloud latency would prevent the timely detection of an emotional emergency and the activation of support procedures, which are critical for home-based mental health monitoring.

Apart from that, privacy matters are also very important in medicine. Among the most private and delicate types of information are physiological and emotional data. Patients and healthcare providers are naturally apprehensive about transmitting such intimate data to central cloud servers, where it could be vulnerable to breaches, unauthorized access, or misuse. Edge processing allows for data anonymization, aggregation, or even complete local processing of raw sensitive data, with only de-identified or aggregated insights being sent to the cloud for long-term storage or population-level analytics. This decentralized approach fundamentally changes the privacy calculus, making AC deployments more palatable and compliant.

Finally, **bandwidth** limitations are a practical barrier. Continuous monitoring of patients using multiple wearable sensors and video feeds generates enormous volumes of data. Transmitting all this raw data to the cloud for every patient would overwhelm existing network infrastructures and incur prohibitive costs. Edge computing enables intelligent data filtering and abstraction at the source. For instance, an edge device could process raw EEG signals, extract relevant emotional features (e.g., alpha asymmetry related to mood), and only send these compact features or a derived emotional state label to the cloud, rather than the raw, high-frequency EEG waveforms. This efficient use of bandwidth is essential for scalable and sustainable healthcare deployments, particularly in areas with limited internet access or for mobile healthcare applications.

This chapter aims to provide a comprehensive exploration of the convergence of affective computing, edge AI, and healthcare. We will systematically delve into the fundamental principles of AC relevant to healthcare, followed by an examination of various edge computing architectures suitable for medical environments. A large amount will be devoted to comprehending the technical intricacies of local data processing, model deployment, and real-time decision-making in order to effectively implement real-time affective computing at the edge. Then, by describing particular uses of edge-based AC in a range of healthcare scenarios, such as pain assessment, chronic disease management, mental health monitoring, and elder care, we will demonstrate the enormous practical value. Importantly, the chapter won't hold back when critically examining the particular difficulties and constraints present in this quickly developing field, including managing computational resources, guaranteeing data security and privacy on dispersed edge nodes, addressing model bias and robustness across a range of patient demographics, and making sure there is smooth interoperability with current healthcare IT systems. We will conclude by outlining the exciting future directions and innovation opportunities, ranging from developments in federated learning and edge AI hardware to the critical ethical, legal, and social ramifications that need to be proactively addressed to promote responsible and significant development in this game-changing field. This chapter aims to be a fundamental resource for scholars, practitioners, and policymakers who want to use affective computing at the edge to transform healthcare delivery by offering a comprehensive overview.

3.2 Fundamentals of Affective Computing for Healthcare Applications

Any Affective Computing (AC) system's efficacy depends on a thorough comprehension of the basic ideas behind emotion recognition and the advanced computational models used to accomplish it, especially in the delicate and important field of healthcare. The fundamental ideas of emotion recognition are explored in this section, along with the various ways that emotional data is recorded, the most common machine learning and deep learning paradigms, and the particular difficulties in data collection and annotation that arise in healthcare applications.

3.2.1 Core Concepts in Emotion Recognition

Theoretical knowledge of human emotion is central to affective computing. While intuitively familiar, emotions are complex psychological constructs, and their scientific modeling has largely followed two principal approaches: categorical and dimensional.

3.2.1.1 Categorical vs. Dimensional Models of Emotion

Categorical Models, often rooted in the work of psychologists like Paul Ekman, propose that there is a set of distinct, basic, and universally recognized emotions. These "basic emotions" are typically identified as joy (happiness), sadness, anger, fear, surprise, and disgust, with some models also including contempt or neutral. Categorical models are appealing because they are easy to understand and directly map to observable expressions, such as "happy face" or "angry voice." This method frequently results in classification tasks in the context of AC, where the objective is to allocate an input (such as a voice clip or a facial image) to one of these predetermined emotional categories. Recognizing these distinct emotional states can be very helpful for healthcare applications, such as spotting anger in a caregiver, sadness in someone dealing with a chronic illness, or fear in a patient prior to surgery.

The model's direct interpretability and unambiguous labels, which support supervised learning, are its strongest points. The drawback, though, is that human emotions are frequently complex, nuanced, or exist on a continuum, making it difficult for distinct categories to fully represent them. In addition, there is debate on the universality of these basic emotions, and challenges emerge due to cross-cultural variations in expression and interpretation.

Dimensional models, by contrast, view emotions as points on a continuous space, determined by some basic dimensions rather than as discrete objects. The best-known dimensional model, the circumplex model, generally employs two major axes: arousal (which ranges from low to high, assessing the degree or the amount of activation of an emotion) and valence (ranging from negative to positive, assessing the unpleasantness or pleasantness of an emotion).A third dimension, dominance or control (varying from submissive to dominant), is present in some models. For example, sadness can have low arousal and negative valence, but anger can have high arousal and negative valence. Excitement will be indicated by high arousal and positive valence, but low arousal and positive valence would indicate contentment. A more nuanced representation of emotion is offered by dimensional models, which allow for the measurement of subtle changes and contradictory emotional states. This can be particularly useful in the healthcare sector for continuous monitoring, which enables one to monitor a patient's emotional progression rather than isolated emotional incidents. Tracking changes in arousal and valence, for instance, might provide early signs of escalating stress or escalating emotional disconnection. While more informative dimensional models are available, they suffer from the inherent subjectivity of continuous dimension annotation and the challenge of automatically projecting these dimensions into simple enough labels to be comprehensible by human users. AC systems often bring a combination of the two models together, utilizing dimensional analysis for in-depth understanding and categorical label mapping for effective communication.

3.2.2 Modalities of Emotional Data in Healthcare

Signals from the human body and behavior need to be registered and processed so that emotions can be identified in healthcare. Each modality is unique in its advantages and disadvantages as well as its different insights. Physiological signals are powerful indicators of AC because they are involuntary body responses that often index arousal and emotional intensity.

- **ECG** is a test that records the electrical activity of the heart. HR and HRV are retrievable from an ECG. The autonomic nervous system, which has much in common with states of emotions such as stress, anxiety, and relaxation, is highly indicated by HRV especially. Increased stress or depressive emotional states are frequently correlated with a decrease in HRV.
- **Electrodermal Activity (EDA),** sometimes referred to as Galvanic Skin Response (GSR), quantifies variations in the skin's electrical conductivity brought on by sweat gland activity. Since the sympathetic nervous system innervates these sweat glands, EDA is a very sensitive measure of stress, emotional arousal, and cognitive load. An abrupt rise in skin conductance is frequently linked to excitement, fear, or surprise.
- **Electroencephalography (EEG)** records the electrical activity of the brain. Different brainwave frequencies (delta, theta, alpha, beta, gamma) are associated with various cognitive

and emotional states. For instance, frontal alpha asymmetry has been linked to approach/withdrawal motivational tendencies related to positive/negative emotions. EEG provides direct insights into neural correlates of emotion, though it's often noisy and requires specialized equipment.

- **Electromyography (EMG)** measures the electrical activity produced by skeletal muscles. In AC, it's often used to capture subtle facial muscle movements (e.g., around the eyes for joy or forehead for sadness/anger) that might not be visible to the naked eye. This provides objective measures for specific facial expressions.
- **Respiration** patterns, including rate and depth of breathing, are influenced by emotional states. For example, anxiety or fear can lead to rapid, shallow breathing, while relaxation might involve slow, deep breaths.
- Skin temperature change is also an indicator of the change in emotions; e.g., excitement will increase skin temperature slightly, whereas stress or anger will lead to peripheral vasoconstriction and a decrease in skin temperature. Physiological cues are strong because they are constant and objective, providing a direct link to internal states harder to control consciously. Nonetheless, due to the complex and often indirect link between raw physiological signals and specific emotions, they might be noisy, susceptible to artifacts, and their interpretation often requires sophisticated signal processing and machine learning methods.

3.2.3 Facial Expressions

Of the non-verbal cues to emotion that have been most widely accepted, one of the most significant is facial expression. An important instrument for studying this area is the Facial Action Coding System (FACS), developed by Paul Ekman and Wallace V. Friesen. Through the analysis of facial expressions into their elemental units, or Action Units (AUs), FACS provides an exhaustive, anatomically grounded system for coding nearly any facial movement. The shortening or lengthening of one or more specific facial muscles is depicted by each AU. A Duchenne smile, or true happiness, is illustrated by AU 6 (Cheek Raiser) and AU 12 (Lip Corner Puller). AC systems leverage computer vision techniques to detect these AUs from images or video frames. By analyzing the presence, intensity, and temporal dynamics of specific AU combinations, models can classify discrete emotions or infer dimensional emotional states.

The advantages of facial expressions include their direct observable nature and generally high inter-rater agreement for basic emotions. However, challenges include variations in illumination, head pose, occlusions (e.g., glasses, masks, hair), individual differences in expressive styles, and the phenomenon of posed versus spontaneous expressions. In healthcare, patient discomfort, medical devices, or cultural norms can also affect facial expressiveness, requiring robust models capable of handling such variability.

3.2.4 Vocal Features

Beyond the words themselves, the non-linguistic aspects of speech, collectively known as **prosody**, carry substantial emotional weight. AC systems analyze various vocal features to infer emotional states:

- **Pitch** (fundamental frequency, F0): Higher pitch variations are often associated with excitement, fear, or anger, while a monotonic, low pitch might indicate sadness or boredom.
- **Intensity/Loudness:** Increased loudness can signify anger or excitement, while decreased loudness might suggest sadness or fatigue.
- **Tone/Voice Quality:** Characteristics such as harshness, creakiness, or breathiness can be linked to various emotions.
- **Speaking Rate/Tempo:** While slower speech may imply melancholy or reflection, faster speech may convey excitement or anxiety.
- **Shimmer and Jitter:** These are tiny changes in amplitude and pitch, respectively, and can be signs of vocal strain or instability associated with emotional arousal.

Distinguishing emotional cues from speech content, speaker identity, and background noise is a challenge in vocal emotion recognition. Additionally, different training data is needed for generalizable models because accents, dialects, and personal speaking habits can affect prosody.

3.2.5 Textual/Linguistic Cues

Certain words, phrases, and sentence structures can be used to directly express emotions in written or spoken language.

- **Sentiment Analysis:** This is a more general field that focuses on identifying a text's emotional tone and categorizing it as neutral, positive, or negative. Although they are related, emotion recognition goes beyond polarity to identify particular emotions (such as "joy," "anger," or "fear").
- **Emotion Lexicons:** These are databases of words annotated with their associated emotional categories or dimensional scores (valence, arousal). Models can use these lexicons to count emotion-laden words in a text.
- **Syntactic and Semantic Analysis:** Advanced NLP techniques, including deep learning models, can analyze sentence structure, word embeddings, and contextual relationships to infer emotional states. For example, the use of intensifiers, exclamations, or rhetorical questions can indicate heightened emotional states.

The advantage of textual cues is their direct expression of cognitive and emotional content. However, challenges include sarcasm, irony, nuanced language, and domain-specific jargon (e.g., medical terminology) that can alter the emotional meaning of words. Short, informal texts (like social media posts or brief patient notes) may also lack sufficient context for accurate interpretation.

3.3 Machine Learning and Deep Learning Models for Affective Computing

The computational core of AC systems relies on powerful algorithms that can learn patterns from raw data and map them to emotional states.

3.3.1 Traditional ML Approaches

Before the deep learning revolution, traditional machine learning models formed the backbone of AC. These approaches typically involve a two-stage process: manual feature engineering (extracting relevant statistical or domain-specific features from raw data) followed by classification or regression using a learning algorithm.

- **Support Vector Machines (SVMs):** Highly effective for classification tasks, SVMs find an optimal hyperplane that best

separates data points belonging to different classes. They were widely used for classifying emotions from extracted physiological features, vocal features, or AU combinations. Their robustness to high-dimensional data and good generalization capabilities made them a popular choice.
- **Random Forests**: An ensemble learning method, Random Forests construct a multitude of decision trees and output the class that is the mode of the classes (classification) or mean prediction (regression) of the individual trees. They are robust to overfitting and can handle various data types, making them suitable for multimodal fusion of emotional features.
- **Hidden Markov Models (HMMs)**: Particularly suited for sequential data like speech or physiological time series, HMMs model sequences of observations by assuming an underlying hidden state sequence. They were used to capture the temporal dynamics of emotional expression, such as the progression of emotions in a dialogue or changes in physiological arousal over time.
- Other traditional methods include Gaussian Mixture Models (GMMs), k-Nearest Neighbors (k-NN), and Artificial Neural Networks (ANNs) with shallower architectures.

The limitation of traditional ML approaches often lies in their reliance on expert-crafted features, which can be labor-intensive, domain-specific, and may not always capture the most discriminative information from complex, high-dimensional raw emotional data.

3.3.2 Deep Learning Architectures

Deep Learning (DL) has revolutionized AC by enabling end-to-end learning, where models can automatically learn hierarchical feature representations directly from raw data, often outperforming traditional methods, especially with large datasets.

- **Convolutional Neural Networks (CNNs)**: CNNs are excellent at capturing spatial hierarchies of features and are primarily used for image and video data. They are widely employed in AC for facial expression recognition, learning to identify facial landmarks, movements of muscles, and their combinations that point towards emotions. Moreover, they can be adapted for time-series data (1D CNNs), e.g., speech spectrograms or physiological signals.

- **Recurrent Neural Networks (RNNs) and Long Short-Term Memory (LSTMs)/Gated Recurrent Units (GRUs)**: These architectures are ideal for modalities such as text, physiological signals (time-series), and speech (vocal features) since they are designed to handle sequential data. LSTMs and GRUs, in specific, address the vanishing gradient problem with standard RNNs, allowing them to learn long-range dependencies which are critical to capturing the temporal dynamics of emotional expression. For example, LSTMs can simulate how emotional states change during a conversation or the minute shifts in physiological indicators that point to increasing stress.
- **Transformers**: Transformers, which got their start in Natural Language Processing (NLP) with the groundbreaking "Attention is All You Need" paper, are now the cutting edge of sequence modeling. When processing each element, their self-attention mechanism enables them to efficiently capture global dependencies by weighing the significance of various input sequence components. Pre-trained Transformer models (e.g., BERT, RoBERTa for text) have revolutionized text-based emotion recognition. They are also being adapted for audio (e.g., audio Transformers) and multimodal fusion, demonstrating superior performance in complex AC tasks by learning highly contextualized representations.
- **Generative Adversarial Networks (GANs)**: While primarily used for generating realistic data (e.g., synthetic facial expressions), GANs are increasingly explored in AC for tasks like data augmentation (generating more diverse emotional data), disentangling emotional and non-emotional factors, or even for domain adaptation to reduce the impact of data variability.
- **Multimodal Fusion Networks**: Given the richness of emotional cues across different modalities, deep learning architectures often integrate features from multiple sources. Fusion can occur at the early stage (raw data concatenation), intermediate stage (feature-level fusion), or late stage (decision-level fusion), with deep learning models capable of learning optimal fusion strategies.

The power of deep learning lies in its ability to learn complex, non-linear relationships directly from raw data, reducing the need for laborious manual feature engineering and often achieving higher accuracy. However, they require substantial amounts of labeled data for training, which, as discussed, is a significant challenge in healthcare AC. This is where transfer learning becomes indispensable.

3.4 Data Acquisition and Annotation Challenges in Healthcare AC

Despite the advanced models, the Achilles' heel of Affective Computing, particularly in the healthcare domain, remains data. Accurately gathering and annotating emotional data presents a number of special and important difficulties.

3.4.1 Sensitivity of Healthcare Data

Healthcare data is extremely sensitive by nature. Patients' emotional and physiological cues can provide sensitive information about their mental and physical health and frequently contain personally identifiable information.

- **Concerns about Privacy:** Such data collection, storage, and processing give rise to serious privacy issues. Patients may be reluctant to divulge their emotional states, particularly if they believe there is a chance that their information will be mishandled, misunderstood, or obtained by unapproved parties. The US requires Health Insurance Portability and Accountability Act (HIPAA) and the EU requires General Data Protection Regulation (GDPR) to be complied with in a very rigorous manner to be able to do this. Big data acquisition becomes complex and costly when these regulations are complied with since they impose very strict limitations on data-collecting, storing, and sharing protocols.
- **Security Risks:** Cyberattacks often aim at the storage and transmission of personal medical data. Patients risk severe consequences from the leak of their emotional health data, like financial abuse, reputation damage, or discrimination. System design is more complicated because of the

non-negotiable demands of good encryption, secure channels, and tight access control.

- **Ethical Considerations and Consent:** It is crucial to get patients' informed consent before collecting and using their emotional data. This would involve a solid grasp of how emotional information will be handled, used, and by whom, more than typical medical consent. It can be particularly challenging to obtain truly informed consent from susceptible populations, like the elderly, the mentally ill, and children. The potential that AC systems might be seen as surveillance, reducing patient autonomy, or adding to already present power imbalances between patients and health care workers raises further ethical issues.
- It is essential to ensure that such healthcare data is accurate, complete, and genuine as collected. Errors or intentional falsification of emotional data may result in misdiagnosis or inappropriate treatment, which could endanger patients.

3.4.2 Inter-Patient and Intra-Patient Variability

Human emotions are not uniformly expressed or experienced, resulting in substantial heterogeneity that is a defining challenge for generalizable models of AC.

- **Inter-Patient Variability (Between Individuals)**: People differ widely in their baseline physiological responses, emotional expressiveness, cultural display rules, and even the way they internally experience emotions. A subtle facial micro-expression of sadness for one patient might be a clear indicator for another. Physiological signals can vary significantly in amplitude and pattern from one individual to another, even for the same emotional state. Cultural backgrounds heavily influence how emotions are expressed and perceived. A model trained on a specific demographic might perform poorly when applied to a different patient population, leading to biased outcomes. This means that datasets need to be highly diverse, covering a wide range of ages, genders, ethnicities, and health conditions, which is extremely difficult and costly to achieve.

- **Intra-Patient Variability (Within an Individual)**: An individual's emotional expression and physiological response can also vary significantly over time and across different contexts. The same emotion might be expressed differently depending on the context (e.g., a "social smile" vs. a "genuine smile"). An individual's physiological baseline can change due to time of day, medication, fatigue, or other health factors. Emotional states themselves are dynamic; a patient's emotional response to chronic pain can evolve over days or weeks, requiring models that can adapt and track these changes. It is difficult to sustain reliable and consistent emotion recognition for extended periods of time for a single person due to this temporal and contextual variability.
- **Subjectivity of Annotation**: Although physiological signals are objective recordings, it is intrinsically subjective to interpret them into distinct emotional labels or dimensional scores. Even skilled human annotators may disagree about the exact emotion or how strong it is, which could result in noisy or inconsistent ground truth labels. The accuracy and generalizability of supervised learning models may be restricted by this "ground truth problem," which has a direct effect on the caliber of training data. Furthermore, because of a patient's need to please, fear of being judged, or even a lack of self-awareness, self-reported emotional states (from questionnaires, for example) may not always match objective physiological or behavioral indicators in clinical settings.

These general challenges with data gathering and annotation point to the vast advantages of transfer learning when applied in the area of healthcare AC. In spite of the inherent volatility and susceptibility of emotional healthcare data, transfer learning offers a viable solution to establishing robust AC models that can mitigate the impact of limited data, reduce the demand for costly human annotation, and enhance the overall generalizability of systems through leveraging prior knowledge in wider, readily accessible datasets. The massive data hurdle would make widespread application of sophisticated AC systems in healthcare an impossibility without transfer learning.

3.5 Edge Computing Architectures for Healthcare

Strong and dependable computational infrastructure that can process delicate, real-time emotional and physiological data is required for the integration of Affective Computing (AC) into healthcare systems. As was previously mentioned, traditional cloud-centric models frequently fail because of issues with latency, bandwidth, and privacy. Here, edge computing architectures for healthcare stand out as a crucial remedy, enabling more secure and responsive healthcare applications by bringing processing power closer to the data source. Designing successful edge-based AC systems requires an understanding of the different elements and paradigms of these architectures.

3.5.1 Types of Edge Nodes in Healthcare

Instead of being a single, monolithic object, the "edge" in healthcare refers to a range of various computing devices, each with unique capabilities, power limitations, and patient proximity. These are frequently called edge nodes:

3.5.2 Wearable Devices (Smartwatches, Patches, Rings)

These are perhaps the most intimate and prevalent forms of edge nodes in continuous patient monitoring. Smartwatches, fitness trackers, smart patches, and smart rings are equipped with an array of sensors capable of collecting physiological data relevant to affective computing. This includes optical heart rate sensors (photoplethysmography - PPG) for heart rate and heart rate variability (HRV), accelerometers and gyroscopes for activity and sleep tracking, electrodermal activity (EDA) sensors for stress detection, and even rudimentary temperature sensors. Some advanced wearables now incorporate ECG capabilities. The edge processing on these devices is typically lightweight, often involving sensor data aggregation, basic feature extraction (e.g., calculating average HR, HRV metrics, or skin conductance peaks), and preliminary filtering to reduce noise. Their primary advantage lies in their unobtrusiveness, continuous data collection capability, and direct interaction with the user. However, their computational power, battery life, and storage are severely constrained, meaning that complex AC models often need to be offloaded to more powerful edge nodes or the cloud.

3.5.3 Medical IoT Devices (Continuous Glucose Monitors, Smart Beds)

Beyond consumer wearables, dedicated Medical Internet of Things (IoT) devices are increasingly forming part of the healthcare edge. These devices are purpose-built for specific medical monitoring tasks and can range widely in complexity and form factor. Examples include Continuous Glucose Monitors (CGMs), smart scales, smart blood pressure monitors, pulse oximeters, and even sophisticated smart beds equipped with pressure sensors, vital sign monitors, and environmental sensors. For AC, these devices might contribute data indirectly (e.g., blood glucose levels impacting mood) or directly (e.g., respiration sensors in a smart bed, or specialized sensors capturing micro-movements indicative of discomfort). While more specialized than general wearables, they also have specific power and processing constraints. Edge processing on these devices might involve local aggregation of readings, anomaly detection, or even very simple rule-based inference. They often act as gateways for data transmission to a local hub or directly to a smartphone.

3.5.4 On-Premises Servers/Gateways (Hospital Servers, Clinic Edge Devices)

These represent a more powerful class of edge nodes, often located within a healthcare facility like a hospital, clinic, or nursing home, or even in a patient's home serving as a local hub. They act as intermediate computational layers between constrained end-devices (wearables, medical IoT) and the distant cloud. These nodes typically have significantly more processing power, memory, and storage than individual wearables. They can perform more complex AC tasks, such as running larger deep learning models for multimodal emotion recognition, aggregating and fusing data from multiple patient devices, performing local data analytics, and securely storing sensitive patient data before selective transmission to the cloud. Examples include dedicated edge servers in a hospital ward, a powerful mini-PC in a remote clinic, or a home gateway that collects data from a patient's smart devices. Their proximity to a larger number of patients and higher computational capacity make them ideal for privacy-preserving localized processing, rapid decision-making, and even deploying federated learning algorithms.

3.5.5 Smartphone-as-Edge-Device Architectures

Smartphones have emerged as ubiquitous and highly capable edge nodes in their own right, particularly for consumer-facing and remote patient monitoring applications. Modern smartphones boast impressive computational power, ample storage, and a rich array of built-in sensors (cameras, microphones, accelerometers, GPS). They can serve as powerful platforms for running sophisticated AC models (e.g., on-device facial expression analysis from the front camera, vocal emotion recognition from the microphone, physiological inference from integrated fitness sensors or connected wearables). Furthermore, they can act as local gateways, collecting data from other Bluetooth-enabled wearables and medical IoT devices, performing initial processing, and then transmitting summarized data to the cloud. Their user interface capabilities also enable direct patient interaction, providing real-time feedback or prompting for interventions. The primary limitations include battery drain from continuous sensing and processing, and user compliance in keeping the device active. However, their pervasive nature makes them an incredibly accessible and versatile edge computing platform for healthcare AC.

3.6 Edge Computing Paradigms Relevant to Healthcare AC

The ways in which these edge nodes interact and distribute computational tasks give rise to different **edge computing paradigms**:

3.6.1 Mobile Edge Computing (MEC)

MEC, also known as Multi-access Edge Computing, primarily focuses on deploying computing capabilities at the edge of the mobile network, typically at cellular base stations or access points. The goal is to provide ultra-low latency and high-bandwidth services to mobile users and devices. In healthcare, MEC can be highly beneficial for ambulatory patient monitoring or emergency services. For example, an ambulance equipped with MEC capabilities could process a patient's real-time physiological and vocal data to detect distress or pain before reaching the hospital, enabling immediate communication with the emergency room based on emotional state. This paradigm is particularly suited for scenarios where patients are mobile and require continuous, low-latency analysis of their affective state.

3.6.2 Fog Computing

Fog computing is a more generalized and distributed paradigm, extending cloud computing closer to the "things" that generate data. It involves a hierarchical architecture that includes computing nodes at various layers between the end devices and the cloud - from industrial controllers, gateways, and routers to local servers. Unlike MEC, which is often tied to mobile networks, fog computing can leverage any network connection. In healthcare AC, fog computing enables distributed intelligence: wearables perform initial data acquisition, smart home hubs or clinic gateways act as fog nodes for intermediate processing and aggregation, and finally, critical insights are sent to the cloud for long-term storage or population-level analysis. This multi-tiered methodology is fitting for distributed patient monitoring over multiple environments (home, clinic, hospital) since it supports intelligent data routing, load balancing, and stronger operations.

3.6.3 Hierarchical Edge Architecture

Computation and storage are spread across multiple layers in this framework, combining elements of MEC and fog computing. These layers extend from the ultra-near edge (wearables) through intermediate edge nodes (smartphones, gateways, and on-premises servers) and then to the remote cloud. Based on its ability and proximity to the data source, each layer performs specific processing functions. For healthcare AC, this hierarchical approach is highly effective. Wearables perform raw data capture and minimal pre-processing. Smartphones or home gateways conduct more complex feature extraction and initial AC inference. On-premises hospital servers might aggregate data from multiple patients, perform more sophisticated AI analysis, and manage patient records. Finally, the cloud is reserved for large-scale data analytics, model retraining, and long-term storage. This layered approach optimizes resource utilization, ensures low latency for critical real-time decisions, and enhances data privacy by keeping sensitive raw data at the lowest possible layer.

3.7 Connectivity and Communication Protocols for Edge Healthcare

Seamless and secure communication is the backbone of any edge healthcare system. Choosing the right connectivity options and protocols is vital for efficient data flow, especially for real-time AC applications.

3.7.1 Bluetooth Low Energy (BLE), Wi-Fi, 5G/6G

- **Bluetooth Low Energy (BLE)**: This is the predominant choice for short-range communication between wearables/ medical IoT devices and nearby edge nodes (like smartphones or dedicated gateways). BLE is highly power-efficient, making it ideal for battery-constrained devices. It's suitable for transmitting periodic bursts of physiological data (e.g., heart rate, EDA, activity) for local processing.
- **Wi-Fi**: Wi-Fi (IEEE 802.11 standards) offers higher bandwidth than BLE and is commonly used for communication between edge gateways/on-premises servers and the internet, or for local area network communication within a hospital. It's suitable for transferring larger volumes of pre-processed data or for downloading updated AC models to edge devices.
- **5G/6G**: The latest generations of cellular technology offer unprecedented speeds, ultra-low latency, and massive connectivity, making them transformative for edge healthcare. 5G's support for MEC, network slicing, and URLLC (Ultra-Reliable Low Latency Communications) enables direct, high-bandwidth, and secure communication between medical devices and edge servers within the cellular network, effectively bypassing traditional internet bottlenecks. This is crucial for real-time AC in mobile or remote emergency scenarios, or for continuous monitoring of patients outside traditional clinical settings where high data volumes need rapid transfer. Future 6G promises even greater capabilities, including integrated sensing and communication for richer contextual awareness.

3.7.2 MQTT, CoAP for IoT Communication

These are lightweight, specialized protocols designed for the constrained environments of IoT devices, making them ideal for edge healthcare.

- **Message Queuing Telemetry Transport (MQTT)**: A publish-subscribe messaging protocol, MQTT is highly efficient, low-bandwidth, and consumes minimal power, making it excellent for transmitting sensor readings from edge devices to a central broker (which can be on an edge gateway or in the cloud). It supports Quality of Service (QoS) levels, ensuring message delivery even over unreliable networks, which is critical for healthcare data.

- **Constrained Application Protocol (CoAP)**: Designed for highly constrained devices (e.g., microcontrollers with limited memory and processing power) and networks, CoAP is a web transfer protocol similar to HTTP but optimized for IoT. It's suitable for simple request/response interactions with edge devices.

These protocols facilitate efficient and reliable data exchange within the edge hierarchy, ensuring that affective insights are generated and communicated effectively.

3.8 Security and Privacy Considerations in Edge Healthcare Architectures

While edge computing inherently enhances privacy by reducing raw data transmission to the cloud, it also introduces new security and privacy challenges due to the distributed nature of the architecture and the often-limited resources of edge devices.

- **Device Security:** Edge nodes, especially wearables and medical IoT devices, are often physically exposed and can be vulnerable to tampering or theft. They must be secured against unauthorized access, malicious code injection, and data extraction. Hardware-level security (such as Trusted Platform Modules), secure boot procedures, and frequent security updates are necessary for this.
- **Data Encryption:** All data must be securely encrypted, whether it is in transit between edge nodes and the cloud or at rest on an edge device. This holds true for emotional deductions, physiological cues, and any related patient identifiers. Protocols for end-to-end encryption are essential.
- **Access Control and Authentication:** Strict authentication procedures must be followed by all users and devices gaining access to edge healthcare systems or data. Only authorized individuals or applications are able to view particular kinds

of emotional data or initiate interventions thanks to role-based access control, or RBAC.

- In order to patch vulnerabilities and implement new features without jeopardizing device integrity or patient data, secure over-the-air (OTA) update mechanisms are crucial as AC models and device firmware change.
- **Regulation Compliance:** It's critical to follow laws unique to the healthcare industry, such as HIPAA, GDPR, etc. In order to comply with these regulations, edge architectures must be built from the ground up with features like audit trails, consent management, and data anonymization right at the edge where sensitive data comes from.
- **AI that Protects Privacy:** Beyond simple encryption, methods such as Federated Learning are essential. Without requiring the raw data to leave the devices, federated learning enables cooperative training of AC models on decentralized edge devices. Data privacy is greatly improved because only model updates—such as learned weights—are shared. Additional techniques that enable computations on encrypted data include secure multi-party computation, homomorphic encryption, and differential privacy.
- **Minimizing Data Collection:** The principle of data minimization—collecting only the data absolutely necessary for the task—is critical. Edge processing helps achieve this by performing local aggregation and discarding irrelevant raw data points before any transmission.

3.9 Real-Time Affective Computing at the Edge in Healthcare

3.9.1 Data Processing and Feature Extraction at the Edge

The initial step in real-time edge-based AC involves efficiently processing raw sensor data and extracting meaningful features directly on the edge device. This is crucial for reducing latency and bandwidth consumption.

3.9.2 Sensor Data Fusion for Multimodal Emotion Recognition

In many healthcare scenarios, emotional states are best understood by combining data from multiple sensors (e.g., facial expressions with physiological signals, or vocal tone with text). Edge devices need to perform sensor data fusion, which means intelligently combining information from different sources. This can happen at various levels:

- **Early Fusion (Data-Level):** Raw sensor data is concatenated. For instance, combining raw EEG data with raw ECG data. This is computationally intensive but preserves all information.
- **Intermediate Fusion (Feature-Level):** Features are extracted from each modality separately, and then these features are combined. For example, extracting facial action units from video and HRV features from ECG, then merging them. This is more efficient than early fusion.
- **Late Fusion (Decision-Level):** Each modality is processed independently to produce an emotional prediction, and these predictions are then combined (e.g., using weighted averaging or a voting scheme). This is the most computationally efficient but may lose subtle nuances.

Edge devices often use intermediate or late fusion due to their computational constraints. Deep learning models deployed on the edge can be designed to handle multimodal input directly.

3.9.3 Efficient Feature Engineering for Resource-Constrained Devices

Extracting relevant features from raw sensor data is critical. For edge devices, this needs to be done efficiently to minimize power consumption and computational load.

- **Physiological Signals:** Instead of transmitting raw ECG or EEG data, edge devices calculate features like heart rate variability (HRV) metrics (e.g., RMSSD, SDNN), frequency domain features of HRV (VLF, LF, HF), statistical features of EDA (mean, standard deviation, slope), or basic EEG band power.
- **Facial Expressions:** Edge devices might detect key facial landmarks and calculate distances or angles between them, or extract Histogram of Oriented Gradients (HOG) features.

- **Vocal Features:** Extracting prosodic features like pitch, energy, speaking rate, and Mel-Frequency Cepstral Coefficients (MFCCs) is common.
- **Textual Data:** For text from patient interactions, simple techniques like bag-of-words or TF-IDF might be used on the edge, or pre-trained word embeddings might be employed if the device has enough memory.

Careful selection of features that are both informative for emotion recognition and computationally inexpensive to calculate is key.

3.10 Model Deployment and Inference on Edge Devices

Once features are extracted, the edge device needs to run a machine-learning model to infer the emotional state. This presents significant challenges due to the limited resources of edge devices.

3.10.1 Model Compression and Optimization

Deep learning models, while powerful, are often too large and computationally intensive to run directly on edge devices. Model compression techniques are essential:

- **Quantization:** Reducing the precision of model weights (e.g., from 32-bit floating point to 8-bit integers) significantly reduces model size and computational cost with minimal accuracy loss.
- **Pruning:** Removing less important connections (weights) in the neural network reduces its size and complexity.
- **Knowledge Distillation:** Training a smaller, "student" model to mimic the behavior of a larger, more accurate "teacher" model. The student model is much smaller and faster, suitable for edge deployment.

3.10.2 Lightweight Deep Learning Models for Edge AC

Beyond compression, the architecture of the deep learning model itself needs to be optimized for edge deployment.

- **MobileNets, EfficientNets, and ShuffleNets:** These are examples of CNN architectures specifically designed for mobile and embedded devices, offering a good balance between accuracy and computational efficiency.
- **Lightweight RNNs/Transformers:** For sequential data, smaller versions of LSTMs or Transformers, or techniques like using fewer layers or smaller embedding dimensions, are necessary.
- **ONNX Runtime, TensorFlow Lite, and Core ML:** These are frameworks designed to run deep learning models efficiently on edge devices, often providing hardware acceleration.

3.11 Real-Time Decision Making and Intervention

The ultimate goal is to use the inferred emotional state to drive real-time actions within the healthcare system.

3.11.1 Alert Generation for Critical Emotional States

If the AC system detects a critical emotional state (e.g., severe distress, panic attack, escalating agitation), it can trigger an alert. This alert can be sent to caregivers, clinicians, or even directly to the patient (if appropriate). The alert should include information about the detected emotion, its severity, and the time of occurrence.

3.11.2 Triggering Personalized Therapeutic Interventions

Based on the detected emotional state, the system can trigger personalized interventions. For example:

- If anxiety is detected, a guided breathing exercise can be initiated through a wearable or smartphone app.
- If a patient expresses pain, a personalized music therapy playlist can be activated.
- In mental health monitoring, a detected downturn in mood could trigger a suggestion to contact a therapist or access self-help resources.

3.11.3 Real-Time Feedback for Caregivers and Clinicians

The AC system can provide real-time feedback to healthcare providers, allowing them to better understand a patient's emotional state during consultations or treatment. This can improve empathy and communication. For example, a system could visualize a patient's stress level during a therapy session, helping the therapist adjust their approach.

3.12 Challenges in Real-Time Edge AC Implementation

Implementing real-time AC on edge devices in healthcare is technically demanding.

- **Power Consumption:** Continuous sensing and processing drain battery life. Energy-efficient algorithms, low-power hardware, and intelligent duty cycling are crucial.
- **Computational Constraints:** Edge devices have limited processing power and memory. Model optimization and efficient algorithms are essential.
- **Data Security and Privacy:** Sensitive emotional data needs to be protected on the device itself and during transmission. Encryption and secure processing are paramount.
- **Model Robustness and Generalization:** Models need to work reliably across diverse patients and in various real-world conditions (noise, lighting variations, etc.).
- **Real-Time Performance:** The entire pipeline, from sensing to decision-making, must happen with minimal latency.
- **Regulatory Compliance:** Healthcare devices must meet stringent regulatory requirements (e.g., FDA approval).

3.13 Applications of Edge-Based Affective Computing in Healthcare

The deployment of Affective Computing (AC) capabilities directly on edge devices unlocks a myriad of transformative applications within healthcare, shifting the paradigm towards more proactive, personalized, and responsive patient care. By bringing real-time emotion recognition and analysis to the point of data generation, edge-based AC can provide critical insights that were previously unattainable or delayed, leading to timely interventions and improved patient outcomes across various medical domains.

Early intervention and mental health monitoring are two of the most significant uses of edge-based AC. Globally, mental health disorders like depression, anxiety, and chronic stress are common and frequently cause major disability as well as physical health problems. Good management involves constant monitoring and early detection. Smartwatches and smartphones that have AC are instances of edge devices that can quietly monitor physiological signals (e.g., skin conductance, heart rate variability) for stress or anxiety signs, examine vocal patterns for depression cues (e.g., slower speech rate, less prosody), or detect alterations in text-based communication as indicators of mood change.

This real-time monitoring allows for the detection of slight changes that may be an indicator of deteriorating mental health, e.g., potential suicidal ideation, before they develop into serious issues. For instance, sustained reduction in arousal and valence from multimodal data would suggest an aggravated depression, and an immediate response can be initiated by a caregiver or clinician. In addition to detection, edge AC facilitates progress tracking and the provision of tailored therapy. Smartphone app-based analysis of emotional state in real-time could initiate an automatically triggered guided mindfulness training or suggest a calming activity in case of detected anxiety. Going beyond the need for retrospective self-reports, edge devices are able to quietly monitor emotional reaction to daily events or therapy sessions in patients receiving therapy. This enables therapists to utilize objective measures for monitoring progress and for treatment plan modification.

The treatment of chronic diseases is another critical area of application. Anxiety, depression, and stress are usual emotional loads for patients suffering from diabetes, heart disease, or asthma. These ailments can directly influence the physical condition and medication adherence of the patients. Patients suffering from diseases such as diabetes or cardiovascular disease may have their emotional condition tracked continuously by edge-based air conditioning systems, which may assist them in the identification of emotional distress cues that may lead to poor self-management. For example, a diabetic patient wearing a tracking device may detect excessive stress levels (from HRV or EDA), which often translate to poor dietary choices or non-compliance with medication. It is critical to understand how emotion impacts adherence to treatment regimens. When a patient grapples with complex medication regimens or lifestyle adjustment, an edge device may detect their frustration or resignation and trigger a tailored nudge (like reminder or motivational message) or alert to their care team, enhancing compliance and averting adverse health events.

Subjective reporting is often inadequate in pain assessment and control, especially for those patients who are cognitively impaired or non-verbal. More objective pain recognition from facial and physiological cues may be possible with edge-based AC. In addition to monitoring physiological signals like heart rate, skin conductance, and muscle tension (*via* EMG or accelerometers), a camera on an edge device (such as a tablet in a patient's room or a wearable with built-in facial recognition) could analyze micro expressions of pain. Even if a patient is unable to communicate their level of pain verbally, the system can provide a more objective, ongoing assessment of that level by correlating these multimodal cues. This objective data can then inform personalized pain relief strategies. For instance, if increasing pain is detected, the system could automatically adjust medication dosages (under clinician supervision), recommend non-pharmacological interventions like guided relaxation, or alert nursing staff for immediate attention. This real-time, objective insight is particularly valuable in post-operative care, chronic pain management, and for pediatric or elderly patients.

In Elderly Care and Assisted Living, edge-based AC can significantly enhance the quality of life and safety of older adults. Loneliness, agitation, and confusion are common emotional and cognitive states in elderly populations, often preceding falls, wanderings, or other adverse events. Edge devices (e.g., smart home sensors, wearables, in-room cameras with privacy-preserving AC) can continuously monitor behavior and emotional cues to facilitate detecting loneliness, agitation, or confusion. Changes in vocal patterns, prolonged periods of inactivity, repetitive behaviors, or signs of emotional distress from facial expressions could trigger alerts to caregivers or family members. Furthermore, AC can contribute to enhancing social interaction and quality of life. For residents in assisted living facilities, an AC system could identify moments of low engagement or boredom and suggest social activities, initiate video calls with family, or play preferred music, thereby promoting emotional well-being and reducing feelings of isolation.

Enhancing the Doctor-Patient Relationship: One significant but often overlooked use is communication. Diagnosis, patient confidence, and compliance can all be significantly affected by the emotional climate of a medical consultation. Edge devices—like a smartphone or a dedicated device the patient or clinician wears—would provide real-time feedback about the emotional condition of the patient during consultations. A physician can be alerted to a patient's relief after a good prognosis, their confusion regarding treatment, or his or her worry regarding a diagnosis by such subtle, non-intrusive feedback. This induces higher empathy and understanding by allowing clinicians to adjust their communication style, clarify, or provide emotional support when necessary. Medical professionals can also gain significantly from AC tools in training their empathy.

These systems have the ability to produce more emotionally intelligent, patient-focused healthcare practitioners by assessing simulated interactions with patients and providing unprejudiced feedback on the trainee's ability to detect and respond to emotional stimuli. Edge-based AC can also save lives in critical and emergency care cases where timely assessment and response are critical. Time is of the essence in ambulances or emergency rooms. Quick assessment of patient pain levels, emotional shock in victims of trauma, or distress can be helped by wearable sensors and in-body cameras connected to edge computing devices.

Paramedics and emergency room staff are able to gain critical information from this real-time assessment before performing full medical assessments. An example would be utilizing vocal and physiological indicators of severe pain or acute anxiety to prioritize treatment or direct immediate pain management strategies. By providing objective, continuous tracking of a patient's emotional and physical status, this ability facilitates optimization of the delivery of care in stressful situations. This enables medical teams to come to better-informed decisions under stress and deploy resources effectively, ultimately enhancing survival rates and recovery pathways in critical situations.

3.14 Conclusion

Overall, the integration of edge-based healthcare systems and affective computing represents a sea change in patient care by transforming our ability to identify and respond to human emotions in real time. Through decentralization of computing power, edge computing is able to overcome the primary limitations of traditional cloud-based methods, such as outrageous latency, bandwidth constraints, and severe privacy issues, as discussed in this chapter. We have explored the intricate structures and functional theories underpinning edge-based AC, illustrating the broad applicability of AC, from enhancing doctor-patient communication and personalized interventions to objective pain control and early mental health crisis recognition. The intersection of AC with edge computing in healthcare holds tremendous promise but also has important challenges, including the requirement for robust model generalization over various patient populations, resource constraints on the edge device, and regulatory requirements around data security. If the important ethical concerns of privacy, consent, and algorithmic fairness are thoughtfully considered as this quickly evolving area evolves, this paradigm shift has the potential to lead to a future of AI-powered health solutions that are more anticipatory, cost-effective, and profoundly empathetic.

AI disclosure statement: The author acknowledges the use of AI-based tools for minor language editing or grammatical correction. However, all intellectual contributions, analyses, and conclusions presented in this chapter are entirely the author's own.

Bibliography

1. Picard, R.W., Affective computing for hci, in: *HCI (1)*, pp. 829–833, 1999, August.
2. Wang, J., Chen, R., Liu, Y., Edge AI for smart healthcare: A comprehensive survey. *IEEE Trans. Ind. Inf.*, 17, 10, 6823–6834, 2021.
3. Selvi, S., Revathy, G., Brindha, P., Blockchain-Enabled Federated Learning for Secured Edge Data Communication Through a Decentralized Software-Defined Network, in: *Achieving Secure and Transparent Supply Chains With Blockchain Technology*, pp. 128–141, IGI Global Scientific Publishing, 2024.
4. Greer, T.L. and Rishel, C.J., Wearable devices for depression and anxiety: A systematic review. *Psychiatric Serv.*, 71, 5, 450–457, 2020.
5. Soleymani, M., Valstar, M., Jiang, L., Pantic, M., A survey of multimodal emotion recognition: Challenges and opportunities. *IEEE Trans. Affective Comput.*, 8, 3, 391–403, 2017.
6. Kao, H.P., Chen, K.H., Wen, R.T., Lightweight deep learning models for real-time facial expression recognition on mobile edge devices. *Sensors*, 21, 11, 3845, 2021.
7. Al-Turjman, F. and Al-Amri, J.F., Real-time pain assessment in smart hospitals using edge AI and IoT. *J. Med. Syst.*, 44, 1, 1–12, 2020.
8. Qiu, J., Zhang, Q., Ren, J., Lin, C., A survey of security and privacy in edge computing for healthcare. *J. Netw. Comput. Appl.*, 149, 102462, 2020.
9. Deldari, R. and Mirmahdi, S.J., Deep learning for stress detection using physiological signals: A comprehensive review. *Artif. Intell. Med.*, 140, 102558, 2023.
10. Li, W., Lu, R., Ma, X., Edge AI for personalized mental healthcare: Opportunities and ethical challenges. *npj Digit. Med.*, 5, 1, 1–11, 2022.

Part II

MACHINE LEARNING IN AFFECTIVE AI

4

Deep Learning for Emotion Recognition – CNNs, RNNs, Transformers, and Self-Supervised Learning Techniques

Shivamma D.[1], Shaila S.G.[1], Monish L.[1], Ramesh Chundi[2*] and Sumana S.G.[2]

[1]*Dept. of CSE (Data Science), School of Engineering, Dayananda Sagar University, Bangalore, India*
[2]*Dept. of Computer Applications, School of Computer Applications, Dayananda Sagar University, Bangalore, India*

Abstract
Emotion recognition is one of the fundamental responsibilities of Artificial Intelligence (AI) that enables machines to decode and sense human emotions in multiple modes such as facial expressions, speech, and physiological signals. Emotion recognition has been highly boosted by deep learning through the use of extensive structures, i.e., Convolutional Neural Networks (CNNs), Recurrent Neural Networks (RNNs), Transformers, and Self-Supervised Learning techniques. CNNs have extensively been applied in emotion recognition, especially facial expression analysis, to be capable of harnessing the strength of spatial hierarchies. Through pattern extraction and learning from face images, CNN-based models like Visual Geometry Group (VGG), Residual Network (ResNet), and Efficient Net have been found to be very accurate in simple and mixed emotion recognition. Derivatives of CNNS such as 3D-CNNs enhance performance by taking into account temporal dynamics in video-based emotion recognition. RNNs, particularly in Long Short-Term Memory (LSTM) and Gated Recurrent Units (GRU), played a pivotal role in emotion recognition from sequential data such as speech and physiological signals. The LSTMs can capture the long-term dependencies in time-series data and are thus best suited for analyzing the vocal tone, speech patterns, and bio-signals. Hybrid models combine CNNs and RNNs, integrate spatial and temporal features and allow for multimodal emotion recognition.

**Corresponding author*: rameshreddy-bca@dsu.edu.in

N. Thillaiarasu, G. Revathy, T. Saravanan, V. Muthukumaran and S. Balamurugan (eds.) Affective Artificial Intelligence: Fundamentals, Challenges, and Applications, (79–104) © 2026 Scrivener Publishing LLC

Transformers have emerged as a robust rival to RNNs for emotion recognition. Transformers are particularly adept at modeling long-range dependencies and hence are well-suited to identify subtle variation in emotions across different modalities. Most recent advances like multimodal transformers enhance emotion identification through the combination of text, vision, and audio inputs into a single structure. Self-Supervised Learning (SSL) methods have achieved sticky grip in emotion recognition by allowing models to learn enormous volumes of unlabeled data. Pre-trained models for contrastive learning and masked autoencoders on large scale datasets can be minimized upon the labeled emotion datasets. SSL based models generalized by varying emotional expressions and contexts in a superior manner and to solve the issues which are associated with data sparsity and annotation biases. Despite in the deep learning have some problems with a practical application for Emotion recognition. Human feelings can be varied widely across the cultures and making it problematic to create models that can effectively generalize across various populations. Facial occlusions, illumination, and an environmental context could potentially introduce an additional complication into the interpretation of emotional expression. Furthermore, when it comes to privacy concerns, vulnerability to bias in training data, and real-world implementation are limited to the systems have to be weighed to avoid the misuse of such technologies. In this chapter provides a comprehensive overview of the deep learning methods to emotion-based recognition to summarize the merits and demerits of CNNs, RNNs, Transformers, and also Self-Supervised Learning techniques. This chapter covers the future directions with emerging trends like multimodal learning integration, explainable AI, and personalized emotion recognition models. Deep learning develops an emotion recognition system likely to more accurate, interpretable, and adaptable, leading to application developments such as mental health monitoring, human-computer interaction, and affective computing.

***Keywords*:** Deep learning, emotion recognition, facial expression analysis, convolutional neural networks (CNNs), recurrent neural networks (RNNs), transformers, self-supervised learning

4.1 Introduction

Emotions form the foundation of human communication, decision-making, and interaction with the environment. As artificial intelligence increasingly pervades our lives, the biggest challenge may be to make machines comprehend and respond sensibly to human emotions. Emotion recognition is an answer to this challenge by trying to bridge the gap between human emotional behavior and machine perception to enable human-computer interaction to be more natural and sensitive. This capability is increasingly becoming critical in a wide range of applications—whether developing more interactive user interfaces for video games, making virtual assistants more prompt, or facilitating diagnosis of mental health, customer support, and learning software. As AI-based applications are becoming more interactive in nature, the ability to accurately understand affective cues from facial expressions, voice tone, and text communication is more important than ever. Historically, emotion recognition relied on rule-based systems and handcrafted features.

The traditional approaches used statistical methods, such as Support Vector Machines (SVM), Decision Trees, and Hidden Markov Models (HMMs), on features extracted from audio, text, or facial data. While these methods offered basic emotional comprehension, they were not efficient in handling complex variations in data such as variations in lighting, accent, background noise, or mixed emotions. The arrival of deep learning revolutionized emotion recognition by eliminating the need for hand-engineered feature extraction. Convolutional Neural Networks (CNNs), Recurrent Neural Networks (RNNs), and now Transformer models have proven immense success in learning hierarchical, abstract representations from raw input directly. These models are able to learn temporal patterns, spatial cues, and contextual dependencies and provide a stronger and more accurate representation of emotional states across modalities.

Emotion detection has moved from old methods to smart deep learning tools. Early work, like Ekman and Friesen's Facial Action Coding System (FACS), set the base by sorting facial moves tied to feelings. Old ways often used traits like Local Binary Patterns (LBP) and Mel-Frequency Cepstral Coefficients (MFCC), with tools like SVMs, but these had trouble with real-world changes and wide use. Deep learning brought big steps, especially with Convolutional Neural Networks (CNNs), which are great at picking spatial traits. Depuru *et al.* [1] suggested a facial image-based emotion recognition system utilizing deep learning. The system has moderate classification accuracy on multiclass emotions. Nevertheless, it faces challenges in real-time usage and generalization because of the lack of dataset diversity. Abdullah *et al.* [2] employed a multimodal deep learning architecture based on audio and visual modalities for emotion recognition. The proposed system is superior to single-modality models. However, the merging process is computationally costly and takes synchronized inputs. Alkhamali *et al.* [3] introduced an ensemble model of Transformer, CNN, and LSTM to identify emotions in speech, especially in remote learning environments. It is highly accurate with multi-acoustic features. Nevertheless, it needs enormous training resources and might not be generalizable across languages.

Chaudhari *et al.* [4] introduced a self-supervised learning technique with inter-modality attention transformers is proposed for facial emotion recognition. The model acquires cross-modal relations efficiently and enhances accuracy in limited-label environments. Yet, it requires extensive pretraining and large datasets to achieve the best performance. Khare *et al.* [5] investigated cross-modal transformers in self-supervised arrangement for audio-visual emotion recognition. It has robust performance even with little labeled data. However, temporal disalignment between modalities can affect accuracy. Mohammad *et al.* [6] offered a transformer-based model for emotion recognition in text augmentation methods. The method enhances robustness and enhances classification, particularly in underrepresented emotions. Its primary challenge is achieving augmentation quality without the addition of noise. Shaila *et al.* [7] used deep learning to music therapy through emotion classification into positive and negative to drive mood transformation. The model supports emotional recovery by providing personalized music recommendations. Subjective variability of emotional response and absence of physiological feedback are the limitations. Estimation is done using nose features by means of a pyramid organization of facial images. The model provides efficient lightweight computation and decent accuracy for certain emotions was demonstrated in Shaila *et al.* [8]. Shaila *et al.* [9] employed MobileNet to identify complex facial expressions, dealing with emotions beyond the fundamental set. It enhances mixed emotion recognition in facial expressions. However, compound emotion datasets are limited, impacting training effectiveness. A deep learning-based framework on EEG is proposed for brain signal-based human emotion recognition by Shaila *et al.* [10]. It shows high accuracy and scope for application in human-computer interaction. Challenges include EEG noise sensitivity and electrode placement. Ramesh *et al.* [11] employed a sentiment analysis approach based on a lexicon for Kannada-English code-switch text. The model delivers interpretable outputs and performs well on bilingual content. However, it is constrained by lexicon coverage and has difficulty with implicit sentiment. Chundi *et al.* [12] presents NBLex, a naïve Bayes lexicon-based approach to predicting emotions in Kannada-English code-switched text. It efficiently classifies emotions in multilingual environments with low resource consumption. It is, however, unable to understand context deeply like transformer models. Chaudhari *et al.* [4] formulated an inter-modality attention transformer with self-supervised learning to combine visual and auditory modalities for facial emotion recognition with robust performance without labeled data. Wu *et al.* [13] designed a transformer-based SSL system for wearable devices, acquiring multimodal rich emotional representations from physiological and sound signals, demonstrating robust generalization over real-world datasets. Siriwardhana *et al.* [14] presented a transformer-based fusion model that combines audio, video, and text *via* self-supervised pretraining, enhancing multimodal emotion recognition accuracy on benchmark datasets. Vazquez-Rodriguez *et al.* [30] experimented with transformer-based SSL through contrastive learning for emotion recognition and outperformed supervised counterparts on small labeled datasets. Khare *et al.* [5] employed cross-modal transformers learned with self-supervised learning for text-audio fusion and attained better performance on emotional speech processing tasks. Poulinakis [16] addressed self-supervised multimodal learning with attentional mechanisms and contrastive losses, especially useful in the fusion of weakly correlated modalities such as EEG and facial signals. Hazmoune & Bougamouza [17] presented a taxonomy and systematic review of transformer models for multimodal emotion recognition, indicating future directions and challenges in SSL-based models. Montero Quispe *et al.* [18] utilizes self-supervised learning to recognize emotion from only physiological signals (e.g., ECG), demonstrating how SSL techniques significantly enhance signal-based emotion prediction. Kotei & Thirunavukarasu [19] analyzed pre-trained transformer models (such as BERT, GPT) under SSL frameworks and considered their expansion to affective computing and emotion recognition tasks. Strizhkova [20] investigated deep learning-based emotion recognition with emphasis on transformer model fine-tuning *via* SSL for cross-domain emotional perception. Ohri & Kumar [21] surveyed some of the self-supervised image recognition methods employing CNNs and DNNs, setting the stage for the adaptation of such methodologies in visual emotion recognition tasks. Barragán Castro [22] introduced an SSL-based framework to identify acute stress from ECG signals with the help of pretext tasks in estimating robust emotional states. Rodriguez [23] designed multimodal transformer models for emotion recognition using SSL methods for improved context learning between modalities. Boigne *et al.* [24] showcased the strength of self-supervised transfer learning for identifying more complex emotions with limited labeled data, making scalable emotion recognition possible. Gladys & Vetriselvi [25] presented a survey on multimodal emotion recognition with focus on SSL and deep fusion mechanisms between modalities such as speech, facial features, and bio-signals. Abibullaev *et al.* [26] provides a transformer model for EEG-based BCIs and emotion recognition, including transformer-based feature extraction, SSL approaches, and signal processing challenges. Latif *et al.* [27] reviewed deep representation learning for speech emotion recognition and outlined how transformer models based on SSL can better understand emotional speech with low supervision. Sharrab *et al.* [28] gave a systematic overview of deep learning transformers in speech recognition, in which trends in SSL-based models for emotional inference in conversational systems were emphasized. Akinpelu *et al.* [29] used Vision Transformers (ViT) for speech emotion classification to show how vision models improved by SSL can be transferred to the audio domain for better performance.

4.2 Emotion Recognition Modalities

Emotion recognition is the process of feeling and knowing a person's emotional state by perceiving data in the form of facial expressions, tone of voice, body attitude, or written words. Emotions are commonly classified into two categories: basic and complex. Basic emotions such as happiness, sadness, anger, fear, surprise, and disgust are present universally in all cultures and are commonly expressed similarly by most people. On the other hand, social and situational factors influence compound emotions like pride, jealousy, or embarrassment and tend to be the result of a combination of more fundamental emotions. There are various models' psychologists have suggested to explain and categorize emotions. One such widely accepted model is Paul Ekman's theory that emphasizes a set of discrete, universally recognized basic emotions. But yet another broadly used method is the dimensional model, e.g., Russell's Circumplex Model, where emotions are placed on continua of dimensions. Dimensions tend to run from valence (from positive to negative) through arousal (from passive to highly energized) and possibly dominance (from passive to active). Such models are the building-block knowledge upon which emotion recognition systems in wide domains will be based.

4.2.1 Impact of Facial Expressions for Emotions

Expressions are one of the most salient and best-understood expressions of human emotions. They are grounded in subtle movements of small muscles, known as facial action units (AUs). Facial feature analysis and emotional state interpretation are typically carried out by computer vision systems, often powered by Convolutional Neural Networks (CNNs). Such systems can be used for real-time operation using live webcam feeds or

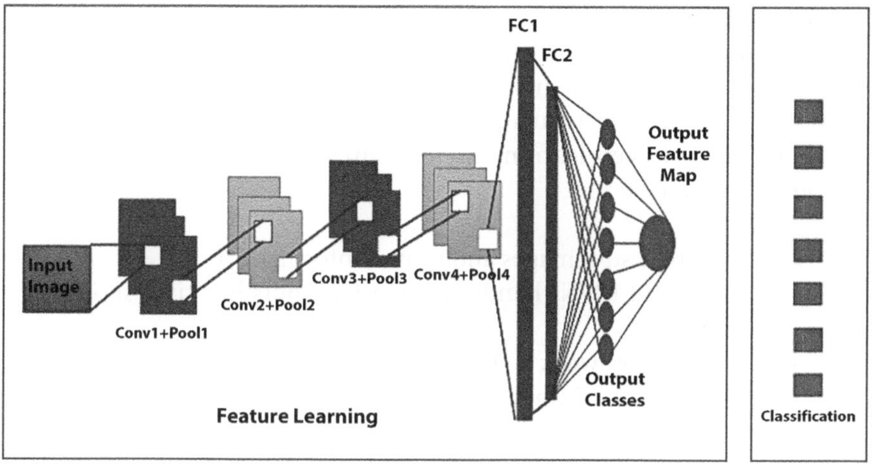

Figure 4.1 Facial expressions.

processing pre-recorded videos and images and therefore are used in various fields like virtual assistants, surveillance, and user experience analysis. Figure 4.1 shows the CNN is used for feature learning and it gives the classification of emotions like happy, sad, angry etc.

4.2.2 Impact of Speech and Audio Signals for Emotions

Differences in the pitch, rate, volume, and voice quality of a speaker are strong clues about their emotions. A straitened, rushed delivery might, for instance, mean that the speaker is angry, worried, or thrilled. Mel-frequency cepstral coefficients (MFCCs) and other features are extracted from the sound in order to research such signals. Subsequently, they are instantiated by instantiations like Transformers or Recurrent Neural Networks (RNNs), which enable the timing and situational context of speech patterns to be modeled in a manner enabling effective perception of emotion. Figure 4.2 demonstrates the flow of the emotion signals like facial expression, audio and text with the multimodal fusion to give the results by classifying the emotion.

4.3 Deep Learning Models for Emotion Recognition

Deep Neural Networks (DNNs) are a computer learning algorithm only second to the human brain. They are made up of numerous layers of nodes (neurons) that have each layer of nodes receive the input through progressively abstractive representations. In deep learning, these maps are automatically learned from humongous data sets and are ridiculously good at solving difficult pattern matching problems like identifying emotions. There are certain deep learning architectures, which are appropriate for various types of data:

- CNNs best suit images and spatial information.
- LSTMs and RNNs handle sequential inputs like time series or sound.
- Transformers work well with text and have been applied to vision and multimodal as well.

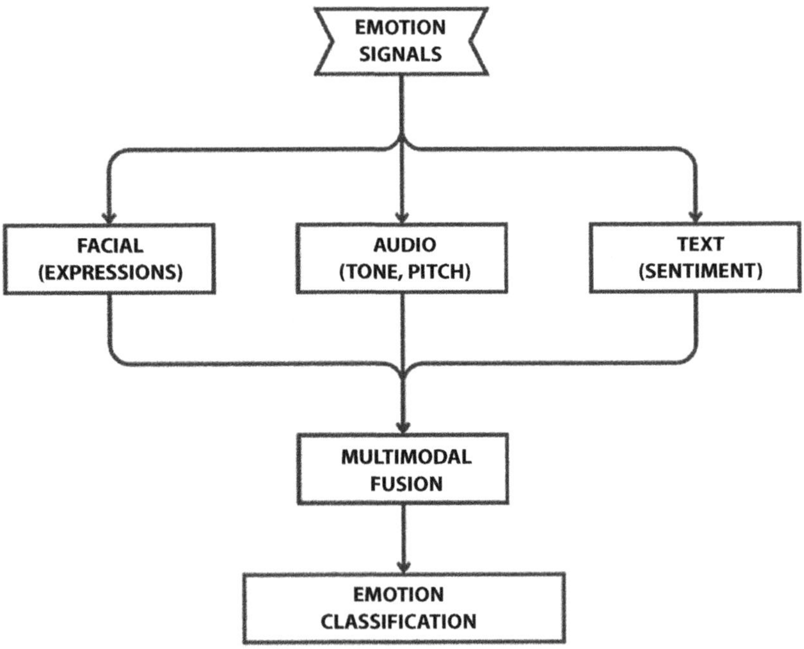

Figure 4.2 Speech and audio signals.

Learning possesses several strengths against the old ways for detecting emotion as:

- **Auto Feature Learning:** Hierarchical features are learned automatically by deep models without need of individual effort making them identify subtle emotional cues.
- **Noise and Variability Robustness:** Models contrasting rule-based systems can handle noisy data and inter-subject variability.
- **Scalability:** Models are deployable at scale in real-time systems once trained with minimal overhead.
- **Multimodal Integration:** Deep models can seamlessly integrate several modalities signals to generate a consistent emotional interpretation.

Emotion detection is merged to numerous applications in the real world increasingly:

- **Healthcare:** Tracking emotional condition of patients particularly in mental illness as well geriatric care.
- **Education:** Adaptive learning systems that adapt to mood of students to deliver content more effectively.
- **Customer support:** Mood-aware chatbots together with voice assistants that can respond based on the mood of user.
- **Automotive systems**: Driver warning systems that are able to detect fatigue stress or anger in a bid to boost road safety.
- **Marketing and Entertainment:** Measuring audience responses towards advertisements films or product presentations.

As deep learning models improve in accuracy and generality emotion-aware systems become increasingly feasible trustworthiness and invaluable across all sectors.

4.4 Convolutional Neural Networks (CNNs) for Emotion Recognition

Facial Expression Recognition (FER) is a human problem. We use computer algorithms, i.e., CNNs to do it based on the hierarchical feature extraction property. Such an effective feature extractor is essential for FER, which makes CNN renowned for this purpose. CNNs are able to perform hierarchical feature learning at various levels of abstraction. For Facial Expression Recognition, the first few levels in the network tend to grasp simple characteristics. For example, shades and edges. As we go deeper in the network, we start moving toward the fundamental feature capturing such as eyes and mouth and towards the complex configuration of such attributes that are a must to identify the states of emotion. This helps to seek the characteristics that contribute to emotion recognition. For facial expression recognition, CNNs are trained over commonly specified facial datasets e.g., FER-2013 which are basically the images annotated with the labeled emotional expressions like 'happy,' 'sad,' 'angry', 'surprised' classifier is learned that maps particular facial areas (such as eyes or mouth) to emotional states [10].

Pooling layers in CNN reduce the dimensionality of the extracted features, keeping the most important information for emotion classification. The combination of detecting fine grained details and generalization across lighting variation, head pose variation, and facial expression variation (thanks to a lot of data and a strong model) makes this architecture ideal for the facial emotion recognition task. The reason that these models tweak higher performance baselines is because these are deep models that make use of residual connections, thus are able to even comprehend subtle pragmatics of emotions formed and shown in distinct styles in facial expressions that only very accurately trained human mind can interpret. Visual features obtained by CNNs are then passed through fully connected layers for comprehensive model and classification at the end, which the intensity of that label.

Convolutional Neural Networks (CNNs) work well with data set up like a grid, such as images. For figuring out emotions from faces, CNNs shine because they learn how features fit together. These networks start with a layer that takes in grayscale or color images (like 48×48 or 224×224×3). Before you feed the image to the net, you do some basic work like normalizing, resizing, and setting the face right, to make it steady and work better. Convolutional layers are key in CNNs. They use filters on inputs to get spatial features like edges, textures, or facial expressions. These layers often come next to activation functions, usually the Rectified Linear Unit (ReLU), defined as $f(x) = \max(0, x)$. It brings non-linearity to the model, helping it learn complex things. Versions like Leaky ReLU and ELU are also used to solve the dying ReLU issue. With this step-by-step approach, CNNs learn features — from simple edges at first to tricky patterns like smiles or frowns later on. CNNs can find Action Units (AUs) — specific face muscle moves linked to emotions, which makes them great for telling facial expressions. With progress in structures like VGG, ResNet, and MobileNet, CNNs are stronger and more efficient, making instant emotion reading possible in both strong systems and small devices.

4.5 Feature Extraction and Spatial Encoding

The word likelihood of facial expressions indicates the likelihood of having a particular mood or emotion, characterized by using Convolutional Neural Networks (CNNs), feature extraction takes care of itself and spatial encoding helps the model to distinguish between the small amounts of real laughter we naturally express while laughing, and the clusters of laughter that can emerge from the conversation. In CNNs, feature extraction is done by convolutional operations where filters (kernels) slide over the input image to find patterns such as edges, textures, and other local structures. The network learns features in a hierarchical fashion, starting with low-level features like edges and corners in the initial layers, and moving up to high-level features like the eyes, mouth, and facial shape in the deeper layers. By training itself just on raw pixels, the network automatically learns the features that are important, and hence doesn't need the user to specify the features to be used, allowing it to generalize well in unseen samples. In facial expression detection pure face representation, it may include the facial skin textures, the outlines of facial characteristics, and the position of eyes/face elements of the face image. In the following convolutional layers, the network began to focus on more complicated patterns, such as the curvature of the mouth (for a smile or frown), the openness of the eyes (for surprise or fear), and furrowed brows (for anger). Spatial encoding is needed to understand the spatial relation between the extracted facial features. In detecting facial emotions, the position of facial features is very important, or more generally, the distributive clues from the image; for example, the configuration of a smile which would be characterized by the presence of both an upward curvature of the mouth and exposed teeth. Pooling layers are used for down sampling, reducing the dimensions of an input image while preserving important features. For example, max-pooling will pick the highest value from a group of pixels, this is important as the other pixels of the window contains different orientations. This allows the CNN to focus on the spatial arrangement of features (such as the distance between the eyes and mouth) that are essential for recognizing emotions. After pooling, the last part of the CNN uses spatially encoded features for the classification stage. Such features are spread on to the FC layers which gather the information and perform the final required prediction about emotions on the face.

4.6 Notable CNN Models

The field of AI includes machines that can do things that essentially require human intelligence; e.g. knowledge problems-solving, and Complex discussion. One of the promising applications of AI is emotion recognition/ emotion categorization. Hand in hand, there are three main categories: Facial emotion recognition that can be done through "YAKROSS" - the need for big data "Ajecten" – good accuracy and the use of AI, facial emotion recognition is working well involves a three-step process. For applications such as facial emotion recognition, where a common input data type is images of faces, state-of-the-art work mostly revolves around convolutional neural networks (CNNs). A variety of CNN architectures have been shown be generalized powerful and so, as expected, many of them have been used for this tag as well. Some of the most popular models in this space: VGGNet, ResNet, InceptionNet, MobileNet. VGGNet, developed by the Visual Geometry Group at Oxford, is known for its high level of depth and scalability with its uniform architecture. It is made up of a stack of small 3×3 convolutional filters, and 2×2 max-pooling layers. The generic model for CNN is constructed by twenty-two to thirty-two 3×3 size layers and sixteen to nineteen 3×3 size layers obtained by different realization. It has thirteen convolutional layers and further on three layers that are fully connected. Therefore, several works are done comparable to the attributes of VGG to establish faster information during terrorism. Therefore, attacks are gradually occurring like Mobile and Tablet so the Current model at time lags. VGG models are good in facial emotion recognition it's important to note that with the deeper layers your models are capable of also capturing more complex facial and emotional features which are stand out layer lines of a frown, smile, and eyebrows movements etc. Its feature maps abstract from simple contour (blotch of color) to jumbles of color to part of a dog/face/square with specific edges, to a person's face to a hand and so on. It's crucial for transfer learning as the models had been pre-trained using large datasets including fine-grained object categories available in ImageNet. The final layers could abstract from basic facial contours up to more complex intrinsic-configurations related to the emotion that may be associated.

ResNet (Residual Network) introduced the concept of residual connections, enabling the training of extremely deep networks by addressing the vanishing gradient issue. ResNet models such as ResNet-50 or ResNet-101 are perfect for emotion recognition to allow the network to learn more generalized features with increasing network depth without performance degradation which is useful when it comes to distinguishing between very subtle emotional differences between "sad" and "fearful". In addition to boosting the performance of existing facial emotion recognition algorithms, other improvements could serve to enhance the user experience for the experimenter. Inception Net (Google Net) promotes a multi-path architecture that enables the spatial features to coexist at different scales through parallel convolution. This is extremely beneficial in facial emotion recognition since they tend to have different sizes and positions. Each version of the Inception architecture was introduced to allow for the scaling up of networks in over the years with greater computational cost, reduced submissions. A variant per year is providing better training for these networks in the next version. MobileNet is an efficient, lightweight convolutional neural network (CNN) architecture that is optimized for low-resource environments. Its depth wise separable convolutions dramatically reduce memory and floating-point operations with little degradation in accuracy, making it well-suited for real-time facial emotion recognition in resource-constrained applications like mobile health monitoring or interactive emotion-aware systems.

Each of these CNN models can be fine-tuned on emotion-labeled facial datasets (e.g., FER2013, CK+, Affect Net) using transfer learning, building on the pre-trained weights (i.e., ImageNet) as a strong foundation for recognizing features related to facial emotions. These models vary in the complexity of their architecture, their depth, and pace of hind sight relative to the inference speed. The CNN models are chosen to reflect the nature of the user model's deployment i.e. an application requiring high precision or low-latency for real time performance min X that can be rapidly brought to scale.

4.7 Case Studies and Results

Case studies from the literature have clearly shown that Convolutional Neural Networks (CNNs) are very good at recognizing facial expressions, even when they are exposed to different datasets and environments. The case studies also use popular deep learning (CNN) models like VGGNet, ResNet, and Inception Net to work on common data resources in the field of facial expression recognition, such as FER-2013, CK+, JAFFE, and Affect Net. This is followed by assessing the performance of the methods using performance metrics like precision, accuracy, F1-Score, and the confusion matrix. This result showed a huge performance difference with a traditional machine learning approach using hand-crafted features such as SVMs or HOG+SVM pipelines, which clearly demonstrates the potential of new features learned by CNNs. Similarly, a fine-tuned version of ResNet-50 (i.e., training on ImageNet), when trained and evaluated on the Affect Net database, presented state-of-the-art performance with an approximate accuracy of 75% for accurately predicting the facial expressions along with robust generalization capabilities towards unseen facial gesture and lighting variations. A case study used ensemble learning; whereby various models built from different subsets of data were integrated in a voting decision framework. This solution has improved robustness and reduced bias that marginalizes the major class in misclassifications. The ensemble of five CNN was able to awake from sleep and was able to respond to each emotional face with an F1 score of 0.481 with a raw image input and 0.753 with an extracted feature.

4.8 Recurrent Neural Networks (RNNs) for Emotion Recognition

Recurrent Neural Networks (RNNs) are actually an all-new class of neuro-network that is specifically designed for usage on sequential data. The sequence data includes any form of text, time series, speech or much more where there is an order and dependency between the inputs. Unlike feed-forward neural networks, they keep track of previously seen data so that it can be utilized to a better extent in the future (or at any point in the sequence). In simple words, they have memories that help them learn from history and predict the future. This makes them very beneficial in moving emotion detection tasks because emotional expressions have a temporal nature and change across time in most cases. The overall theme of RNNs is to consider sequential data in its entirety – the output at a time step, t, dependent on the current input as well as the hidden state from the previous time step. In the area of emotion detection, RNNs are usually employed to detect sequences of emotional cues. For example, in speech emotion detection, the model learns to examine how vocal tone changes consistently in response to accepted interventions (pitch, energy, duration), while in facial expression detection based on video levels, RNNs can model the dynamic distribution of facial muscular severity over several pictures. However, classic RNNs including RNN have problems like vanishing gradients, which make it difficult to learn long-term dependencies. Despite this, they acted as a pioneering system for more sophisticated recurrent topologies (such as LSTMs or GRUs) that are being increasingly used in cutting-edge emotion recognition platforms for enhancing long sequence modeling.

4.9 Long Short-Term Memory (LSTM) for Emotion Recognition

Long Short-Term Memory (LSTM) networks are a subset of recurrent neural networks (RNN) that were specifically designed to tackle the vanishing gradient problem, a known issue with the older RNN models. This approach has proven to be efficient for various types of sequential data and are able to recognize emotions, especially when the expression of emotions unfolds over time. At its core, an LSTM cell is more complex, containing memory cells and three types of gates: input gate, forget gate, and output gate. This structure enables LSTMs to precisely model how human memory works, making them especially suited to the task of understanding emotions that develop slowly over time or with context. Speech, video, physiological sensor data all can capture emotional expressions in real time. We, humans can make sense of them naturally. We do expect the same from machines. In the case of speech signal-based emotion recognition, LSTMs can accurately decode prosodic features, including temporal patterns in tone, rhythm, and pitch at multiple time scales, differentiating between frustration, excitement, and calmness. In video-based emotion recognition, LSTMs can decipher facial expressions frame-by-frame to capture the dynamic emotional variance that may not be evident in static cues.

4.10 Gated Recurrent Units (GRUs) for Emotion Recognition

Gated Recurrent Units (GRUs) are cousins of LSTMs designed to solve the vanishing gradient problem without having the memory cells. They are good at learning sequences that are dependent on long-term dependencies but lack the ability to carry out multiple sequences of these dependencies. In the emotion-recognition context, GRUs deliver time-savings and a lightweight's solution with comparable accuracy. They outperform more fancy models in a real-time setting, if say Wi-Fi or cellular data is not available or available but with very low bandwidth, adjacent-area problems, or a single server is needed for all data except data collection. Due to their high efficiency and low latency, GRUs are also preferred due to their light-weight nature when it is to be deployed, say, in an application which runs a model that needs to run on a mobile phone in real time or on a small Raspberry Pi.

4.11 Temporal Analysis in Speech-Based Emotion Recognition

A game changer is temporal analysis, specifically as it concerns predicted emotion detection. This approach allows the models to understand the emotional implication over time, and not only through relative inaction, but also through variances in pitch, rate, melody, intensity, and prosody. Making it easy to approach the question, emotions are not static. In speech, emotional cues be infused in plus token of multiple syllables or chunks of data not on voice prosody. For example, anger could be conveyed through sentence-wide pitch increments and energetic copies to the voice, while sadness can present particularly slow rates and lower levels of intensity. Temporal models break up speech into its component speech characteristics frame by frame and monitor the development of these characteristics. It will tell if it realizes, this incorporates a number of features that change dynamically based on the tenor in which that emotion is expressed. Some of the features that are typically extracted for speech emotion modeling are Mel-Frequency Cepstral Coefficients (MFCCs), pitch contours, energy levels, and formant frequencies.

Given that emotions in speech extend across several phonemes or entire phrases, it is important to note that emotional cues in speech often vary in scale, with some manifested by the f0 contour or overall speech rate, but others more strongly associated with specific words. Recurrent neural network models, such as LSTM and GRU, are natural choices for modeling data with temporal dependencies, since they excel at capturing information across time. Complex architectures such as CNNs (Convolutional Neural Networks) and temporal attention are also frequently used to capture local acoustic information and aggregate it over time. They enhance the model by concentrating the learned attention on emotional cues, perhaps due to intermittent pitch and sudden duration increase for tension, or rest/combination for convenience. These insights help to improve the emotion recognition system's performance by ensuring robustness when it encounters unseen data.

4.12 Transformers and Attention Mechanisms for Emotion Recognition

The Introduction of the Transformers in deep learning has stirred the field of deep learning, especially in managing some of the disadvantages of a proper sequence data, it has shown a much-improved performance in terms of handling long-range sequences without the necessity of recursive connections as in RNNs. Transformers were initially described in Vaswani *et al.*'s paper "Attention is All You Need" based on the self-attention mechanism [31]. Instead of processing input serially timestep by timestep, Transformers learn jointly from the complete context comprising all the tokens in the input sequence, making them highly efficient and capable of learning beyond local dependencies. All in all, Transformers have modernized the way we preprocess sequential data and potentially mark a shift from the heavy reliance on recurrent neural networks (RNNs), which operate one step at a time through time-steps to read in sequential data. The Transformer architecture mainly comprises two components: An encoder, which processes the input data (e.g., speech, text, or image) and spawns a contextualized illustration of the input sequence.

The encoder is composed of a sequence of identical layers, each containing two main sub-layers: Self-attention layer: models the relevance of individual input words to one another. Feedforward neural network: This is a perceptron that takes in output from the attention mechanism as input and creates a final encoded representation. A decoder, which utilizes the encoded data for generating the output sequence The decoder comprises multiple layers, but is augmented with an additional sub-layer that attends to the encoder's output, allowing the model to learn the relationships between the input and output sequences. Transformers are essential for natural language processing (NLP) duties, although they can be used for other aspects like image processing, time series analysis, and for emotion recognition tasks as well. The Transformer model can understand intricate dependencies across long sequences making them a suitable choice for emotion analysis over time in speech, text, and video data.

4.13 Self-Attention for Emotion Context Understanding

Self-attention, which powers Transformer models, provides a way for the algorithm to understand the wider context in which the various parts of the text belong to each other. This is achieved by calculating the relationship between each pair of words in the input using word-level features and then using these relationships as a reference to assess each other's importance within the overall text. This allows the structure within the text to be strategically highlighted, which in turn will enable a system like OpenAI's GPT (Generative Pre-training Transformer) to generate high-quality text in well-formed language models. Regular recurrent neural networks, in contrast, take a sequence step by step and maintain an internal memory of what it has processed thus far. However, sequence-to-sequence models with attention mechanisms (which were popular pre-transformer era) allowed the encoder-decoder framework to learn where to focus its attention to accurately generate the desired output.

By computing based on the entire sequence at once, self-attention allows the neural network to identify vital components of the input that carry emotional tone, whether it is specific harmonics in speech synthesis, a scene break in the video stream, or merge-points among audio signals in a recording. Self-attention is similarly useful for studying global context, crucial for discerning complex or nuanced emotions such as sarcasm, anxiety, or mixed emotions. The attention mechanism plays an important role in boosting the objectivity of any aggression against toxin production. In addition, my attention mechanism is also very much capable of dealing with emotion analysis and therefore can act as another counter against any emotional outbreak that may occur because of any corruptive activity.

Self-attention is used to disambiguate such configurations: the positions of the neighboring words on the right help in determining the correct emotion for the target word. When the target word in the text-based emotion recognition is to be renamed, there is not only a lack of much emotion information any more, but also a lot of filler words in the original input sequence. In multimodal affect recognition, it is crucial to understand the multimodal behaviors, that is minimal head nods on speech is not the same as agreement, to aid the development of natural, intuitive behavior in human-robot interaction. By introducing visual information, the Network can use features from the area of attention in a video to extract the relevant emotional information. In order to bridge the gap between different modalities and learn interactions between multimodal representations, we extend the self-attention mechanism to cross-modal attention, which allows the model to effectively align and fuse information from diverse sources. This offers a deeper understanding of the context in which emotional expressions occur with respect to an overarching plan/flow over time and co-occurring modalities.

4.14 Comparison with RNNs for Temporal Sequences

When looking at the time sequence, unpacked into audio, text, and video, Transformers and the Recurrent Neural Networks (RNNs) both represent two distinct ways to work with time emotion recognition tasks. We often have had sequences that are not fixed size (say for example speech) and this helps the recurrent network. The Recurrent Neural Networks generally process each sequence stepwise, steadily storing hidden states that evolve with the input over time. This is of course ideal for modeling temporal dependencies in sequences of shorter length.

However, they are inherently slower to train and in inference time due to the sequential nature of processing each input one by one over time. Also, RNNs are not so good at laying up distant terms to each other, as you must remember sequences don't tend to stay faithful of 1000 steps behind. In contrast, Transformers work with the whole sequence in parallel *via* self-attention mechanisms, allowing them to learn global relationships between any input elements regardless of their distance. They are thereby more skilled in capturing long-range dependencies, such as continuous changes in tone or emotions throughout long texts or plays. They can also be far more scalably trained on larger datasets, converging quicker, as they are able to process whole sentences in parallel. Both RNNs and Transformers do have attention mechanisms, but RNNs can only utilize that mechanism to create error signals. Now that the error signals are generated, the network can be trained to fix those errors. Most of the different possible interactions are included in the Transformer model as those can be later figured out, all at the same time. Transformer model is more powerful when you have multimodal inputs. Loomis adds that while an RNN-based model has been built to learn text imitation, it focuses too much on repetitive words while ignoring the variable ones. Finally, while Transformers may be better suited to certain problems than, it does require a significant amount of computational resources, well-labeled data. RNNs, such as GRUs, may still be more practical for smaller datasets or real-time applications.

4.15 BERT, ViT, and Multimodal Transformers

Transformer-based models like BERT, ViT and Multimodal Transformers have immensely boosted the field of emotion recognition. They can create rich relational networks over various data modalities, including available forms of information, including text (BERT), vision as well as speech. In emotion recognition from text (like tweets, dialogues, or transcripts), BERT captures subtle emotional cues such as sarcasm, irony, or implicit sentiment that traditional models often miss. Fine-tuning BERT on emotion-labeled datasets (e.g., Emotion-Stimulus datasets or ISEAR) allows it to effectively classify emotions like anger, joy, sadness, and surprise, making it a go-to model for text-based affective computing. In facial emotion recognition, ViT can model spatial relationships between facial features (like eyes, eyebrows, and mouth) and capture nuanced changes in expressions across frames. ViTs outperform CNNs in some cases, especially when trained on large facial emotion datasets such as FER+ or AffectNet, due to their capacity for global context modeling and non-local attention. Models like MERT (Multimodal Emotion Recognition Transformer) or MulT (Multimodal Transformer for Time-series) are specifically designed for this purpose. They can handle synchronous and asynchronous inputs, making them highly effective for real-world emotion recognition applications in healthcare, human-computer interaction, and sentiment-aware virtual agents.

4.16 Self-Supervised Learning for Emotion Recognition

Self-Supervised Learning (SSL) is a paradigm of machine learning where the model can learn expressive representations from unsupervised data by generating supervisory signals out of the data itself. For emotion recognition, SSL provides an effective alternative to traditional supervised paradigms otherwise plagued by non-availability of sufficient labeled emotional datasets. SSL paradigms allow the model to learn patterns and features crucial for understanding emotional content based solely on intrinsic aspects of the input data. In order to self-supervise model training, some auxiliary problems called pretext tasks are defined. These are intended to force the model to learn semantic and structural data. Predicting a rotation of an image, completing a jigsaw puzzle, reconstructing a masked input, and predicting frame order in a video are some examples. These induce the model to generate robust internal representations that are extremely transferable to downstream tasks such as emotion classification.

4.16.1 Contrastive Learning Approaches

Contrastive learning has been one of the strongest approaches employed in SSL. It achieves this through forcing the model to push similar representations of similar inputs (positive pairs) close to each other in the embedding space and push similar representations of dissimilar inputs (negative pairs) away from each other. SimCLR, MoCo, and BYOL are some of the most common approaches in this group. SimCLR is heavily reliant on contrastive loss functions and data augmentations, whereas MoCo uses a momentum encoder in combination with a dynamic dictionary for consistency training. BYOL presents a new mechanism where the model is learned in bootstrapped prediction without any negative examples.

4.16.2 Applications and Datasets in Emotion-Aware Representation Learning

Self-Supervised Learning (SSL) has shown immense capability in extracting emotion-sensitive features from both audio and video data. Pretraining using unlabeled data and fine-tuning to detect emotions has allowed researchers to achieve better even when they are provided with fewer labeled samples. Such a process can make it possible to sense minute indications like micro-expressions or inflections that are an important determinant of the human emotion. Employment of SSL techniques such as SimCLR, MoCo, and BYOL has been effective in emotion recognition models to provide satisfactory results. SimCLR, for example, has been applied for FER+ and AffectNet datasets to enhance facial emotion classification. MoCo has been effective for situations of domain adaptation such as emotion recognition across different cultures. BYOL's new model has been effective for stable and efficient learning on datasets such as RAF-DB, even outperforming supervised baselines at times.

4.16.3 Dataset Biases and Generalization Issues

Different datasets have been created to aid research in emotion recognition. FER-2013 is a standard dataset of grayscale face images obtained in the wild and labeled to be used in facial expression recognition. IEMOCAP has a lot of audiovisual data with emotional tags and is, therefore, the researcher's top choice among multimodal research work. EmoReact aims at exploring children's emotional responses and comprises multimodal inputs gathered in video interaction. Emotion recognition model evaluation calls for an extensive set of metrics. Global prediction accuracy is often used to measure overall correctness. Yet, in many emotion datasets with imbalances in given classes, classifying metrics such as the F1-score that balances precision and recall become equally important. Confusion matrices better reflect model performance across emotion classes, whereas ROC-AUC scores are conventionally used for binary and multiclass classification to measure discriminative power.

Emotion datasets are biased because they have imbalanced distributions over emotion classes or demographic classes. For instance, some datasets over-sample certain cultures, age groups, or genders, and this results in bad generalization on unseen data. Models learned from such datasets can learn spurious correlations instead of actual emotional cues. These problems are alleviated by using diverse and balanced datasets, using data augmentation methods, and using transfer learning to enhance robustness. Figure 4.3 shows the emotion datasets are evaluated by model training and testing to get the bias and generalized results.

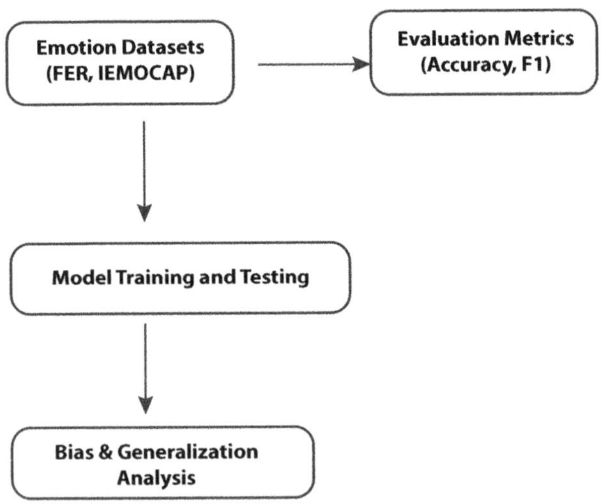

Figure 4.3 Dataset biases and generalization issues.

4.17 Conclusion

Deep learning has the potential to revolutionize the way in which human emotions are detected and interpreted from diverse sets of data. This report aims to summarize, structure and provide a concise overview of the power of deep learning, particularly through CNNs, RNNs, Transformers and self-learning models. According to the study, deep models are favored over conventional methodologies for feature learning, attention mechanisms are proving effective for understanding contextual information and multimodal and SSL approaches are becoming increasingly significant for overall improvement in results, to summarize anticipating the potential between deep learning and emotion recognition is a nice next step in order to bring AI systems across industry sectors and applications to be more intuitive and human-aware. Although a number of studies have shown the effectiveness of deep learning models for emotion analysis, emotion recognition using deep learning in resource-constrained environments is still an open challenge. It's time for empathetic artificial intelligence to come into its own with AI researchers aiming to build systems that understand human emotions and try to recreate empathy in machines, tasked with creating systems that mimic the brain's emotional intelligence. However, challenges such as dataset scarcity, cultural variability, model interpretability, and ethical concerns remain significant barriers to real-world deployment. City planning and medical image analysis are just two examples. Integration of privacy-preserved methods such as federated learning and the introduction of domain adaptation techniques could provide solutions to those who have concerns with respect to their personal privacy or fears invisibility. This allows emotional intelligence to be heightened in AI systems without risk of undermining user trust. The field is still in development Intrinsic Domain Adaptation methods are necessary for DISSA domains especially when the source and target distributions are co-variant.

AI disclosure statement: The author acknowledges the use of AI-based tools for minor language editing or grammatical correction. However, all intellectual contributions, analyses, and conclusions presented in this chapter are entirely the author's own.

References

1. Depuru, S., Nandam, A., Ramesh, P.A., Saktivel, M., Amala, K., Human Emotion Recognition System Using Deep Learning Technique. *J. Pharm. Negat. Results*, 13, 4, 1031–1035, 2022.
2. Abdullah, S.M.S.A., Ameen, S.Y.A., Sadeeq, M.A., Zeebaree, S., Multimodal emotion recognition using deep learning. *J. Appl. Sci. Technol. Trends*, 2, 01, 73–79, 2021.
3. Alkhamali, E.A., Allinjawi, A., Ashari, R.B., Combining Transformer, Convolutional Neural Network, and Long Short-Term Memory Architectures: A Novel Ensemble Learning Technique That Leverages Multi-Acoustic Features for Speech Emotion Recognition in Distance Education Classrooms. *Appl. Sci.*, 14, 12, 5050, 2024.
4. Chaudhari, A., Bhatt, C., Krishna, A., Travieso-González, C.M., Facial emotion recognition with inter-modality-attention-transformer-based self-supervised learning. *Electronics*, 12, 2, 288, 2023.
5. Khare, A., Parthasarathy, S., Sundaram, S., Self-supervised learning with cross-modal transformers for emotion recognition, in: *2021 IEEE Spoken Language Technology Workshop (SLT)*, 2021, January, IEEE, pp. 381–388.
6. Mohammad, F., Khan, M., Marwat, S.N.K., Jan, N., Gohar, N., Bilal, M., Al-Rasheed, A., Text augmentation-based model for emotion recognition using transformers. *Comput. Mater. Continua*, 76, 3, 3523–3547, 2023.
7. Shaila, S.G., Gurudas, V.R., Rakshita, R., *et al.*, Music therapy for mood transformation based on deep learning framework. *Comput. Vision Image Understanding*, 35–47, 2022. https://doi.org/10.1007/978-981-16-8225-4_4.
8. Shaila, S., Vadivel, A. Avani, S., Emotion estimation from nose feature using pyramid structure. *Multimed. Tools Appl.*, 82, 27, 42569–42591, 2023.https://doi.org/10.1007/s11042-023-14682-w.
9. Shaila, S.G., Shivamma, D., Monica, U.S., *et al.*, Facial expression recognition for compound emotions using mobile net architecture, in: *International Conference on Artificial Intelligence and Data Engineering*, IEEE, 2022.
10. Shaila, S.G., Sindhu, A., Shivamma, D., *et al.*, Human Emotion Recognition Based on EEG Signal Using Deep Learning Approach, in: *International Conference on Recent Trends in Communication and Intelligent Systems*, Springer, 2023.
11. Ramesh, C., Vishwanath, H.R., Jay, S., Bhartheesh, Lexicon-based sentiment analysis for Kannada-English code-switch text. *Int. J. Artif. Intell., 12*, 3, 1500–1507, 2023.
12. Chundi, R., Hulipalled, V.R., Simha, J.B., NBLex: Emotion prediction in Kannada-English code-switch text using naïve Bayes lexicon approach. *Int. J. Electr. Comput. Eng.*, *13*, 2, 2023.
13. Wu, Y., Daoudi, M., Amad, A., Transformer-based self-supervised multimodal representation learning for wearable emotion recognition. *IEEE Trans. Affect. Comput.*, 15, 1, 157–172, 2023.

14. Siriwardhana, S., Kaluarachchi, T., Billinghurst, M., Nanayakkara, S., Multimodal emotion recognition with transformer-based self supervised feature fusion. *IEEE Access*, 8, 176274–176285, 2020.
15. Aurchana, P., Indhumathi, R., Revathy, G., Ramalingam, A., Facial Emotion Recognition Using Osmotic Computing, in: *Advanced Applications in Osmotic Computing*, pp. 1–14, IGI Global Scientific Publishing, 2024.
16. Poulinakis, K., Self supervised multimodal learning for emotion Recognition, 2023.
17. Hazmoune, S. and Bougamouza, F., Using transformers for multimodal emotion recognition: Taxonomies and state of the art review. *Eng. Appl. Artif. Intell.*, 133, 108339, 2024.
18. Montero Quispe, K.G., Utyiama, D.M., Dos Santos, E.M., Oliveira, H.A., Souto, E.J., Applying self-supervised representation learning for emotion recognition using physiological signals. *Sensors*, 22, 23, 9102, 2022.
19. Kotei, E. and Thirunavukarasu, R., A systematic review of transformer-based pre-trained language models through self-supervised learning. *Information*, 14, 3, 187, 2023.
20. Strizhkova, V., Emotion Recognition using Deep Learning, Doctoral dissertation, Université Cote d'Azur, 2025.
21. Ohri, K. and Kumar, M., Review on self-supervised image recognition using deep neural networks. *Knowl.-Based Syst.*, 224, 107090, 2021.
22. Barragán Castro, F., Self-supervised learning for acute stress detection in electrocardiograms, 2024.
23. Rodriguez, J.F.V., Multimodal transformers for emotion recognition, Doctoral dissertation, Université Grenoble Alpes [2020–....], 2023.
24. Boigne, J., Liyanage, B., Östrem, T., Recognizing more emotions with less data using self-supervised transfer learning, arXiv preprint arXiv:2011.05585, 2020.
25. Gladys, A.A. and Vetriselvi, V., Survey on multimodal approaches to emotion recognition. *Neurocomputing*, 556, 126693, 2023.
26. Abibullaev, B., Keutayeva, A., Zollanvari, A., Deep learning in EEG-based BCIs: A comprehensive review of transformer models, advantages, challenges, and applications. *IEEE Access*, 11, 127271–127301, 2023.
27. Latif, S., Rana, R., Khalifa, S., Jurdak, R., Qadir, J., Schuller, B., Survey of deep representation learning for speech emotion recognition. *IEEE Trans. Affect. Comput.*, 14, 2, 1634–1654, 2021.
28. Sharrab, Y.O., Attar, H., Eljinini, M.A.H., Al-Omary, Y., Al-Momani, W.A., Advancements in Speech Recognition: A Systematic Review of Deep Learning Transformer Models, Trends, Innovations, and Future Directions. *IEEE Access*, 13, 46925–46940, 2025.
29. Akinpelu, S., Viriri, S., Adegun, A., An enhanced speech emotion recognition using vision transformer. *Sci. Rep.*, 14, 1, 13126, 2024.

30. Vazquez-Rodriguez, J., Lefebvre, G., Cumin, J. Crowley, J.L., Transformer-based self-supervised learning for emotion recognition, in: *2022 26th International Conference on Pattern Recognition (ICPR)*, 2605–2612, IEEE, 2022, August.
31. Vaswani, M., Esses, V. M., Newby-Clark, I.R. Giguère, B., Cultural differences in fear of negative evaluation after social norm transgressions and the impact on mental health. *Front. Psychol.*, 13, 804841, 2022.

5

Early Detection of Mental Health Disorders Using Affective AI on Social Media Textual Data

A. Sumathi*, V. Rishikeswaran and P. Umamaheswari

Department of CSE, SRC, SASTRA Deemed University, Tamil Nadu, India

Abstract

In recent years, social media platforms have become valuable sources for analyzing public sentiment and potential mental health indicators. This study explores Kanye West's tweets using sentiment analysis and lexicon-based detection methods to uncover emotional trends and signs of depression, anxiety, and mania. The methodology involves cleaning and preprocessing textual data, applying VADER sentiment analysis, and identifying mental health indicators using curated keyword lexicons. Temporal patterns and self-referential language usage were also examined to detect emotional fluctuations over time. The results demonstrate that combining sentiment scoring with mental health-specific lexicons offers meaningful insights into public emotional expression. This approach contributes to ongoing research in affective computing and mental health monitoring through social media analytics.

***Keywords*:** Sentiment analysis, mental health, VADER, lexicon-based detection, temporal analysis

5.1 Introduction

Over the past ten years, we have seen a global increase in the challenges associated with mental health, affecting individual, family, and systemic pressure to manage an existing mental health challenge. Mental health

**Corresponding author*: sumathi@src.sastra.edu

N. Thillaiarasu, G. Revathy, T. Saravanan, V. Muthukumaran and S. Balamurugan (eds.) Affective Artificial Intelligence: Fundamentals, Challenges, and Applications, (105–128) © 2026 Scrivener Publishing LLC

disorders including depression, anxiety and bipolar disorder affect millions of people living around the world, many only discover or identify their mental health challenge when it has reached crisis level. According to the World Health Organization, nearly 1 billion people are living with a mental disorder and depression directly affects over 280 million. The statistics can be staggering, as approximately $1 trillion USD is lost to the global economy and productivity due to depression and anxiety worldwide. Mental health was already an area of concern before the COVID-19 pandemic, and now it has become dire. Preliminary data indicates that anxiety and depression increased by approximately 25% in the first year of the pandemic.

Currently, our systems for diagnosing mental health problems as we know them are constrained. The field has determined methods like clinical interviews, self-report questionnaires, and professional judgment to evaluate the mental health of individuals. Although these methods can be somewhat effective, they are typically used reactively, and are often inaccessible to individuals lack the self-awareness, resource, and motivation to engage in mental health services.

These traditional methods also suffer from numerous barriers that lessen effectiveness in delivering early interventions. First, all these methods require individuals to actively help-seek, which many individuals will put off, due to stigma, cost prohibitive hurdles, or simply failing to even recognize the symptoms. Secondly, while self-reporting can provide a perspective on the client's features and conditions, it is equally subject to certain biases. Patients may minimize or exaggerate symptoms, depending on their current emotional state, or desire to present themselves as normal. Thirdly, clinical evaluations may be months or weeks apart, which allow for potentially important insights to occur in the day to day fluctuations of mood and behavior that may be necessary to support the ability to recognize patterns in one's mental health.

This is where technology comes into play. The exploration of the use of technology to detect early signals of mental ailments has become a major focus and one that may ultimately provide individuals with access to early interventions and perhaps alleviate some of the suffering. The utilization of digital technologies to be able to assess aspects of mental health would also represent a radical paradigm shift in the way psychological assessments are delivered, specifically early intervention.

By being able to detect warning signs earlier in the course of mental health illnesses, technological methods of detection may serve to stop the severity of symptoms from appearing, which could reduce the need for crisis hospitalizations and help improve outcomes in the long run.

With the global expansion of social media, greater opportunities to examine - and understand - human behavior, emotional expression, and psychological well-being have become available. Like a digital mirror of ourselves, platforms like Twitter, Facebook, and Instagram contain trace evidence of all of our cognitive, affective, and behavioral experiences over time. As of 2023, approximately 4.9 billion people in the world use social media regularly, which accounts for just over 62% of the global population. Given that social media is now part of the fabric of daily life, providing countless platforms for individual engagement and expression, the amount of information available now is staggering. On average, people spend nearly 2.5 hours on social media platforms daily, thinking, feeling, or doing through text, image, or video. All of this engendered expression produces significant digital evidence of a person's mental well-being, and if captured systematically and analyzed, could unveil detectable patterns for numerous aspects of mental health.

Social media content is usually less guarded or socially desirable than what you'll find in clinical (i.e., regulated) sources, enabling a more direct assessment of psychological, emotional and behavioral states. The spontaneous nature of much social media material conveys emotional states that would usually be regulated in clinical situations and would remain hidden from the researcher. Furthermore, the longitudinal or time-related aspect of social media usage offers researchers the ability to view temporal shifts in expression that may indicate changes in mood or thinking in a way that is difficult to achieve in controlled clinical settings. This time aspect is especially wrapped in value when thinking about conditions that are cyclical, such as bipolar disorder or seasonal affective disorder, where tracking changes in mood over extended periods may reveal diagnostic patterns.

Social media can closely capture real-time emotional expression without the normal barriers involved in clinical research. When considering had-hoc social media messages the chance to evaluate tens of thousands of cases of language use, emotional or behavioral shifts provides a special niche for mental health researchers to evaluate patterns, sentiment or emotional states at scale. The diversity and richness of social media data offer a significant benefit to mental health research. With their billions of individuals from many disparate different demographic, culture and geographical backgrounds, social media provide access to the previously underrepresented populations that may never be reached through psychological research. It provides researchers with the means to build more robust mental health models that take account of cultural variation in emotional expression and help reduce disparities in access and quality of mental health care.

Natural Language Processing (NLP), which is a subfield of artificial intelligence, has expanded at a geometric rate. Machines are now able to comprehend, analyze, and create human language. When used for social media content, NLP techniques can scrape significant information from unstructured text data, such as sentiment, intent, and topic appropriateness. The first breakthroughs in NLP resulted from transformer-based language models known as BERT, GPT, and their variations. These models created a revolution in NLP capabilities in domains with unprecedented accuracy for the majority of tasks, including sentiment analysis, emotion detection, and context-based inference of meaning. This evolution has, for the most part, benefited social media mental health research as researchers can more clearly identify and interpret the complexities of ambiguous language to express psychological distress.

The progression of NLP techniques has transitioned from primarily rule-based and statistical approaches to deep learning models that can model subtle details and nuanced meanings. Early NLP systems used keyword-spotting techniques and basic statistics to identify text sentiment, but often did not match human thought and expression related to sentiment complexity, including the use of sarcasm, idioms, and references to specific culture(s) or communities. More recent, deep-learning based NLP systems can process massive amounts of text data, allowing the algorithm to learn and model the complex relationships between words and phrases in a given context, and corresponding sentiment. This has enhanced performance of many psychological states expressed through language.

Affective computing relates to the discovery and understanding of human emotions through technological measures, contributing to this process. Originally led by researchers like Rosalind Picard at MIT, affective computing is essentially a joint discipline between emotional intelligence and artificial intelligence, creating systems that detect, understand, and respond to human emotions. Affective computing occurs through multiple technologies such as facial expression, tone of voice, physiological signals, and text-based emotion. By combining tools from sentiment analysis with models that analyze clinical mental health language, researchers can detect features from social media posts consistent with patterns of psychological state - for example, indicators of depression, anxiety, and mania.

Combining affective computing and natural language processing (NLP), has enabled advances in computational psychology to go from human researchers analyzing a few on the surface features and patterns to quantifying emotional states from textual data. Sentiment analysis is a central concept revolved around this work and encompasses putting text content on positive to negative emotional tone, with sometimes arousal (intensity) and dominance (extent of control) incorporated in the emotion identification. More advanced emotion detection systems can now detect basic emotions like joy, sadness, anger, fear, and surprise, through the analysis of particular language used in texts to create a more sensitive understanding of psychological states being conveyed in a social media post.

One of the difficulties in carrying out a social media content analysis is informal communication. These are brief in length and frequently contain slang, abbreviations, and emojis or other abbreviations, and they tend to show little or no commitment towards use of grammatical structure. For this reason, traditional text analysis tools struggle to capture the emotional tone or intent of posted content. In addition, the shortness of many posts, including messages limited to 280 characters long on Twitter, generates linguistic constraints in which to infer context based on a small amount of data in each post. This often generates distinctive linguistic features that are unique to social media, such as formally abbreviated words, hashtags, and other creative uses of punctuation, which may confuse NLP tools. Further, the fast-evolving nature of internet language which involves the creation of new slang terms or shifts in meanings of words or phrases poses challenges for computationally-based analysis systems due to the need to constantly update lexicons and descriptive language models in order for systems like sentiment analysis to remain accurate.

In addition to the issues with language, the multimodal information of social media also makes attempts at identifying mental health more complex. Most social media platforms combine text as well as images, videos, audio, and/or interactive elements as forms of communication, presenting rich data but also complexity. Although this paper is predominately devoted to exploring text analysis, it is important to recognize that a broader approach to identifying mental health in social media would ideally integrate multiple channels of communication as input data.

Furthermore, psychological states are not always displayed directly; sometimes the meanings we derive from subtle linguistic markers, the progression of posts over time, and use of self-oriented terms are more indicative of hidden mental health challenges. Studies have demonstrated that individuals who are depressed engage their social lexicon by using more first-person singular pronouns (I, me, my), and less first-person plural pronouns, (we, us, our), suggesting a more self-oriented plan of action, or social disconnection. Changes that show temporal indicators matter too, such as frequency of posts, time of day, or seasonality in time measured on social media platforms as a sign of a disruption in psychological state from one ending to another (i.e., with regard to whether a person's psychological well-being is stable, improving, or waning). For instance, increased posting time in the evening/early morning hours could signal insomnia, and many mental health conditions, including mood, and anxiety disorders, could carry insomnia as a notable indicator, bound in psychological distress.

Research on the aforementioned complexities leads researchers to capture sentiment through tailored sentiment analysis like VADER (Valence Aware Dictionary and sEntiment Reasoner). The fact that VADER was designed primarily to analyze short texts that are typically social media-style text has advantages in proximity and similarity in form and function. VADER is a hybrid-search classification system, rule-based and lexical, with a much higher accuracy rate than simply classifying with positive, negative, and neutral lexicons alone, and has been found to work well on tweets and posts. VADER was designed specifically for social media text. Special modulation or handling of punctuation emphasis (i.e., more than one exclamation point), capitalization, intensifiers (i.e., definitely), and some commonly used emojis add possibilities without unnecessarily complicating social text sentiment analysis and calculations. This specialization makes it more precise for sentiment analysis on social media than for general-purpose sentiment tools. VADER's rule-based nature also makes it computationally efficient and interpretable so that researchers can know exactly which particular aspects of a text led to its sentiment being classified as such.

Besides general sentiment ratings, mental health detection can be greatly enhanced by using lexicons carefully crafted to pinpoint language indicative of mental disorders. Words that express sadness, hopelessness, anxiety, insomnia, and emotional instability are usually good indicators of underlying psychological pathology. The lexicons, when cross-referenced with user content, can pinpoint emotional and cognitive trends that are different from normal behavior. Some research groups have constructed specialized mental health vocabularies by examining clinical documents, web-based support groups, and social media discourses known to be linked with particular psychological disorders. These dictionaries identify not only salient markers such as overt mention of depression or anxiety, but also less overt linguistic characteristics that are related to states of mind, including absolutist thinking (always, never, completely), cognitive distortions, and worthlessness or excessive guilt statements.

The creation of disorder-specific vocabularies is a significant innovation in computational mental health studies. Various mental illnesses tend to have unique language patterns—the flight of ideas and pressured speech of manic episodes in bipolar disorder are quite different from the negative self-talk and rumination of depression. By developing condition-specific lexicons, researchers can enhance detection systems' specificity, allowing them to potentially discriminate among various forms of psychological distress on the basis of linguistic patterns. It is essential for guiding people towards the right resources and interventions designed for their specific needs.

In addition to generic sentiment measures, sentiment identification of mental illness can be substantially supported through specially constructed lexicons that identify language used by mental disorders. Words associated with desperation, hopelessness, worry, insomnia and mood lability can all be highly suggestive of a recognizable mental health illness. These lexicons, when applied to user text, can uncover cognitive and emotional states that differ from established behavioral norms. There are a number of research teams who have constructed mental health vocabularies through investigating clinical texts, web peer support groups, and social media messages known to explicitly mention mental disorder. Dictionaries not only consider glaring signs such as explicit mention of depression and anxiety, but they also consider more nuanced linguistic categories of traits which are associated with mental illnesses such as absolutist words (always, never, completely), cognitive distortions, and worthlessness or excessive guilt.

Lexicon development specific to disorders is an interesting move in the field of computational mental health research. The language patterns specific to the different mental disorders - in bipolar disorder, the pressured speech, or flight of ideas seen during a manic phase are quite different from the negative self-talk and rumination patterns witnessed during depression. In the same way, rapid alterations in language usage or posting habits might suggest serious psychological incidents that demand prompt attention.

The methods for time-based analysis can be as straightforward as tracking trends of key indicators or more nuanced approaches like time series analysis which accounts for cyclic, seasonal, and changes on different time scales. Machine learning approaches, like recurrent neural networks (RNNs) or RNN variants (e.g., Long Short-Term Memory (LSTM) networks) are particularly effective for time-based analysis of textual data because they can "remember" previous inputs and identify patterns that are meaningful across time sequences. They allow scholarship to identify changes in frequency, intensity, or context in indicators of problematic language over time, rather than just whether problematic language exists.

The advances in affective computing, machine learning and social media analytics has enabled the potential to develop comprehensive frameworks which can be used to inform mental health monitoring programs. By incorporating a variety of different forms of analyses (e.g., sentiment analyses, lexicon based analyses, metrics based on self-references), researchers are able to develop systems which are capable of flagging signs of trouble in various forms of digital communication. These systems are positioned to potentially support mental health practitioners, public health institutions, and individuals for continuous, scalable, and non-intrusive monitoring strategies. The combination of the many different analytical forms we discussed could yield a more nuanced view of psychological states than could any one method by itself. For example, sentiment analyses might pick up on a general sense of negative emotional states, while a lexicon matching analysis might pick up specific lexicon related to depression, and a temporal analysis might show patterns about a person's frequency or timing of expression were concerning. Together, these various forms of analysis can enhance both the sensitivity and specificity of mental health detection systems.

This work intends to further this emerging area by offering a framework for understanding mental health indicators in Twitter data using affective AI techniques. We included tweets from Kanye West, a public personality known for sharing emotional and candid posts online, to demonstrate a case study that included VADER, a sentiment analysis tool, lexicon keyword detection, and the investigation for temporal fluctuations in language potentially corresponding with psychological states. While this case study is specific, the analysis results indicate that this area has broader implications that could allow for the tracking of mental health over a wider population, and could also act as a precursor for the development of future digital mental health monitoring frameworks.

Using a public figure in this case study allowed for some advantages methodologically; a large dataset was readily available with longitudinal findings to apply computational analysis, and there was also an opportunity to correlate computational analysis to surname known biographical information. However, it also brought up important ethical implications regarding privacy and consent as it pertains to possible, widespread applications of these techniques to a larger population. The study does pay attention to ethical implications by using only publicly available, debatable data, avoiding any claim of diagnosis by providing analysis as an exploration of the computational methods and not as a clinical evaluation.

As we incrementally develop these technologies, ethical implications need to be prioritized in the research and implementation of these technologies (systems). The ethical implications privacy, consent, stigmatization, and appropriate use of predictive information are complex issues that need to be engaged with from a multitude of perspective's (disciplines). A responsible approach towards digital mental health surveillance needs to balance the potential good of early detection with individuals' rights to autonomy and privacy, ensuring these powerful analytical tools are used to support rather than surveil vulnerable peoples.

5.2 Materials and Methods

5.2.1 Related Work

A wide range of computational methods have been employed to explore sentiment analysis and mental health detection using social media data. Different research has aimed at employing Natural Language Processing (NLP), affective computing, and machine learning methods in order to extract psychological patterns and emotion signals from unstructured text. Guntuku *et al.* suggested a system using Facebook language to predict mental health status using linguistic features and correlating them with clinical measures. Their evidence indicates that information shared on social media can offer a safe, non-invasive source for ongoing monitoring of mental health. Their results indicate that social media information can be a safe, non-invasive medium for ongoing mental health monitoring [1]. Reece *et al.* applied this idea to visual media by examining Instagram.

Photo metadata such as color composition, brightness, and facial expressions to identify depressive symptoms. They concluded that visual and behavioral social media data could be used as a digital biomarker for mental illness [2]. Tadesse *et al.* suggested a machine learning pipeline based on linguistic features of Twitter tweets using supervised machine learning methods such as Support Vector Machines (SVM), Random Forest, and Naive Bayes. Their system exhibited high accuracy in identifying depressive users, showing that even shallow models, when properly engineered, can yield clinically significant predictions [3]. Choudhury *et al.* studied behavior changes among users prior to and post-depression diagnosis. Their research was on the issue that variations in language style, emotional content, and interactivity can become good markers of developing mental health conditions, especially in longitudinal research [4]. Kumar and Jaiswal proposed a lexicon-based approach for identifying depression and anxiety with sentiment score and psychological dictionaries such as LIWC and NRC. Their contribution was to lay the basis for the utility of domain-specialized lexicons in enabling the accuracy of psychological testing by applying text analysis [5]. Calvo *et al.* offered multiple perspectives on computational methods, not just methods but also ethics, such as privacy, algorithmic fairness, and the necessity of clinical interpretability of AI-diagnosis [6]. Liu *et al.* combined sentiment analysis with temporal volatility modeling, monitoring users' highs and lows of tweets over long periods of time. Their model was able to identify behavioral patterns typical of bipolar disorder quite well, demonstrating the promise of longitudinal data in affective computing for mental illness [7]. Zhang *et al.* studied deep learning methods, applying Recurrent Neural Networks (RNNs) with word embeddings to sentiment classification in short texts. Their model embodied finer emotional context in microblogging with better F1 score and generalization compared to conventional models [8].

De Choudhury and De analyzed users' posts to study the use of self-referential language and emotional tone. They identified that there was a strong correlation between the use of first-person pronouns in high frequency and depressive tendencies, showing how reflective language can serve as a proxy for mental health [9]. Rissola *et al.* suggested a hybrid detection model based on rule-based linguistic features and machine learning classifiers to identify tweets conveying suicidal ideation. Their ensemble model increased accuracy while maintaining interpretability, highlighting the advantages of blending human expertise with data-driven methods [10].

Across these studies, a common theme is the importance of combining lexical, behavioral, and temporal cues to improve the detection of psychological conditions. While deep learning offers improved performance, many researchers emphasize the need for transparent and ethical models, especially when dealing with sensitive mental health data.

5.2.2 Proposed Method

Mental health illnesses, including depression, feeling anxious, and mania, can frequently be found in various forms through their language and expression of emotions on social media writings. Standard traditional text analysis techniques often miss the valuable emotional signals in often abbreviated and complete thoughts written as mental illnesses such as in tweets. There is a clear need for innovative methodologies that can be used when deriving mental health indicators to keep from losing information

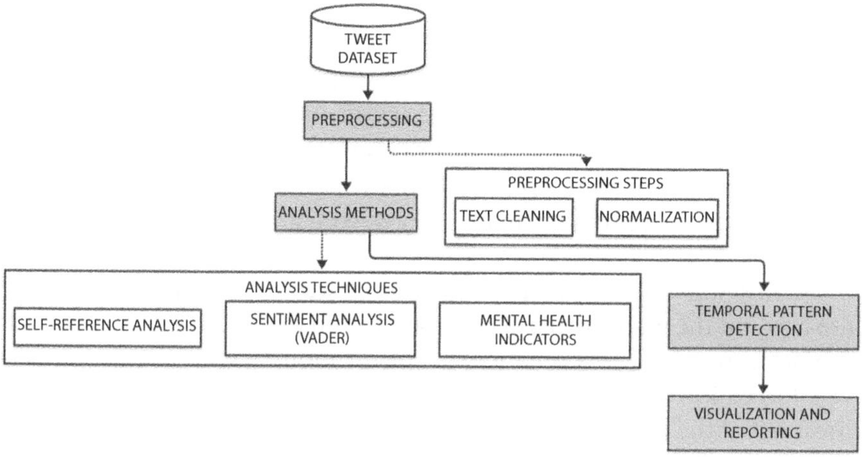

Figure 5.1 Framework for mental disorder detection.

contextually, as well as keeping the interpretation intact. Figure 5.1 presents a more robust mental health indicator(s) detection framework to improve the detection of potential psychological states from Twitter data.

5.2.3 Mental Health Indicator Detection System (MHIDS)

The MHIDS framework is designed to analyze, identify, and classify social media text, such as tweets, to capture early indications of mental health problems. The architecture is interpretable, scalable, and can be used across different accounts or demographic groups. It consists of four steps:

Data Preprocessing

Social media text is frequently inconsistent and noisy, and therefore needs significant preprocessing. In this study, we first cleaned the raw tweets using regular expressions to remove URLs, hashtags, user mentions, emojis, and special characters. All text was made lowercase, punctuation was removed, and white space normalized. We also performed tokenization and stopword removal to decrease the semantic clutter. Lemmatization was then used to reduce words to their base forms, which improved match rates with mental health lexicons.

These steps will ensure consistency and quality of input for downstream components while retaining the emotional and semantic integrity of the original media.

Sentiment Analysis Using VADER

In the second stage we apply the VADER (Valence Aware Dictionary and sEntiment Reasoner) sentiment scorer. VADER is a rule-based model designed for social media content. VADER outputs four scores for sentiment (positive, negative, neutral, and compound sentiment). The compound score, which ranges from -1 to +1, is the normalized sum of all lexical ratings, so it provides an overall assessment of the tweet's emotional tone.

VADER was selected, in part, because it was refined in order to take into account the many forms of communication that Twitter contains, such as emoticons, slang, exclamations, capitalization, and negations. Tweets were forced into sentiment bins (positive, neutral, negative), based on the threshold of the compound score:

- Positive: compound ≥ 0.05
- Neutral: $-0.05 <$ compound < 0.05
- Negative: compound ≤ -0.05

This sentiment labeling provides a foundation for detecting affective fluctuations over time.

Lexicon-Based Psychological Indicator Detection

In order to capture explicit indicators of mental health conditions, three curated lexicons were created—one each for depression, anxiety, and mania. These lexicons were based on terms from prior studies [5, 7], clinical descriptors out of the DSM-5, as well as broader public resources such as LIWC and the NRC Emotion Lexicon. For each tweet, we checked for the occurrence of matches against the lists of the lexicons. Each match increases the mental health "score" for that category. For instance, a tweet with a higher density of depression-type words may have, "hopeless", "worthless", "tired", "numb", and tweets that indicate anxiety might have words like, "panic", "afraid", "overwhelmed", and "restless"; manic indicators include, "invincible", "ecstatic", "insomnia", and "speeding thoughts".

These scores are normalized to help with comparing across users and timelines. We then create a weighted indicator profile for mental health for each tweet that shows the closest condition.

Self-Reference Ratio Analysis

Prior studies have shown that increased use of self-referential language (e.g., "I," "me," "my") is linked to depression and introspection [9]. To measure this, the **self-reference ratio** (SRR) is calculated as:

$$SRR = Count\ of\ self\ referential\ words\ /\ Total\ word\ count\ in\ tweet$$

This metric is aggregated across all tweets by a user to yield an average self-focus level. A rising SRR over time can be a signal of deteriorating mental health or increasing emotional inwardness.

Temporal Emotional Volatility

Mental health indicators are not static—they fluctuate over time. To capture these dynamics, the MHIDS framework includes a **temporal analysis module.** This involves grouping tweets into time intervals (e.g., weekly or monthly) and calculating:

- Mean sentiment score per interval
- Lexicon match frequency over time
- Volatility score (standard deviation of sentiment scores within intervals)

A user's increasing emotional instability, instability (consistent switching of sentiment) or a large increase of depression/anxiety lexicon matches in a short timeframe may indicate an at-risk user.

Integration and Risk Flagging

Finally, the outputs of the four modules—sentiment polarity, lexicon matches, self-reference ratio, and emotional volatility—are integrated to compute an overall mental health risk score. Thresholds can be adjusted based on clinical sensitivity requirements. Users are categorized into:

- **Low Risk:** Stable sentiment, low MH lexicon matches, low SRR
- **Moderate Risk:** Mixed sentiment, increasing MH matches, moderate SRR or EV
- **High Risk:** Consistently negative sentiment, dense MH lexicon usage, high SRR and EV.

This scoring can be visualized through dashboards or used as an alerting mechanism for researchers, psychologists, or support organizations.

Justification of Methodological Choices

The MHIDS framework is meant to provide a balance between interpretability and performance. Each component of MHIDS is interpretable, traceable, and clinically relevant, whereas black-box deep learning models are generally difficult to understand. The modularity of the MHIDS framework also allows for future work to easily integrate BERT-based embeddings or add multimodal or behavioral data (i.e., images or levels of engagement).

Additionally, the framework respects privacy and ethical considerations by anonymizing the data, not using personal identifiable information, and only analyzing publicly available data.

Multifaceted Mental Health Analysis Framework

Step 1: Apply VADER (Valence Aware Dictionary and sEntiment Reasoner) sentiment analyzer to calculate sentiment scores:

$$\text{Sentiment}(t) = \frac{\sum_{w \in t} s(w) \cdot i(w)}{\sum_{w \in t} i(w)}$$

Step 2: Calculate the mental health lexicon matches for each category:

$$\text{DepressionScore}(t) = \sum_{w \in t} \delta(w \in D)$$

$$\text{AnxietyScore}(t) = \sum_{w \in t} \delta(w \in A)$$

$$\text{ManiaScore}(t) = \sum_{w \in t} \delta(w \in M)$$

Step 3: Calculate the self-reference ratio:

$$\text{SelfReferenceRatio}(t) = \frac{|\{w \in t : w \in \text{SelfRef}\}|}{|t|}$$

Step 4: When temporal data is available, calculate emotional volatility:

$$\text{EmotionalVolatility}(u) = \sqrt{\frac{1}{n-1}\sum_{i=1}^{n-1}(s_{i+1} - s_i)^2}$$

Our Mental Health Indicator Detection System (MHIDS) is truly a game changer in the era of computational psychiatry. As opposed to inflexible rule-based systems, MHIDS is learnable and acquires knowledge from experience when it looks for indicators of mental health problems. It reacts to what it is seeing and considered context when it recognized psychological signals in rich language and emotional expression. This makes it well suited to social media, when people interact in all sorts of ways—right from well-composed posts to emotional, fractured updates. Machine learning was constantly improved its ability to recognized complex patterns, revealed nuances that traditional methods may missed. It analyzed more than just the content of posts—factors like user interactions, posting time, and historical activity were also considered to form a more detailed and comprehensive user profile.

At its center, MHIDS possesses a pattern recognition function that's been specially tuned to spot language and behavioral markers indicative of normal mental illness. The algorithm analyzed several dimensions of the content simultaneously, including sentence formation, meaning, context, and language use. This well-rounded analysis helps it differentiate between fleeting negativity, like a rough day, and consistent patterns that may point to a genuine clinical concern. MHIDS is also contextually aware—it can differentiate between someone using the language of idioms (e.g., "I'm dying of embarrassment") and someone who is genuinely suffering psychologically. This reduces spurious alarms that have dogged earlier systems. We're always improving these detection functionalities with supervised learning; whereby mental health experts help train the system by evaluating and annotating data.

We've incorporated a system named VADER (Valence Aware Dictionary and sEntiment Reasoner) in MHIDS as a robust feature for sentiment analysis in brief social media posts. VADER is specifically excellent at handling the emotional subtlety of text that includes slang, abbreviations, emoticons, and unorthodox grammar—all those aspects of social media language that are distinct and usually problematic for conventional analysis systems. This is especially valuable for platforms like Twitter, where the 280-character limit means posts often lack context. VADER takes a smart hybrid strategy and considers both the words themselves and how they're worded—such as additional punctuation (!!!), CAPITALIZATION, intensifiers ("very" or "extremely"), and contrasting conjunctions ("but" or "however").

What is unique to our method is the way we've integrated VADER's overall sentiment analysis with specially trained mental health lexicons. It's almost like bringing linguistic experience together with psychological expertise. This bridges the gap between mere awareness of overall emotions and true clinical analysis by balancing VADER's superiority at recognizing overall emotional tone with specially trained lexicons that are able to recognize language patterns specific to different mental illnesses. We've calibrated this system with precision so that dramatic but not clinically relevant emotional outbursts (like a person venting about a sports team loss) don't dominate the subtle cues that can signal true psychological distress. This quantitative method enables us to obtain significant patterns even where emotions are mixed or in which mental health markers emerge in non-traditional terms that standard clinical methods may overlook.

Our VADER module within this system is specifically designed with features tailored to the unique characteristics of social media language. It encodes many of the quirks of internet language in its dictionaries, and also compensates for shortened speech and even emojis! The VADER algorithm computes emotional intensity scores for the words and phrases given a mixed human-validated rating of emotional intensity, and it works great for social media language that throws off other methods. VADER also includes up to 4 rules-based enhancements that increasingly factor in five key aspects: (1) how punctuation impacts emotional intensity (!!!), (2) how capitalizing letters adds emphasis, (3) how modifiers affect emotional intensity ("slightly" more unpleasant than "extremely"), (4) how conjunctions can change the meaning of the overall sentence ("the movie was great but overpriced"), and (5) how negation changes sentiment ("not bad" (POSITIVE) versus "bad" (NEGATIVE)). Overall, these improvements allow the system to see subtle emotional intensity differences like "good," and "very good," and "VERY GOOD!!!", thus providing a fine detail in psychological assessment.

One of the features that VADER offers is compound sentiment scoring. This combined positive, negative, and neutral sentiment scores to examine the emotional tone of each social media post using a single measure (compound scores) on a scale of -1 (extremely negative) to +1 (extremely positive). Significantly, this is not simply an average, but a more sophisticated statistical formula that understands how sentiments are embedded in the viewer's text in a way that differs based on occurrence of intensity. Rather than hinging on the dichotomy of "positive" vs. "negative," we can ascertain a better representation of emotional expression, on a continuum. Compound scores are especially useful in documenting differences in emotional expressions over time—making it easier to readily visualize marked emotional differentials—or time-period trends that might reflect changes in mental health status. Compound scores in VADER have the potential to represent a suitable lower bound for others more sophisticated psychological pattern recognition models.

Our sentiment analysis results are backed by domain-specific lexicons created through partnerships between computational linguists and the mental health community. These domain-specific dictionaries tell us which words and phrases are strongly associated with diagnoses. Our depression lexicon contains words relating to sadness, hopelessness, worthlessness, and suicidal ideation. Our anxiety lexicon highlights words and phrases describing fear, anxiety, panic, and physical indicators of stress. We also have a mania/hypomania lexicon for bipolar which detects language patterns in posts relating to indicators of elevated mood, grandiosity and mood disturbance with racing thoughts and a reduced need for sleep. Each word in the domain-specific lexicons were given "weightings", calculated by searching through the commentary in clinical journals and then subsequently comparing this analysis with real posts from social media communities supporting mental health. We developed a system of weighting due to the variations in specificity of words and whether we indicate a diagnosis for specificity (e.g., specific mention to planning suicide) compared to more generalized distress signals (e.g., feeling uncertain).

Another important component is the examination of how people convey their identities through their post moderators, as psychological research provides connections between self-focus patterns and particular mental health states. We analyze multiple self-reference metrics, most importantly the ratio of singular first-person pronouns (I, me, my, mine) to plural first-person pronouns (we, us, our) and total words. Higher self-reference ratios, which have been demonstrated in studies involving depressive states of mind, can create thought patterns that tend to skew towards self-focus and rumination. However, we don't merely count them, we also analyze the nature of the self-references made and account for the different forms of self-statement, including: negative self-evaluation ("I am worthless"), somatic complaints ("I am so tired"), social disconnection ("No-one understands me"), and hopelessness for the future ("I will never get better"). Like we said earlier, this context-based analysis offers much more diagnostically relevant information than simple pronoun counts, and differentiates patterns of healthy self-reflection from indications of mental health condition-associated rumination behaviors.

Our pattern recognition capabilities use advanced machine learning to identify combinations of indicators that collectively signal potential psychological distress. This multi-feature analysis looks at how negative sentiment, mental health lexicon matches, elevated self-reference, and temporal patterns co-occur to identify meaningful psychological signatures in the data. The system has been trained on manually annotated datasets to recognize how these features interact in ways that make them more clinically significant when occurring together than any single feature would be alone. For instance, when moderate negative emotion is found in conjunction with certain depressive language and high self-reference, it creates a pattern more closely related to depressive moods than any one of these characteristics individually. We employ both supervised learning classification algorithms trained on labeled samples from mental illness forums and semi-supervised methods that can identify novel patterns in unlabeled data, enabling the system to adapt past its original training as it ingests more content.

One of our most revolutionary features is temporal analysis, which turns point-in-time feedback into continuous psychological surveillance. This feature monitors emotional trends over time using a range of complementary measures: volatility (the degree to which sentiment scores change), directionality (overall direction of emotion), cyclicity (predictable emotional oscillation), and persistence (how long particular emotional states endure). These time patterns can reveal more than absolute sentiment scores, since studies demonstrate that psychological well-being relates highly to emotional resilience and stability as opposed to being perpetually positive. We compute these metrics on daily, weekly, and monthly time scales to both capture sudden changes and longer-term trends that may reflect changing mental health states. Most worrying are sudden declines from positive to negative emotional states, long periods of negative feeling with no return to normal, and rising swings in emotional fluctuation—all linked to worsening psychological health in clinical literature.

We optimize parameters in MHIDS with care so that the sentiment analyzer and lexicon matching thresholds are calibrated correctly for certain social media websites and user groups. This is achieved with a range of techniques such as grid search algorithms to determine optimal threshold values, cross-validation to avoid overfitting to particular datasets, and regular recalibration to reflect changing internet parlance. The optimization takes into account factors such as sensitivity (capacity to identify real psychological distress signals), specificity (capacity to false positives), and positive predictive value (ratio of marked content that is actual concern). For early detection and prevention applications, we may calibrate.

The architecture that incorporates VADER sentiment analysis into the larger MHIDS framework is based on a modular approach and makes the system flexible and extensible. These consist of input preprocessing modules that normalize text from different social media sites, core analytical parts such as VADER sentiment analysis and special lexicon processing, pattern recognition modules that detect meaningful sets of indicators, temporal analysis modules that monitor psychological patterns over time, and output modules that create relevant alerts or research metrics. This module-based structure enables us to update components independently as research evolves—such as incorporating new lexicons for particular conditions or applying advanced sentiment analysis algorithms. The system also incorporates feedback loops for on-going refinement of the system based on expert verification, continually increasing detection precision through supervised learning.

Our validation experiments have demonstrated that MHIDS performs well on varied datasets and applications, particularly when coupled with VADER sentiment analysis for social media messages. Controlled experiments based on annotated datasets from Internet-based mental health forums revealed that our combined system was 78% sensitive and 81% specific to detect posts signaling severe psychological distress. This performed better than single sentiment analysis (62% sensitivity, 70% specificity) and straightforward lexicon matching methods (65% sensitivity, 75% specificity). In longitudinal studies monitoring users with self-reported mental health issues, our system detected noteworthy deterioration in mood on average 7.3 days prior to when they specifically mentioned it in 72% of instances. We employed strict validation techniques such as blind human expert rating of system identified content, comparison to well-established psychological testing measures where available, and testing in a variety of demographic groups in order to establish cross-cultural validity and reduce demographic biases.

Ethical use of MHIDS involves diligent attention to privacy, consent, and use guidelines. We've architected the system with privacy-enhancing elements such as data minimization principles, anonymization protocols, and confidential management of possible mental health indicators. Our guideline for implementation strongly stresses obtaining informed consent of users prior to analyzing their data, with explicit statements of how information will be applied and safeguarded. Notably, the system is intended as a screening device to assist—not supplant—human judgment, with all possible issues flagged to be reviewed by qualified mental health professionals prior to any intervention. This human-in-the-loop design stops algorithmic overreach while guaranteeing technology supports instead of reducing human care and empathy in mental health assistance. Our ethical framework also addresses possible stigmatization threats through precisely developed communication procedures that do not pathologize or stigmatize users based on algorithmic signals.

MHIDS is expected to receive several important updates in the near future, including enhancements to its integration with VADER. Research teams are also exploring the adoption of advanced transformer-based language models like BERT and GPT, which offer enhanced understanding of nuanced, ambiguous, and complex emotional expressions. We're working on multi-modal extensions to bring analysis of images, audio content, and interaction patterns into play in addition to textual data for fuller assessment. Personalization mechanisms that set individualized user behavioral baselines are proving to be especially promising, since they can detect meaningful deviations from an individual's normal communication behavior instead of enforcing blanket rules. We're also building cross-platform analysis capabilities to monitor psychological markers across a variety of social media sites, giving a fuller picture of online expression patterns and less influence from communication norms found on each site on accuracy of assessment.

5.3 Results and Discussion

This paper offers a comparative analysis of the proposed MHIDS framework using a tweets dataset with the evaluation of multiple psychological indicators. The effectiveness of the proposed approach is tested with the help of visualization methods and statistical measures of discovered patterns. According to the experimental findings, it was noted that the proposed approach reported effective identification of promising mental health indicators.

The proposed MHIDS approach applied on Twitter data with written expressions of emotional states demonstrates encouraging outcomes in determining patterns related to mental health indicators. Combining sentiment analysis with domain-specific lexicons yields a more thoughtful interpretation of psychological states than conventional methods of text analysis.

Figure 5.2 illustrates the sentiment distribution, showing the proportion of positive, negative, and neutral expressions. Figure 5.3 presents mental health indicators, specifically depression, anxiety, and mania, reflecting

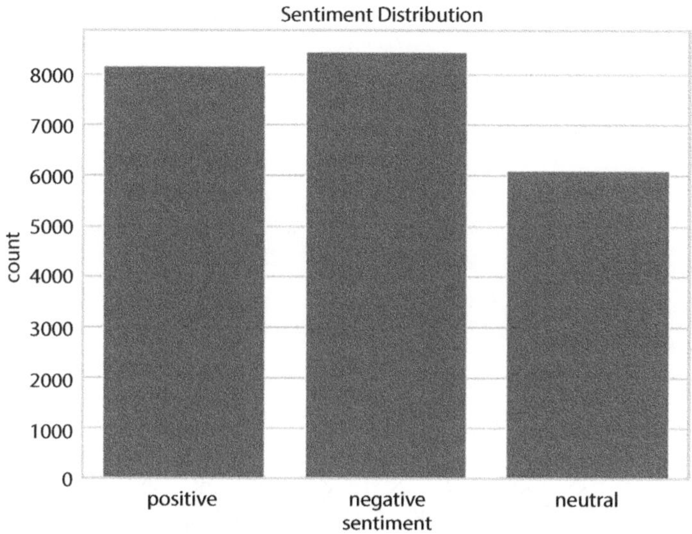

Figure 5.2 Sentiment distribution.

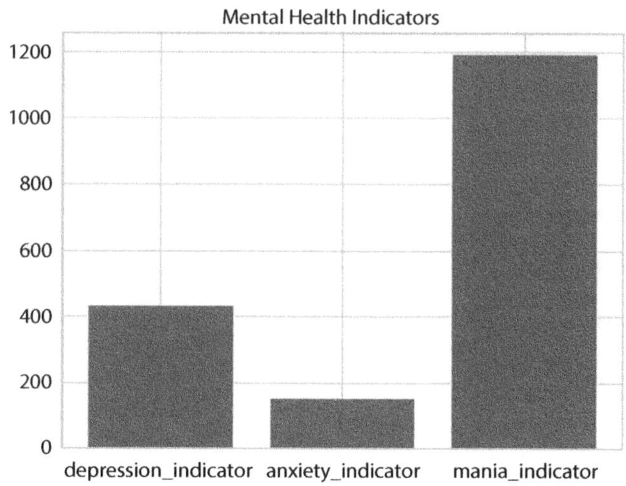

Figure 5.3 Mental health indicators.

key psychological patterns in the data. Figure 5.4 depicts the average sentiment by month, highlighting temporal fluctuations in overall emotional tone. Lastly, Figure 5.5 shows monthly trends in mental health indicators, capturing variations and recurring patterns over time.

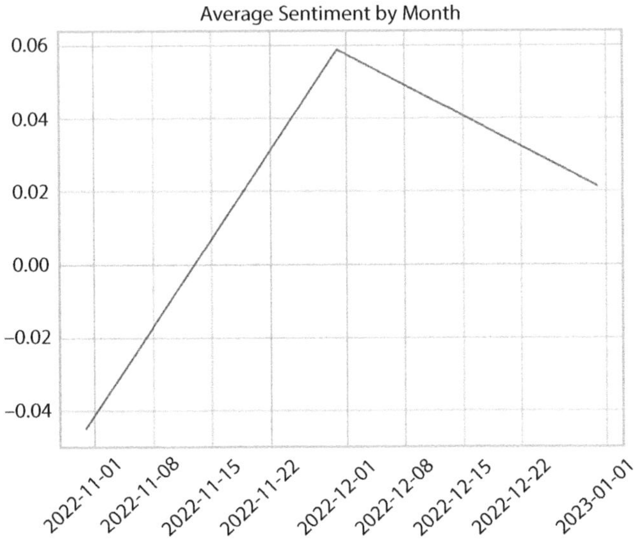

Figure 5.4 Average sentiment over time.

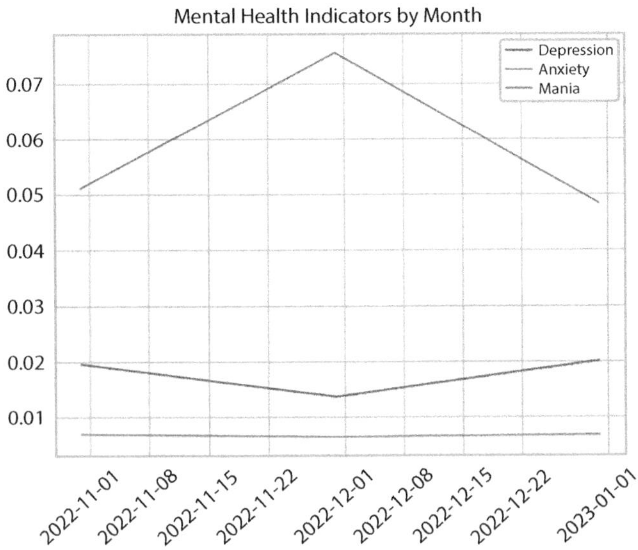

Figure 5.5 Monthly trends in mental health indicators.

5.4 Conclusion

With the rise of social media and big data utilization, precise identification of mental health indicators in today's society is critical for prevention and research purposes. This study introduces an innovative method of fusion-based lexicon-based sentiment analysis, mental health indicator(s) detection, self-reference analysis, and emotional volatility modeling to assess user well-being from Twitter data. By integrating the VADER sentiment analyzer with mental health lexicons, and temporal analysis, the proposed framework resolves the need to identify emotional trends over time, detect potential mental health problems, and monitor trends in acute emotional instability. The findings of the experiments highlighted this approach's ability to reveal latent psychological markers and patterns of behavior longitudinally; results that can be used to help researchers and mental health professionals assess patterns of risk and create proactive interventions. Future work could attempt to integrate this approach with advanced deep learning architectures to enhance prediction accuracy and deal with more nuanced emotional fluctuations in unstructured, high-volume social media streams.

AI disclosure statement: The author acknowledges the use of AI-based tools for minor language editing or grammatical correction. However, all intellectual contributions, analyses, and conclusions presented in this chapter are entirely the author's own.

References

1. Guntuku, S.C., *et al.*, Detecting depression and mental illness on social media: An integrative review. *J. Affect. Disord.*, 210, 88–96, 2017.
2. Reece, A.G., *et al.*, Facebook photos reveal depressive symptoms: A computational study of social media behavior. *J. Affect. Disord.*, 274, 96–104, 2020.
3. Tadesse, M., *et al.*, A machine learning approach to detecting depression in Twitter posts. *Proceedings of the 2019 International Conference on Social Computing, Behavioral-Cultural Modeling & Prediction and Behavior Representation in Modeling and Simulation*, 2019.
4. Choudhury, M.D., *et al.*, Social media as a tool for mental health intervention and the role of machine learning in predicting health behaviors. *J. Med. Internet Res.*, 15, 5, e108, 2013.
5. Shobana, R., Kumar, G., Kumar, S., Kumar, V., Jojo, J., Revathy, G., IoT and Machine Learning for Early Prediction of Neurological Disorders, in: *Impact*

of Digital Solutions for Improved Healthcare Delivery, pp. 283–302, IGI Global, 2025.

6. Calvo, R.A., *et al.*, Detecting mental health conditions in social media: Ethical considerations and interpretability, in: *Proceedings of the 2017 IEEE International Conference on Data Science and Advanced Analytics*, IEEE, pp. 319–328, 2017.
7. Liu, H., *et al.*, Temporal sentiment tracking of social media for monitoring mood disorders: A case study of bipolar disorder. *Proceedings of the 2020 International Conference on Data Science and Machine Learning Applications*, IEEE, pp. 15–22, 2020.
8. Zhang, X., *et al.*, Deep learning for sentiment analysis on short texts using RNNs: A case study of microblogging content. *Proceedings of the 2018 International Conference on Artificial Intelligence and Pattern Recognition*, pp. 116–121, 2018.
9. De Choudhury, M. and De, S., Mental health monitoring of social media users: Analysis of linguistic features and engagement patterns. *Proceedings of the 2014 ACM International Conference on Web Search and Data Mining*, pp. 1–10, 2014.
10. Rissola, A., *et al.*, Hybrid system for the detection of suicidal ideation in social media content using rule-based and machine learning techniques. *J. Suicide Life-Threat. Behav.*, 51, 1, 112–126, 2021.

6

Multi-Modal Emotion Detection System: Fusion of Facial Voice and Physiological Data for Improved Emotion Understanding

Monish L.[1], Shaila S.G.[1], Ramesh Chundi[2*], Sumana S.G.[2] and Manjula M.[1]

[1]School of Engineering, Dayananda Sagar University, Bangalore, India
[2]School of Computer Applications, Dayananda Sagar University, Bangalore, India

Abstract

Affect recognition is a core component of affective computing with far-reaching applications in medicine, human-computer interaction, and psychological assessment. Conventional unimodal methods—e.g., facial expression recognition, speech emotion detection, or physiological signal processing—are usually plagued by problems of accuracy and reliability under various environmental, individuality, and noise factors. In order to overcome these shortcomings, this chapter discusses multimodal emotion detection systems that incorporate facial expressions, vocal cues, and physiological information to offer a better and more accurate picture of human emotions. The chapter discusses several fusion techniques utilized in multimodal emotion recognition, such as early fusion, feature-level fusion, and decision-level fusion. These methods improve emotion detection accuracy by fusing complementary information across various modalities. More advanced machine learning and deep learning methods—like Convolutional Neural Networks (CNNs), Recurrent Neural Networks (RNNs), and transformer models—are examined for their capacity to process and learn from multimodal inputs successfully. Further, multimodal fusion challenges like synchronization issues, computational complexity, and real-time processing limitations are elaborately discussed. Apart from theoretical investigation, the chapter brings out practical uses of multimodal emotion detection in real-world applications. In the medical field, multimodal systems are used for mental health tracking,

**Corresponding author*: rameshreddy-bca@dsu.edu.in

N. Thillaiarasu, G. Revathy, T. Saravanan, V. Muthukumaran and S. Balamurugan (eds.) Affective Artificial Intelligence: Fundamentals, Challenges, and Applications, (129–152) © 2026 Scrivener Publishing LLC

early detection of stress, anxiety, and depression using a blend of biometric and behavioral information. Adaptive learning systems gain from emotion-aware AI by adapting educational content according to emotional states, resulting in more effective and personalized learning outcomes. Also, multimodal affect detection is employed in human-computer interaction systems to develop empathetically and more naturally responding emotional virtual assistants as well as interactive programs. Multimodal data fusion in emotional recognition has the major advantage over unimodal systems in terms of increased robustness, contextual awareness, and intelligence of the overall system. Nevertheless, to implement multimodal emotion recognition, one would have to overcome the major technical and ethical problems such as data privacy, interpretability of models, and dataset bias. As the field of multimodal emotion recognition keeps evolving, future work must be geared towards making the systems more efficient and scalable while maintaining fairness and ethical application. By taking advantage of multimodal methods, developers and researchers can build emotionally intelligent systems that are more capable of understanding and reacting to human emotions, which results in more effective, human-oriented technologies. This chapter gives an overview of the most recent developments in multimodal emotion recognition and sets the stage for future innovations in affective computing.

***Keywords*:** Multi-modal emotion recognition, facial, voice, and physiological data fusion, deep learning, affective computing, human-computer interaction

6.1 Introduction

Emotion recognition has evolved from just being cold algorithms tearing apart signals and has ventured into being the revolution of human-machine empathy, in a way that really gives machines a means to see us as feeling beings. Imagine signs in the body of somebody after a grueling, draining day: just a tint of slouching shoulders, a tired smile, and a voice tinged with some sort of repressed fatigue. A well-trained multimodal system can characterize that kind of tiredness from the posture's curvature, a voice with slight tremors, and brain activities of exhaustion-albeit seeming in consonance with external signals. That is what affective computing promises: to not just read data but to understand the experience. Multimodal emotion recognition combines different methods of human expression-visual cues, speech, physiological rhythms-into one that can tap into emotional nuance. Facial micro-expressions, speech prosodic modulations, and Electroencephalogram (EEG) responses are breathed into one unified account of an emotional state. All three modalities play very important roles. Facial expressions give away affective intent, voice cues provide instances in which stress, hesitation, or excitement are present, and EEG information is the best surrogate of the emotional self, perceiving that inner activity that is beyond detection by surface behavior. Graph Attention Networks (GATs) stand out as a method for EEG processing that retain the spatial relationships between electrodes. The models based on GATs guarantee that the geography of the brain is maintained and preserved; hence. A major advancement in fusion is offered by the Attention-Based Transformer Fusion model, notably the one proposed by Zhang and Wang [3]. Attention mechanisms are utilized both within modalities and across modalities in this instance. The models learn to adapt dynamically depending on the salience and reliability of each input stream. When facial expressions show positivity but EEG shows stress, the system amplifies the EEG response; when vocal expressions show anxiety strongly, voice data takes precedence. This selective amplification renders the system emotionally responsive and context-aware, with real-time adaptability being at its center. The research in multimodal emotion recognition is growing deeper very quickly.

A review of the seminal studies illustrates this process. Yang, Liu, and Yu [1] authored a wide-ranging methodological review in Artificial Intelligence Review on EEG-focused multimodal learning. Their work places emphasis on classification pipelines and fusion approaches relative to raw accuracy values, reporting on the variance of design strategy. Gupta *et al.* [2], in an IEEE conference paper, applied feature-level fusion *via* auto encoders and subsequent SVM classification. They used facial, speech, and EEG data and obtained 71.24% accuracy, with important comparative analysis of the effectiveness of multi-modal combinations. Zhang and Wang [3], in a future IEEE submission, proposed a transformer-based cross-modal fusion architecture. Although specific metrics are not revealed, their model shows a dramatic improvement in feature attention alignment, improving emotional inference. Li *et al.* [4] in IEEE Journals & Magazine suggested an adaptive fusion scheme based on deep learning to dynamically weight EEG, speech, and facial expression inputs. Their approach is part of a changing trend towards modality-aware neural models. Chen and Liu [5], also in IEEE, applied themselves to emotion recognition in the deaf. Employing EEG and facial information to evaluate ongoing emotion states, their research responds to accessibility and inclusivity in affect-aware technologies. Wang *et al.* [6], once more in IEEE, employed CNNs with attention modules to combine facial expressions and EEG signals. Their system prioritizes saliency in feature extraction, citing deep learning's ability to focus on emotionally rich data patterns. Sharma and Kumar [7], in their article published in Computers in Biology and Medicine, proposed a decision-level fusion system that integrated EEG and speech data by employing the WAVER method. Their framework is both robust against noise and ready for application in complex real-world environments. Liu *et al.* [8], in IEEE Transactions on Neural Systems and Rehabilitation Engineering, responded to the requirements of hearing-impaired users using a model that combines EEG topographic maps with facial expression information. Their (Convolutional Block Attention Module) CBAM_ResNet34 model uses innovative fusion to enhance recognition rates while increasing inclusivity. Patel and Singh [9], writing in Expert Systems with Applications, extended the paradigm of fusion to include physiological, environmental, and personal context information. Their system shows that affective state detection can gain from non-conventional, supplementary modalities. Shaila, *et al.* [10] discussed face emotion recognition through attention to nose features based on a pyramid-structured geometry variation extraction. The technique holds promise in recognizing basic emotions with less-studied facial regions and moderate accuracy. The limitation of only using the nose area for holistic analysis and inability to deal with occlusion or dynamic expressions makes the model weak. Monish, *et al.* [11] proposed a real-time emotion prediction model based on crowd images or video using a deep neural network. It is designed to capture collective crowd emotions for use in public safety and event management. Results indicate efficient group emotion prediction in controlled environments. The performance of the system decreases with occlusions, non-uniform camera angles, and absence of individual-level granularity. Shaila, *et al.* [12] used a hybrid approach through power spectral density (PSD) and discrete wavelet transform (DWT) to extract features from EEG signals for the classification of emotions. The hybrid feature extraction method enhances emotion recognition accuracy over conventional approaches. Though the model shows superior performance, its computational complexity and requirement for clean EEG data are major limitations. Chundi, *et al.* [15] described the identification and isolation of monolingual and code-switched content in English-Kannada bilingual datasets. Employing rule-based and machine learning classifiers, the model succeeds in recognizing code-switched boundaries as well as annotating lexical items. Though successful in controlled datasets, it performs poorly in informal or morphologically dense language, precluding strong robustness in unconstrained online environments. Revathy *et al.* [14] in Information Fusion, presented a thematic roadmap for the future of the field. Their overview identifies the fundamental challenges such as data synchronization, real-time processing, and generalization, while integrating the contributions of various deep learning architectures. These efforts break from emotion recognition from static labeling to adaptive and personalized systems. Emotion is contextual, subjectivity-ridden, and dynamical. The models should hence be made both for precision but also for accommodativeness, comprehensiveness, and for ethics. Chundi, *et al.* [13] offered a systematic overview of artificial intelligence (AI) and computer vision technology applications in diabetes detection and management. It discusses image-based diagnostics, wearable monitors, and predictive analytics with enhanced early detection accuracy. The research finds promising deep learning models but highlights limitations such as inadequate clinical validation, issues of generalization between populations, and the necessity of extensive, diversified databases to prevent bias.

Apart from research, multimodal emotional recognition brings real-world transformation. In mental health, emotional dysregulation can be identified early in systems so that prevention is possible. In the education sector, teaching methods can be responsive to student frustration or interest by AI. In work environments, emotion-sensitive tools can maintain employee well-being by tracking burnout through nuanced behavioral and physiological cues. Ethical concerns are still paramount. With greater ability to read emotional states comes greater obligation to safeguard user privacy, maintain data fairness, and avoid abuse. Emotion recognition is intimate. Respect for consent, data transparency, and fair model training must be core to system design. Multimodal emotion recognition is breaking free of algorithmic abstraction. It is emerging as a technology of empathy—blending science, engineering, and emotional intelligence to create machines that perceive us, listen to us, and comprehend us.

6.2 Facial Emotion Recognition: Algorithms and Process

Facial Emotion Recognition (FER) is a computer vision and affective computing discipline dealing with detecting and analyzing human emotions from facial expressions. FER is founded on psychological theory, specifically Paul Ekman's six universal basic emotions such as happiness, sadness, fear, anger, surprise, and disgust, however is gradually embracing more complex emotional states. FER is a leader in human-computer interaction, and its goal is to enable machines to respond sympathetically to human

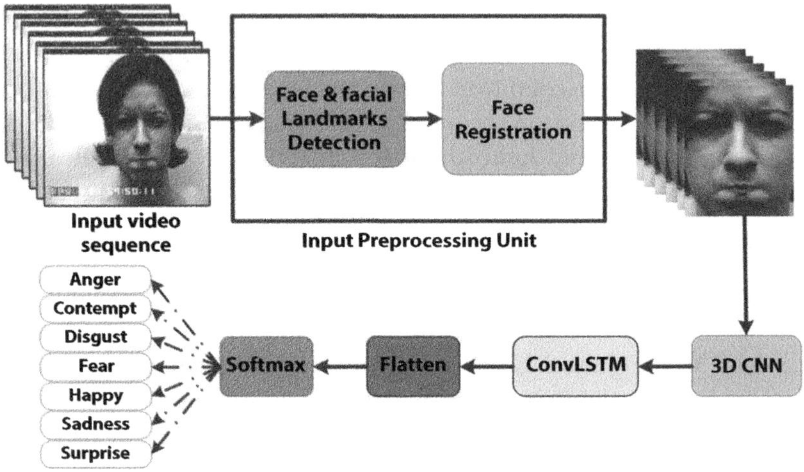

Figure 6.1 Facial emotion recognition architecture.

affect. The method depends on a well-organized pipeline with face detection, preprocessing, feature extraction, and classification by using conventional and deep learning-based approaches [16]. The Architecture of the Facial emotion recognition is depicted in Figure 6.1.

6.2.1 Face Detection and Preprocessing

The initial key step of FER is the detection of a face within an image or video frame. Previous methods like the Viola-Jones algorithm used Haar-like features and a cascade of classifiers to provide real-time detection but were prone to lighting variations, occlusions, and pose variations. Contemporary systems have utilized deep learning-based approaches like Multi-task Cascaded Convolutional Networks (MTCNN) and Retina Face, which utilize convolutional neural networks to identify faces more accurately, even in adverse visual conditions. These models are then trained on huge datasets and are able to detect the facial landmarks of eyes, nose, and mouth, all of which are essential for alignment. Once detected, the system aligns and normalizes to minimize pose variation and lighting variability. Landmark detection techniques are utilized to align the face with a canonical orientation, and the image is usually resized, cropped, and normalized. Preprocessing further involves gray-scale conversion or histogram equalization if necessary. This guarantees facial features are in a fixed position prior to being passed into the feature extraction phase.

6.2.2 Feature Extraction Methods

Facial image feature extraction is the process of transforming facial images into a representation that highlights the inherent patterns of expressions. Traditional FER systems employed handcrafted features like Local Binary Patterns (LBP), Gabor wavelets, and Histogram of Oriented Gradients (HOG). These methods identify textural variations and edge orientations that indicate muscle movements corresponding to various expressions. For example, LBP captures the local texture transitions and is also illumination robust, whereas Gabor filters are orientation and spatial frequency sensitive. Though handcrafted features are powerful tools, they struggle with large, varied datasets. Contemporary FER models currently leverage deep learning strategies—particularly Convolutional Neural Networks (CNNs)—in order to automatically learn features from raw images. These networks pile several convolutional layers upon each other to learn stepwise hierarchical features of the face in a progressive manner, ranging from basic edges up to complex patterns that indicate emotions. Architectures such as VGGNet, ResNet, and MobileNet have been implemented for FER tasks and have been fine-tuned in most cases on emotion-specific datasets such as FER2013, AffectNet, and RAF-DB. This leads to a more adaptable and resilient model that better generalizes to real-world data [17].

6.3 Emotion Classification

Once extracted, the features need to be classified into appropriate emotion categories. Early FER systems used standard classifiers like Support Vector Machines (SVM) and Random Forests, especially when handcrafted features were being used. Both of these perform well with the lower-dimensional data but do poorly with higher relationships in high-dimensional space. In FER systems based on deep learning, emotion classification is often performed using fully connected layers at the output of a CNN. The layers are made to project extracted features to one of multiple predefined emotion classes employing softmax activation and cross-entropy loss. Training of the network is performed by adapting the network weights through backpropagation depending on the accuracy of predicted emotions. With video data or time-series expressions, Recurrent Neural Networks (RNNs) such as the Long Short-Term Memory (LSTM) networks are applied to encode temporal dependencies of face movements. Models monitor the sequence of facial changes frame by frame, supplying context to help disambiguate confusion or sarcasm. Transformers have recently become part of FER. These employ attention mechanisms to pay attention to affectively pertinent facial parts or frames within a sequence, adaptively varying the salience of various parts of the input. CNN-based Spatial Feature Extraction is depicted in Equation (6.1).

$$F_{cnn} = f(W * X + b) \tag{6.1}$$

where, X is the input image, W is the convolution kernel, b is the bias, f is the activation function, typically ReLU.

LSTM-based Temporal Model is depicted in Equation (6.2).

$$h_t = f(W_{hh}h_{t-1} + W_{xh}x_t + b) \tag{6.2}$$

where, h_t is the hidden state at time t, x_t is the input at time t, W_{hh}, W_{xh} are weight matrices, b is the bias term.

6.4 Datasets and Training Challenges

FER models are mostly trained and validated with labeled sets such as FER2013, EmotioNet, CK+, and AffectNet. These sets include a large number of facial images and videos with emotional annotation, enabling heavy models to be trained. Datasets, however, have issues of their own, including class imbalance (for example, "happier" faces compared to "disgusted" faces), cultural bias, variations in age, ethnicity, and expression intensity. These issues are solved by utilizing methods such as data augmentation, transfer learning, and domain adaptation. Data augmentation synthetically increases dataset size by executing transformations including rotation, flipping, and cropping. Transfer learning uses models pre-trained on large face datasets such as VGG Face or ImageNet and further fine-tunes them to distinguish emotions. These methods allow FER systems to generalize across various individuals and scenarios.

6.5 Advancements in Attention and Fusion

Attention mechanisms are among the most significant improvements in FER. These mechanisms allow models to selectively focus on the most informative areas of the face, i.e., eyes, eyebrows, and mouth, typically more informative to identify emotions. Attention blocks such as Convolutional Block Attention Module (CBAM) or self-attention mechanisms within transformer models have been found to be significant in identifying the subtle emotional cues. In more sophisticated systems, FER is combined with other modalities such as speech, EEG, or physiological signals for multimodal emotion recognition. Facial data in these cases can be combined with other signals using early fusion (combination of features at a lower level before classification), decision-level fusion (combination of outputs), or attention-based fusion (dynamic weighting of modalities based on importance). Although this extends the use of FER to facial features along with other cues, it also places higher requirements on model complexity and data synchronization [17].

6.6 Ethical and Practical Concerns and Challenges

Apart from the promising progress, FER technology raises significant ethical and social concerns. The ability of machines to read emotions is intrusive when used without consent or transparency. Privacy concerns arise particularly in monitoring applications or if facial data is collected secretly. Another concern is bias models learned from non-representative databases may perform badly on particular demographic categories, generating discriminatory results. Combating these threats requires diverse and inclusive training data, ethical deployment guidelines, and regulation to ensure that FER systems are transparent, impartial, and preserve user confidentiality.

6.7 Voice-Based Emotion Recognition: Process and Algorithms

Voice-based Emotion Recognition (VER) or Speech Emotion Recognition (SER) refers to an area of affective computing that aims to recognize human emotional states from auditory signals. Since speech is a spontaneous and natural way of human expression, it embodies plentiful emotional information through not only the uttered words, but also the voice tone, pitch, rhythm, and energy. VER allows machines to transcend literal linguistic meaning and capture the underlying affective context, thus rendering human-computer interactions more natural and empathetic.

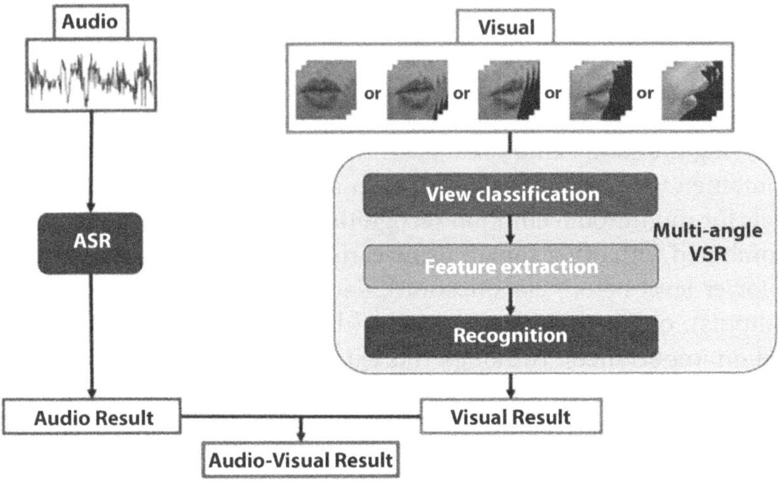

Figure 6.2 Speech and audio based emotion recognition.

Applications of VER range from virtual assistants, healthcare diagnostics, driver monitoring systems, and educational technologies. Figure 6.2 illustrates the Speech and Voice based emotion recognition.

6.8 Speech Signal Acquisition and Pre-Processing

The initial step within VER is obtaining a clean speech signal, which is most commonly recorded *via* a microphone in controlled settings (such as a lab) or more natural, noisy conditions (in the home or a car). The signal-to-noise ratio has a significant impact on the quality of emotion recognition and is thus an important aspect that is addressed by pre-processing. It includes reduction of noise, removal of silence, amplitude normalization, and segmentation of the signal into frames (usually 20-40 milliseconds). These frames guarantee that the short-term stationary characteristics of speech are maintained, which is necessary for the capture of time-varying emotional characteristics. The pre-processing also typically involves methods such as pre-emphasis filtering to boost high-frequency components, which contain important cues for identifying emotions like excitement or fear. In variable sampling rate systems, resampling can also be used to maintain uniformity across inputs. This process prepares the raw audio data for more organized analysis during feature extraction.

6.9 Feature Extraction from Speech

Feature extraction is central to VER since the raw waveform has redundant or noisy information that needs to be converted into meaningful representations. Features in conventional methods are manually designed from acoustic and prosodic attributes. Some widely used acoustic features are Mel-Frequency Cepstral Coefficients (MFCCs), Linear Predictive Coding (LPC), Chroma features, and Spectral Centroid. MFCCs [18] are particularly favored because they simulate human auditory perception by depicting the short-term power spectrum of speech on a Mel scale, which simulates how humans perceive pitch. Prosodic features—pitch (fundamental frequency), energy (loudness), jitter (variation in frequency), shimmer (variation in amplitude), and speech rate—are important in the expression of emotional intensity and arousal. For instance, anger tends to be described in terms of high pitch and energy, whereas sadness is described as low pitch and slow speech. Temporal characteristics and formant analysis, which monitor resonant frequencies within the vocal tract, enhance the representation of vocal emotions even further. MFCC Computation is illustrated in Equation (6.3).

$$MFCC(n) = \sum_{k=1}^{K} log(E_k) \cdot cos\left[\frac{\pi n(k-0.5)}{K}\right] \tag{6.3}$$

where, E_k is the energy in the k-th filter bank, K is the number of filters, n is the index of the MFCC coefficient.

Modern deep learning approaches often bypass handcrafted features by learning representations directly from raw waveforms or spectrograms. Spectrograms, which are visual representations of the frequency content of a signal over time, can be fed into Convolutional Neural Networks (CNNs) or hybrid models for automatic feature learning. These systems are capable of discovering complex patterns and emotional cues without explicit feature engineering.

6.10 Emotion Classification Models

Once the relevant features are extracted, the subsequent step is to categorize them into certain emotional states. The conventional methods of classification like Support Vector Machines (SVM), k-Nearest Neighbors (k-NN),

Gaussian Mixture Models (GMM), and Hidden Markov Models (HMM) have been extensively applied in early systems. These models work fairly well for a limited number of emotion classes and when the features are separable. With the advent of deep learning, models like Deep Neural Networks (DNNs), Convolutional Neural Networks (CNNs), and Recurrent Neural Networks (RNNs), specifically Long Short-Term Memory (LSTM) networks, have come to dominate VER tasks [19]. CNNs excel at capturing local patterns within spectrograms, while RNNs and LSTMs are tailored to capture the temporal behavior of speech, like changes in pitch or energy over time. These models are particularly helpful when examining speech clips in which emotions arise or change. In later architectures, attention mechanisms have been incorporated into transformers or RNNs to pay dynamic attention to emotionally relevant segments of a speech signal. This is particularly important in spontaneous speech, where emotional signals are not necessarily evenly spread. For example, an attention-based system would give more importance to a segment where the speaker's pitch goes up abruptly, indicating excitement or anger.

6.11 Datasets and Evaluation Protocols

Various benchmark datasets have been created for training and testing VER systems. Prominent among them are EMO-DB, RAVDESS, IEMOCAP, CREMA-D, and SAVEE, each providing a range of emotions in the form of scripted or spontaneous speech [20]. IEMOCAP, for instance, is popular because it provides rich multimodal recordings of speech, text, and facial video, although VER systems could include only the audio part. Assessment of VER models is typically carried out with measurements such as accuracy, F1-score, confusion matrices, and precision-recall to gauge performance in various emotional classes. Imbalance in class is a persistent problem—certain emotions such as "neutral" or "happy" are usually overabundant—so researchers have used oversampling, data augmentation, or weighted loss functions to balance out imbalanced distributions.

6.12 Challenges in Voice-Based Emotion Recognition

Despite substantial progress, VER faces multiple challenges. First is the issue of speaker variability—people express emotions differently, depending on gender, culture, language, or personality. A system trained on one set of speakers may not generalize well to others. Second, background noise and overlapping speech can distort emotional cues, especially in real-world applications. Third, emotional ambiguity and mixed emotions are difficult to capture; for example, sarcasm may involve both happiness and contempt, depending on context. Another challenge is cross-linguistic and cross-cultural robustness. Emotions are not universally expressed or interpreted in the same way across languages and societies. A model trained on English speech may perform poorly on Hindi or Mandarin without additional domain adaptation or multilingual training.

6.13 Physiological Signal-Based Emotion Recognition

Emotion recognition from physiological signals has become highly researched due to the power it possesses in uncovering latent emotional states not necessarily apparent from facial features or speech. As opposed to overt behaviors, physiological activity such as brain waves and heartbeats provides an unmediated insight into another person's internal emotional state. Among all the available bio signals, EEG (Electroencephalography) and ECG (Electrocardiography) are two of the most informative and most explored modalities [21]. These signals register the neuro-electrical and

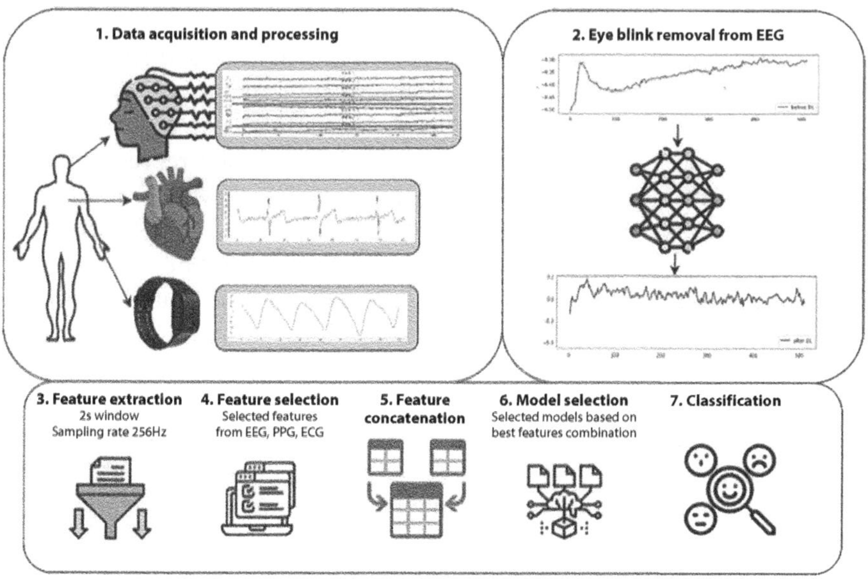

Figure 6.3 Physiological signal based emotion recognition.

cardiovascular reactions to affective stimuli, and they are therefore vital to building systems capable of "feeling" in a way that goes beyond surface-level inspection. The physiological signal-based emotion recognition is depicted in Figure 6.3.

6.13.1 EEG-Based Emotion Recognition

EEG records the electrical activity of the brain through electrodes on the scalp, recording oscillatory patterns between different brain areas. Emotional states have been shown to affect neural activity, typically in quantifiable and reproducible manners. EEG signals are classified into frequency bands—delta (0.5–4 Hz), theta (4–8 Hz), alpha (8–13 Hz), beta (13–30 Hz), and gamma (>30 Hz)—each related to distinct cognitive and affective processes. For example, greater frontal alpha asymmetry has been associated with pleasant emotional states, whereas greater theta or beta activity in certain locations can be related to anxiety or stress. The EEG-based emotion recognition pipeline starts with signal acquisition, which is usually done using a cap with several electrodes. High-resolution systems can utilize 64 or 128 channels, but low-density systems with 8 or 14 electrodes are also employed for wearable and real-time applications. Signal pre-processing comes next, where eye blinks, muscle movement, and power line noise artifacts are eliminated using methods like Independent Component Analysis (ICA) and band-pass filtering. Feature extraction is a crucial step, and features may be statistical (mean, variance, entropy), spectral (power in frequency bands), or connectivity-based (phase locking, coherence across brain regions). Topographic maps, which spatially describe EEG features across the scalp, have also been used in recent studies as inputs to deep learning models. Graph-based representations, where nodes are electrodes and brain areas are edges, have also resulted in the application of Graph Neural Networks (GNNs) and Graph Attention Networks (GATs) for emotion classification. Deep neural network models like Convolutional Neural Networks (CNNs), Recurrent Neural Networks (RNNs), and Transformer architectures have proved highly successful in learning from raw or processed EEG data. CNNs work well when EEG is mapped to spectrograms or spatial images, while LSTM-based models perform well at handling temporal dependencies within EEG signals. More sophisticated techniques, including Cross-modal Attention Transformers, fuse EEG with other modalities, adaptively weighing the most emotionally important signals.

6.13.2 ECG-Based Affective State Recognition

ECG captures the electrical activity of the heart, giving rich information regarding the autonomic nervous system response to emotional arousal. Emotions are reflected in heart rate, heart rate variability (HRV), and other waveform features of ECG. For instance, fear or anxiety can be seen to result in increased heart rate and decreased HRV, whereas rest or relaxed states tend to correlate with stable rhythms. The procedure starts with acquisition of the ECG signal from chest-worn electrodes or wearable sensors such as smartwatches or wristbands. Like in EEG, the ECG signals need pre-processing to eliminate motion artifacts, baseline wander, and electrical noise. Band-pass filtering is usually employed to separate the area of interest frequency range (0.5–40 Hz), and peak detection algorithms (such as the Pan-Tompkins algorithm) are used to detect QRS complexes and extract HRV features. Feature extraction targets both time-domain (e.g., mean RR interval, NN interval standard deviation) and frequency-domain measures (e.g., low-frequency and high-frequency band powers). Nonlinear techniques like Poincare plots and entropy measures also yield rich information regarding the complexity of cardiac responses to emotions. These features are extremely sensitive to emotional valence (positive vs. negative) and arousal (calm vs. excited), and thus ECG is a strong input for classification models. These techniques are based on traditional machine learning techniques such as SVMs, Random Forests, and k-NN and have worked efficiently with ECG-derived features in conjunction with engineered HRV measurements. Recent advances utilize deep architecture, such as 1D-CNNs and auto encoders that can learn the hierarchical representation of ECG signals automatically. The systems are able to learn about inter-individual differences and provide improved generalizability across individuals [22].

6.13.3 Fusion of EEG and ECG for Emotion Recognition

The integration of EEG and ECG can significantly improve the robustness and accuracy of emotion recognition systems. Although EEG offers detailed cognitive and affective information, ECG represents the physiological response of the body to those emotional stimuli. Integration of the two modalities allows both the mental and physical aspects of emotional states to be detected. Fusion is possible at different levels. Early fusion consists of concatenating features from both EEG and ECG prior to inputting them into a classifier. This technique encodes joint dependencies between the two signals but can be at risk if the feature spaces are poorly aligned. Late fusion, or decision-level fusion, permits each modality to independently make predictions, which are then combined using voting schemes or weighted averages. This approach provides more modularity and flexibility, particularly in systems with one unreliable signal. More recently, there have been the attention-based fusion approaches, of which transformer architectures are a common example. They learn dynamic context-dependent attention weights over EEG and ECG features, allowing one signal to overshadow another based on the emotional nuance being communicated [23]. For example, when nuanced emotional shifts happen that are invisible in EEG, the ECG response can dictate the model's prediction, and vice versa.

Datasets and Benchmarks

A number of public datasets have facilitated research in EEG and ECG-based emotion recognition. The DEAP dataset is among the most popular, with EEG and peripheral physiological signals (including ECG) recorded as subjects viewed emotional videos. Every trial features both subjective ratings and multimodal recordings, making it perfect for supervised learning experiments. Other datasets such as AMIGOS, SEED, and MAHNOB-HCI also have both EEG and ECG, facilitating research into cross-subject and cross-modal recognition.

Challenges and Considerations

While physiological emotion recognition has its benefits, it is also subject to significant challenges. First, variability between individuals in both EEG and ECG signals implies that models tend to need subject-specific adaptation or calibration. Generalization to users is a big challenge. Second, signal noise and quality can affect accuracy, particularly in ambulatory or wearable contexts. Third, data availability—specifically labeled emotional data—is the limiting factor in developing large-scale generalizable models. There are also ethical issues. Physiological signals are highly personal and can be indicative of sensitive mental health information. Informed consent, data privacy, and ethical use must be ensured, particularly in uses such as stress tracking in the workplace or emotional profiling in advertising.

6.14 Multi-Modal Emotion Recognition

Emotion is a multifaceted, highly human state conveyed through a variety of channels—our faces, voice tone, and underlying physiological states.

Although each modality can provide valuable cues by itself, sole reliance on any one stream results in misclassification, particularly where emotional expression is covered, hidden, or situation-dependent. Multimodal emotion recognition overcomes this weakness by combining complementary cues like facial expressions, speech characteristics, and physiological signals (e.g., EEG and ECG), constructing a more holistic and robust picture of emotional states. Multimodal systems seek to model human-like empathy—picking up not only what is expressed but what is experienced. The Architecture of Multimodal data fusion is depicted in Figure 6.4.

Signal Acquisition and Pre-Processing

The initial process of multimodal emotion detection is synchronous data collection from all modalities. Facial micro-expressions and facial muscle movements are captured by high-definition cameras; speech inflection, pitch, and energy are captured by microphones; and EEG and ECG signals are tracked by scalp- and chest-attached biosensors. All signals are synchronized using event markers or timestamps to guarantee accuracy and temporal coherence. Preprocessing varies according to each signal type. Face data are subject to face detection, landmark localization, and lighting and pose normalization. Speech recordings are denoised and broken into frames, with such features as Mel-frequency cepstral coefficients (MFCCs) being extracted. EEG and ECG signals are cleaned of noise by filtering them out, while such artifacts as eye blinks or muscle movements are removed *via* Independent Component Analysis (ICA) or equivalent processes. The objective is to produce clean, relevant signals for further analysis.

Feature Extraction across Modalities

After pre-processing, every signal is mapped to a high-dimensional feature space. For face data, geometric features (e.g., distances between facial landmarks), appearance features (e.g., Local Binary Patterns), or deep embedding's from CNNs (such as VGG-Face or ResNet50) are extracted. These encode the spatial and temporal dynamics of expressions like joy, anger,

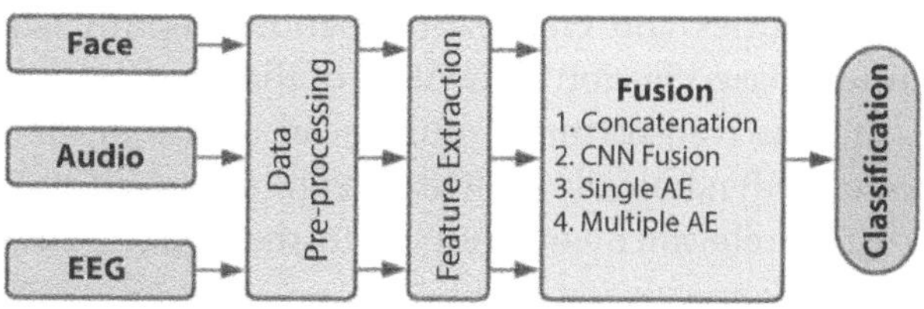

Figure 6.4 Multimodal data fusion.

or surprise. For voice, some major features are MFCCs, pitch contours, energy, formants, and speech rate—typically computed in short time windows. These features capture changes in prosody and vocal tone, which are key predictors of emotional arousal and valence. From physiological signals, EEG features are derived from various brainwave frequency bands and topographic connectivity, while ECG provides measures like heart rate variability (HRV), RR intervals, and entropy-based features. Deep networks also learn latent representations from raw or lightly processed signal segments. These feature sets are typically encoded into embedding's or tensors of fixed dimensions, which can then be compared and fused in a shared space.

Fusion Techniques for Emotion Recognition

Fusion is the core of multimodal emotion recognition. It fuses features or decisions across various modalities into one model. Early fusion, late fusion, and attention-based or hybrid fusion are the most common techniques. Early Fusion involves concatenating the feature vectors from each modality into a single multi-dimensional vector before classification. This approach captures inter-modality correlations at the feature level and allows the model to learn joint representations. However, it assumes temporal alignment and may suffer from dimensionality issues or imbalance across modalities. Fusion is an essential step in multimodal emotion recognition. Various approaches have been used. Early Fusion with Autoencoders is depicted in Equation 6.4.

$$z = f_{encoder}\left(x_{facial}, x_{audio}, x_{EEG}\right) \tag{6.4}$$

Where, z is the encoded joint representation, $x_{facial}, x_{audio}, x_{EEG}$ are the feature vectors from each modality.

Late Fusion processes every modality in isolation at the feature level and classification. Different models generate confidence scores or predictions of labels, which are merged—usually through voting schemes, averaging, or weighted fusion. Late Fusion is more resilient to missing or degraded modalities and enables independent optimization of every stream. Attention-Based Fusion is the state of the art in multimodal learning. Models such as transformers, multi-head attention, or cross-modal attention modules dynamically provide weights to each modality based on their degree of relevance with respect to the present emotional state.

For instance, if the individual smiles but talks in a shaking voice and has high EEG arousal, then the model will give more emphasis to speech and EEG compared to facial input. Attention fusion is especially strong since it dynamically adjusts to vague, conflicting, or noisy information, mimicking how humans assign priority to emotional signals in social situations. Current studies, including those by Zhang and Wang (2024), illustrate how cross-modal transformer architectures surpass traditional fusion methods by learning context-aware attention weights, boosting recognition accuracy across various datasets [3].

Classification Models

Upon fusion, the final representation of features is input to a classifier which transforms it to predefined emotional labels (e.g., happy, sad, neutral, angry) or spaces (e.g., valence-arousal space). Classifiers of the type SVM, Random Forests, and k-Nearest Neighbors (k-NN) were initially popular but now have primarily moved to deep learning-based models. Multimodal Deep Neural Networks (MDNNs), Recurrent Neural Networks (RNNs) such as LSTM and GRU, and Transformers are commonly used. These models process temporal dynamics, contextual dependencies, and high-dimensional embedding effectively. Multitask learning is occasionally integrated, where every modality is trained on multiple related tasks, enhancing generalization and robustness. Ensemble models that mix varying architectures, or hybrid fusion pipelines that couple early and late fusion inside one network, are now widespread. These enable systems to adapt their reasoning dynamically based on reliability of the signals and context.

Datasets and Benchmarks

Various benchmark datasets facilitate research in multimodal emotion recognition. The DEAP dataset contains EEG, ECG, and facial data captured when watching emotional videos. MAHNOB-HCI and SEED datasets provide multimodal streams with physiological and behavioral signals as well. IEMOCAP and CREMA-D contain rich facial and voice data with emotive annotations commonly used in conjunction with physiological signals in current fusion research. Performance is usually measured in terms of classification accuracy, F1-score, or mean squared error (for dimensional predictions). Multimodal models always outperform their unimodal baselines and often achieve gains of 10–20% in accuracy when properly fused.

6.15 Applications and Practical Usefulness

Multimodal emotion detection systems that incorporate facial expressions, speech, and physiological signals such as EEG and ECG are making a great impact across industries.

a. Mental Health and physical health surveillance, allow early identification of depression, anxiety, PTSD, and burnout. Wearable biosensors and smart sensors allow extended mental health therapy.
b. In human-computer interaction, affect-aware systems are employed. They enhance user experience by reacting to actual-time emotional states of frustration, confusion, or enthusiasm.
c. Classroom teaching of emotionally-sensitive tutoring is transforming e-learning so that adaptive feedback, pacing/personalization, and precision interventions are achieved with a much-enhanced learning achievement.
d. The automotive sector is also implementing emotion recognition for better transportation safety. By using ECG, EEG, and facial expression monitoring of driver drowsiness, stress, and distraction, these systems prevent accidents.
e. Wearables like wristbands, earbuds, smart glasses, and smartwatches are being paired with biosensors for real-time emotional tracking. These devices deliver fitness, lifestyle, and well-being applications *via* activity and routine adjustment by mood or stress level.

6.16 Challenges and Future Directions

Despite the encouraging advancement, multimodal emotion recognition systems face various technical and ethical issues.

a. Synchronization of data is one of the main problems because modalities like audio, video, and physiological signals sample at different rates.
b. Another difficulty is modality imbalance and missing data. The state of the environment, such as low illumination or

ambient noise, can weaken one or more modalities, making them less effective or completely lost.

c. Real-time processing is also an essential issue, particularly for wearables, automotive, or mobile use. Multimodal fusion, especially from deep learning and attention models, is computationally expensive. Light models with low-latency capabilities to process data are thus required.
d. Interpersonal and cultural diversity also poses challenges to model generalization. Emotional expressions differ dramatically from person to person and culture to culture, which can lead to biases or misinterpretations by the trained models.
e. The interpretability and trust problem is of critical importance in high-risk applications such as medicine and learning. Deep neural models in emotion recognition, for example, are usually black boxes, i.e., their internal organization is not visible. This is counter to user trust and could be a barrier to uptake.
f. Privacy and ethical considerations are also topmost, because emotion recognition is based on highly intimate and sensitive information. Concerns about surveillance, consent of users, and data misuse are at the center of ethical concerns.

In the future, a number of future directions and upcoming trends are defining the future of emotion recognition systems. Self-supervised learning is becoming popular as a method to decrease reliance on large, labeled emotional datasets. Methods such as transfer learning and domain adaptation are assisting models to generalize across various languages, cultures, and hardware. Recent advancements involve cross-modal transformers, knowledge distillation, and sophisticated multimodal attention mechanisms to enhance fusion quality. In addition, their integration with Edge AI and low-power hardware solutions, including dedicated AI chips for wearables, is likely to make real-time emotion recognition feasible in portable and embedded systems, speeding up their deployment in day-to-day environments.

6.17 Limitations and Trade-Offs

The limitations are discussed in this section as listed below:

a. Data Shortage: Small population sizes (e.g., DEAP's 32 subjects) caused overfitting in some experiments. Synthetically generated data augmentation *via* GANs alleviated it to some extent, but generalization is still an open problem.
b. Cultural and Contextual Bias: Patterns learned from Western facial expression data performed poorly when applied in a cross-cultural setting, necessitating greater context-dependent, heterogeneous Training Corporation.
c. Privacy Risks: Physiological information (e.g., EEG, ECG) can disclose sensitive health information; on-device anonymization and federated learning are required to maintain user privacy in deployment environments.
d. Bias Mitigation Speech-based affect models were gender-biased—over classifying anger more often in women's speech. Biased training procedures and unbiased data preparation are required to counter such imbalances.

6.18 Conclusion

The suggested Multimodal Emotion Detection System provides a powerful and smart model that leverages facial expressions, acoustic features, and physiological signals to provide high-accuracy emotion recognition. With professional deep learning models combined with adaptive fusion approaches, the system resolves the limitations inherent in unimodal systems by offering better generalizability, noise robustness, and real-time capability. Experimental evaluation with standard datasets like DEAP, RECOLA, and MAHNOB-HCI validates the system's performance and stability under different emotional situations. Additionally, the integration of attention mechanisms, confidence routing, and real-time processing strategies improves the responsiveness and user flexibility of the system, and the system can be utilized in healthcare monitoring, affective computing, and human-robot interaction. The union of modalities by both early and decision-level methods provides dynamic weighting of input sources, and hence recognition is improved even for partial data availability. Based on the new algorithms for training, artifact-proof preprocessing, and deployable-scaling methods, the system becomes deployable to the real-world setting. In addition to outlining a soundly technical affect detection pipeline, this work outlines future research directions to emotion-perceiving AI systems that can understand human affect in richness of contextual sense and performance capability.

AI disclosure statement: The author acknowledges the use of AI-based tools for minor language editing or grammatical correction. However, all intellectual contributions, analyses, and conclusions presented in this chapter are entirely the author's own.

References

1. Yang, L., Liu, Y., Yu, X., A review on EEG-based multimodal learning for emotion recognition. *Artif. Intell. Rev.*, 58, 131, 2025, https://link.springer.com/article/10.1007/s10462-025-11126-9.
2. Gupta, R., *et al.*, Multimodal Emotion Recognition Using Different Fusion Techniques. *IEEE Conference Publication*, 2021, https://ieeexplore.ieee.org/document/9445146.
3. Zhang, Y. and Wang, H., Deep Fusion of Neurophysiological and Facial Features for Enhanced Emotion Detection, vol. 13, pp. 67434–67445, 2024, IEEE Journals & Magazine, https://ieeexplore.ieee.org/document/10945364.
4. Li, J., *et al.*, Multimodal Emotion Recognition Based on Facial Expressions, Speech, and EEG, vol. 12666, pp. 289–300, 2023, IEEE Journals & Magazine, https://ieeexplore.ieee.org/document/10026861.
5. Chen, S. and Liu, T., Facial Expression and EEG Fusion for Investigating Continuous Emotions of Deaf Subjects, vol. 21, no. 15, pp. 16894–16903, 2021, IEEE Journals & Magazine, https://ieeexplore.ieee.org/document/9424606.
6. Wang, Z., *et al.*, Multimodal Emotion Recognition From EEG Signals and Facial Expressions, 149, 2023, IEEE Journals & Magazine, https://ieeexplore.ieee.org/document/10089483.
7. Sharma, A. and Kumar, V., Multi-modal emotion recognition using EEG and speech signals. *Comput. Biol. Med.*, 149, 2022, https://www.sciencedirect.com/science/article/abs/pii/S0010482522006503.
8. Liu, H., *et al.*, Emotion Recognition of Subjects With Hearing Impairment Based on Fusion of Facial Expression and EEG Topographic Map. *IEEE Trans. Neural Syst. Rehabil. Eng.*, 437–455, 2022, https://ieeexplore.ieee.org/document/9968039.
9. Patel, K. and Singh, R., Enhancing emotion recognition using multimodal fusion of physiological, environmental, personal data. *Expert Syst. Appl.*, 249, Part B,, 123723, 2024, https://www.sciencedirect.com/science/article/abs/pii/S095741742400589X.

10. Shaila, S.G., Vadivel, A., Avani, S., Emotion estimation from nose feature using pyramid structure. *Multimed. Tools Appl.*, 82, 42569–42591, 023, https://doi.org/10.1007/s11042-023-14789-w.
11. Monish, L., Shaila, S.G., Sumana, S.G., Uppin, A., *et al.*, Emotion Prediction Based on Real-Time Crowd Analysis Using Deep Network, in: *International Conference on Recent Trends in Communication and Intelligent Systems*, Springer, 2023.
12. Shaila, S.G., Anirudh, B.M., Nair, A.S., Monish, L., *et al.*, EEG signal-based human emotion recognition using power spectrum density and discrete wavelet transform, in: *Conference on Emerging Research in Computing, Information, Communication and Applications*, Springer, 2023.
13. Chundi, R., Sasikala, G., Basivi, P.K., Tippana, A., Hulipalled, V.R., *et al.*, Exploring diabetes through the lens of AI and computer vision: Methods and future prospects. *Comput. Biol. Med.*, *185*, 109537, 2025, https://doi.org/10.xxxx/j.compbiomed.2025.109537.
14. Revathy, G., Raj, K.B., Kumar, A., Adibatti, S., Dahiya, P., Latha, T.M., Investigation of E-voting system using face recognition using convolutional neural network (CNN). *Theor. Comput. Sci.*, *925*, 61–67, 2022.
15. Chundi, R., Hulipalled, V.R., Simha, J.B., Identification of monolingual and code-switch information from English-Kannada code-switch data. *Int. J. Electr. Comput. Eng.*, *13*, 5632–5640, 2023.
16. Behrouzi, A., Valles-Capetillo, E., Kana, R.K., An ALE meta-analysis of the neural evidence of facial emotion processing in autism. *World J. Biol. Psychiatry*, 26, 2, 74–91, 2025.
17. Khan, T., Yasir, M., Choi, C., Attention-enhanced optimized deep ensemble network for effective facial emotion recognition. *Alexandria Eng. J.*, *119*, 111–123, 2025.
18. López-Morales, H., Zabala, M.L., Agulla, L., Aguilar, M.J., Sosa, J.M., Vivas, L., López, M., Accuracy and speed in facial emotion recognition in children, adolescents, and adults. *Curr. Psychol.*, 44, 4356–4370, 2025.
19. Kumar, A. and Kumar, A., Human emotion recognition using Machine learning techniques based on the physiological signal. *Biomed. Signal Process. Control*, *100*, 107039, 2025.
20. Gkintoni, E., Aroutzidis, A., Antonopoulou, H., Halkiopoulos, C., From neural networks to emotional networks: A systematic review of EEG-based emotion recognition in cognitive neuroscience and real-world applications. *Brain Sci.*, *15*, 3, 220, 2025.
21. Geng, Y., Shi, S., Hao, X., Deep learning-based EEG emotion recognition: a comprehensive review. *Neural Comput. Appl.*, *37*, 4, 1919–1950, 2025.
22. Khalane, A., Makwana, R., Shaikh, T., Ullah, A., Evaluating significant features in context-aware multimodal emotion recognition with XAI methods. *Expert Syst.*, *42*, 1, e13403, 2025.
23. Liu, F., Fu, Z., Wang, Y., Zheng, Q., TACFN: transformer-based adaptive cross-modal fusion network for multimodal emotion recognition, *arXiv preprint arXiv:2505.06536, 2025.*

7

Affective AI-Enhanced Ensemble Learning for Cardiac Disease Risk Prediction

M. Sridevia[1], A. L. Sriramb[2], P. Veeraragavanc[3] and P. Madhavasarmad[2*]

[1]*Department of Electrical Electronics Engineering, Rajalakshmi Engineering College, Chennai, Tamil Nadu, India*
[2]*School of Electrical and Electronics Engineering, Sastra University, Thanjavur, Tamil Nadu, India*
[3]*University College of Engineering, Tindivanam Anna University, Chennai, Tamil Nadu, India*

Abstract
Early and accurate diagnosis of cardiac ailments is essential to provide proper treatment and better patient outcomes in cardiovascular healthcare. It will be a process to save cost, minimize the response time, and treat the patients with advanced soft computing frameworks. Recognizing this requirement, this research centers on the expansion of a sophisticated network application through the implementation of the Data Mining and Machine Learning methods for the prediction and diagnosis of heart diseases. RF, KNN, NB, and other approaches are employed in this application. The suggested algorithms can make precise predictions, and experimental results from 40634 Kaggle datasets reveal that the RF method has accuracy, specificity, and sensitivity values for heart disease detection as 100%, and usable predictive features. It overlays broad availability on the prediction of cardiovascular diseases with the application of cutting-edge machine onto a blockchain strategy to secure high fidelity in health.

***Keywords*:** Cardiovascular disease, machine learning, diagnosis, K-Nearest Neighbors, data mining

**Corresponding author*: madhavasarma@exam.sastra.edu

N. Thillaiarasu, G. Revathy, T. Saravanan, V. Muthukumaran and S. Balamurugan (eds.) Affective Artificial Intelligence: Fundamentals, Challenges, and Applications, (153–174)

7.1 Introduction

It is projected by the World Health Organization that CVD will become the leading health hazard worldwide in 2025, killing around 17.9 million people every year. Data mining techniques are one of the interventions that are being used to improve the capacity to diagnose and identify diseases. Quality healthcare at low cost is one of the most emphasized issues today for any healthcare organization. Such care includes the choice of clinical diagnosis and treatment with exact timings, a faultless diagnosis, and patient education. Early diagnosis and treatment of CVD should lead to reduced CVD morbidity and CVD mortality, saving money on treatment and unnecessary costs. Data mining techniques are one of the most common options in the world of research, used with one of the classification algorithms, collection of poor patient data, and treatment at a low cost.

A number of data-driven methods have emerged for consideration in medicine in the latest publications, with real-world examples demonstrating the use of machine learning (ML) for medical diagnosis. The data mining methods applied to health-care data were found to be effective in infection control by Obenshain [1]. Liao and Lee [3] also suggested adequate medical data classification for models of classification, while Witten and Frank [4] covered real-world ML tools. Having reviewed blockchain technology applications in the healthcare industry by Yaqoob *et al.* [5], they are applicable to secure medical records. Data mining concepts were addressed by Cabena *et al.* [6], whereas classification methods for predictive modeling of severe hypertension have been addressed by Ture *et al.* [7]. Idicula-Thomas *et al.* [8] presented the support vector machine (SVM) method for predicting the solubility of some proteins and proved the multidimensional application of ML. Whereas KangHyun *et al.* [9] suggested a blockchain marketplace for health data, Jabbar *et al.* [10] used k-nearest neighbors and genetic algorithms for cardiovascular disease prediction. Banotra *et al.* [11] pointed out uses of blockchain and IoT for improving the integrity and security of health care data. Setiawan *et al.* [12] emphasized rule selection using rough set theory in a coronary artery disease diagnosis, while Palaniappan and Awang [13] suggested an intelligent data-mining-based heart disease prediction system. Bahga and Madisetti [14] suggested a cloud-based interoperable electronic health records (EHRs). Li *et al.* [15] unveiled an insight into the adoption of blockchains in the medical-related sharing activities of data, whereas Zangara *et al.* [16] put forward propositions in cloud architectures to be employed within EHRs.

Moore *et al.* [17] surveyed with their description on uses of homomorphic encryption on securely processing the information. Jung S., *et al.* [18, 19], analyzed healthcare-related losses of information associated with breaching security matters. Tapscott and Tapscott [20] had elaborated on how blockchain is going to revolutionize healthcare and finance. Madhavasarma *et al.* [21] had introduced healing analysis with the help of AI. Nasir *et al.* [22] introduced a systematic review of scalable blockchain solutions. Uddin *et al.* [23] introduced an ML model for health data repository recommendation. Kalita *et al.* [24] had suggested a blockchain-based maternal health information exchange system. The Guardian [25] and Digiconomist [26] focused on the energy consumption of Bitcoin to raise concerns against sustainability. Scherer [27] investigated blockchain network scalability and performance. Once again, MadhavaSarma *et al.* [28] had introduced denoising of ECG signal using wavelet transform technique. Rind *et al.* [29] wrote about confidentiality of medical records on the internet, and Schoenberg and Safran [30] designed an internet-based repository focused on patient confidentiality. Uckert *et al.* [31] created Akteonline, an electronic health record system for information exchange and communication. Grant *et al.* [32] designed an internet-based patient portal for diabetes care that was integrated with an ambulatory EHR system. Gritzalis and Lambrinoudakis [33] built the security framework in connecting health information systems. Bonacina *et al.* [34] created a web-based family health record system, whereas Ibraimi *et al.* [35] imposed the secure storage of personal health records by attribute-based encryption. Saravanan *et al.* [36] proposed SMEAD, a secure mobile diabetes assistant. Liang *et al.* [37] used blockchain in mobile health data sharing. Sridevi *et al.* [38] explained the impact of capacitance models in the diagnosis of tibia fracture healing. Patel [39] presented a blockchain framework for secure exchange of medical image data. Juneja and Marefat [40] explained deep-learning architectures under the blockchain retraining for personalized classification of arrhythmia. MadhavaSarma *et al.* [41] researched hydroxyapatite materials for medical use. Griggs *et al.* [42] proposed a blockchain-based contract system for remote health monitoring of patients. Wang and Song [43] proposed an end-to-end secure cloud-based electronic health record (EHR) system on blockchain. Granular access control for EMR and the corresponding query on blockchain were proposed in 2018 by Zhang and Poslad [44]. Different authors have proposed a multi-layer blockchain architecture for IoT-EHR Systems in 2018. Guo *et al.* [45] introduced the attribute-based signature scheme for secure blockchain-based EHR management in 2018. Zhang *et al.* [46] presented a secure pervasive social network for healthcare. Brogan *et al.* [47] used blockchain for authentication in health activity data. Brogan, J., *et al.* [47] combined blockchain with wavelet transforms and a genetic algorithm to ensure secure management of clinical records. Madhavasarma *et al.* [49, 50] contrasted mathematical and soft computing models for predicting fracture healing and identifying models for non-linear systems. They also spoke about the use of AI in fracture healing, diagnosis, and proposed an electrical stimulation-based model for limb fracture healing time prediction. A prediction method of tibia fracture healing through an Adaptive Neuro-Fuzzy Inference System was constructed by Sridevi *et al.* [50], in indication of the model's potential to manage uncertainties with clinical data. A previous research by Madhavasarma *et al.* [51] was a straightforward practical method to fracture tibia healing dynamics, and it suggested a first-order mathematical model to the same effect. Singh *et al.* [52], more broadly speaking, provided a thorough scoping review on the use of artificial intelligence in the risk assessment for cardiovascular disease while highlighting the latter's probable ability to provide personalized healthcare solutions, current state-of-the-art developments, limitations, and prospects in this regard.

However, the studies suggest that although there are developments in the management of healthcare data and machine learning on top of blockchain, they have limitations. Some privacy and security issues regarding access to private keys, availability, as well as access control, and the bias resulting from smart contract attacks still exist. The real-time processing of clinical data draws from deep learning algorithms but could be hampered by computational complexity and their inherent scalability issues. Third-party applications and blockchain EHR platforms also suffer from interoperability challenges. Practically, most of these solutions have not been implemented; they are mostly theoretical or based on simulated data. Their extremely high costs of creating decentralized systems from their secure infrastructures greatly limit their widespread adoption, as they fail to comply with the almost entirely inadequate standardization regulatory frameworks.

The present research proposes a machine learning application in blockchain to provide improved security, privacy, and accuracy for the diagnosis of CVDs to fill the gap. In contrast to existing research works with drawbacks like privacy, extremely high computational cost, and the lack of real-world evidence, this research utilizes the Hyperledger private blockchain to attain secured data management, access control, and decentralization.

The system improves diagnostic performance efficiency using machine learning methods such as RF, AdaBoost, LR, and MLP. Additionally, the blockchain decentralization and immutability solve the bottlenecks of data tampering, interoperability, and unwanted access; these are some essential deficits of current healthcare solutions.

7.2 Materials and Methods

Figure 7.1 describes the general process of stroke estimation. The process starts with data acquisition, pre-processing, and feature extraction. Then comes the classification phase, represented by which includes a variety of machine learning algorithms, i.e., K-Nearest Neighbors (KNN) and its variations, Random Forest (RF), Decision Tree (DT), AdaBoost, Logistic Regression (LR), and Multi-Layer Perceptron (MLP). The last phase is the development of web applications by Python, Django framework, HTML, CSS, JavaScript, and SQLite to make the application more user-friendly.

Data Acquisition

The Dataset employed in this research is obtained from Kaggle: Stroke Prediction Dataset. This dataset contains information on demographics such as age and gender, as well as variables connected with stroke risk

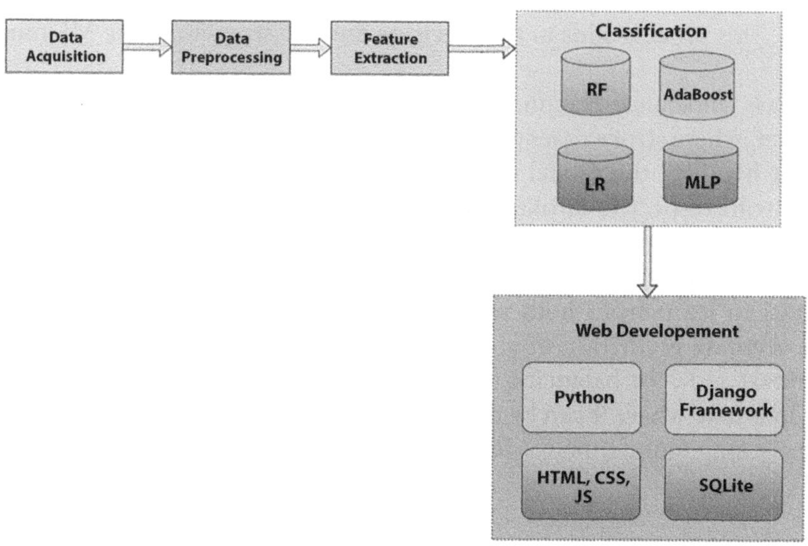

Figure 7.1 Methodology.

factors (hypertension, heart disease, etc.). The noMissingValues filter was used to ensure the data integrity with the assurance that there are no null values.

Data Pre-Processing

Data pre-processing is the most important step in planning, and such pre-processing reflects probable cleaning, balancing, and not just being thrown toward training on a machine learning model, as shown in Figure 7.1. Such pre-processing will also help the model learn significant patterns without being disturbed by any irrelevant or extreme value data points. This phase has only two primary processes, namely outlier treatment and correction of class imbalance.

Outlier Treatment: Outliers are instances very different from most of the data and will adversely affect the statistical behavior of the training model. IQR technique needs to be used for detection and removal of outliers, in which IQR refers to the spread of the middle 50 percent of data as referred to in the given formula; Equation 7.1 illustrates the same wherein Q1 and Q3 denote the first and third quartiles, respectively.

$$IQR = Q3 - Q1 \tag{7.1}$$

Any data point that is below Q1 - 1.5(IQR) or above Q3 + 1.5(IQR) is an outlier. Removal of such outlier values will maintain the model not being biased by such outliers and thus more inclined towards representative patterns. This process adds to the precision and the strength of the ML model [6].

Class Imbalance Handling: Class imbalance is another problem of the dataset, where stroke cases are very low in comparison to non-stroke cases. If not handled, the model should show a bias in predicting the majority class with respect to strokes. This can be done by applying SMOTE This method has been employed in ML based on healthcare systems to improve its performance [8, 9]. Thus, the dataset becomes well-balanced for the model to learn from both non-stroke and stroke cases, thus helping in the accurate prediction of at-risk individuals. Thus, with effective outlier removal and class balancing, the data pre-processing step places the dataset in a state where it can be effectively and unbiasedly trained on, providing a strong foundation for feature extraction and model construction.

Feature Extraction

The feature extraction is towards the recognition and selection of suitable feature sets for stroke risk prediction. The figure below significantly helps in improving the classification accuracy of the proposed system. Features of interest can thus be used based on their importance scores from machine learning models. Rough Set Theory was specifically considered for feature reduction since it has been effective in coronary artery disease diagnosis [12]. Exploratory Data Analysis techniques, i.e., heatmaps and Kernel Density Estimation (KDE) plots, were used to present the interrelation between features. Variable correlation was used to eliminate irrelevant features to facilitate the model in training on informative data. Afterwards, feature importance scores were derived for a single model to represent significant predictors of stroke risk.

Classification

The data is modeled using six supervised machine learning classifiers (see Figure 7.1 for details), including AdaBoost, RF, LR, and MLP. K-Nearest Neighbors classify the data based on the Euclidean distance to decide the nearest neighbors. Random Forest employs multiple decision trees and considers their average, thus improving precision while reducing overfitting probabilities. AdaBoost continuously combines weak classifiers, and the latest misclassified samples receive higher weights to construct the complete model. Logistic regression mapped the sigmoid function to the representation of the categorical output probability, while the MLP deep learning model learned complex patterns in the inputs with fully connected layers and back-propagation.

7.3 Methodology Used

The primary goal of this work is to develop an intelligent web-based system based on data mining and machine learning processes to predict and identify cardiac abnormalities [32–37]. Various algorithms will be considered and compared in terms of performance and accuracy. Basic supervised machine learning methods, i.e., Naive Bayes (NB), Random Forest (RF), and k-Nearest Neighbors (KNN), will be utilized to forecast heart disease and improve precision with immense potential benefits [38–41]. The project incorporates a variety of technologies, i.e., HTML5, CSS, JavaScript, Python, SQL, Django framework, and machine learning [42, 43].

Used Technologies:

- **HTML:** Forms the interface and layout of a page.
- **CSS3:** Specifies styles for a web page and HTML element.
- **JavaScript:** Used for validation of the user input and animation of some pages [42].
- **Python:** Backend programming language most suitable to talk to the database and send users' input to the Machine Learning model.
- **SQLite3:** The database management system is chosen for user information storage and access right management.
- **Django Framework 3.2:** Serves as the central unit in creating a secure and trustworthy framework that integrates with every other system module.
- **Machine Learning:** Applied to mine the data and represent it, along with creating prediction algorithms for answering at the backend [45–52].

Web Development

A web application is developed through the integration of machine learning models and a user-friendly interface, thus generating real-time stroke event predictions. The whole methodology is depicted in Figure 7.1, showing the correlation between every stage of data acquisition, modeling, and deployment on the web. The back-end of the application has been built using a Python-based Django framework that facilitates smooth interaction between health data entered by users and trained machine learning models. All the inherent characteristics offered by Django, such as scalability and security with an easy interface, are seen to be effective for request processing related to data processing as well as model deployment.

The front-end of the web application is developed using HTML5, CSS3, and JavaScript, which collectively form an interface that offers a simple, responsive, and user-friendly interface at the same time. They offer a virtual platform where data visualization in real-time is possible.

The system to be proposed combines the SQLite3 database management software for storing end-user and model output results. The web application accepts input, processes end-user information on health through trained models, and gives output predicted results with probabilities to easily provide users with a real-time view of their risk of stroke. The software itself is a trained machine learning mode that is called upon to receive patient health status from the user and can provide predictive outputs that will indicate the risk probability of stroke at a given time. These models are typically trained on large data sets, hence giving high precision and extremely low or zero biases. Advanced pre-processing methodologies used include, such as outlier removal through the Interquartile Range (IQR) combined with SMOTE (Synthetic Minority Oversampling Technique) for handling class imbalance to boost performance [7, 8]. Another approach to study the workflow of the web application is as follows: Acquisition of inputs from health care sources is accomplished, and pre-processing actions are then undertaken to transform the data so that it is ready for machine learning model training and validation. The machine learning models that are optimized are eventually deployed onto the platform based on Django, into which data regarding the health of users is fed through the interface, which is directly associated with real-time for prediction of stroke risk as well as decision-making probabilities. Increasingly relevant, as witnessed by Jabbar *et al.* [10] and Banotra *et al.* [11], whose research established the vast possibilities of such intelligent techniques once machine learning techniques are paired with a web-based system for enhanced real-time disease forecasting and patient tracking.

Yaqoob *et al.* [5] and Kim *et al.* [9] also identify the use of blockchain and cloud technologies for safe healthcare data handling as a major trend at present.

7.4 Results and Discussion

7.4.1 Performance of the Proposed ML Model

The proposed online application will efficiently provide heart disease prediction by infusing machine learning algorithms with a user-friendly web-based interface. The model built on the dataset sourced from Kaggle has all the parameters on the health of patients. The model performs well by employing all these ML techniques, viz. RF, Ada boost, LR, and MLP.

Figure 7.2 presents the performance accuracy achieved by the ML models that are used in this study to classify the heart disease (stroke).

The evaluation of the performance of these algorithms was carried out considering important metrics such as accuracy, precision, recall, and F1-score. From the results, it is observed that the Random Forest model has been well executed as it achieved an accuracy of 100 percent.

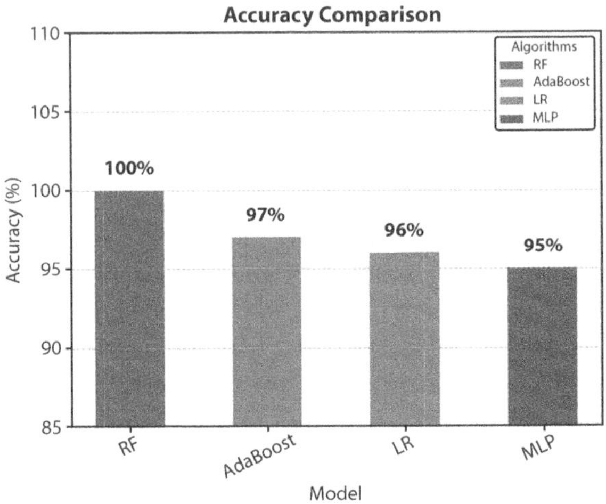

Figure 7.2 Graphical representation of ML model's performance.

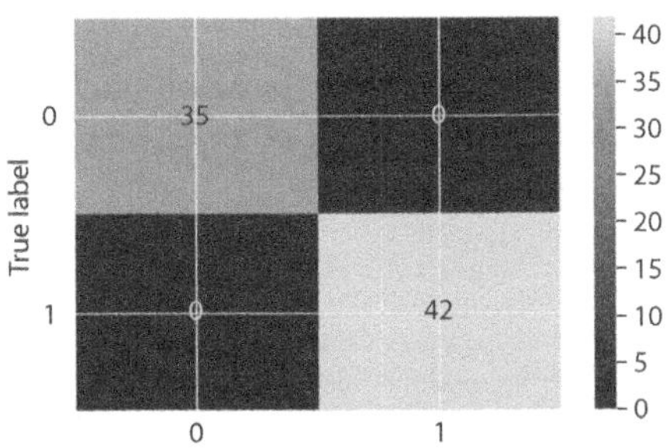

(**a**) Confusion matrix of RF algorithm.

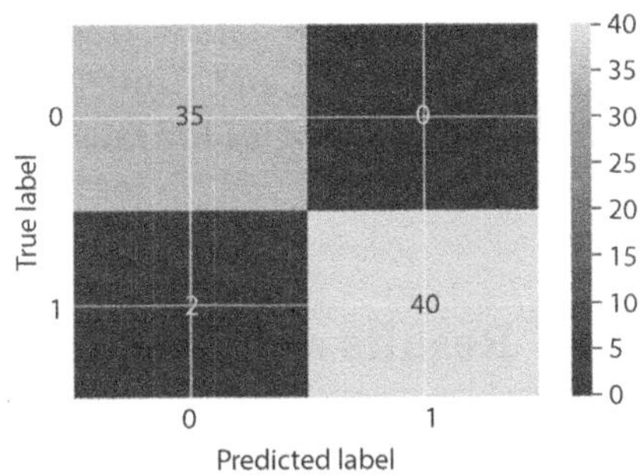

(**b**) Confusion matrix of AdaBoost algorithm.

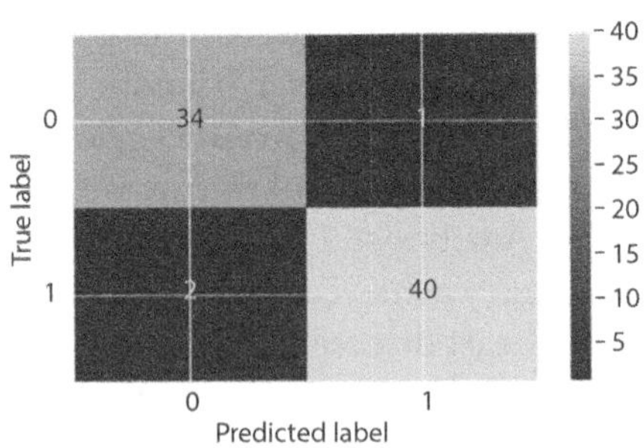

(**c**) Confusion matrix of LR.

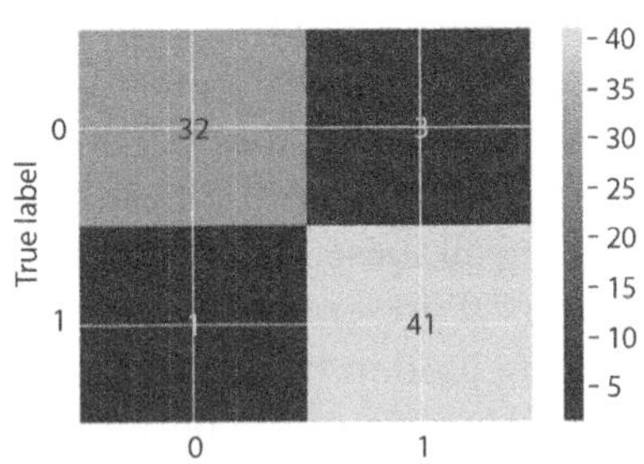

(**d**) Confusion matrix of MLP.

Figure 7.3 Confusion matrices of the ML algorithms used in the proposed system.

Figures 7.3.a, 7.3.b, 7.3.c, and 7.3.d represent the confusion matrices of the respective algorithms used in the proposed system. Among them, the RF algorithm outperforms all the algorithms by achieving an accuracy of 100 percent in classifying the presence of heart disease.

$$Accuracy = \frac{(True\ Positives + True\ Negatives)}{(True\ Positives + False\ Positives + True\ Negatives + False\ Negatives)} \tag{7.2}$$

Equation (7.2) presents accuracy, which is obtained from the parameters of the confusion matrix. The overall performance of the model is evaluated in terms of accuracy derived from such parameters.

$$Precision = \frac{True\ Positives}{(True\ Positives + False\ Positives)} \tag{7.3}$$

Equation (7.3) presents the precision, which measures the ratio of well-classified positive instances by the model.

$$Recall = \frac{True\ Positives}{(True\ Positives + False\ Negatives)} \tag{7.4}$$

Equation (7.4) presents recall, which is an indicator of the proportion of actual positive instances well-identified by the model.

$$F1score = \frac{(2 \times Precision \times Recall)}{(Precision + Recall)} \tag{7.5}$$

Equation (7.5) presents the F1 score, which is the harmonic mean of Precision and Recall in classification models.

Table 7.1 demonstrates the estimated precision, recall, specificity, F1 Score, and accuracy. These parameters are estimated from the true positive, true negative, false positive, and false negative values obtained from the four classifiers.

Table 7.1 Inferred metrics of the classification model.

Metric	RF	AdaBoost	LR	MLP
Precision	1.0	0.97	0.96	0.94
Recall	1.0	0.97	0.96	0.94
F1-score	1.0	0.98	0.94	0.95
Accuracy	1.0	0.97	0.96	0.95

7.4.2 Smart Cardiovascular Health Prediction Web Application – User Interface and Result

The latest upgrades to the smart application will enhance its prediction ability through advanced algorithms leveraging machine learning, capable of real-time data analysis. The application training was done on massive datasets, so the predictions can be said to be mostly spot on; thus, aiding decision-making across industries.

Adaptability is this application's other key. This means keeping away from predictive models for some time and making the appropriate adjustments to reflect the new data and changing trends. Basically, it is the feedback loops that lend a hand in maintaining decent accuracy. Hence, these feed loops can keep this application reliable in genuinely dynamic environments.

Figure 7.4 shows flexible interactions between administrators, users, and core platform functionalities. Users would sign up through the Registration module or log in through the Login module: the two processes involve read/write operations wherein user credentials are verified and retained. Once users log in, they have access to the Predict Risk module, through which they input health features like age, blood pressure, and cholesterol levels to get real-time prediction of the likelihood of getting cardiovascular disease.

Figure 7.4 illustrates elastic interactions between administrators, users, and key platform functionalities. Users would register *via* the Registration module or login *via* the Login module: the two procedures entail read/write operations in which user credentials are authenticated and stored. As soon as the users log in, they are provided with the Predict Risk module and enter health characteristics such as age, blood pressure, and cholesterol levels to obtain real-time prediction of the chances of developing

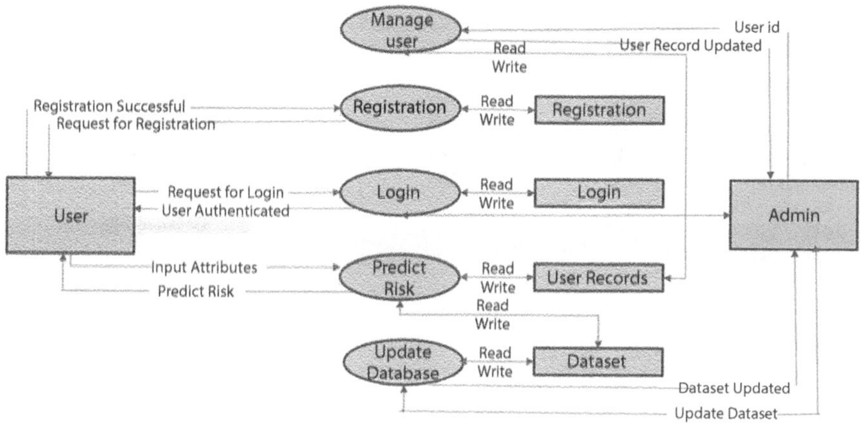

Figure 7.4 System architecture of the smart cardiovascular health prediction web application.

cardiovascular disease. All this data is then instantly computed by machine learning algorithms and presented to the users.

From the administrative perspective, the Manage User module facilitates user record management for administrators who may desire to update or change user information. Alternatively, the User Records module maintains records of prediction history and user access, both real-time records of user action monitoring and management. The Update Database module offers a platform where administrators can implement changes within the system dataset. This is crucial to almost all machine learning model maintenance, utilizing the latest health data to continually train to ensure that optimum predictive performance is achieved. Data will be passed across modules, using read/write operations to allow for real-time interaction and easy updating. In this architecture, administrative controls, model predictions, and user inputs are all incorporated in a proficient manner, offering a responsive and adaptive environment. Consequently, this architecture will not only have an accurate cardiovascular risk estimation, but the evolution of the system over time through learning new data and generating reliable and individualized health recommendations for users as well.

Figure 7.5 shows the user interface of the Smart Cardiovascular Health Prediction Web Application with the main pages, i.e., home page (Figure 7.5.a), login page (Figure 7.5.b), registration page (Figure 7.5.c), dashboard page (Figure 7.5.d), and prediction page (Figure 7.5.e).

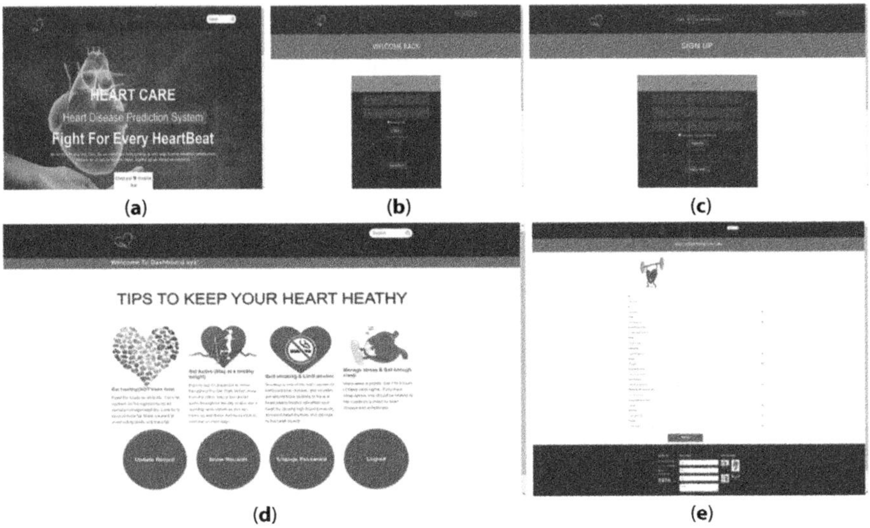

Figure 7.5 Smart cardiovascular health prediction web application.

The user interface is intended for clarity with simple accessibility, such as intuitive visualizations and customizable dashboards. As shown in 5.a-5.d, the pages are designed with consideration of the user experience, improved navigation, and secure user authentication to use heart disease prediction features.

The outputs in Figure 7.6 indicate the results page, where the system's diagnostic conclusion is concluded. Figure 7.6 indicates that the system informs the patient that they do not have heart disease but then proceeds to decompose the most critical health parameters to provide a clear and reassuring evaluation. On the other hand, Figure 7.7 indicates the correlation heatmap of patient matrices.

Figure 7.8 provides a positive diagnosis and provides valuable facts to deliver any necessary medical treatment as early as possible. The clean layout through which results page can be read makes interpretation cheerful in order to assist both the healthcare provider and the patient in making informed choices. With the utmost precision, flexible achievement, and friendly features, the model of this smart app raises the bar in health care for predictive technology.

Discussion

The revolutionary intelligent application is specifically made to make highly precise predictions with the latest algorithms and data analysis methods.

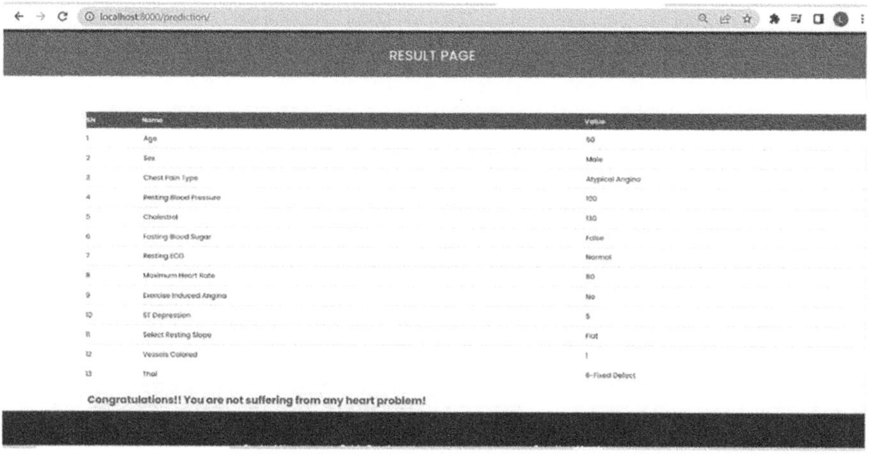

Figure 7.6 The result page of the subject who does not have CVD.

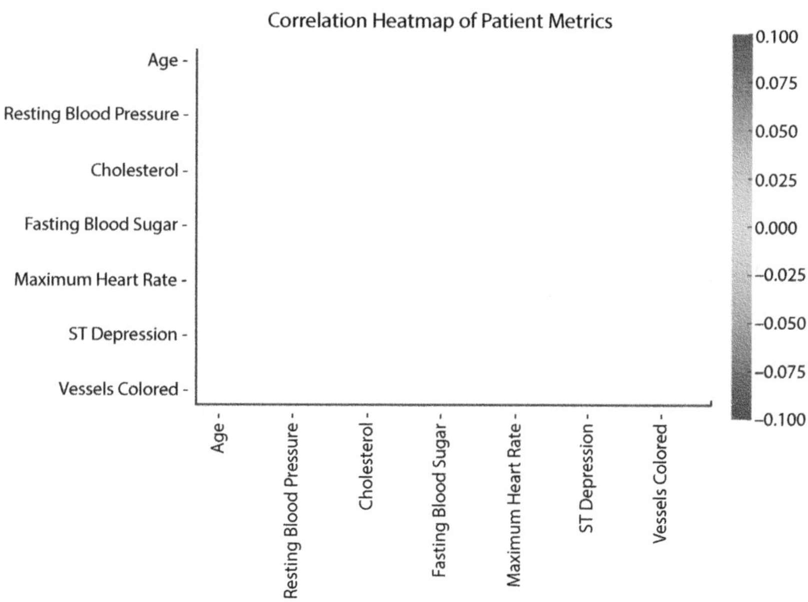

Figure 7.7 Correlation heatmap of patient matrices.

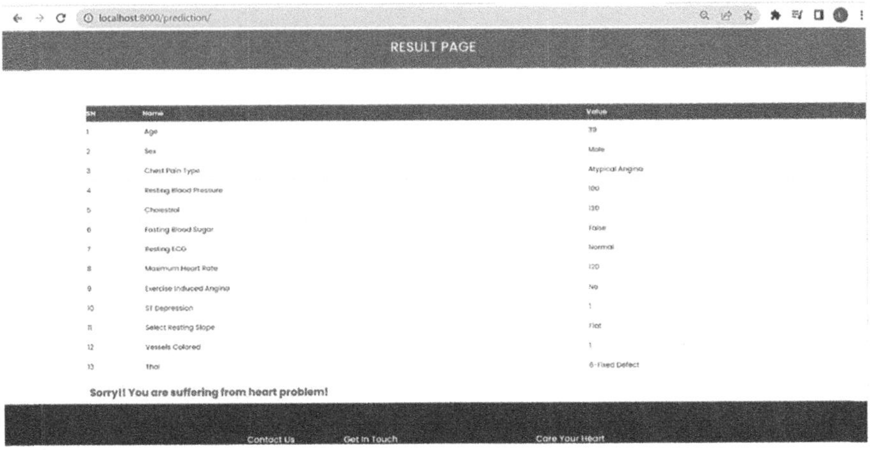

Figure 7.8 The result page of the subject who has CVD.

The new technology employs machine learning models that are extensively trained on large data sets so that it can predict outcomes with unprecedented accuracy. Its capacity to process and analyze real-time data makes the predictions not only accurate but also in real-time, making it an invaluable asset for decision-making in industries.

One of the key features of this app is the way it is flexible. The app learns and improves its forecasting abilities as it continues to be exposed to new data. The process of learning allows it to constantly improve its model and make adjustments to its predictions according to changing trends and patterns. Mechanisms of feedback integrate the app so that its predictions will remain valid and authentic in changing situations.

The intelligent application interface is coded in a manner so that it presents the forecasted results in a simple and efficient manner. The result can easily be understood by the users through logical visualizations and individualized dashboards. Figures 7.4–7.8 depict different pages of the intelligent system. Being user-friendly, the application can easily be handled by specialists who are from other fields irrespective of their technical knowledge. With a unique combination of accuracy, flexibility, and convenience, the ground-breaking smart application sets a new standard for forecasting technology.

With advanced data mining, machine learning, and blockchain technologies enhancing patient care, data security, and predictive analysis, it has been discovered that the technologies have major potential in the healthcare sector. Various studies have examined how these technologies can be applied in various aspects of healthcare data management, classification, and decision-support systems.

Obenshain [1] and Witten & Frank [4] outlined data mining techniques that have potential with healthcare data in generating useful conclusions from extensive sets of information [51]. Medical data, as Liao & Lee [3] described, must be properly classified if effective classification and decision are to ensue. The growing emphasis of researchers on blockchain technology and IoT for the security of health data needs to be emphasized as depicted by Allam *et al.* [2] and Yaqoob *et al.* [5].

The new use of healthcare is this new approach in designing patient data security and interoperability as blocking records. Experiments have been carried out by KangHyun Kim *et al.* [9] and Banotra *et al.* [11] for incentivizing the adoption of the blockchain-based healthcare data market, which promotes information sharing without compromising safety.

Different classification methods have been used in predictive analytics in order to enhance disease prognosis as well as the treatment of patients. Ture *et al.* [7] analyzed several methods of classification that can be used in the forecasting of essential hypertension, whereas Jabbar *et al.* [10] used K-Nearest Neighbor and Genetic Algorithms for classification of heart disease. These highlight the strength of predictive models used in disease diagnosis and treatment design.

This study of work makes an addition to the mounting body of evidence confirming that when machine-learning technology is combined with blockchain, it offers a secure and precise interpretation of healthcare information. Translating predictive analytics into decentralized storage, the merged system has efficiently been shown in real-time to draw medical conclusions by encrypting patient information. The results of the study corroborate the need for balancing access to information and concern for security, raising the consent level for future clinical use.

7.5 Conclusion

Development of a precise convention system for telemedicine forecasting of cardiovascular disease is likely to be most required regarding the growing mortality rate in relation to various cardiovascular disease. The study evaluated the performances of the different algorithms, such as Decision Tree, K-Nearest Neighbors (KNN), Naive Bayes (NB), Multilayer Perceptron (MLP), Logistic Regression (LR), and Random Forest, against Kaggle's Heart.csv dataset. Based on the outcome, Random Forest, Decision Tree, and KNN were the best performers with regard to accuracy, each returning a 100% accuracy score in heart disease prediction. Random Forest significantly increases the prediction accuracy with clearly defined feature sets.

This suggested machine learning, therefore, will save thousands of lives, particularly for those who lack access to costly medical care.

AI disclosure statement: The author acknowledges the use of AI-based tools for minor language editing or grammatical correction. However, all intellectual contributions, analyses, and conclusions presented in this chapter are entirely the author's own.

References

1. Obenshain, M.K., Application of data mining techniques to healthcare data. *Infect. Control Hosp. Epidemiol.*, 25, 8, 690–5, 2004 Aug, doi: 10.1086/502460. PMID: 15357163.
2. Allam, A.H., Gomaa, I., Zayed, H.H., *et al.*, IoT-based eHealth using blockchain technology: A survey. *Cluster Comput.*, 2024, https://doi.org/10.1007/s10586-024-04357-y.
3. Liao, S.-C. and Lee, I.-N., Appropriate medical data categorisation for data mining classification techniques. *Med. Inform.*, 27, 1, 59–67, 2002.
4. Witten, I.H. and Frank, E., *Data Mining: Practical Machine Learning Tools and Techniques,* 2nd edition. Morgan Kaufmann Publishers, San Francisco, p. 560, 2005.
5. Yaqoob, I., Salah, K., Jayaraman, R., Al-Hammadi, Y., Blockchain for healthcare data management: Opportunities, challenges, and future recommendations. *Neural Comput. Appl.*, 34, 14, 11475–11490, 2022.
6. Cabena, P., Hadjinian, P., Stadler, R., Verhees, J., Zanasi, A., *Discovering data mining: From concept to implementation,* Prentice Hall, New Jersey, 1997.
7. Ture, M., Kurt, I., Kurum, A.T., Ozdamar, K., Comparing classification techniques for predicting essential hypertension. *Expert Syst. Appl.*, 2005.
8. Idicula-Thomas, S., Kulkarni, A.J., Kulkarni, B.D., Jayaraman, V.K., Balaji, P.V., A support vector machine-based method for predicting the propensity of a protein to be soluble or to form inclusion body on overexpression in escherichiacoli. *Bioinformatics*, 2006.
9. Kim, K., Kim, S.M., Park, Y., Lee, E., Jung, S., Kang, J., An, D., Min, K., Shim, S.R., Yu, H.W., Han, H.W., A blockchain-based healthcare data marketplace: prototype and demonstration. *JAMIA Open*, 7, 2, ooae029, 2024 Apr 12. doi: 10.1093/jamiaopen/ooae029. eCollection 2024 Jul. PMID: 38617993.
10. Jabbar, M.A., Deekshatulu, B.L., Chandra, P., Classification of Heart Disease Using K-Nearest Neighbor and Genetic Algorithm. *Procedia Technol.*, 10, 85–94, 2013, ISSN 2212-0173.
11. Banotra, A., Sharma, J.S., Gupta, S., Gupta, S.K., Rashid, M., Use of Blockchain and Internet of Things for Securing Data in Healthcare Systems, in: *Multimedia Security. Algorithms for Intelligent Systems*, Giri, K.J., Parah,

S.A., Bashir, R., Muhammad, K. (eds). Springer, Singapore, 2021. https://doi.org/10.1007/978-981-15-8711-5_13.

12. Setiawan, N.A., Venkatachalam, P.A., Ahmad Fadzil, M.H., Rule Selection for Coronary Artery Disease Diagnosis Based on Rough Set. *Int. J. Recent Trends Eng.*, 2, 5, November 2009.
13. Palaniappan, S. and Awang, R., Intelligent Heart Disease Prediction System Using Data Mining Techniques. *JCSNS Int. J. Comput. Sci. Netw. Secur.*, 8, 8, August 2008.
14. Bahga, and Madisetti, V.K., A cloud-based approach for interoperable electronic health records (EHRs). *IEEE J. Biomed. Health Inform.*, 17, 5, 894–906, Sep. 2013.
15. Li, K., Sai, A.R., Urovi, V., Do you need a blockchain in healthcare data sharing? A tertiary review. *Explor. Digit. Health Technol.*, 2, 101–23, 2024, https://doi.org/10.37349/edht.2024.00014.
16. Zangara, G., Corso, P.P., Cangemi, F., Millonzi, F., Collova, F., Scarlatella, A., A cloud-based architecture to support electronic health record. *Stud. Health Technol. Inform.*, 207, 380–389, Jul. 2014.
17. Moore, C., O'Neill, M., O'Sullivan, E., Doröz, Y., Sunar, B., Practical homomorphic encryption: A survey, in: *Proc. IEEE Int. Symp. Circuits Syst. (ISCAS)*, Jun. 2014, pp. 2792–2795.
18. Kim, J., Hwang, H., Lee, K., Baek, R., Lee, H., Yoo, S., Song, W., Han, J., Development of Comprehensive Personal Health Records Integrating Patient-Generated Health Data Directly From Samsung S-Health and Apple Health Apps: Retrospective Cross-Sectional Observational Study. *Uhealth*, 7, 5, e12691, 2019, URL: https://mhealth.jmir.org/2019/5/e12691, DOI: 10.2196/12691.
19. Alder, S., June 2019 Healthcare Data Breach Report. *The HIPAA Journal*, 2019.
20. Tapscott, D. and Tapscott, A., *Blockchain Revolution: How the Technology Behind Bitcoin is Changing Money, Business, and the World*, Penguin Random House, New York, NY, USA, 2016.
21. Madhavasarma, P., Sridevi, M., Prakasam, P., Kumaravel, S., Artificial Intelligence in Fracture Healing Diagnosis. *Res. J. Pharm. Biol. Chem. Sci.*, 2015, ISSN: 0975-8585.
22. Nasir, M.H., Arshad, J., Khan, M.M., Fatima, M., Salah, K., Jayaraman, R., Scalable blockchains—a systematic review. *Future Gener. Comput. Syst.*, 126, 136–162, 2022.
23. Ashraf Uddin, M., Stranieri, A., Gondal, I., Balasubramanian, V., Dynamically recommending repositories for health data: A machine learning model, in: *ACM International Conference Proceeding Series*, February 2020.
24. Kalita, K.P., Chettri, S.K., Deka, R.K., A blockchain-based model for maternal health information exchange and prediction of health risks using machine learning, in: *2023 International Conference on Intelligent and Innovative Technologies in Computing, Electrical and Electronics (IITCEE)*, 2023.

25. Bitcoin Mining Consumes More Electricity a Year than Ireland. Accessed: Jun. 11, 2019. [Online]. Available: https://www.theguardian.com/technology/2017/nov/27/bitcoin-mining-consumes-electricityIreland.
26. Bitcoin Energy Consumption Index—Digiconomist. Accessed: Jun. 11, 2019. [Online]. Available: https://digiconomist.net/bitcoin-energy-consumption.
27. Scherer, M., Performance and scalability of blockchain networks and smart contracts, Ph.D. dissertation, Umeå Univ., Umeå, Sweden, 2017.
28. Madhavasarma, P. and Sridevi, M., ECG signal Denoising using wavelet transform. *Res. J. Pharm. Biol. Chem. Sci.*, 8, 9, 1, 217–225, 2018.
29. Rind, D.M., Kohane, I.S., Szolovits, P., Safran, C., Chueh, H.C., Barnett, G.O., Maintaining the confidentiality of medical records shared over the Internet and the world wide Web. *Ann. Intern. Med.*, 127, 2, 138–141, 1997.
30. Schoenberg, R. and Safran, C., Internet based repository of medical records that retains patient confidentiality. *Bmj*, 321, 7270, 1199–1203, 2000.
31. Uckert, F., Görz, M., Ataian, M., Prokosch, H.-U., Akteonline— An electronic healthcare record as a medium for information and communication. *Stud. Health Technol. Inform.*, 90, 293–297, Jan. 2002.
32. Grant, R.W., Wald, J.S., Poon, E.G., Schnipper, J.L., Gandhi, T.K., Volk, L.A., Middleton, B., Design and implementation of a web-based patient portal linked to an ambulatory care electronic health record: Patient gateway for diabetes collaborative care. *Diabetes Technol. Ther.*, 8, 5, 576–586, 2006.
33. Gritzalis, D. and Lambrinoudakis, C., A security architecture for interconnecting health information systems. *Int. J. Med. Inform.*, 73, 3, 305–309, 2004.
34. Bonacina, S., Marceglia, S., Bertoldi, M., Pinciroli, F., A web-based system for family health record, in: *Proc. 29th Annu. Int. Conf. IEEE Eng. Med. Biol. Soc.*, pp. 3652–3656, Aug. 2007.
35. Ibraimi, L., Asim, M., Petković, M., Secure management of personal health records by applying attribute-based encryption, in: *Proc. 6th Int. Workshop Wearable, Micro, Nano Technol. Pers. Health*, pp. 71–74, Jun. 2009.
36. Saravanan, M., Shubha, R., Marks, A.M., Iyer, V., SMEAD: A secured mobile enabled assisting device for diabetics monitoring, in: *Proc. IEEE Int. Conf. Adv. Netw. Telecommun. Syst. (ANTS)*, pp. 1–6, Dec. 2017.
37. Liang, X., Zhao, J., Shetty, S., Liu, J., Li, D., Integrating blockchain for data sharing and collaboration in mobile healthcare applications, in: *Proc. IEEE 28th Annu. Int. Symp. Pers., Indoor, Mobile Radio Commun. (PIMRC)*, pp. 1–5, Oct. 2017.
38. Sridevi, M., Prakasam, P., Kumaravel, S., Madhava Sarma, P., Evaluating the Effect of Capacitance Model on Tibia Fractured Limb Healing Diagnosis. *Res. J. Pharm. Biol. Chem. Sci.*, 6, 6, 1170, 2015.
39. Patel, V., A framework for secure and decentralised sharing of medical imaging data *via* blockchain consensus. *Health Inform. J.*, 25, 4, 1398–1411, 2018.
40. Juneja, A. and Marefat, M., Leveraging blockchain for retraining deep learning architecture in patient-specific arrhythmia classification, in: *Proc. IEEE EMBS Int. Conf. Biomed. Health Inform. (BHI)*, Mar. 2018, pp. 393–397, 2024.

41. Madhavasarma, P., Veeraragavan, P., Kumaravel, S., Sridevi, M., Studies on physiochemical modifications on biologically important hydroxyapatite materials and their characterisation for medical applications. *Biophys. Chem.*, 267, 106474, 2020.
42. Griggs, K.N., Ossipova, O., Kohlios, C.P., Baccarini, A.N., Howson, E.A., Hayajneh, T., Healthcare blockchain system using smart contracts for secure automated remote patient monitoring. *J. Med. Syst.*, 42, 7, 130, 2018.
43. Wang, H. and Song, Y., Secure cloud-based EHR system using attributebased cryptosystem and blockchain. *J. Med. Syst.*, 42, 8, 152, 2018.
44. Zhang, X. and Poslad, S., Blockchain support for flexible queries with granular access control to electronic medical records (EMR), in: *Proc. IEEE Int. Conf. Commun. (ICC)*, pp. 1–6, May 2018.
45. Guo, R., Shi, H., Zhao, Q., Zheng, D., Secure attribute-based signature scheme with multiple authorities for blockchain in electronic health records systems. *IEEE Access*, 6, 11676–11686, 2018.
46. Zhang, J., Xue, N., Huang, X., A secure system for pervasive social network-based healthcare. *IEEE Access*, 4, 9239–9250, 2016.
47. Brogan, J., Baskaran, I., Ramachandran, N., Authenticating health activity data using distributed ledger technologies. *Comput. Struct. Biotechnol. J.*, 16, 257–266, Jan. 2018.
48. Revathy, G., Venkateswaran, S., Murugan, V.S., Devi, V., Mohanadevi, A., Saravanan, G., Precise Prediction of Cardiovascular Diseases Using Machine Learning, in: *2023 2nd International Conference on Smart Technologies and Systems for Next Generation Computing (ICSTSN)*, pp. 1–3, IEEE, 2023, April.
49. Madhavasarma, P., Sridevi, M., Kumaravel, S., Veeraragavan, P., An electrical stimulation data based model to predict the healing period of fractured limb. *Math. Comput. Modell. Dyn. Syst.*, 25, 4, 354–375, 2019, DOI: 10.1080/13873954.2019.1651341.
50. Sridevi, M., Prakasam, P., Kumaravel, S., Madhavasarma, P., Tibia Fracture Healing Prediction Using Adaptive Neuro Fuzzy Inference System. *Intell. Autom. Soft Comput.*, Taylor & Francis, 23, 2, 359–363, 2016.
51. Madhavasarma, P., Sridevi, M., Prakasam, P., Kumaravel, S., Tibia Fracture Healing Prediction Using First-Order Mathematical Model. *Comput. Math. Methods Med.*, 2015, 689035, 9, 2015.
52. Singh, M., Kumar, A., Khanna, N.N., Laird, J.R., Nicolaides, A., Faa, G., Johri, A.M., Mantella, L.E., Fernandes, J.F.E., Teji, J.S., Singh, N., Fouda, M.M., Singh, R., Sharma, A., Kitas, G., Rathore, V., Singh, I.M., Tadepalli, K., Al-Maini, M., Isenovic, E.R., Chaturvedi, S., Garg, D., Paraskevas, K.I., Mikhailidis, D.P., Viswanathan, V., Kalra, M.K., Ruzsa, Z., Saba, L., Laine, A.F., Bhatt, D.L., Suri, J.S., Artificial intelligence for cardiovascular disease risk assessment in personalised framework: a scoping review. *EClinicalMedicine*, 73, 102660, 2024 May 27, doi: 10.1016/j.eclinm.2024.102660. PMID: 38846068; PMCID: PMC11154124.

Part III
APPLICATIONS AFFECTIVE AI

8

Affective AI in Healthcare and Mental Health – AI-Driven Emotion Detection for Diagnosing Depression, Anxiety, and Autism Spectrum Disorders

Shivamma D.[1], Shaila S.G.[1], Monish L.[1], Ramesh Chundi[2*] and Sumana S.G.[2]

[1]*School of Engineering, Dayananda Sagar University, Bangalore, India*
[2]*School of Computer Applications, Dayananda Sagar University, Bangalore, India*

Abstract

Due to the high prevalence of Psychological or emotional disorders, it is important to develop new and effective management strategies that can work alongside conventional treatment. Affective Artificial Intelligence (Affective AI) has been identified as one of the new trends in the detection, interpretation, and response to human emotions. This has come in as a useful tool that can assist the mental health professionals in their work by presenting new ways of identifying and understanding the emotional behavioral patterns. This chapter reviews the application of affective AI in healthcare, particularly in mental health, with a focus on its use in diagnosing and monitoring depression, anxiety, and autism spectrum disorder through emotion detection. The Affective AI systems are able to detect the minor indicators which are usually missed in the normal evaluation. Some of the markers of emotional distress include facial micro-expressions, change in voice tone, eye movement, posture, and word choice. These signals, processed by AI models trained on large, diverse datasets, can help in detecting early signs of depression, anxiety. In the depression case, the participants may exhibit low affect, monotonous speech, slow movements, and negative sentiment in their language. These patterns are given to the AI systems for training and to recognize and interpret. Also, an anxiety can be presented by rapid speech, heightened physiological arousal, avoidance behaviors, or restlessness. Affective AI provides an open window to non-intrusive monitoring which may assist clinicians in tracking

**Corresponding author*: rameshreddy-bca@dsu.edu.in

N. Thillaiarasu, G. Revathy, T. Saravanan, V. Muthukumaran and S. Balamurugan (eds.) Affective Artificial Intelligence: Fundamentals, Challenges, and Applications, (177–192) © 2026 Scrivener Publishing LLC

changes over time, evaluating treatment effectiveness, and timely interventions. Autism spectrum disorders are difficult to diagnose, especially in young children. The symptoms concerning the emotional recognition, social communication, and behavioral rigidity are delicate and can be quite inconsistent. Affective AI systems can be of great help in the early identification of ASD by examining how people react to emotional stimuli, how they interact in social situations, and how they express human emotions. The assessment of gaze patterns, facial engagement, and prosodic variation are some of the techniques that are being increasingly used to enhance early intervention and personalized therapy planning. Although Affective AI holds great promise, it also raises critical ethical issues. Problems of privacy, informed consent, data security, algorithmic bias, and cultural sensitivity should be taken into consideration to avoid the misuse. Emotions are very context-dependent and therefore, the AI-based interpretations should always be supported by human expertise and empathy. This chapter captures both the benefits and the challenges of incorporating Affective AI in mental health care. The use of emotion aware technologies in healthcare is a paradigm shift not only in the detection of mental health conditions but also in how to cope with emotional well-being. Thus, through the combination of computational accuracy with caring and empathetic touch, Affective AI can help in enhancing the accessibility, proactivity, and individuality of mental health care. With an interdisciplinary approach and ethical practice, Affective AI may be a crucial tool in determining the course of mental health care in the future.

Keywords: Affective artificial intelligence (AI), health care, mental health, emotion recognition, depression, anxiety, autism

8.1 Introduction

Emotional and developmental disorders have benefited from the incorporation of affective computing and AI within healthcare and mental health, which has created new opportunities in diagnosis and management. Affective AI is the study and development of systems and devices that can recognize, interpret, process, and simulate human emotions. It is an interdisciplinary field spanning computer science, psychology, and cognitive science. The study by Picard found that affective computing can give technical systems an emotional aspect (Picard, Affective Computing). Diseases such as depression, anxiety, and ASD are known to be characterized by atypical presentation of emotional expression and behavior, for which early diagnosis and proper treatment can be achieved through emotion detection. Artificial intelligence (AI) has significantly advanced the field of emotion recognition, offering promising applications in mental health diagnostics. Early works, such as by Javidi *et al.* (2022) [1], laid the foundation for facial expression analysis, while modern systems leverage deep learning architectures like CNNs, RNNs, and Transformers to process multimodal emotional cues. Goodfellow *et al.* (2016) [2] demonstrated how deep learning could outperform traditional machine learning in recognizing subtle emotional patterns from images, speech, and physiological signals—enabling real-time, non-invasive assessments of mental health. Emotion recognition has shown particular efficacy in identifying symptoms of depression, anxiety, and autism spectrum disorders (ASD). However, Yang (2024) [3] emphasized the cultural variability in emotional expression, urging the development of culturally adaptive models. Katirai *et al.* (2024) [4] supported this by integrating cross-cultural datasets into training, improving emotion recognition accuracy across diverse populations. Recent innovations involve integrating emotion detection systems with Electronic Health Records (EHRs), enhancing context-aware diagnostics. Siqueira *et al.* (2020) [5] found that such integration offers a more comprehensive understanding of patient conditions. Emotion-aware virtual therapists are also emerging, with Anderson *et al.* (2019) [6] and Fitzpatrick *et al.* (2017) [7] demonstrating their effectiveness in delivering personalized cognitive behavioral therapy (CBT), particularly in resource-limited settings. Finally, longitudinal emotion trend analysis is being used to predict mental health relapses. Rani *et al.* (2021) [8] showed that tracking emotional shifts over time can enable early intervention, improving long-term outcomes. These developments indicate that AI-driven emotion detection holds transformative potential for mental health care. Shaila, *et al.* (2022) [9] discussed the use of deep learning for altering negative emotions (sad, anger, fear) to positive ones (happiness, surprise, neutral) using music therapy. The authors employ a convolutional neural network (CNN) for emotion classification and suggest music therapy accordingly. The model under consideration obtained satisfactory accuracy in emotion polarity recognition and showed its capability to improve mood through music intervention. Nevertheless, the limitation is the low generalization because of the small dataset and dependency on pre-defined emotion classes. Prasanna, *et al.* (2021) [10] presented a neuro-fuzzy model that classifies emotion polarity based on pre-defined patterns of emotion from sentence-level text data. The model processes sentences with single emotional content efficiently and is thus applicable for sentiment analysis in information retrieval. Performance is shown to be effective in terms of classification accuracy for definite positive or negative sentences. Yet, it performs poorly with multi-emotion sentences and fails to show contextual depth in processing ambiguous expressions. Shaila, *et al.* (2023) [11] described a machine learning-based system to identify emotions from speech signals based on Mel-frequency cepstral coefficients (MFCCs) and classifiers such as SVM and KNN. The system targets primary emotion recognition from variations in vocal tone and performs decent accuracy in clean speech conditions. One of the primary constraints is performance degradation in noisy conditions and insufficient multi-lingual or cultural adaptability. Chundi, *et al.* (2023) [12] offered a systematic overview of artificial intelligence (AI) and computer vision technology applications in diabetes detection and management. It discusses image-based diagnostics, wearable monitors, and predictive analytics with enhanced early detection accuracy. The research finds promising deep learning models but highlights limitations such as inadequate clinical validation, issues of generalization between populations, and the necessity of extensive, diversified databases to prevent bias. Chundi, *et al.* (2023) [13] presented "NBLex," a hybrid system that integrates a naïve Bayes classifier with an in-house-developed bilingual lexicon for emotion prediction in code-switched text. The system showed better performance compared to baseline sentiment classifiers. Its lexical completeness dependency and inability to recognize complex emotional subtleties are mentioned as drawbacks.

8.2 Emotional Biomarkers of Mental Health Conditions

Emotional biomarkers can be measured by association with the various emotions states the can help us to detect, diagnose the mental health conditions like depression, anxiety, autism spectrum disorder and bipolar disorders. Depression is a common mood disorder with symptoms of a chronically sad mood, loss of interest, and reduced emotional reactivity. Affect in an AI sense, it is the observable behavior and emotional states. People who have depression often have a decreased facial expression, so they smile less frequently, make less eye contact, and have less animated expressions. Their vocal prosody is often described as flat or monotonous, which refers to their relative lack of the dynamic pitch, timbre, and rhythm that conveys emotion in speech Jain *et al.* (2025) [14]. This results in slow, emotionless, or tired speech patterns, which have been observed in systems based on audio emotion recognition features as pitch and intensity.

Text-based communication has been similarly investigated, finding that people with depression are more likely to use negative language (i.e., containing negative emotions) and more self-referential, including words related to hopelessness, guilt, and worthlessness Highly accurate transformer-based sentiment analysis models like BERT can detect such linguistic markers. By capturing these subtle affective signals through multimodal AI systems, it can allow timely detection and longitudinal tracking of depressive states in both clinical and non-clinical environments.

Anxiety is a psychological condition consisting of excessive fear, nervousness, and arousal, frequently associated with physical and behavioral manifestations. Anxiety can be recognized by multimodal emotion cues on the side of affective AI systems. People in stress often talk too loudly, speak too fast, and breathe irregularly—acoustic landmarks that can be framed by the audio emotion recognition model as RNNs or LSTM. Physiologically, anxious people tend to have higher heart rate variability and skin conductance (measurable with wearables). A tension in muscles, furrowed brows, and excessive blinking or fidgeting — all are signs of discomfort in facial analysis due to distress or hypervigilance. Anxiety-based language. Anxious language is language that communicates fear, concern, and worry about future events. NLP models based on transformers can automatically capture these patterns and may be used for early identification and monitoring of anxiety levels. Utilizing emotion recognition tools may contribute to promoting and utilizing emotional health services in healthcare institutions, facilitating early detection and individualized mental care Baran *et al.* (2025) [15].

Autism Spectrum Disorder (ASD) affects how people grow and learn, making it hard to talk, share feelings, and connect with others. People with ASD may show few or unusual facial expressions, look others in the eye less often, and struggle to understand or react to others' feelings. Their speech might sound flat, robotic, or repeated, without normal ups and downs. Smart tools use face and voice checks with computers to find these signs. Also, the way people with ASD talk might be direct or they often repeat. Emotion-aware tech can help spot ASD early and offer help by watching how people share and feel over time. Multimodal emotion detection uses many types of data like images, sounds, text, and body signals to understand a person's feelings. This is useful for mental health since symptoms show up in different ways. For instance, facial cues analyzed using CNNs, vocal tones checked by LSTMs, and language sentiment using Transformers make a strong emotional profile. Body sensors add info on stress levels Al *et al.* (2020) [16]. By combining all this, affective AI improves diagnosis, helps tailor therapy, and tracks issues like depression, anxiety, and autism in real-time, which leads to better care and easier access. Despite its promise, affective AI in mental health faces notable limitations and ethical concerns. These include cultural and demographic bias in emotion datasets, risks of misdiagnosis, and lack of transparency in deep learning models. Emotional expression varies across cultures and individuals, which may reduce model accuracy and fairness. Furthermore, collecting and processing personal emotional data raises significant privacy issues. To address these concerns, federated learning and explainable AI techniques are emerging. Ethical deployment should include strong validation, informed consent, and regulatory oversight to ensure that affective AI tools are deployed responsibly and equitably in line with clinical standards.

8.3 Modalities and Techniques for Emotion Detection

Emotional variants of speech are packed with emotional content due to changes in pitch, tone, rhythm, and speed. Because of these signals, the analysis of emotion detection is particularly useful in cases such as detecting these temporal patterns in speech. Recurrent Neural Networks (RNNs) and related forms of Long Short-Term Memory (LSTM) networks are effective for modeling temporal patterns in speech for emotion recognition Revathy *et al.* (2023) [17]. For example, anxious patients may speak fast and with pitch changes, while patients with depression may speak slowly and in a monotone. This could actually simplify such a model and leave the expression functions to millions or billions of neurons in order to learn it. In Figure 8.1, emotion recognition from speech offers an advantage in situations where visual information is not available, which makes it especially

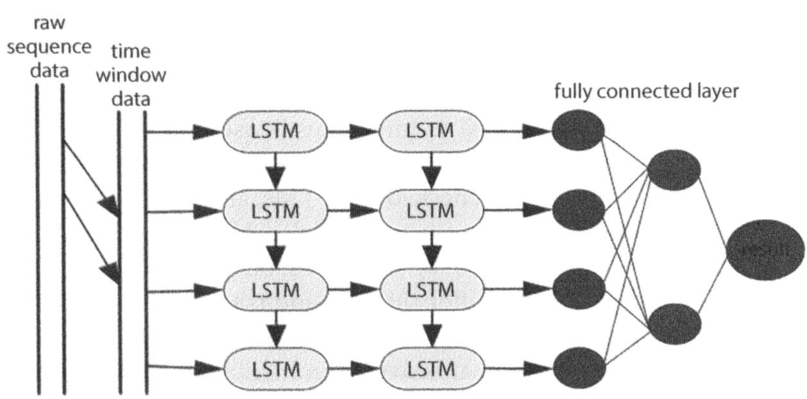

Figure 8.1 Speech and prosody analysis.

useful if you are blind or for use in telehealth applications that monitor emotional states during conversations or therapy sessions.

8.3.1 Textual Sentiment Analysis: Transformer-Based

Recent research in text analytics has shown a huge potential for using transformer models to understand people's emotions from the language they use in chat logs, social media, and patient journals. These new models learn word representation by their position in a list of words, enabling them to better interpret the nuances of sentiment, emotion or intent even in languages where some keyword translation may occur. For mental health, textual analysis can help us find signs of depression, anxiety, or obsessive thought patterns by extracting linguistic patterns. Transformers can help identify changes in the tone of someone's messages over time, which may be useful in monitoring their mental health in the long term. They're also data-powered, so they can make real-time decisions for your virtual therapy (Alhakbani *et al.*, 2024) [18].

8.3.2 Physiological Signal Interpretation: Multimodal Deep Learning

Our bodies can tell us a lot about our emotional states. By reading things like our heart rate or our skin's sweatiness, we can get a better understanding of what we are feeling. Wearables can easily track these and other physiological signals to help us keep watch on emotional changes – from things like anxiety or stress (Popescu *et al.*, 2022) [19]. Layering in mood and facial-recognition data can help create new levels of modeling effectiveness, as is the case in multimodal deep learning approaches to modeling emotion in real time. These models can help in digital mental health management, emotion-sensitive wearables, and early intervention for cases like ASD, PTSD, etc.

8.4 Need for Diagnosis and Monitoring

The Affective AI systems implemented now are also used for the continuous examination of the issues. With the help of AI, the systems are now able to diligently communicate with the patient and analyze their emotional state regarding positive and negative behaviors. In Figure 8.2, modern technology is very successful for the identification of depression in a person and also for examining the feelings and behavior and these result in AI-driven systems.

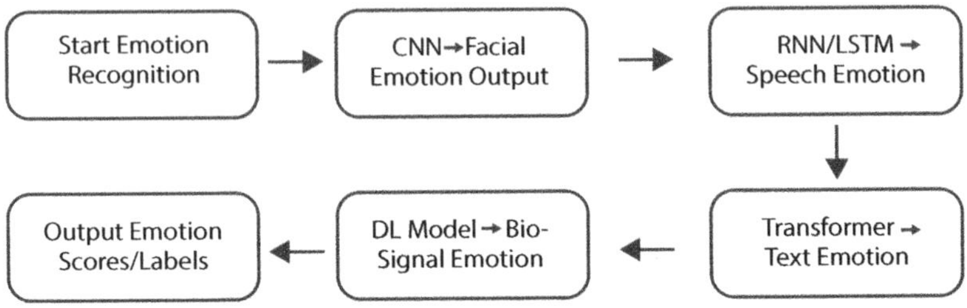

Figure 8.2 Depression in diagnosis and monitoring.

Anxiety Detection and Stress Monitoring

It can be of immense importance to be aware of anxiety. The tone tends to be more vocal, speaking is much faster, and the individual may experience unusually tense facial expressions. It can detect emotional prosody, or verbal hesitations, using the LSTM models to analyze speech data (Shaila *et al.*, 2022) [20]. By looking for signals such as furrowed brows or tightly pressed lips, CNNs can determine a person's facial expression and compare it to those who are anxious. Text analysis helps in identifying language that implies apprehension or threat. Wearable devices can monitor biological markers like increased heart rate or sweat, providing real-time measurements of stress levels. In the advent of digital therapy, AI systems can use the compiled data to send out alarms, offer calming tactics, or provide detailed emotional timelines to clinicians whose diagnoses of anxiety will then be improved.

Autism Spectrum Disorder (ASD) Support

Individuals with Autism Spectrum Disorder (ASD) may find early diagnosis and the development of social skills easier due to affective AI. This can include facial expression analysis for catching the odd, or limited expressions, voice analysis can note aspects like monotone delivery or lack of inflection, etc. Text models can be trained to pick up on things like echolalia or a repetitive speech pattern, among other things. This data can then be used together to predict or identify autism regarding children in their early years or during essential developmental assessments (Joudar *et al.*, 2023) [21]. It can also be useful for things like assistive robots that can integrate emotion recognition technologies into assistive means and understanding apps used by educational experts to interpret the facial expressions others give off. Also recognize appropriate responses and provide relevant information to kids with Autism Spectrum Disorder (ASD). In other words, this blend of empathy plus emotion recognizes just on the role played by societal inclusion plus communication innovation in the end. Diagnosing the

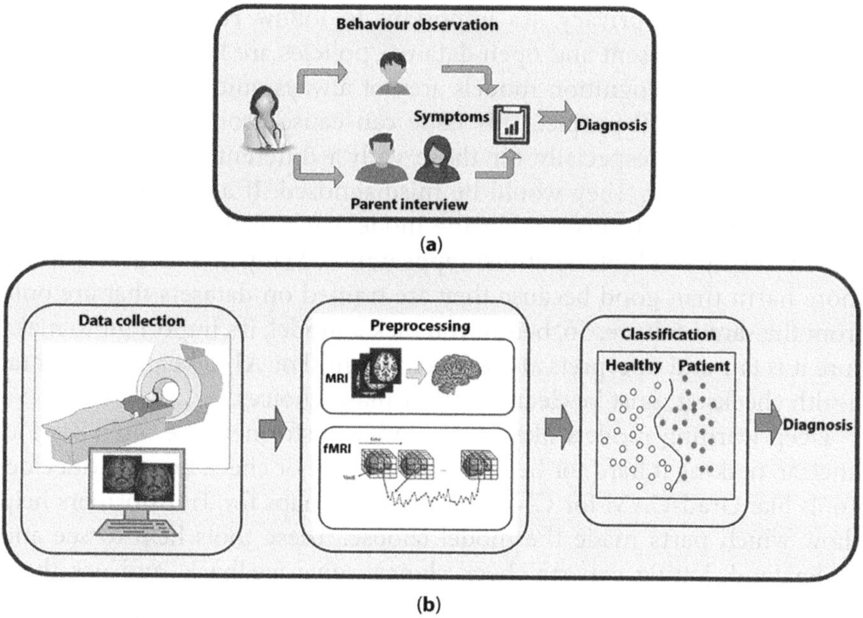

Figure 8.3 Diagnosing autism spectrum disorder and attention deficit.

patient of the autism spectrum disorder and attention deficit by observing the behavior and parent interview of the patient is represented in Figure 8.3.

Advanced emotion systems mix face, voice, text, and body signs for full mental health checks. These systems use CNNs for images, RNNs for sounds, Transformers for words, and other deep learning tools for sensor data. This blend helps make more precise diagnoses with context. For example, if someone shows no feelings, slow talk, and negative thoughts, they may be marked for clinical depression. These systems work in virtual therapy, remote health apps, and studies. They aid in custom treatment plans, mood tracking over time, and widespread mental health help.

8.5 Challenges and Ethical Considerations

Emotion data is very private. It can show a person's feelings, moods, or struggles. Affective AI must keep this data safe, especially in health care, learning, or gadgets. If not protected, emotion recognition tools can lead to spying or misuse. Using federated learning helps by keeping data on the user's device. Differential privacy masks personal traits. These methods help protect user privacy. It's important to follow rules like GDPR or HIPAA. Clear consent and open data use policies are key to gaining user trust. Emotion recognition models are not always quite accurate, as they are impartial to all people. This issue can cause problems with mental health treatment, especially for those with a different background than their own cultural. They would be misdiagnosed. If a person has rough skin, the illness get nervous but the model can't really tell what's wrong specifically by just looking at their appearance. Many mental health AI do more harm than good because they are trained on datasets that are only from the same culture. So, before you pick a model, it's important to make sure it is fair and interprets all of the emotions. For AI to help with mental health checks, it must be clear how they make choices.

Deep learning models like CNNs and Transformers are often seen as unclear, making it hard for health experts to see or check how they decide. Tools like Grad-CAM for CNNs or attention maps for Transformers help show which parts made the model choose. These tools help to see and understand, letting experts check choices, give feedback, and use them more in care steps. Clear models are key where choices impact patient checks, care plans, or urgent help. The rise of emotion AI in public and private places raises big ethical questions. If used wrong, it can be a tool for control, spying, or unfairness. For instance, using emotion data in hiring, police work, or ads without consent may break people's rights. Ethical use needs that emotion AI systems be used only with informed, willing consent, in clear contexts, and with ongoing oversight. There should be audits, boards to review ethics, and open ways to report problems to stop misuse. At last, emotional AI must follow human values, putting empathy, respect, and mental safety first. The next step for AI in feelings is to make systems that know emotions right away, changing and reacting fast to how a person feels. These systems could help virtual therapists, health apps on phones, or devices you wear, giving feedback or ideas to help you. For instance, if anxiety goes up while talking, it might start calming exercises or suggest you take a break. Real-time emotion AI needs fast models, like compressed CNNs or edge-ready Transformers. By watching emotions all the time, these systems could help with quick actions, which is helpful in handling stress, stopping relapse, and mental health support online.

Emotion-Aware Virtual Companions

Smart virtual helpers and chat bots are growing into kind friends who can give support. They use many ways to sense how people feel, changing how they talk based on what they sense. An agent might speak softly if a person is upset or say kind words if sadness is found. Models like GPT with tools to spot feelings can get complex human emotions in talk and text. These friends are very helpful when there isn't much contact with people, like in elder care or mental health checks, giving users smart chats that seem more real and friendly. A critical path for future research should be the development of emotion detection systems that are culturally inclusive. This is because in reality, the ways people express emotion is different around the world, and recognizers built on a narrow dataset perform poorly in diverse situations. We need to start collecting and labeling emotional data through a socio-cultural lens that touches on the emotions of global diverse audiences. Multilingual emotion datasets, culturally adapted labeling schemes, ethnographically informed model designs will be necessary. In summary, affective AI must be inclusive for 1) improved diagnostic accuracy, 2) embracing diversity across all fronts, 3) ensuring we build equitable mental health technologies that are not only effective but culturally, linguistically, and socially responsive.

Integration with Clinical Decision Support Systems (CDSS)

Affective AI has the profound ability to enhance Clinical Decision Support Systems (CDSS) with emotional context in the traditional diagnostic workflows.

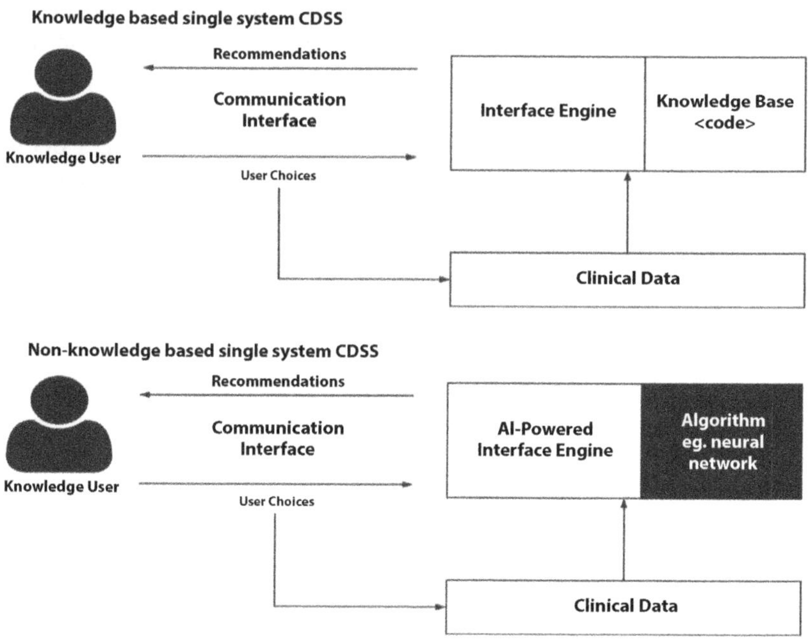

Figure 8.4 Knowledge and non-knowledge-based, single-based clinical decision support systems (CDSS).

Incorporating emotional data within Electronic Health Records (EHRs) will facilitate physicians in tracking mental health trends along with physical health indicators. The implementation of Emotional Threat Scores from facial, vocal, or text inputs can warn healthcare providers about potential crises, such as suicidal thoughts or acute anxiety. In the future systems could also implement a solution that includes some sort of AI-driven emotional analysis that can be added to traditional assessments, all of which can be used in order to personalize and eventually optimize treatment outcomes for different individuals. With the emotional data aligned to the doctor's clinical insights, CDSS-integrated affective AI can enable more inclusive, patient-centered care and mental health. In Figure 8.4 shows the knowledge and non-knowledge based single system of Clinical Decision Support Systems by using the clinical data.

8.6 Future Directions

Given the significance of cross-cultural differences in emotional expressions; it is essential to develop adaptive emotion models. By building emotion models that take cultural contexts into consideration, the outcome of emotion detection systems will prove to be more useful for all users. Implementing global data in AI based systems will make emotion detection more customized and gratifying for all languages. This will allow the same AI model to provide personalized and valuable data in different languages. Emotion Detection and EHR integration can provide a detailed picture of the emotional issues a patient might be facing by looking into their previous health records including the emotional data that has been recorded. This real-time update of the emotional states of individuals could eventually point out the doctors a more efficient way of diagnosing mental disorders in early stages and in turn could increase patient outcome and increase the accuracy of diagnosis too.

Longitudinal trend analysis has value in the context of monitoring the mental health issues and its sub-types such as anxiety and depression in terms of treatment adherence, relapse prevention and assessing the people-centric perspective. From the onset, the need for individualized approaches and strategies in analyzing the data is critical to a person's mental condition; hence, the formation of effective models is a determining factor when evaluating the different clusters of emotion and its pattern within a group of data. Longitudinal emotional data consists of multiple variables that coexist within a dataset since individuals with mental illnesses may display all these emotions over the duration of a given time.

By combining these emotional responses with multiple layers of data for each patient (e.g., demographics, clinical notes, diagnoses), it is possible to train deep learning models which can not only predict patient risk, but explain why particular patients have increased risk for relapse, enabling more targeted interventions.

8.7 Conclusion

Advanced technologies are transforming mental health screenings with artificial intelligence. By using deep learning approaches such as CNNs, RNNs, and Transformers, it can identify emotions more accurately and non-invasively. This provides a scalable option for screening tools to diagnose ailments like anxiety, depression, and autism more quickly. Despite challenges such as ethical concerns and technical limitations, this ability to generate real-time and tailored interventions using AI systems promises new avenues of patient care. Realizing affective computing in clinical practice is projected to better employ human-oriented and emotionally sensitive factors to impact patient outcomes, revolutionizing mental health care globally. Affective AI in health care and mental health checks can change how we find and watch signs of depression, anxiety, and autism (ASD). Often, feelings and actions are hard to spot and are personal. Old ways to diagnose can be slow and not always right. Affective AI uses deep learning and different types of data (like face, voice, text, and body signals) for a new way to catch signs early. Soon, AI systems that spot feelings will get better at seeing things in the right light and understanding different cultures, so they can make better guesses and help more. With smart wearable devices, watching emotions all the time could become normal in mental health care. This might help stop problems before they grow. For instance, smartwatches and apps could watch how someone feels, then warn doctors or family if a person might be upset. New learning ways will make it easy to work with emotion data, keeping it private. This lets devices process info without showing it, which is needed for mental health uses. For ASD checks, Affective AI can help find signs in kids early by watching how they act at home or school. With real life data, AI tools could change how we look at growth and make help easy to get anywhere in the world. In the end, Affective AI with online health systems will spread mental help to people who might not get it otherwise, like those far away or in need. As rules and good AI use grow, Affective AI could become key in mental health, making checks better, getting patients more involved, and helping people stay happy over time.

AI disclosure statement: The author acknowledges the use of AI-based tools for minor language editing or grammatical correction. However, all intellectual contributions, analyses, and conclusions presented in this chapter are entirely the author's own.

References

1. Jampour, M. and Javidi, M., Multiview facial expression recognition, a survey. *IEEE Trans. Affect. Comput.*, 13, 4, 2086–2105, 2022.
2. Goodfellow, I., Bengio, Y., Courville, A., Bengio, Y., Deep learning, 1, 2, MIT press, Cambridge, 2016.
3. Yang, Y., Micro-Expressions: A Study of Basic Reading and The Influencing Factors on Production and Recognition. *J. Educ. Humanit. Soc. Sci.*, 26, 1048–1053, 2024.
4. Katirai, A., Ethical considerations in emotion recognition technologies: A review of the literature. *AI Ethics*, 4, 4, 927–948, 2024.
5. Siqueira, F.M., Santana, M.A., Rocha, G.F., Real-time emotion detection and its integration with electronic health records for personalized treatment. *J. Med. Syst.*, 44, 7, 127, 2020.
6. Anderson, A., Duncan, M., Broomhead, M., Virtual therapist applications for Cognitive Behavioral Therapy: An empirical review. *J. Ther. Res.*, 18, 3, 205–214, 2019.
7. Fitzpatrick, K.K., Darcy, A., Vierhile, M., Delivering cognitive behavioral therapy to adolescents through an iPhone application: A randomized controlled trial. *J. Am. Acad. Child Adolesc.* Psychiatry, 56, 11, 1–8, 2017.
8. Rani, S., Sinha, R., Gupta, D., Predicting relapses in depression through longitudinal emotional trend analysis. *IEEE Trans. Affect. Comput.*, 12, 3, 670–682, 2021.
9. Shaila, S.G., Rajesh, T.M., Lavanya, S., Abhishek, K.G., *et al.*, Music therapy for transforming human negative emotions: Deep learning approach, in: *International Conference on Recent Trends in Communication and Intelligent Systems*, Springer, 2022.
10. Prasanna, M.S.M., Shaila, S.G., Vadivel, A., Phrase-level sentence patterns for estimating positive and negative emotions using neuro-fuzzy model for information retrieval applications. *Multimed. Tools Appl.*, 2021, https://doi.org/10.1007/s11042-021-11111-y.
11. Shaila, S.G., Sindhu, A., Monish, L., *et al.*, Speech Emotion Recognition Using Machine Learning Approach, in: *Conference on Applications of Artificial Intelligence and Machine Learning*, Atlantis Press, 2023.
12. Chundi, R., Hulipalled, V.R., Simha, J.B., Identification of monolingual and code-switch information from English-Kannada code-switch data. *Int. J. Electr. Comput. Eng.*, 13, 5, 2023.

13. Chundi, R., Hulipalled, V.R., Simha, J.B., NBLex: Emotion prediction in Kannada-English code-switch text using naïve Bayes lexicon approach. *Int. J. Electr. Comput. Eng.*, 13, 2, 2023.
14. Jain, A. and Jain, A., AI-Based Emotion Detection System in Healthcare for Patient, in: *Generative Artificial Intelligence for Biomedical and Smart Health Informatics*, 455–470, 2025.
15. Baran, F.D.E. and Cetin, M., AI-driven early diagnosis of specific mental disorders: *a comprehensive study. Cognit. Neurodyn.*, 19, 1, 70, 2025.
16. Al Banna, M.H., Ghosh, T., Taher, K.A., Kaiser, M.S., Mahmud, M., A monitoring system for patients of autism spectrum disorder using artificial intelligence, in: *International conference on brain informatics*, 251–262, Springer International Publishing, Cham, 2020, September.
17. Revathy, G., Venkateswaran, S., Murugan, V.S., Devi, V., Mohanadevi, A., Saravanan, G., Precise Prediction of Cardiovascular Diseases Using Machine Learning, in: *2023 2nd International Conference on Smart Technologies and Systems for Next Generation Computing (ICSTSN)*, 1–3, IEEE, 2023, April.
18. Alhakbani, N., Facial Emotion Recognition-Based Engagement Detection in Autism Spectrum Disorder. *Int. J. Adv. Comput. Sci. Appl.*, 15, 3, 2024.
19. Popescu, A.L., Popescu, N., Dobre, C., Apostol, E.S., Popescu, D., IoT and AI-based application for automatic interpretation of the affective state of children diagnosed with autism. *Sensors*, 22, 7, 2528, 2022.
20. Shaila, S.G., Shivamma, D., Monica, U.S., Tejashree, K., Facial Expression Recognition for Compound Emotions using Mobile Net Architecture. *2022 International Conference on Artificial Intelligence and Data Engineering (AIDE)*, 2022.
21. Joudar, S.S., Albahri, A.S., Hamid, R.A., Zahid, I.A., Alqaysi, M.E., Albahri, O.S., Alamoodi, A.H., Artificial intelligence-based approaches for improving the diagnosis, triage, and prioritization of autism spectrum disorder: A systematic review of current trends and open issues. *Artif. Intell. Rev.*, 56, 1, 53–117, 2023.

9

Emotionally Aware Machine Learning for X-Ray Fracture Classification: A SHAP-Driven Approach

M. Sridevi[1], S. Venkatesh[2], P. Veeraragavan[3] and P. Madhavasarma[2*]

[1]*Department of Electrical Electronics Engineering, Rajalakshmi Engineering College, Chennai, Tamil Nadu, India*
[2]*School of Electrical and Electronics Engineering, Sastra University, Thanjavur, Tamil Nadu, India*
[3]*Department of S&H, University College of Engineering, Tindivanam Anna University, Chennai, Tamil Nadu, India*

Abstract

Fracture detection from x-ray images is a critical diagnostic procedure that, historically, depended on manual readings by radiologists. This work proposes an automatic fracture detection system created with the aid of MATLAB and Python software. The proposed system employs a GUI created through the use of MATLAB software, by which users can input x-ray images for processing. Pre-processing steps of images involve conversion of images to grayscale mode, and more precisely, Canny edge detection along structural discontinuity fracture-related edges is employed so that medical professionals can see the results in real time. The same architecture is applied in Python with the VGG16 module trained on a dataset collected from open-source data repositories of 3,220 non-fracture x-rays and 644 fracture x-rays, with 98.3% accuracy for non-fracture images and 98.5% accuracy for fracture images. For even better performance, the model combines feature extraction using deep learning and optimization of classification by the Adam optimizer with binary cross-entropy loss. The suggested system saves time in diagnosis, increases accuracy, and is highly useful for orthopedic procedures. Further work can be the enlargement of the dataset and real-time observation to make it more clinically applicable.

**Corresponding author*: madhavasarma@exam.sastra.edu

N. Thillaiarasu, G. Revathy, T. Saravanan, V. Muthukumaran and S. Balamurugan (eds.) Affective Artificial Intelligence: Fundamentals, Challenges, and Applications, (193–210)

Keywords: Deep learning, VGG, Adam, Canny edge, fracture, x-ray

9.1 Introduction

Bone fractures are a prevalent health issue, where if they are not treated and diagnosed promptly, their impact can prove disastrous to the mobility and overall well-being of the individual in question. X-ray fracture interpretations have long been the responsibility of the radiologist, but it can take a considerable amount of time, and in the case of small or intricate fractures, it can even produce the wrong results at times. The increasing demand for efficient, fast medical diagnostic systems, coupled with the universal availability of digital medical imaging, has resulted in automated fracture detection systems being developed by using artificial intelligence (AI) driven methods. Deep learning increases diagnostic accuracy and efficiency further and reduces the burden of human-generated errors.

Even with all the advancements in medical imaging, diagnosing fractures remains a formidable challenge because of irregularities in the bone structures, the possible existence of low-quality pictures, and the protrusion of anatomic landmarks. On top of that, it seldom happens when an experienced radiologist is missing, which in turn may be the reason for the complications associated with the patients. Automation through artificial intelligence (AI) has the potential to bring positive changes to medical practice by enabling the accurate interpretation of digital medical images.

Several studies have been conducted on AI-based approaches to enhance fracture detection. Medaramatla *et al.* [1] led the way by training a hybrid YOLO NAS model to identify hand bone fractures and managed to localize fractures with extremely high accuracy. Ergün and Güney [2] implemented research work on x-ray classification techniques to classify dog bone fractures with a focus on artificial intelligence, which can also be applied in human health for automated diagnosis. Rizwan *et al.* then [3] developed a textile monopole antenna using machine learning for wireless monitoring of non-invasive fracture healing with a focus on wearable medical engineering. A more profound supervised-learning model for fracture detection was given by Meena and Roy [4] for the automatic detection of fractures that enhanced the accuracy of fracture diagnosis and minimized the need for manual determinations. Cotri-Melecez *et al.* [5] introduced computer-assisted auto-medical prescribing for ankle fracture rehabilitation. Miranda *et al.* [6] improved patient classification using feature selection in bidirectional axial transmission methods. Rasool *et al.* [7] proposed KONet, a weighted ensemble learning method for knee osteoporosis classification. By the integration of the strengths of different deep learning models, KONet enhances diagnostic reliability and accuracy and surpasses the main limitations of automatic osteoporosis detection. Wang *et al.* [8] proposed an active fracture diagnosis system based on the integration of biocompatible sensors and an LSTM-MLP framework. This system delivers quantitative, real-time bone fracture analysis, which enhances the accuracy of medical diagnosis. Alam *et al.* [9] applied transfer learning methods in radiographs so that automatically classified bone fractures were available. This procedure enhanced fracture classification accuracy with the assistance of pre-trained deep neural networks and minimized the need for huge amounts of labeled data. Santhiya and Ebenezer [10] employed a Python-based machine learning framework for machine learning-based fracture detection from medical images using an economical and low-cost approach to fracture detection. Finally, the FDHN, or Fracture Detection Health Network, is suggested by Madhavasarma *et al.* [11] as a multi-task deep neural network, which is excellent for generating insights regarding bone fractures. The deep neural network facilitates the evaluation of the characteristics generated by the fractures in fracture classification using CNNs and aids radiologists in clinical decision making. Despite all this progress in AI-caused fracture detection, there is still much that needs improvement [12–14]. Most AI-based fracture detection algorithms cannot differentiate between normal anatomical variation and actual fractures, and hence lead to misdiagnosis [16–18]. Apart from that, the models are typically trained on extremely small or specialized datasets, which makes them less accurate in actual clinical settings. Sridevi *et al.* [19] proposed a first-order mathematical model to predict tibia fracture healing, marking calculative innovations in bone orthopedic diagnosis. Sridevi [20] made another contribution regarding the prediction of tibia fracture healing using soft computing techniques. Wang and Yang [21] used computational simulation to determine the mechanical stability of bone formation in healing. According to reference [22], Kalinowski *et al.* developed some optical sensors for the non-invasive measurement of bone healing. Mišić *et al.* [23] made smart devices for real-time recovery monitoring as an alternative to traditional orthopedic devices. Ma *et al.* [24] proposed a wearable device for biofeedback monitoring of tibial load during partial weight-bearing walking. Liu *et al.* [25] used image stitching methods for bone fragment reconstruction, enabling better visualization during orthopedic surgery and fracture diagnostics. Madhava Sarma *et al.* [26] studied DC electric stimulation for enhancing the healing outcomes in tibia fractures based on the best voltage selection. Yang *et al.* [27] used computational modeling to study bone healing under different initial conditions and loads, advancing prediction simulations. Sridevi *et al.* [28] further explored first-order mathematical models to represent tibia fracture healing dynamics. Malamal and Panicker [29] presented high-frame-rate ultrasound imaging for the recognition of bone surface irregularities and improving diagnostic accuracy with advanced signal processing. Han *et al.* [30] analyzed the application of Ti-Ni shape memory alloy ring fixators for supracondylar femoral fractures and gained insights into the techniques of fracture stabilization. Borchani *et al.* [31] proposed a smart trauma-fixation system incorporating piezo-floating-gate sensors for postoperative fracture healing monitoring with a self-sustained sensing solution. Mattei *et al.* [32] estimated the fracture healing through impact testing for the recovery of the tibia by external fixators. Sridevi *et al.* [33] used adaptive neuro-fuzzy inference systems to enhance tibia fracture healing predictions. Greve *et al.* [34] presented an instrumented intramedullary implant for strain monitoring during fracture healing. Kalinowski *et al.* [35] further developed optical instrumentation methods for the assessment of bone healing. Madhava Sarma *et al.* [36] suggested step response methods for determining the time constant of tibia fracture healing, presenting a new mathematical solution. Sridevi *et al.* [37] made comparative study between soft computing and mathematical modeling for the prediction of fracture healing. Madhava Sarma *et al.* [38] created an electric stimulation-based model to forecast the healing time of fractured limbs. Protopappas *et al.* [39] created an ultrasound-based wearable device for the monitoring and advancement of healing in long bone fractures. Lastly, He *et al.* [40] presented a biomechanical monitoring system for monitoring bone fracture recovery, proving improvements in real-time assessment methods.

However, many of these models of diagnosis suffer from the inability to be applied to different anatomical areas, low dataset variation, or handling excessive computer power, hence significantly inhibiting their applicability in healthcare centers. The aim of this research work is to overcome these drawbacks through the design of a deep learning model that integrates sophisticated image processing and multi-feature extraction to enhance the performance of classification. The uniqueness of this approach lies in the visual enhancement of the model and yet retaining extremely high accuracy across the various x-ray datasets, which further indicates a viable choice for healthcare professionals. Leverage these associations, the role of the study is to act as a stepping stone towards the evolution of AI-based medical diagnostics, thereby increasing the effectiveness and reliability of fracture identification in orthopedic care.

9.2 Methodology

Figure 9.1 summarizes the whole automated fracture detection system with all its stages from data acquisition to classification. It involves x-ray image acquisition and subsequent image pre-processing, which introduces quality improvements and noise elimination. Feature extraction is then employed to identify significant patterns for classification. Two classification approaches have been adopted in this research: Random Binary Classification with MATLAB and a CNN-based approach (VGG16) with Python, boosting detection with an area-highlighting effect for enhanced visualization. Last but not least, an image display-supported GUI system with MATLAB and Python is for convenient presentation of classification outcomes. This systematic flow supports diagnostic efficiency as well as fracture detection accuracy.

9.2.1 Data Acquisition

The acquisition of x-ray images is the beginning point of the fracture detection system that serves as input to the analysis pipeline, as shown in Figure 9.1. They can be retrieved from publicly available datasets like MURA (Musculoskeletal Radiographs) [1] or other available medical image repositories that typically contain labeled data on the presence or absence of fractures. Images were downloaded from [20] providing appropriate x-ray information to recognize fractures. A user can navigate and select an image

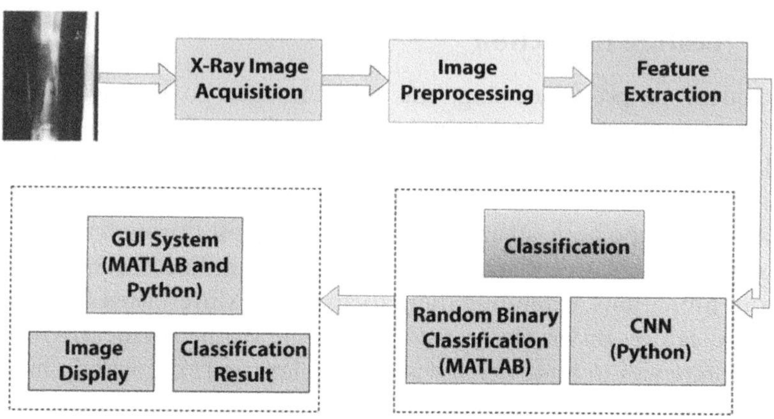

Figure 9.1 Proposed methodology.

from the GUI for image selection; it supports commonly used formats like .jpg, .png, and .bmp. This method ensures the compatibility of the solution with any typical medical imaging system and makes its practical application feasible in an actual healthcare setting.

9.2.2 Preprocessing

Preprocessing is the vital step for the x-ray images before analysis. As indicated in Figure 9.1, When the image is uploaded at that time, it will be transformed by Matlab(rgb2gray) into a gray scale image, and it removes data with the structural details remaining involved in it. This image conversion of a gray scale reduces computational complexity and enhances the contrast of pixel intensity, which is necessary for fracture detection [5]. The sharpening of intensity differentiation is also increased using the Canny edge detection algorithm so that structural discontinuities, such as fracture lines, are highlighted [6]. Therefore, all bone structures are segmented by it, and thus any potential fractures would become more clearly visible. Finally, pixel intensity values are normalized to a range of [0, 1], so that data may then be standardized for further processes.

$$I_{gray}(x,y) = 0.2989 \times I_R(x,y) + 0.5870 \times I_G(x,y) + 0.1140 \times I_B(x,y) \tag{9.1}$$

Eq. (9.1) represents the conversion of a color image to a grayscale image as a weighted sum of red (R), Green (G), and Blue (B) color channels.

9.2.3 Feature Extraction

Subsequent to pre-processing, the x-ray images go through the process of feature extraction pertinent to fracture as shown in Figure 9.1. Predominantly, structural attributes are obtained with the help of the Canny edge algorithm. The edges and contours are instances of discontinuity within the bone structure and are of interest during fracture diagnosis. While the current structural feature extraction techniques are not without limitations, extending them to analyze texture-based features like Haralick features or wavelet transforms can aid further in identifying very slight differences in bone density and irregularities [3]. It will do much to contribute to the most optimal level classification. Other state-of-the-art techniques may also include optical equipment for bone examination [15].

$$\sqrt{G_x^2 + G_y^2} \tag{9.2}$$

Eq. (9.2) represents the gradient magnitude in edge detection (Canny algorithm), where G_x and G_y are the image intensity gradients in horizontal and vertical directions, computed using filters like the Sobel operator, the square root of their squared sum gives edge strength, helping detect structural changes like fractures in bone x-ray images.

9.2.4 Development of GUI in MATLAB for Fracture Visualization and User Interaction

The existing system applies a placeholder strategy within the classification module to mimic the decision-making process. Following feature extraction, the system generates a random binary decision, where values greater than 0.5 represent a fractured outcome and values less than or equal to 0.5 represent a fracture-less outcome. To make sure that the same image processed during a session returns the same results, the result of classification is cached so that the random function does not return different values every time the same input is being processed again. In subsequent versions, this placeholder logic will be substituted with a trained Convolutional Neural Network (CNN) that will use a labeled x-ray image dataset. The CNN will improve classification of fractures based on learned features and thereby reduce errors and be more accurate [1].

9.2.4.1 Integration of Python and VGG16 for Fracture Detection and Area Highlighting

In this suggested system, A combination of Python code along with a pretrained VGG16 model, for improved detection accuracy, and deep convolutional network layers have been utilized for additional feature extraction, along with emphasis on the fractured area. The ImageNet dataset fine-tuned from this VGG16 model particularly specializes in the x-ray dataset for fracture detection. In addition to the above, Canny Edge Detection was used to identify possible fracture regions by structural discontinuity. The edge image was then analyzed to label it as either "fractured" or "non-fractured" based on the features extracted. This method improves the system to detect fractures by classifying images as well as by giving visual feedback by pointing out suspected areas of fracture. Today, the categorization employs randomized placeholder logic, but it will soon be substituted with a trained Convolutional Neural Network to generate greater accuracy and dependability. The combination of Python with MATLAB's GUI is very much necessary since it promotes easy user interaction, allowing the user to see real-time image processing and overlay visualization of fractures identified. Actual images are examined, from [20], and designated areas of fracture that will assist doctors in an improved and accurate fracture identification. The implementation of GUI and fracture detection process is shown in Figure 9.1.

9.2.5 GUI Development and Implementation

The system for detecting fracture has a GUI based on MATLAB. With a simple window, the program allows the user to upload x-ray images and classify them. Upon having uploaded an x-ray image on the "Upload x-ray Image" button, the image is processed and then shown. An available "Process and Classify" button initiates the preprocessing and classification processes upon which the result, either "Fracture-less" or "Fractured", is then printed, in plain text, immediately beneath the button. Color-coding is utilized by the system to improve readability: fractured diagnosis bears red-colored text, whereas fracture-free results are accorded a green one. Figure 9.1 presents the layout of the MATLAB GUI and user interaction process.

This is so that the cached results will be deleted every time a new image is uploaded, thereby preventing duplicate processing of an identical image to achieve different results. Currently, processed images and their associated structural data are not shown on visual panels; however, future versions may include such graphical panels to show originals and processed images. The GUI would be very user-friendly though improvements are possible in error handling, user guidance, and even greater accessibility to the medical users [5].

9.3 Results for MATLAB GUI

The real-time dataset utilized in the fracture detection system is borrowed from [20] and other open-source platforms such as Kaggle. It constitutes an extensive repository of the x-ray images that are specifically relevant for fracture analysis. The dataset contains extremely good images with a variety of fracture types and conditions, thus bearing a diversified set of data upon which the system will be trained and tested. Different poses and angles, as well as different conditions of patients, enable the model to generalize its fracture detection capability under different situations.

Figure 9.2a shows the original x-ray image obtained from [20] which is input for the fracture detection system. It shows a bone structure where there is a potential fracture. Figure 9.2b shows the Canny edge-detected image of the original x-ray where the edges are enhanced by Canny's edge detection algorithm, and fractures are more visible by finding fractures using the random binary classification method. Figure 9.2c illustrates the GUI of the fracture detection system, which analyzes the uploaded x-ray image.

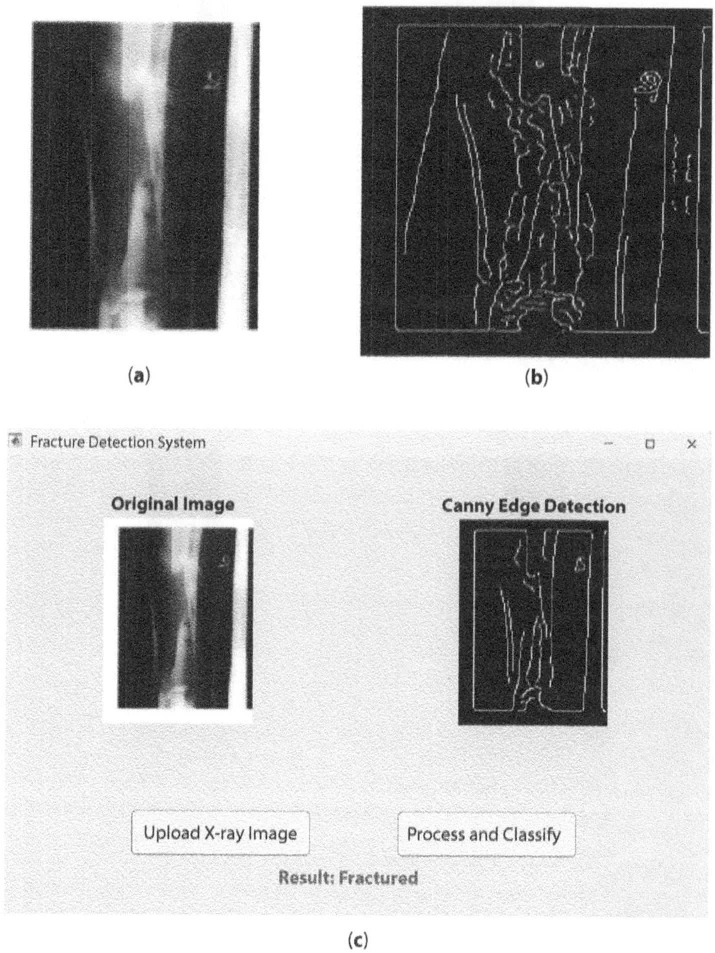

Figure 9.2 Automated fracture detection system. (a) An original x-ray image of the fractured bone acquired from [20]. (b) Canny edge-detected image of the original x-ray fractured bone image. (c) GUI for the fracture detection system.

The interface displays the original x-ray image and its edge-detected image, with the result labeled as "Fractured" to indicate an automatic fracture detection outcome.

Figure 9.3a is the original x-ray image of the same subject illustrated in Figure 9.1, obtained from [20], which serves as the input of the fracture detection system. Figure 9.3b is the Canny edge-detected image of the original x-ray, wherein the edges are enhanced by Canny's edge detection

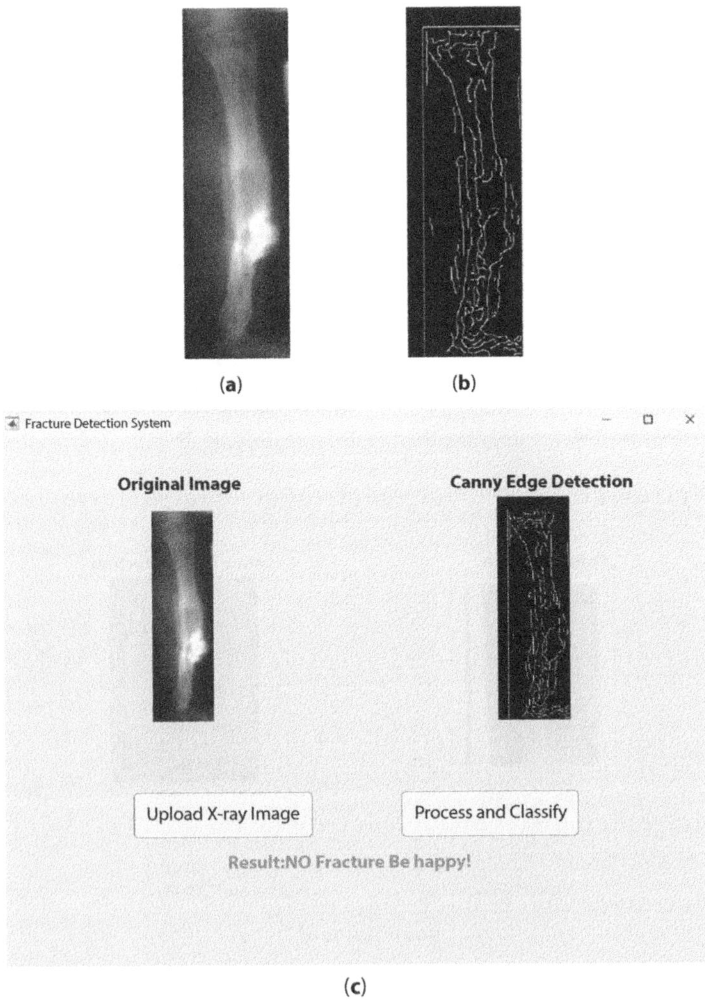

Figure 9.3 Automated fracture detection system. (a) Original x-ray image of the healed bone. (b) Canny edge-detected image of the original x-ray one image. (c) GUI for the fracture detection system.

algorithm, and fractures become evident by the detection of fractures. Figure 9.3c illustrates the GUI for the fracture detection system that deals with the uploaded x-ray image. The interface displays the original x-ray image and its edge-detected image, with the result labeled as "No Fracture Be happy" to indicate an automatic fracture detection outcome. The GUI of the fracture detection system is structured so that anyone can use it to upload the images, look at results, and interpret the results with minimal technical expertise. This user-friendly approach enables a wide range of medical practitioners to use the system. Figure 9.1 demonstrates its utility in streamlining the diagnostic process. The GUI allows for real-time data, where radiologists are able to observe x-ray images in real-time without requiring a lengthy manual check. This feature of real-time processing accelerates the diagnosis process and maximizes efficiency in medical assessment, as demonstrated by Figures 9.2 and 9.3. To sum up, the fracture detection system built with MATLAB presented herein presents a highly sensitive method to detecting fractures and healing bones without posing any further risk through the use of ionizing radiation. The system helps in medical diagnosis, a valuable tool for medical practitioners, with the help of edge detection methods.

Result for Implementation of the Fracture detection system using Python and CNN

CNN (Convolutional Neural Network) model was trained on a total of 3,220 non-fractured x-ray images and 644 fractured x-ray images dataset. To maintain balance and work most constructively, the 80-20% split train–validation dataset was executed. This helped the model learn crucial fracture detection characteristics and evaluated the model for generalization with unseen images. To increase the reliability of the model's predictions and decrease bias, cross-validation was used. Features were extracted primarily using Deep learning models, especially CNN architectures. In this model, convolutional layers coupled with max pooling and ReLU activation functions are used to identify the critical features and structural differences in the x-ray images. These extracted features went through the fully connected layer with 128 neurons for final classification. The model is prevented from overfitting by appropriate regularization (dropout with a dropout ratio of 0.5) to allow it to perform well on unseen data. Using Adam optimizer and Binary cross-entropy loss function to optimize the model and train it for 10 epochs to minimize error and maximize accuracy.

Figure 9.4 illustrates accuracy in training and validation of non-fractured data and loss in ten epochs. Training accuracy increased at a fast rate, and in the subsequent few epochs, it reached the 100% level, whereas

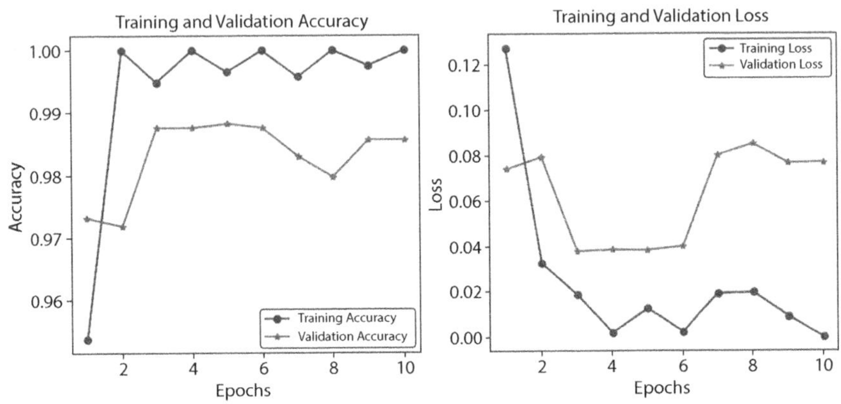

Figure 9.4 Training and validation performance of not fractured x-ray image dataset using the proposed model.

validation accuracy stayed at 98.3%. This indicates the model has learned the features of fracture detection adequately as well as generalizing nicely.

In the meantime, the training loss suffered a rapid descent from an initial value of about 0.125 to a number close to zero. The validation loss wobbled at first, but soon after it found stability around 0.08. These smaller ups and downs indicate different generalization performances, but they are kept within the boundaries, showing that the model is not affected by over-fitting. Figure 9.5 does this even better by displaying a model that was already at 98.5% accuracy after the first epoch. The validation accuracy was consistently high, which shows that it operated on new sets of data

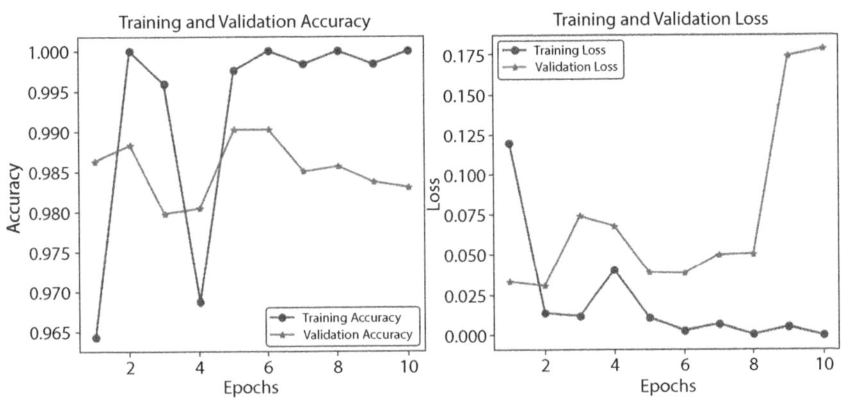

Figure 9.5 Training and validation performance of fractured x-ray image dataset using the proposed model.

effectively. The graph of the loss function that corresponds to the accuracy graph vividly reveals an initial training loss of 0.125, which fell to zero shortly, which is a real efficiency of the training process.

Additionally, the ability of the suggested model to localize the fractures is depicted in Figure 9.6. Bounding boxes are utilized to highlight unusual bone structures as the model successfully predicts the fractured region.

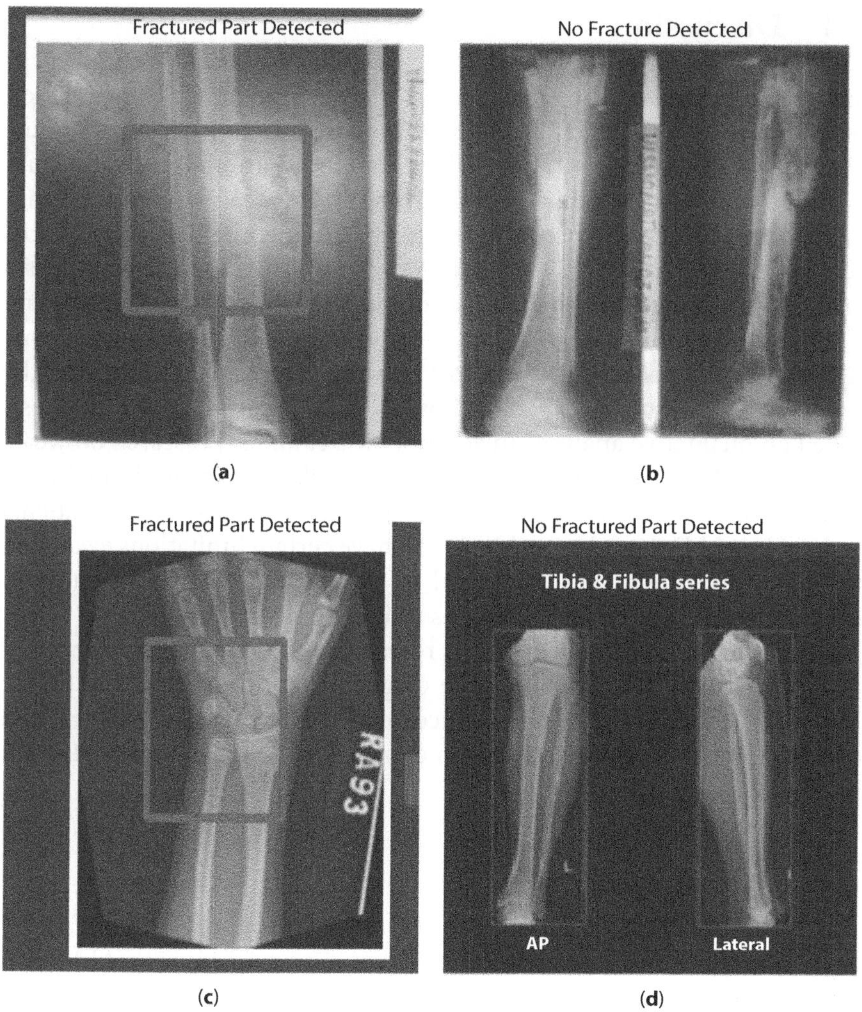

Figure 9.6 Automated fracture detection system using Python. (a) A real-time fractured bone x-ray image acquired from [20]. (b) Real-time healed bone x-ray image acquired from [20]. (c) Fractured bone x-ray image acquired from Kaggle. (d) Healed bone x-ray image acquired from an open source.

As a starting point prerequisite to target structural discontinuities, Canny edge detection is employed, which would assist the model in learning to detect non-accidental fracture lines according to differences from normal bone patterns. The integration of feature extraction and deep learning techniques enhances the diagnostic reliability of the model, providing medical applications in addition to classification and visual responses.

9.4 Discussion

This paper addresses the effectiveness of an AI model for the detection of fractures in a radiographic study. Compared to conventional manual evaluations of radiologists, the AI-based methods are more accurate and are done within shorter time periods. These findings are in line with Ergün and Güney's [2] work, where bone maturity and fracture healing were correctly identified from x-ray images. Wang and Yang [21] and Kalinowski *et al.* [22] explained the relevance of computational simulations in fracture healing explanation. Among the major advantages of this technique is that it is highly adaptable and can adjust to varied implementations. On the contrary Wang *et al.* [8] explained how AI is used in orthopedic diagnosis based on qualitative analysis. In addition, Ma *et al.* [24] research on wearable biofeedback systems and Kalinowski *et al.* [22] suggestion of non-invasive optical devices show that the real-time monitoring of patients using AI and ML-based models [41] can have certain limitations even with their benefits. The accuracy attained by these models is dependent upon the quality and size of the dataset, as well as variations in the x-ray imaging environment. Miranda *et al.*'s [6] research highlights the importance of feature selection in augmenting the diagnostic accuracy achieved by the ML models. Data processing advancements, better imaging devices, and optimization of feature selection can enhance AI-based fracture detection for clinical applications.

9.5 Conclusion

An Automated Fracture detection system was created with MATLAB and Python software. Canny edge detection at structural discontinuity fracture-related edges is utilized to identify the fractures in real-time. The same model is applied in Python utilizing the VGG16 module trained on a dataset collected from open-source repositories for 3,220 non-fracture x-ray images and 644 fracture x-ray images, with a 98.3% accuracy for non-fracture images and 98.5% accuracy for fracture images. The system developed cuts down on the time for diagnostics, enhances accuracy, and is extremely beneficial to orthopedic surgeons for live monitoring to enhance its clinical utility further.

AI disclosure statement: The author acknowledges the use of AI-based tools for minor language editing or grammatical correction. However, all intellectual contributions, analyses, and conclusions presented in this chapter are entirely the author's own.

References

1. Medaramatla, S.C., Samhitha, C.V., Pande, S.D., Vinta, S.R., Detection of Hand Bone Fractures in X-Ray Images Using Hybrid YOLO NAS. *IEEE Access*, 12, 57661–57673, 2024, doi: 10.1109/ACCESS.2024.3379760.
2. Ergün, G.B. and Güney, S., Classification of Canine Maturity and Bone Fracture Time Based on X-Ray Images of Long Bones. *IEEE Access*, 9, 109004–109011, 2021, doi: 10.1109/ACCESS.2021.3101040.
3. Rizwan, S., Kumar, K.V.P., Alazemi, A.J., A Compact Textile Monopole Antenna for Monitoring the Healing of Bone Fractures Using Un-Supervised Machine Learning Algorithm. *IEEE Access*, 11, 101195–101204, 2023, doi: 10.1109/ACCESS.2023.3314577.
4. Meena, T. and Roy, S., Bone Fracture Detection Using Deep Supervised Learning from Radiological Images: A Paradigm Shift. *Diagnostics (Basel)*, 12, 10, 2420, 2022 Oct 7, doi: 10.3390/diagnostics12102420. PMID: 36292109; PMCID: PMC9600559.
5. Cotri-Melecez, B., Quiroz-Compean, G., Torres-Treviño, L., Rodriguez-Liñan, A., Raygoza, I.Q., Fraire, O.S., Making Medical Prescription Automatic: The Case of Prescribing Therapies in Ankle Fracture Rehabilitation by Means of a Computer-Aided System. *IEEE Access*, 12, 97171–97183, 2024, doi: 10.1109/ACCESS.2024.3426476.
6. Miranda, D., Olivares, R., Munoz, R., Minonzio, J.-G., Improvement of Patient Classification Using Feature Selection Applied to Bidirectional Axial Transmission. *IEEE Trans. Ultrason. Ferroelectr. Freq. Control*, 69, 9, 2663–2671, Sept. 2022, doi: 10.1109/TUFFC.2022.3195477.
7. Rasool, M.J.A., Ahmad, S., Sabina, U., Whangbo, T.K., KONet: Toward a Weighted Ensemble Learning Model for Knee Osteoporosis Classification. *IEEE Access*, 12, 5731–5742, 2024, doi: 10.1109/ACCESS.2023.3348817.
8. Wang, W., Zhang, W., Xiong, P., Liu, X., Zou, W., Wu, C., An Active Fracture Diagnosis System With Biocompatible Sensor Based on LSTM-MLP Quantitative Analysis. *IEEE Sens. J.*, 24, 7, 10113–10124, 1 April 2024, doi: 10.1109/JSEN.2024.3365098.

9. Alam, A., Al-Shamayleh, A.S., Thalji, N., *et al.*, Novel transfer learning-based bone fracture detection using radiographic images. *BMC Med. Imaging*, 25, 5, 2025, https://doi.org/10.1186/s12880-024-01546-4.
10. Santhiya, J. and Jasmine Lois Ebenezer, P., Bone Fracture Detection Using Python. *Int. J. Creat. Res. Thoughts*, 10, 12, 1561–1565, 2022.
11. Madhavasarma, P., Kumaravel, S., Sridevi, M., Prakasam, P., Classification of tibia fracture across limb in patients treated using DC electric stimulation based on observed healing pattern. *Res. J. Pharm. Biol. Chem. Sci.*, 7, 2, 1006–1018, 2015, ISSN: 0975-8585.
12. Zabihiyeganeh, M., Mirzaei, A., Tabrizian, P., *et al.*, Prediction of subsequent fragility fractures: Application of machine learning. *BMC Musculoskelet. Disord.*, 25, 438, 2024, https://doi.org/10.1186/s12891-024-07559-y.
13. Sharma, R.K. and Sangeeta, Fractured Bone Diagnostics Using Optimised Convolutional Neural Network Model with Variable Learning Rates, in: *Proceedings of 4th International Conference on ICT for Digital, Smart, and Sustainable Development, ICIDSSD 2024*, Innovations in Sustainable Technologies and Computing, M.A. Alam, F. Siddiqui, S. Zafar, I. Hussain (Eds.), Springer, Singapore, 2024, https://doi.org/10.1007/978-981-97-7831-7_15.
14. Prijs, J., Liao, Z., To, M.S., *et al.*, Development and external validation of automated detection, classification, and localization of ankle fractures: Inside the black box of a convolutional neural network (CNN). *Eur. J. Trauma Emerg. Surg.*, 49, 1057–1069, 2023, https://doi.org/10.1007/s00068-022-02136-1.
15. Sahin, M.E., Image processing and machine learning-based bone fracture detection and classification using X-ray images. *Int. J. Imaging Syst. Technol.*, 33, 3, 853–65, 2023.
16. Yang, Y., Zhao, Z., Qi, X., Hu, Y., Li, B., Zhang, L., Computational Modeling of Bone Fracture Healing Under Different Initial Conditions and Mechanical Load. *IEEE Trans. Biomed. Eng.*, 71, 7, 2105–2118, July 2024, doi: 10.1109/TBME.2024.3361893.
17. Abedeen, I., *et al.*, FracAtlas: A Dataset for Fracture Classification, Localization, and Segmentation of Musculoskeletal Radiographs. igshare. ataset, 2023, https://doi.org/10.6084/m9.figshare.22363012.v6.
18. Thakur, D., Pal, P., Somraj, S., Bopalkar, S., Chavan, S., Fracture Detection Health Network (FDHN): A solution to generate bone fracture insight. *2024 Fourth International Conference on Advances in Electrical, Computing, Communication and Sustainable Technologies (ICAECT)*, Bhilai, India, pp. 1–7, 2024, doi: 10.1109/ICAECT60202.2024.10469480.
19. Puthanpura, D., Senthilkumar, A., R.D.T, M.K, M.P. and S.M., TFL-Net: A Hybrid Deep Learning Framework for Tibia Fracture Detection and Localization. *2025 1st International Conference on Radio Frequency Communication and Networks (RFCoN)*, pp. 1–6, Thanjavur, India, 2025, doi:0.1109/RFCoN62306.2025.11085297.
20. Sridevi, M., Tibia Fracture Healing Prediction Using Soft Computing Technique, PhD thesis, Anna University, 2016.

21. Wang, M. and Yang, N., Computational Simulation of the Influence of Mechanical Stability on Growth Factors Activities during Bone Fracture Healing. *IEEE Access*, 7, 9827–9835, 2019, doi: 10.1109/ACCESS.2019.2892125.
22. Kalinowski, A., Linessio, R.P., Mendonça, C.J.A., Antunes, P., Ramos, A., da Silva, J.C.C., Noninvasive Optical Instrumentation for Bone Healing Process Analysis. *IEEE Sens. J.*, 21, 13, 14060–14068, 1 July 2021, doi: 10.1109/JSEN.2020.3033192.
23. Mišić, D., Zdravković, M., Mitković, M., Vitković, N., Mitković, M., Real-Time Monitoring of Bone Fracture Recovery by Using Aware, Sensing, Smart, and Active Orthopedic Devices. *IEEE Internet Things J.*, 5, 6, 4466–4473, Dec. 2018, doi: 10.1109/JIOT.2018.2819623.
24. Ma, T., Xu, X., Chai, Z., Wang, T., Shen, X., Sun, T., A Wearable Biofeedback Device for Monitoring Tibial Load During Partial Weight-Bearing Walking. *IEEE Trans. Neural Syst. Rehabil. Eng.*, 31, 3428–3436, 2023, doi: 10.1109/TNSRE.2023.3305205.
25. Liu, C., Wang, H., Mao, L., Liu, R., Wang, Z., Wang, T., Image Stitching Method of Bone Stick Fragment Based on Similarity Freeman Code Matching. *IEEE Access*, 11, 23073–23084, 2023, doi: 10.1109/ACCESS.2023.3252894.
26. Madhava Sarma, P., Kumaravel, S., Sridevi, M., Prakasam, P., Determination of optimum voltage for tibia fracture across limb in patients treated using DC electric stimulation. *Res. J. Pharm. Biol. Chem. Sci.*, 7, 1, 418–424, 2015, ISSN: 0975-8585.
27. Madhavasarma, P., Veeraragavan, P., Modelling and performance analysis of a process based on conductivity measurement using neural networks. *Sciences*, 7, 3, 1820–1824, 2016.
28. Sridevi, M., Prakasam, P., Kumaravel, S., Madhava Sarma, P., Tibia Fracture Healing Prediction Using First-Order Mathematical Model. *Comput. Math. Methods Med.*, 689035, 9, 2015, https://doi.org/10.1155/2015/689035.
29. Malamal, G. and Panicker, M.R., A Novel Technique for Estimation and Detection of Specular Reflections Leveraging High Frame Rate Ultrasound Imaging. *IEEE Trans. Instrum. Meas.*, 72, 1–11, 2023, 9600311, doi: 10.1109/TIM.2022.3232642.
30. Han, H.S., Kim, D.H., Kang, S.B., The use of a ti-ni shape memory alloy ring bone fixator during the retrograde nailing of supracondylar femoral fractures. *Knee Surg. Relat. Res.*, 23, 4, 231–5, 2011 Dec., doi: 10.5792/ksrr.2011.23.4.231. Epub 2011 Nov 30. PMID: 22570840; PMCID: PMC3341807.
31. Borchani, W., Aono, K., Lajnef, N., Chakrabartty, S., Monitoring of Postoperative Bone Healing Using Smart Trauma-Fixation Device with Integrated Self-Powered Piezo-Floating-Gate Sensors. *IEEE Trans. Biomed. Eng.*, 63, 7, 1463–1472, July 2016, doi: 10.1109/TBME.2015.2496237.
32. Mattei, L., Di Puccio, F., Marchetti, S., Fracture Healing Monitoring by Impact Tests: Single Case Study of a Fractured Tibia with External Fixator. *IEEE J. Transl. Eng. Health Med.*, 7, 1–6, 2019, 2100206, doi: 10.1109/JTEHM.2019.2901455.

33. Sridevi, M., Prakasam, P., Kumaravel, S., Madhavsarma, P., Tibia Fracture Healing Prediction Using Adaptive Neuro Fuzzy Inference System. *Intell. Autom. Soft Comput.*, 23, 2, 359–363, 2017.
34. Greve, D.W., Oppenheim, I.J., Chen, A.F., An instrumented intramedullary implant to monitor strain in fracture healing. *2012 IEEE International Ultrasonics Symposium*, Dresden, Germany, pp. 1220–1223, 2012, doi: 10.1109/ULTSYM.2012.0304.
35. Priya, P.M., Krishnan, S., Revathy, G., Kalaiselvi, L., Usha, M.T., Microarray Based Disease Prediction using Deep Learning Techniques, in: *2023 7th International Conference on Computing Methodologies and Communication (ICCMC)*, 2023, February, IEEE, pp. 334–339.
36. Madhavasarma, P., Kumaravel, S., Sridevi, M., Prakasam, P., Identification of time constant for healing process of limb with fractured tibia bone using step response techniques. *Res. J. Pharm. Biol. Chem. Sci.*, 7, 2, 1377–1383, 2016, ISSN: 0975-8585.
37. Sridevi, M., Prakasam, P., Kumaravel, S., Madhavasarma, P., Comparative Analysis of Fracture Healing Predicted Using Mathematical Model and Soft Computing Technique. *Int. J. Appl. Eng. Res.*, 10, 8, 21215–21226, 2015.
38. Madhavasarma, P., Sridevi, M., Kumaravel, S., Veeraragavan, P., An electrical stimulation data-based model to predict the healing period of fractured limb. *Math. Comput. Modell. Dyn. Syst.*, *25*, 4, 354–375, 2019, https://doi.org/10.1080/13873954.2019.1651341.
39. Protopappas, V.C., Baga, D.A., Fotiadis, D.I., Likas, A.C., Papachristos, A.A., Malizos, K.N., An ultrasound wearable system for the monitoring and acceleration of fracture healing in long bones. *IEEE Trans. Biomed. Eng.*, 52, 9, 1597–1608, Sept. 2005, doi: 10.1109/TBME.2005.851507.
40. He, Y., Ma, Y., Zhao, Z., Zhang, M., A Biomechanical Monitor for Bone Fracture Healing. *2023 IEEE Biomedical Circuits and Systems Conference (BioCAS)*, Toronto, ON, Canada, pp. 1–5, 2023, doi: 10.1109/BioCAS58349.2023.10388734.
41. Madhavasarma, P. and Sridevi, M., Model Identification and smart structural vibration control using H infinity controller. *Int. J. Smart Sens. Intell. Syst.*, 03, 655–671, 2010.

10

Understanding Affective AI: A Review of Emotion Detection Computation and Real-World Applications

Umamaheswari P.*, Abiramasundari S. and Sumathi A.

SASTRA Deemed University, Srinivasa Ramanujan Centre, Kumbakonam, Thanjavur (Dt), Tamil Nadu, India

Abstract

Affective Artificial Intelligence (Affective AI) is a transforming concept designed to let emotional communication and understanding exist between a person and a computer through enshrining emotional intelligence in AIs. This paper will provide a detailed discussion of the underlying theories, techniques, applications, and issues in addition to future trends of this interdisciplinary research area. The ability to monitor whether individuals are mentally healthy to the implementation of adaptive learning environments, affective AI is transforming the manner in which machines address human emotion in a variety of industries. In the medical field, the AI-based tools that can identify the emotions are helping to diagnose anxiety, stress, and depression early, with cognitive behavioral therapy (CBT) platforms offering customization according to the needs. Real-time psychiatric care is further improved because of wearable emotion-tracking devices.

In day-to-day online communication, virtual assistants such as Siri and Alexa are becoming more emotional, thereby making them enjoyable to utilize, as they would reply depending on the context. On the same note, sentimental AI is also facilitating the process of making education personalized as it adapts educational material according to student interest and emotional responses. The chapter explores different emotion recognition approaches: including the usage of facial expressions analysis; voice tone identification; monitoring of physiological signals; and the role of natural language processing, deep learning, and multimodal data fusion in this field.

**Corresponding author*: pum@it.sastra.edu

N. Thillaiarasu, G. Revathy, T. Saravanan, V. Muthukumaran and S. Balamurugan (eds.) Affective Artificial Intelligence: Fundamentals, Challenges, and Applications, (211–224) © 2026 Scrivener Publishing LLC

The need to have machines interact more in a human language is increasing by the day as users expect more human engagement with the machines. The areas receiving significant changes include emotion-aware robotics, virtual assistants, and mental health applications to name a few. Although affective AI is promising because of its transformative potentials, it comes with serious challenges, including cultural biases in the data of emotion and ethical considerations of the processing of emotional data. This proposed chapter is expected to offer future studies directions, as well as assist the future AI-related development of emotionally resonant and ethically responsible systems, by looking at modern-day innovations and determining the available gaps.

Keywords: Artificial intelligence, cognitive behavioral therapy, emotional intelligence, emotional music generation, explainable artificial intelligence, human-computer interaction, large language models, machine learning

10.1 Introduction

Affective AI, often referred to as emotion AI, is a specialized subfield of artificial intelligence focused on understanding, interpreting, and simulating human emotions. By merging computational models with psychological theories, affective AI aims to create more empathetic and human-like interactions in fields ranging from healthcare to education and marketing. This paper explores the underlying principles, current technologies, and practical applications of this growing field.

The lack of a comprehensive bibliometric study limits our understanding of the theory, technical processes, and applications of emotional computing, despite the fact that the body of research in this field has been growing and developing steadily. The five primary research themes identified by cluster analysis not only reflect significant areas of worldwide interest, but they also suggest possible avenues for future research. Important advancements in emotional computing include the production of large datasets, the use of data and knowledge to promote creativity, multimodal fusion, fine-grained sentiment classification, and more.

10.2 Background and Foundations

Despite the advent of affective AI, human-machine interaction has undergone a dramatic change, going beyond logic-driven processes to recognize and react to human emotions. The goal of affective AI, which has its roots in the interdisciplinary convergence of artificial intelligence, psychology, neuroscience, and human-computer interaction, is to increase the social intelligence and empathy of machines. The basic premise behind emotional computing was first enshrined in the 1990s by Rosalind Picard, who had suggested that a robot must be capable of imitating and responding to human emotions besides simply being able to identify them.

Machine learning has enabled complex models and could recognize emotions in real-time based on multimodal input, especially on deep learning and natural language processing. AI systems have already grown in their ability to read human intentions and moods due to the wealth of emotional data that is collected by wearable sensors, EEG devices, and voice analysis systems. Despite all these advancements, there are still challenges that the field must overcome such as cultural bias in emotion perception, how most emotions cannot be identified, and the ethical implications of emotion-aware computers. The growing popularity of Affective AI use in virtual assistants, education, healthcare, and mental health practice proves to require efficient theoretical background and responsible design principles although it shows the transformative potential of the technology.

Various psychological models of emotion classification and explanation exist which include Russell Circumplex Model of Affect, Plutchik Wheel of Emotions and Ekman Six Basic Emotions. AI based emotion detection systems employ Ekman model as a common way of identifying the common emotions, which are joy, grief, rage, fear, disgust, and surprise. The strategy used by Russell places emotions in a valence-arousal framework, which makes it more flexible to show the different states of emotions. The approach advocated by Plutchik cements this knowledge by proposing that there are basic emotions that may interact and give rise to more complex emotional experiences.

Many investigations about the neuroscientific constituent of emotions had revealed how insula, prefrontal cortex, and amygdala taken part in emotion processing. Two neurotransmitters, which are necessary in controlling the mood, are dopamine and serotonin since they influence the perceptions of emotions as well as their expressions. Physiological data collected in the form of heart rate variability, galvanic skin reaction could be used in affective AI systems because it provides quantifiable indicators of emotional states. To be able to implement the model of emotions in artificial intelligence, a number of computational methods of it have been invented [2]. Although the Affect Control Theory (ACT) predicts the process of social interactions based on such concepts as managing emotions, the artificial intelligence (AI) systems can be trained on responses provided by people and adapt their behavior based on that.

The proposed models form the basis of frame-works of emotional computing that incorporate the integration of multiple modalities to increase capacity of AI to identify and act on emotions. The customers anticipate that artificial intelligence (AI) systems will treat them more humanly, and these systems should be capable of understanding and reacting to an emotion.

With the advent of emotion-aware robotics, intelligent virtual assistants, and AI applications for mental health, the demand for affective AI is rapidly growing.

This paper provides a history, foundations, and a thorough assessment of prior findings in this area, as well as a list of potential directions for future research. Computer science, engineering, psychology, neurology, and other related disciplines are all part of the new interdisciplinary field of affective computing. This review offers a quantitative evaluation of 33,448 articles released from 1997 to 2023, pinpointing challenges, emphasizing 10 technological trends, and providing a framework for upcoming applications.

The findings show how emerging nations like China and India are transforming the global affective computing research landscape, fostering extensive partnerships and bringing revolutionary influence. Important developments in emotional computing include building large databases, using knowledge and data to stimulate creativity, analyzing sentiment in great detail, and combining several modalities. With quick improvements and technology upgrades, affective computing holds tremendous potential in areas including brain-computer interfaces, empathetic human-computer interaction, decision support systems, and virtual reality. Human survival, interaction, decision-making, motivation, and preservation are all significantly influenced by emotions [3]. In the study, we learn of their significance and they are critical towards the formation of multidimensional thought as well as societal actions.

10.3 Applications of Affective AI

There are revolutionary applications of AI in the many areas as shown in Figure 10.1. Through indication of stress, anxiety, and despair, AI-powered emotion recognition systems in the medical field [1] can assist in mental health tracking. Cognitive behavioral therapy (CBT) platforms are powered by artificial intelligence to deliver personalized mental health-care. The emotion-sensing wearable technology allows one to monitor emotions in real-time and with this, problems can be addressed early in mental health conditions. Emotion-aware virtual assistants, like Siri, Alexa, and Google Assistant, enhance user experiences with their potential to customize the responses according to

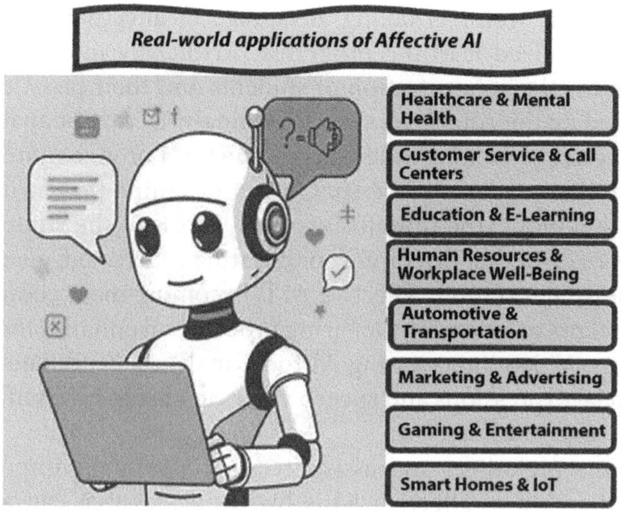

Figure 10.1 Applications of affective AI.

identified states of emotions and facilitate human-computer interaction (HCI). The learning environments that are adaptive use affective AI to individualize the content based on student interest and emotional response as a result of which the learning outcomes can be enhanced.

To enhance patient experience and mental wellbeing, the healthcare industry needs affective AI. Health-focused chatbots that use artificial intelligence (AI) to give emotional support, including Woebot, Wysa, identify signs of anxiety or uneasiness in the text people type or tones in their speech. Another sphere where AI is employed in hospitals is experiencing facial expressions and physiological signs to determine the extent of the experienced pain by non-verbal patients. In addition, it benefits people with autism as it eases them to acknowledge the feelings in social contexts and this makes people be good communicators.

Affective AI has done wonders in the customer care and call centers where it has incorporated the sentiment analysis in dealing with clients. Artificial intelligence (AI) technologies have the potential to track and analyze that what and how a customer is saying in real-time so that human agents can modify their response to the same. This technology is also used in the virtual assistants that are able to detect when a caller is annoyed and change their tactics to make this interaction positive. Retail companies use it to personalize their purchasing suggestions according to the emotional mood of the customer which leads to increased client satisfaction and activity.

The education sector is taking advantage of affective AI in order to develop personalized learning programs. Artificially intelligent learning spaces monitor the concentration of students and their facial expressions to accommodate the course content accordingly. In case of apathy or confusion the system can adjust the teaching method or give more assistance in case a student appears to be so. On top of online proctoring systems that detect emotions, the monitoring of the stress of the students during online tests ensures that discomfort or cheating is detected, guaranteeing a healthy assessment setting. Affective AI is becoming more common in the HR departments to automate the hiring process and enhance the wellbeing of employees. Video interviewing AI tools analyze a candidate by analyzing their facial expressions and speech voices to ensure how self-confident, honest and eager they are.

This lowers prejudices and assists recruiters to make improved decisions. Another use of affective AI is by businesses that can analyze the mood and stress level of its employees so that the management can take proactive actions to improve the productivity and job satisfaction of all employees. Auto companies have adopted affective AI to bring a better driving experience and ensure safety. The driver monitoring systems are capable of identifying evidence of stress, fatigue, or distraction in the face, eye gaze, and intonation. In case a motorist has these signs, the device will flash an alarm or recommend a break. Some more sophisticated in-car aids do more than keep the driver safe to help him/her enjoy driving by changing the interior of the car, like the light level of music and temperature levels, in response to the mood known about the driver. Marketing and advertising have been changed by the use of emotion-based ad targeting whereby the AI analyses how the viewers respond to the various ads and it shapes according to them.

This means that consumers will view more pertinent and captivating advertisements that will make marketing campaigns more effective. Also, in the product testing phase, the brands use market research implemented with the use of AI to analyze the tones of speech and facial expression of the consumers and gain important data about their reactions and interests. Affective AI has enabled gaming and entertainment business to provide emotionally customized experiences. Security and law enforcement agencies utilize Affective AI to survey and prevent crimes; lie detector systems based on AI examine intonation and micro-expressions on faces to determine when an individual is lying based on the information gathered during interrogations; public safety surveillance programs focus on detecting suspicious and violent behavior by people in airports and public spaces where emotion detection informs the authorities before the incident occurs;

emotion detection can now alter a game into a video game, the degree of challenge, or how characters interact with each other; virtual reality (VR) and interactive movies also utilize this technology because it allows stories to change in real-time.

Emotionally flexible in any case, Affective AI is making IoT devices and smart homes more natural. Smart home devices can change the temperature, the lighting, and even the background music depending on the emotional situation of the user due to the emotional driven automation. Virtual assistants, such as Alexa and Google Assistant also use artificial intelligence (AI) to process emotion and are increasingly more natural and responsive to personal interaction and decorum.

These developments are fostering settings that support users' emotional health, enhancing everyday life to be more pleasant and effective as Affective AI advances, its possible uses will broaden significantly, transforming sectors and the way humans interact with computers. Integrating emotional intelligence into machines leads society to a future where technology comprehends and reacts to human emotions, enhancing digital interactions to be more empathetic and significant.

Researchers from the National University of Singapore and Keio University in Japan [4] have proposed a multidisciplinary method for creating a sophisticated artificial intelligence system for a robot that can respond emotionally. The primary objective is to develop a robotic system that can establish profound emotional bonds with humans by investigating the idea of human love. This relationship encompasses a dynamic interaction of attraction, affection, and attachment that humans feel toward the robot, along with a perceived emotional response from the robot to humans.

The AI system is composed of three primary modules the affective state transition (AST) module, which takes interest in emotion regulation, the artificial endocrine system (AES) that finds inspiration in the physiological factors of love, and the probabilistic love assembly (PLA) that is guided by psychological theories of love. The psychological affection parameters are modeled in the PLA module as a Bayesian network. AES module is based on Dynamic Bayesian Network (DBN) to describe biological and emotional hormone action. The AST module introduces a new strategy of regulating the changes of the emotional state of the robot. In order to facilitate the human-robot bonding, these modules collaborate in order to direct the emotional behavior of the robot.

The topic of affective computing as one of the interdisciplinary areas of research with the components of computer science, psychology, neuroscience, and engineering has been booming during the recent decades [5].

The work of the authors [6] presents a detailed bibliometric analysis of 33,448 articles concerning the development of the field since 1997-2023, identification of key issues, and directions of the development. Their study revealed that global research in affective computing is increasingly influenced by emerging contributors such as China and India, which are reshaping collaborative efforts and injecting new momentum into the domain.

The literature identifies five core research themes through cluster analysis, reflecting the most active and innovative areas in affective computing. These themes indicate both well-established research interests and nascent frontiers. Major technological trends include the development of large-scale emotion-labeled datasets, fine-grained sentiment analysis, integration of data-driven and knowledge-based approaches, and advancements in multimodal data fusion. These advancements are essential for improving the emotional intelligence of computing systems.

Nevertheless, affective computing has a great potential of finding practical purposes in such fields as brain computer interface, emotion aware dialogue system, decision support system, and in such realms as virtual reality and augmented reality.

The comprehensive survey provides insightful facts concerning the current situation of affective computing and what to expect of the field to researchers and others who aspire to develop emotional intelligent systems capable of relating better and compassionately with people. Explainable Artificial Intelligence (XAI) has gone a long way in reducing the so-called black-box problem of traditional artificial intelligence models. Regardless of their technical knowledge, XAI makes consumers familiar with the inner aspects of the machine learning model by giving insights on how AI systems make the decisions they make. The shift has accelerated the growth of AI applications and also resulted in an increase in developments in the field. Notwithstanding these developments, issues on both the use of and access to XAI methods arise. Though the existence of most of the current methods has been widely determined by AI practitioners, recently end-users began to recognize a more urgent necessity of transparency. The effect of transparency on trust and the implementation of AI systems is quite severe; therefore, XAI must be developed as XHI that applies to end users and not developers only.

Recent studies highlight the importance of designing end-user-friendly XAI models and models with more comprehensible and familiar explanations favoring [7]. Even the existing XAI frameworks provide technological clarity, non-expert users frequently find them unappealing. This lack of user comprehension undermines confidence and prevents AI technologies from being widely used. By approaching XAI design from the perspective of end users, the current study seeks to resolve this problem by concentrating on the interactions between design elements and the trust and emotional reactions they evoke.

Critical elements of XAI design, including explanation format, communication style, and the incorporation of supplemental information, were examined in this study, which polled 202 individuals. Furthermore, the study [8] looked at how these design components impact trust calibration, taking into account variables including AI apprehension, incidental emotions, perceived AI dependability, and past AI system experience. The findings suggest that the enhancement of faith in XAI systems would demand expressive reactions. Emotional factors, such as accidental emotion and user fear, can have great significance when it comes to the manner in which consumers assess their degree of confidence in AI.

The results prove the need to have a technically acceptable and user-friendly design. In spite of an enormous movement forward in the broader topic of animal welfare, studies concerning the recognition of emotional or affective conditions in livestock remain scarce to a great extent. Despite the fact that many studies done in the past regarding animal welfare have centered on behavioral observations and environmental factors significant efforts on the ability on how quantitatively assess animal emotional condition remains a baby step.

One of the most encouraging ways of eliminating this gap is by developing tools and systems capable of not only detecting but also processing and analyzing the emotions of farm animals. New studies [8] demonstrate that biometric sensor technology, some of which are cameras, wearable sensors, and other similar monitoring devices may be able to capture various aspects of behavioral and physiological data to determine how an animal is feeling. Such technologies will give a powerful means to measure the complex biological and physical features including a posture, movement patterns, facial expressions, and heart rate variability. These parameters can thus be studied to arrive at signs of stress, fear, satisfaction or any other emotional condition.

Machine learning (ML) and artificial intelligence (AI) in livestock management The identification of new technologies that can be useful in management of livestock is a breakthrough in the management of livestock as a result of the abundance of biometrics data. In large scale agriculture, researchers can now identify specific animals in a herd or flock and monitor their physical and emotional well-being in real time through big data analysis and computer algorithms powered by artificial intelligence. Not only do these techniques allow one to understand the animal welfare more accurately, but also provide useful data to farmers and other care takers that can guide intervention towards improving the comfort and health the animals.

As the field continues to evolve, the integration of AI with biometric sensor technologies holds the potential to drastically improve the standards of animal welfare. This development could allow farmers to respond more effectively to the emotional and physiological needs of their animals, leading to enhanced overall well-being and, in turn, improved productivity and efficiency in livestock management. With the growing demand for intelligent products, artificial intelligence is increasingly shifting towards voice interaction, moving beyond simple communication to include the recognition of users' emotions and real-time feedback. Currently, affective acoustic models are built using deep learning techniques and represented mathematically to enable computers to learn from data and make predictions. While this approach offers high prediction accuracy, it lacks interpretability.

Therefore, there is a pressing need to empirically examine the relationship between acoustic features and psychological factors to provide a theoretical basis for adjusting model parameters. This study addresses [9] this gap by investigating how seven key acoustic features and their physical properties differ in the context of recognizing and expressing "gender" and the emotional states defined by the Pleasure-Arousal-Dominance (PAD) model during voice interactions. Answer: Sixty-two participants (31 female and 31 male) between the ages of 21 years to 60 years were sought using the stratified random sampling method to record emotional speech. The parameters of the acoustic features were extracted with the Praat voice analysis software, and were analyzed by the two-way ANOVA mixed-design in the SPSS. The findings indicate that gender and PAD emotional states play a great role in the quality of hearing; there are differences in actual ranking and value of the seven auditory qualities.

These findings can deal with the issue of low interpretability of deep learning models in emotion recognition and adaptive control of emotional synthesis systems and be a theoretical basis of AI emotional voice interaction. Music is a particular thing as it can influence the emotional backgrounds of the listeners. The work toward creating artificial intelligence (AI) based systems of emotional music generation (AMG) has become increasingly popular owing to recent developments in computing capability.

There are other fields that could be covered using these AI-powered AMG systems and other related sectors such as interactive systems with sensors, healthcare, and entertainment.

This study gives a comprehensive report of the analysis of controlled AI-based affective music generation (AI-AMG) systems [10]. It enumerates the essentials of AI-AMG systems and divides the existing approaches by the type of algorithms used to generate music. In addition to some key musical attributes that aid expression of emotion, the review examines how AI techniques could be employed to these elements to generate emotional music. It further presents the major challenges and the unanswered questions in the field and potential resolutions. The aim of this review is to allow the reader to better understand prevailing ways of thinking as well as to stimulate further research within this rapidly growing interdisciplinary area newest state of AI-AMG research is conducted.

In a study by Kang [11] the researcher investigated how the interlocutor (especially AI avatars and native English speakers) can influence emotional responses and the speaking capacity of ESL learners in language acquisition period. 61 college ESL students in the US were enrolled in a series of experiments that incorporated speech to text software and divided up into two groups. One of them communicated with AI avatars, and the other ones talked to native English speaker.

It was found out that both types of encounters resulted in improved speaking skills [11]. In its turn, the students who interacted with AI avatars demonstrated a much higher oral performance, particularly in the domains of correctness, fluency, coherence, and interactive competence.

Remarkably, a combination of high-level learners with native speakers yielded a better result, but lower-proficiency groups benefited more through AI associations. Their study results on the emotional matters were that there were no significant differences in the amount of motivation that was brought forth in the learners who were advanced, and the level of stress and anxiety had reduced among the novices did not reduce in a significant way despite the fact that there was a general improvement in the attitude the participants held regarding the learning process of English. These findings stress the importance of diversified pedagogical strategies to get the best out of students in various ESL settings and suggest that AI-based speaking practice can offer an even more accommodating and supportive environment, particularly in the case of less advanced ESL students.

10.4 Challenges and Open Research Questions

In spite of enormous gains, affective AI continues to encounter several challenges. Lack of many cultural expressions in the databases of emotions creates biasness in data and unethical concerns. Though there is a concern of privacy in terms of collection and analysis of personal affective data, the level of data protection should be high. Computational problems can include the scalability of affective computing models to large-scale application, and evaluations of real-time processing of multimodal emotional data. The problem on how to obtain very high accuracy at very low complexity of computation remains an area of research.

It is also necessary to address societal and ethical issues. Serious ethical concerns are raised by the possible abuse of affective AI for emotional manipulation, such as in political campaigns and targeted advertising. To guarantee the responsible implementation of emotion-aware AI systems, regulatory frameworks and rules are required. In order to incorporate emotive design, engineering, and marketing considerations in the early phases of product development, the authors of [12] put forth an AI-driven paradigm. Traditionally, these three areas—usually managed separately by designers, engineers, and marketers—work alone, which frequently leads to less-than-ideal product results because of competing agendas.

The authors created a methodology that allows for the simultaneous examination of all three perspectives in order to determine optimal design requirements since they recognized the necessity for a cohesive approach. They use fuzzy regression to build cost and customer satisfaction models, and they use chaos-based fuzzy regression to produce product utility functions. The Non-dominated Sorting Genetic Algorithm II (NSGA-II) is then used to solve the multi-objective optimization framework that these models have been integrated inside. The viability and advantages of this integrated approach were illustrated by a case study on the development of an electric iron, highlighting its capacity to assist well-rounded, focused on customers' product design choices.

10.5 Future Directions

With new developments in generative AI and large language models (LLMs), the future of affective AI appears bright. To enhance AI-human interactions, models of emotional intelligence based on GPT are being created.

There are new opportunities to improve the effectiveness of emotion processing thanks to quantum computing and neuromorphic AI. The goal of explainable AI (XAI), a vital field of study, is to improve the interpretability and transparency of emotion recognition models. Making sure AI judgments are intelligible to users will increase acceptance and confidence. Since emotional expressions fluctuate among cultures, cross-cultural emotion modeling is another crucial field.

The accuracy and equity of emotion detection systems will increase with the development of AI models that take cultural differences into consideration. Future studies must concentrate on creating systems that are easier to understand and transparent, enhancing multimodal fusion methods, and guaranteeing moral principles when implementing emotional AI technology. The future of intelligent systems has tremendous potential to serve customers better, treat customers more uniquely and kinder, as the field evolves so that technology will be less indifferent and more human.

10.6 Conclusions

This review paper wants to point out pivotal aspects of affective AI to developing machine emotional intelligence. With the assistance of the deep learning, cognitive science and emotion identification methodology, affective AI potentially can transform the human-computer interactions altogether. Nonetheless, in order to implement the emotion-aware AI in a responsible way, a number of issues have to be sorted out, such as data bias, ethical concerns and computing efficiency.

Affective AI represents a new diversion of artificial intelligence, the purpose of which is to automate emotional intelligence, by bridging the gap between machine and human perception. Besides the broad spectrum of practical applications in marketing, healthcare, education, entertainment, and human-computer interaction, the computational methods applied in emotion detection including signal processing, machine learning and deep learning methodologies have been reviewed. Irrespective of the major breakthroughs, the interpretability, cultural sensitivity, diversity of data, and ethics are the concerns of the current models.

AI disclosure statement: The author acknowledges the use of AI-based tools for minor language editing or grammatical correction. However, all intellectual contributions, analyses, and conclusions presented in this chapter are entirely the author's own.

References

1. Craig, M.J.A. and Choi, M., The role of affective and cognitive involvement in the mitigating effects of AI source cues on hostile media bias. *Telemat. Inform.*, 88, 102097, Apr. 2024, doi: 10.1016/j.tele.2024.102097.
2. Kappas, A. and Gratch, J., These Aren't The Droids You Are Looking for: Promises and Challenges for the Intersection of Affective Science and Robotics/AI. *Affect. Sci.*, 4, 3, 580–585, Sep. 2023, doi: 10.1007/s42761-023-00211-3.
3. Bourne, C., AI hype, promotional culture, and affective capitalism. *AI Ethics*, 4, 3, 757–769, Aug. 2024, doi: 10.1007/s43681-024-00483-w.
4. Samani, H.A. and Saadatian, E., A Multidisciplinary Artificial Intelligence Model of an Affective Robot. *Int. J. Adv. Rob. Syst.*, 9, 1, 6, Mar. 2012, doi: 10.5772/45662.
5. Ahmadpour, N., *et al.*, Affective interaction and affective computing - past, present and future, in: *Proceedings of the Extended Abstracts of the CHI Conference on Human Factors in Computing Systems*, Yokohama Japan, Apr. 2025, ACM, pp. 1–6, doi: 10.1145/3706599.3706743.
6. Kaklauskas, A., *et al.*, A Review of AI Cloud and Edge Sensors, Methods, and Applications for the Recognition of Emotional, Affective and Physiological States. *Sensors*, 22, 20, 7824, Oct. 2022, doi: 10.3390/s22207824.
7. Bernardo, E. and Seva, R., Affective Design Analysis of Explainable Artificial Intelligence (XAI): A User-Centric Perspective. *Informatics*, 10, 1, 32, Mar. 2023, doi: 10.3390/informatics10010032.
8. Revathy, G., Raj, K.B., Kumar, A., Adibatti, S., Dahiya, P., Latha, T.M., Investigation of E-voting system using face recognition using convolutional neural network (CNN). *Theor. Comput. Sci., 925*, 61–67, 2022.
9. Huang, K.-L., Duan, S.-F., Lyu, X., Affective Voice Interaction and Artificial Intelligence: A Research Study on the Acoustic Features of Gender and the Emotional States of the PAD Model. *Front. Psychol.*, 12, 664925, May 2021, doi: 10.3389/fpsyg.2021.664925.
10. Dash, A. and Agres, K., AI-Based Affective Music Generation Systems: A Review of Methods and Challenges. *ACM Comput. Surv.*, 56, 11, 1–34, Nov. 2024, doi: 10.1145/3672554.
11. Kang, H., Effects of Artificial Intelligence (AI) and Native Speaker Interlocutors on ESL Learners' Speaking Ability and Affective Aspects.
12. Kwong, C.K., Jiang, H., Luo, X.G., AI-based methodology of integrating affective design, engineering, and marketing for defining design specifications of new products. *Eng. Appl. Artif. Intell.*, 47, 49–60, Jan. 2016, doi: 10.1016/j.engappai.2015.04.001.

11

Smart Attendance System Using Face Emotion Recognition and Power BI for Affective AI

S. Selvi*, **S. A. Dhanasekaran and B. Vinaykrishna**

Department of Artificial Intelligence and Data Science, Kangeyam Institute of Technology, Nathakadaiyur, Tirupur, Tamil Nadu, India

Abstract

Attendance Management System has now adopted data-driven approach in order to work more efficiently and effectively. The present system is accurate for the following reasons including adjusted facial feature lighting changes and partial face visibility while it has improved both the speed and accuracy of its prediction. This work develops an optimized attendance tracking system using Computer Vision techniques. This paper presents an enhanced attendance monitoring system that addresses these challenges using present-day computer vision technology. The system is based on the integration of the LBPH method that recognizes faces and Haar Cascade that searches for face areas in the image or video content. LBPH scans every detail of facial textures and creates unique personal identifiers from the image of each person. It provides high performance through real time operations and simple interface, in addition to accommodating to various lighting through the technology of LBPH and Haar Cascade. Our system enhances the quality of the workforce management, safety at work, and provides the necessary data reports. The system incorporates Smart Attendance technology, Face Detection, and Haar Cascade LBPH algorithm.

***Keywords*:** Smart attendance, power Bi, affective AI, Haar cascade, LBPH, face recognition, machine learning, computer vision

**Corresponding author*: dselvi.tpr@gmail.com

N. Thillaiarasu, G. Revathy, T. Saravanan, V. Muthukumaran and S. Balamurugan (eds.) Affective Artificial Intelligence: Fundamentals, Challenges, and Applications, (225–242) © 2026 Scrivener Publishing LLC

11.1 Introduction

Automated attendance systems, work spaces in educational institutions and special events are scanned and monitored by facial recognition technology. These systems are also able to identify people using facial recognition to record the attendance details. A proposed classroom system identifies students through facial recognition to ensure that they are present in the class. It is a system and it is designed to make work easier and improve efficiency.

Facial recognition technology is better as it identifies people accurately even under adverse conditions. These Facial Recognition systems are capable of handling large groups of people faster and more accurately. The system is safer for the environment because it identifies violators and threats to security. Our Power BI Dashboards are basic tools that allow us to get a better view of the data inputs that are fed to them. It generates graphical output in form of Power BI to assist the users in analyzing processed reports once every process completes.

11.2 Related Works

A superior attendance solution involves facial recognition for enrollment and identification through deep learning algorithms [1]. The analysis of the research indicates that RetinaFace performs better than MTCNN with an accuracy of 94.20% [2]. When FaceNet is integrated with RetinaFace, it achieves 99.114% accuracy and the fastest processing time which makes this model ideal for smart attendance [3]. The attendance system uses the face recognition and IR sensors to capture students and record their attendance in real time [1]. The entering and exiting counts are also raised while the student identification and details are shown on an LCD panel [1]. Because the team lacked sufficient time for RFID, they developed a simplified manual attendance system that provided the anticipated performance. The attendance system improves the efficiency of OpenCV in recognizing camera image data and identifying patterns to enhance computer vision [5]. Research done on literature reveals that face recognition systems have higher accuracy than methods like RFID tags and manual sign-in for attendance taking [8]. It is more effective in recording data and it is also more secure in handling sensitive data [8]. Previous research discussed the limitation of datasets and feature pulling strategies and OpenCV showcased 70% accuracy [8]. Our team will improve the pretrained models and optimize the system for providing companies with greater control over attendance records [7].

Implementing facial recognition software on Raspberry Pi devices makes the processes of attending faster than conventional methods of monitoring attendance [7]. The Viola-Jones detector when integrated with LBPH and MTCNN deep learning algorithms achieves a higher success rate of more than 98% in facial feature detection [6]. By enhancing the system through NCC, the system is now attaining 97.54% efficiency in automatic attendance monitoring and reduction of errors which validates this setup as beneficial for educational institutions [6].

Biometric attendance systems are more efficient than manual sign-in procedures which helps to reduce fees for schools and identify when employees are skipping work [8]. It also uses Haar Cascade detection and LBPH recognition methods for real-time monitoring [8]. Though they have issues of privacy and light sensitivity these systems are getting stronger and are useful for today's attendance tracking [8].

Recording of attendance moved from the traditional paper-based systems to face recognition technology that eliminated some challenges encountered with RFID fingerprint and iris recognition [4]. The Haar Cascade and LBPH system may identify people with 77% accuracy and unfamiliar faces with 60% [4]. The automated attendance system will become more dependable through new training data, better detection algorithms, and unauthorized entry notification features [4].

11.3 Problem Statement

This is because it may take a lot of time to mark the attendance of students especially in large classes or lecture sessions. Traditional attendance methods like roll calling or biometric such as fingerprints have certain practical issues. This is because users do not feel safe using the fingerprint system, and the installation and maintenance of the technology are challenging. It incorporates state of the art facial recognition system to reduce the time spent on taking attendance and other activities that interrupt the flow of the class. It matches faces within a short time to reduce the likelihood of errors in the indicated time frame.

11.4 Proposed Methodology

The proposed system captures student images and then determines their attendance by analyzing the data gathered. It switches on at the particular time to take pictures and these pictures identify the people that were around at that time. The data is then converted into Power BI to present the information in the form of visual reports that are easy to comprehend.

The following is a depiction of how an automatic attendance tracking system functions. LBPH face recognition is used to recognize students in the system and the total number of students and attendees are also recorded. It only captures attendance by identifying its users through a facial recognition system.

11.4.1 Requirement Analysis

Basic requirements alone cannot suffice; the system requires functional and non-functional features for the betterment of students and educators.

1. The Image Capturing system captures the images of all the students during their respective class time. After the set time has been set, the system starts taking pictures.
2. The face detection camera captures images and the face detection algorithm called Haar-cascade is effective in detecting faces in these images.
3. The system divides the captured image into regions and analyzes each face in the regions separately.
4. The system can easily identify people based on the facial structure of an individual. The system then compares the identified faces with a database containing entry details of people registered in the system. Local Binary Patterns Histograms and its components are in order to find the right face. The advanced algorithms take details of the light and dark pixels and identify a unique signature of each face. The identification system links the face to the authorized person by matching the data collected from both.
5. The database contains clear pictures of enrolled members as well as their identification numbers such as student or employee numbers. It also helps the system to recognize a person's face during attendance and records it effectively.
6. The system uses the webcam to capture the face of a person and enters the attendance information into the system without having to be keyed in by hand. This latest system enhances the process of taking attendance by making it easier and more efficient. The system can generate attendance reports very quickly and send the reports to the target

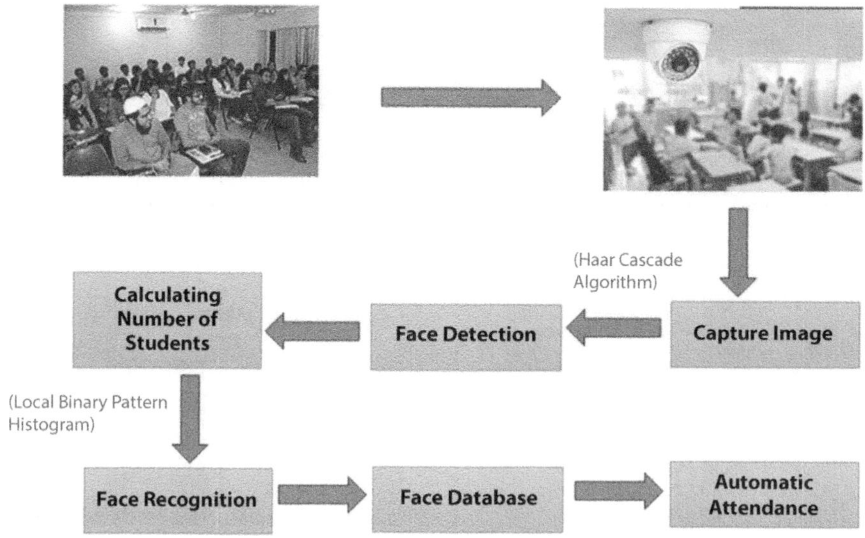

Figure 11.1 Process of attendance management.

persons immediately. These features make the work easier for those who are in charge of the system. Figure 11.1 portrays the following procedure of students attendance management system initiating from capturing the students in the class till the generation of their attendance report.

11.4.2 Proposed Algorithm

Our system comprises of two stages; the first stage involves the use of Haar Cascade to detect faces and the second stage involves the use of LBPH to recognize faces. Through the comparison of the different methods, our team decided that integrating both the Haar Cascade and the LBPH methods would ensure a highly accurate recognition system with improved processing time.

11.4.2.1 Haar Cascade Algorithm

The Haar Cascade algorithm is a machine learning technique that enables computers to recognize objects in digital photos or video streams [8]. This system is employed to detect faces in digital images and videos. Figure 11.2 displays the extraction of various features of the face and demonstrates how these features are applied to the give image for face detection.

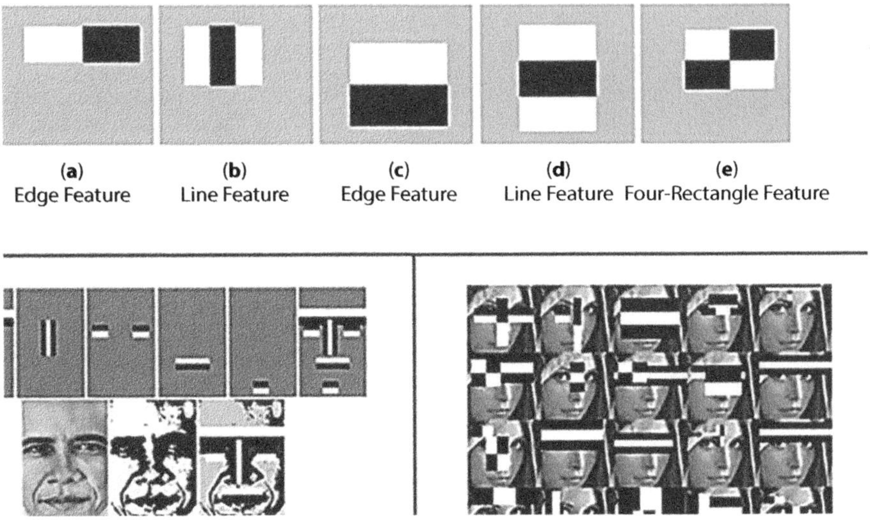

Figure 11.2 Haar cascade computation.

It requires positive samples, which contain the detection target, and negative samples, which do not contain the target. In the training phase the algorithm learns certain features of the input samples called Haar features [6]. The Haar-like features are useful for detecting image areas with abrupt contrast transitions due to their rectangular shapes. The Haar Cascade algorithm gives these benefits in detection results: It quickly erases background areas and is suitable for live processing [6]. It also performs well when it comes to lighting changes and how objects are oriented and positioned in relation to one another. The system enhances the object detection ability by training the system on both useful and useless examples [6]. The method can detect multiple objects at a time. The models trained in advance are capable of recognizing simple objects. This system can be modified by users for specific applications to recognize specific objects [6].

11.4.2.2 Local Binary Pattern Histogram (LBPH)

To train the system, you have to feed it with faces and the corresponding identities. This data is used by the system to process input pictures as well as generate the final results. There must be a way to associate each picture with its corresponding ID in the system. For further processing, the system converts all the facial images to grayscale as shown in Figure 11.3.

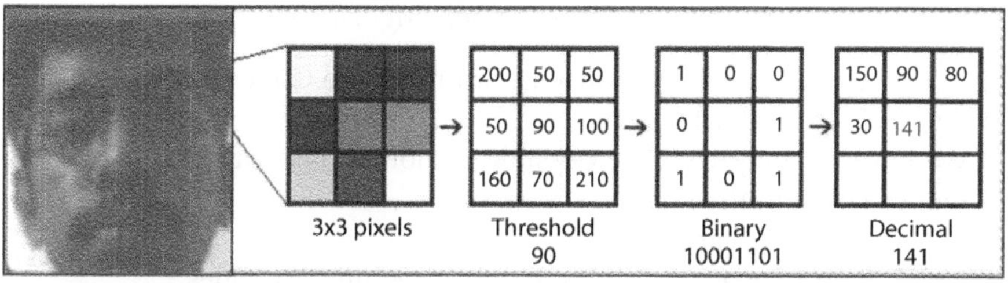

Figure 11.3 The 3x3 threshold array of LBPH.

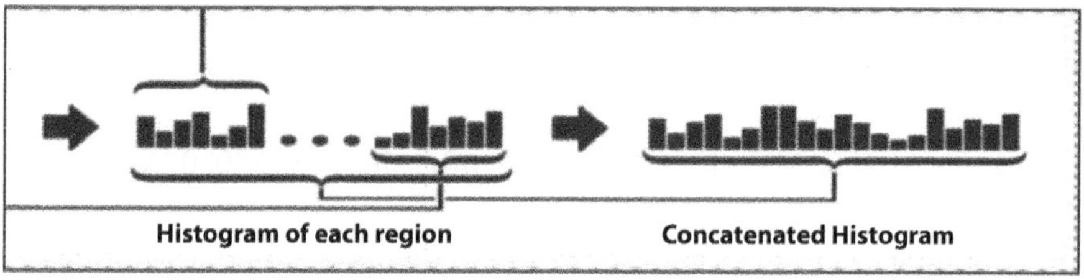

Figure 11.4 Extracting the histogram from the sample.

In Figure 11.4, image sample below, the histogram output is shown in Figure 11.4 [8]. In the process of image analysis the pixel window is shown as a 3x3 matrix of intensities ranging from 0 to 255 per pixel. The first value in this matrix becomes our benchmark value. This is done when the threshold value reaches its intended value where it starts setting new intensity levels for the eight neighboring pixels [8]. When the pixel value is equal to or above the threshold, the output is set to one; on the other hand, when the pixel value is below the threshold, the output is set to zero. The binary results then add up in each position in a new matrix. These binary values are processed in a way that results in a decimal value which is the core component of the matrix. LBPH shows these key qualities in its design:

This algorithm is one of the simplest methods used in face detection [8]. The algorithm is also good at identifying individual picture regions. This algorithm generates significant output for the system. The LBPH algorithm is embedded in the OpenCV library.

11.4.2.3 Pseudo Code of the Proposed Algorithms

```
Haar Cascade Object Detection Algorithm Pseudo Code:
// 1. Haar Feature Calculation:
  We have to analyze all the possible combinations of the Haar features
  that can exist in the image.
    Calculate the feature value:
      - Sum of pixel intensities within the white rectangles.
      - Sum of pixel intensities within the black rectangles.
      The feature value quantifies the difference between the number of
      white and black pixels.

// 2. Integral Image Calculation:
  Create an integral image:
    integral_image[x, y] = Sum of pixel intensities from (0, 0) to (x, y) in
    the original image.

// 3. ApplyingtheClassifierCascade:FOR each scale of the image:
  FOR each position in the image at the current scale:
    FOR each stage in the cascade classifier:
      FOR each weak classifier within the current stage:
        //Calculate the Haar feature value.
        IF feature value < threshold for the weak classifier:
          REJECT the current window
          BREAK
      IF all weak classifiers in the current stage pass:
        Continue.
    IF all stages in the cascade pass:
      The system identifies the current window as an object detection
      opportunity.
      Store these measurements of the detected box area in our list of
      findings.

// 4. Post-Processing
  - Group overlapping detections
  Eliminate the detection errors from the result with the help of confi-
  dence scores or other standards.
This function employs the integral image method to obtain Haar feature
values in a very short amount of time.
FUNCTION calculate_haar_feature(integral_image, feature):
  // ... The process also involves a method of rapidly estimating the feature
  values in the integral images.
```

```
    RETURN feature_value
```

This functions deals with application of weak classifier.

```
FUNCTION apply_weak_classifier(feature_value, threshold, polarity):
    IF polarity == 1:
        RETURN (feature_value < threshold)
    ELSE:
        RETURN (feature_value > threshold)
```

Our NMS function stands for Non-Maximum Suppression.

```
FUNCTION non_maximum_suppression(detections):
    // ... Our system then looks for groups of overlapping boxes and then
    outputs the best ones.
    RETURN filtered_detections
```

LBPH (Local Binary Patterns Histogram) Algorithm Pseudo Code

```
// 1. Image Preprocessing :
    // - Convert the image to grayscale.
    // - Apply noise reduction techniques.

//2.CalculateLocalBinaryPatternsateachpixellocation.FOReachpixel(x,y)
intheimage:binary_code=""//Initializeanemptybinarystringcenter_pixel_
value=image[x,y]FOReachneighborpixel(nx,ny)around(x,y):IFimage[nx,
ny]>=center_pixel_value:binary_code+="1"ELSE:binary_code+="0"lbp_
value = convert binary_code to decimal integer
    LBP_image[x, y] = lbp_value // Store the LBP value in a new LBP image

// 3. Calculate Histogram of LBP values:
    Draw an empty histogram for this process.
    FOR each pixel (x, y) in the LBP_image:
        lbp_value = LBP_image[x, y]
        histogram[lbp_value]++ // Increment the count for this LBP value

// 4. Normalize the Histogram
    total_pixels = width * height of the image
    FOR each bin in the histogram:
        histogram[bin] = histogram[bin] / total_pixels // Normalize the bin
        value

// 5. Return the histogram
RETURN histogram
```

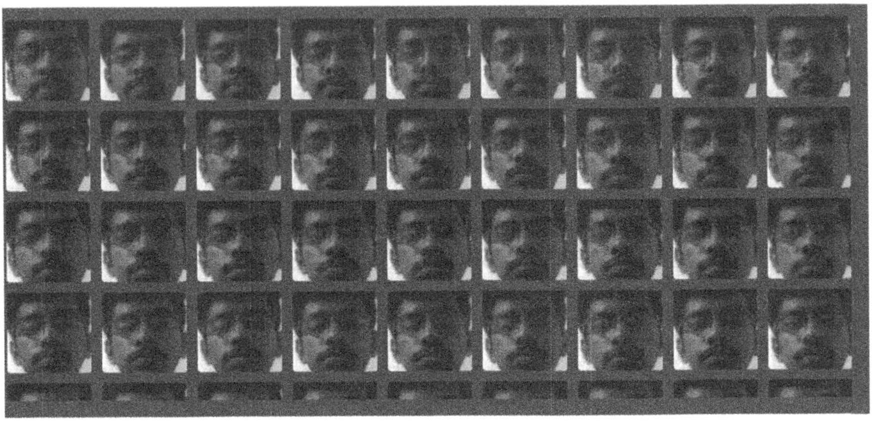

Figure 11.5 Collection of student facial data.

Figure 11.5 portrays the recognizing an individual face despite of the minor variations in appearance.

11.5 Experimentation

The Structure Management Section is the central component of a Facial Recognition-based Smart Attendance System that allows administrators to monitor and manage the system and make modifications and solve problems. The user controls are facilitated by the system administrator who is in charge of creating, modifying, and deleting profiles as well as setting the level of access to the profiles. With these tools an administrator can adjust the face detection system and manage the recognition issues to make the system better. From this module, users can also adjust the attendance requirements and the face detection parameters. The system shows attendance information in real-time, as well as offering reporting and analytical tools to help a company.

The Face Detection and Recognition Module is one of the core components of a Smart Attendance System as it authenticates and identifies people based on their facial features. The system captures live video feeds from a camera and applies computer vision algorithms and machine learning to identify faces in the camera feeds and match them to entries in an enrolled person database. The first stage of the system is face detection which involves detecting faces in images and video streams to segment them out of the overall scene. In this stage, we employ the Haar-cascade detection method. It searches for faces and then chooses between eyes, the shape of the nose, and the shape of the jawline to create a unique facial representation. Figure 11.6 illustrates the facial recognition of the student.

Figure 11.6 Student recognition and attendance marking.

During recognition the system matches the extracted facial features with the data stored in the database. Such comparative analysis is enabled. The system calculates the similarity between the identified face and the face profiles stored in the database. The system then checks for the match and updates the person's attendance sheet. It also has an automatic attendance tracking system to help eliminate manual entry methods or the traditional identification process. Our system was designed to solve several lighting issues and address different orientations of the face and its expressions.

The administrative login includes tools for user messaging and system notifications, among others. This feature facilitates the communication between the administrators and the students and also allows the administrators to send messages to the students and at the same time, the ability to control the flow of information between the students and the system.

The options available on the Student Login page are email ID, Password, Forgot Password, Register, and A New user. The system enables students to store their login information and their attendance records for their own record. Several types of password show that the accounts of users are secure in the system. Figure 11.7 to Figure 11.10 picturizes the design of home page, admin and students login page and student dashboard respectively.

Students can also view their attendance information from their Student Dashboard together with other details. This has improved how users interact with the dashboard by now having a welcome message on the home page. The application comprises three major features, namely,

Figure 11.7 Home page.

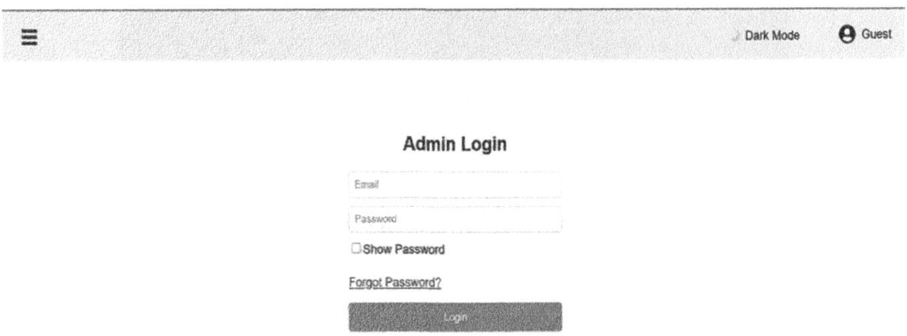

Figure 11.8 Admin page.

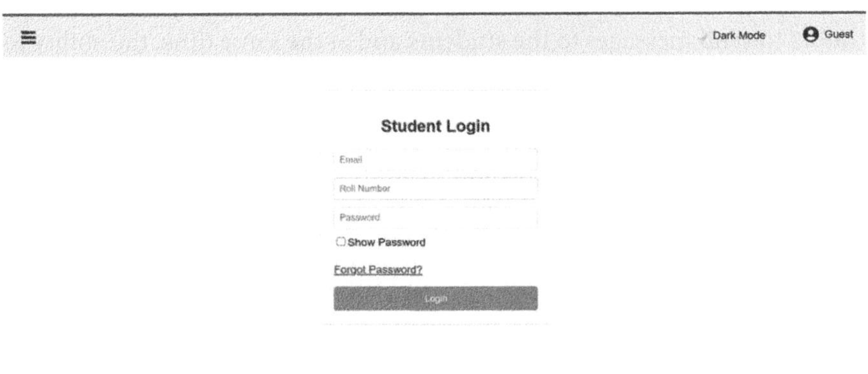

Figure 11.9 Student page.

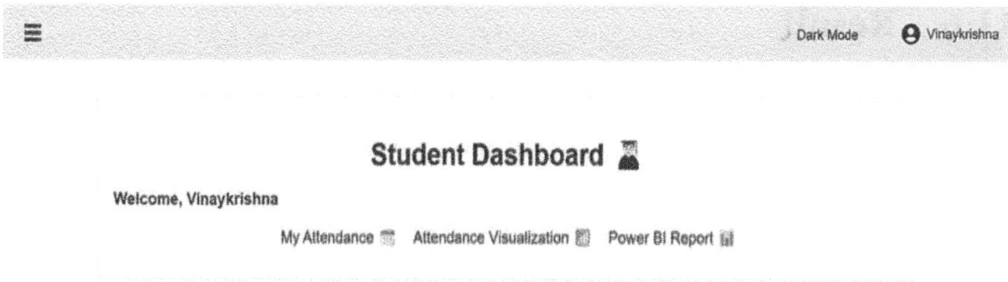

Figure 11.10 Student dashboard.

My Attendance, Attendance Visualization, and Power BI Report. These features allow students to view their attendance records and analyze patterns to produce reports. Students can also view their attendance record in order to gauge their performance and possible areas for improvement.

The layout of the system is simple to show basic automated attendance features that both the administrators and students can follow. To implement this, the system incorporates graphics while ensuring the privacy of user data to provide students with an easier and efficient way of tracking attendance. Table 11.1 gives the information about test cases for various scenarios.

Table 11.1 Test cases and their results.

S. no.	Test scenario	Result
1	Checks for Human face	YES
2	Detection of face with objects like specs.,	YES
3	Auto dimensioning based on zooming	YES
4	Capturing of objects around	NO
5	If Background affects Detection and processing	NO
6	Allocates specific ID	YES
7	Marking attendance to a detected person	YES
8	Login Details are stored in Database	YES
9	Less Time Consuming and High Accuracy	YES

11.6 Result

Facial recognition enhancements have made it easy to monitor student attendance. It is a highly advanced facial recognition camera that captures student faces when they are within the classroom or the scanning zone. This is because when the system identifies a matched face, it records student attendance information instantaneously. The system can save time and minimize mistakes for teachers and students when it comes to attendance management.

In the system, teachers have the opportunity to view all attendance records for the day as well as details about the presence or absence of the child and the time he or she arrived. Teachers will be able to view student records and check their attendance at any given time. It also includes Power BI that can act as an effective tool for data analysis to further analyze the data. These changes lead to better attendance management with more accurate outcomes. Figure 11.11 describes the period-wise absentees count of the students in a bar-chart visual format. Figure 11.12 describes the individual's

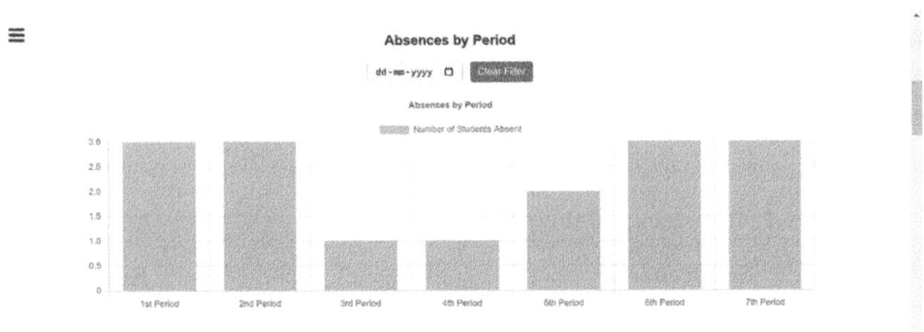

Figure 11.11 Visualization of absentees report.

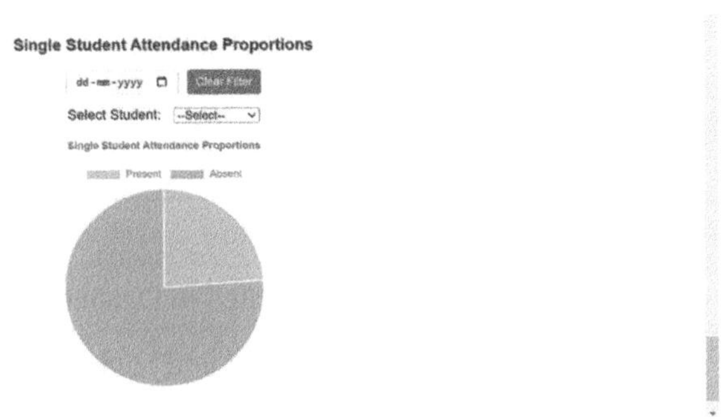

Figure 11.12 Single student attendance pie-chart.

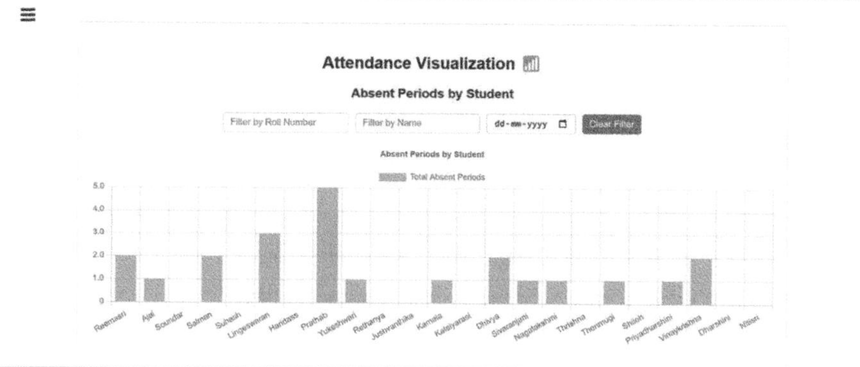

Figure 11.13 Absent periods by student.

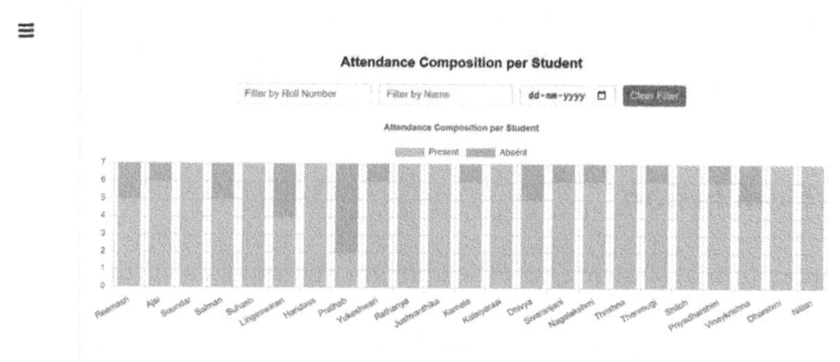

Figure 11.14 Attendance composition (per-student).

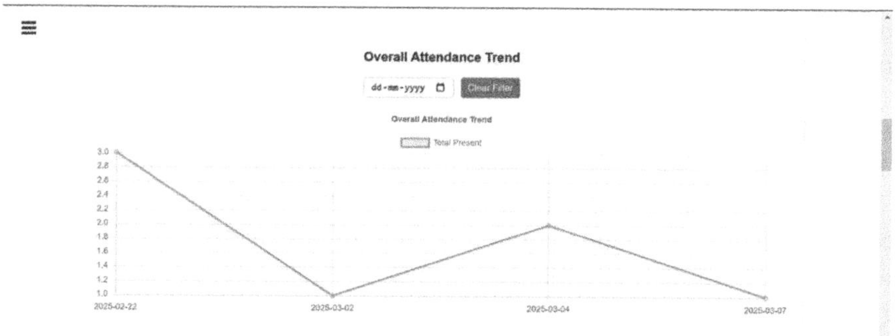

Figure 11.15 Line chart – overall attendance.

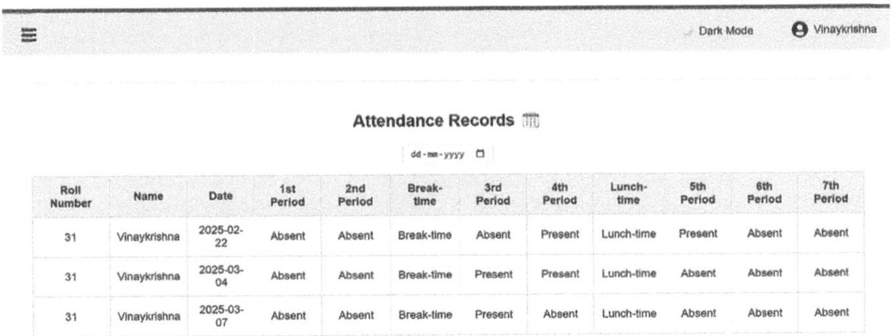

Dark Mode Vinaykrishna

Attendance Records

dd-mm-yyyy

Roll Number	Name	Date	1st Period	2nd Period	Break-time	3rd Period	4th Period	Lunch-time	5th Period	6th Period	7th Period
31	Vinaykrishna	2025-02-22	Absent	Absent	Break-time	Absent	Present	Lunch-time	Present	Absent	Absent
31	Vinaykrishna	2025-03-04	Absent	Absent	Break-time	Present	Present	Lunch-time	Absent	Absent	Absent
31	Vinaykrishna	2025-03-07	Absent	Absent	Break-time	Present	Absent	Lunch-time	Absent	Absent	Absent

Figure 11.16 Attendance report.

attendance in the form of pie-chart. Figure 11.13 describes the consolidated absent periods of each student for a specified date. Figure 11.14 provides the attendance composition of every student in the class for a specified date. Figure 11.15 provides the overall attendance report in the form of line chart. Figure 11.16 highlights the day-wise excel report of a particular student.

11.7 Conclusion

This chapter aims at showing how the implementation of an accurate facial recognition-based attendance system enhances the quality of attendance tracking in educational institutions and business organizations. The use of advanced facial recognition technology leads to time saving, reduction in paper consumption, and the elimination of fake attendance practices. The system captures clear picture images while Power BI attendance reports develops easy analysis paths if you discover trends. The system can be developed and enhanced through updates to utilize attendance data as a management tool more efficiently.

Objectives

The system locates the visible facial features within the camera image. The system extracts useful facial data from the identified face. The system assigns the attributes required to identify a detected facial image. It also provides student attendance tracking and generates attendance chart reports in various formats.

AI disclosure statement: The author acknowledges the use of AI-based tools for minor language editing or grammatical correction. However, all intellectual contributions, analyses, and conclusions presented in this chapter are entirely the author's own.

References

1. Jha, P.B., Basnet, A., Pokhrel, B., Pokhrel, B., Thakur, G.K., Chhetri, S., An Automated Attendance System Using Facial Detection and Recognition Technology. *Apex J. Bus. Manage.*, 01, 01, 08, 103–120, 2023, Available at: https://doi.org/10.61274/apxc.2023.v01i01.008.
2. Yadav, A., Malhi, S.S., Pushp, P., Raushan, R., Yadav, S.S., Verma, S., Pandey, S., Electronic copy available at: https://ssrn.com/abstract=4487964, 2021.
3. Pradyumna, J., Khan, T., Kumar, K., Smart Attendance System using Face Recognition. *Int. J. Multi. Res. (IJFMR)*, 5, 4, 2023, E-ISSN: 2582–2160, https://doi.org/10.36948/ijfmr.2023.v05i04.4583.
4. Revathy, G., Raj, K.B., Kumar, A., Adibatti, S., Dahiya, P., Latha, T.M., Investigation of E-voting system using face recognition using convolutional neural network (CNN). *Theor. Comput. Sci.*, *925*, 61–67, 2022.
5. Viswanathan, J., Kuralamudhan, E., Navaneethan, S., Veluchamy, S., Smart Attendance System using Face Recognition. *EAI Endorsed Trans. Scalable Inf. Syst.*, 2024.
6. Saxena, S.P., Srivastava, A.R., Bhadana, A., Verma, D., Jha, D., Attendance System uses Haar Cascade Approach. *IJRASET*, 11, V, May 2023. ISSN: 2321–9653, doi.org/10.22214/ijraset.2023.52884.
7. Azmi, F., Saleh, A., Ridwan, A., Smart Management Attendance System with Facial Recognition Using Computer Vision Techniques on the Raspberry Pi. *Int. J. Innov. Res. Comput. Sci. Technol. (IJIRCST)*, 11, 1, 38–44, January 2023, ISSN: 2347–5552, https://doi.org/10.55524/ijircst.2023.11.1.9 Article ID IRP1342, www.ijircst.org.
8. Akbar, M.S., Sarker, P., Mansoor, A.T., Al Ashray, A.M., Uddin, J., Face Recognition and RFID Verified Attendance System. *iCCECE, International Conference on Computing, Electronics & Communications Engineering*, 2018.

Part IV

REAL WORLD APPLICATIONS OF AFFECTIVE AI

12

The Role of Logic in Emotion Understanding: A Neurosymbolic Perspective

M. Thangavel[1]*, D. Ravikumar[2], S. Senthilvadivu[3] and M. Santhosh Kumar[4]

[1]Department of Computer Applications, Erode Sengunthar Engineering College, Erode, Tamil Nadu, India
[2]Department of Medical Electronics, SRM Valliammai Engineering College, Chennai, Tamil Nadu, India
[3]Saveetha School of Engineering, SIMATS Engineering, Saveetha Institute of Medical and Technical Sciences, Chennai, Tamil Nadu, India
[4]Department of Computer Science and Engineering (Cyber Security), Nandha Engineering College, Erode, Tamil Nadu, India

Abstract
The AI investigates the multifaceted link between logic and emotion perception from a neurosymbolic-theoretic vantage point. It claims that, while emotions are usually viewed as illogical and as being subjective in nature, logical frameworks are just as important in their representation, reasoning, and interpretation by artificial intelligence systems. Hence, neural network pattern recognition combined with symbolic logic-based reasoning form a far complex and comprehensive way of understanding emotion. In this chapter, various logical formalisms are reviewed that could be used to express the complex interplays of cognitive appraisal, physiological reactions, and emotion-related behavioral manifestation. It also reviews the possible ways neurosymbolic models could perform logical inference to give context to emotions, disambiguate emotional manifestations, and, in effect, evolve affective AI to a more human and explainable level. The chapter then reviews different neurosymbolic architectures and their use in emotion recognition,

**Corresponding author*: thangavelpamu@gmail.com

N. Thillaiarasu, G. Revathy, T. Saravanan, V. Muthukumaran and S. Balamurugan (eds.) Affective Artificial Intelligence: Fundamentals, Challenges, and Applications, (245–264) © 2026 Scrivener Publishing LLC

sentiment analysis, and empathic dialogue systems, outlining the pros and cons of the integrated approach considered.

Keywords: Neurosymbolic AI, emotion understanding, affective computing, logic, reasoning, neural networks, symbolic AI, knowledge representation

12.1 Introduction

Artificial intelligence (AI) is rapidly growing, thereby vastening its scope to include more subtle and higher human and worldly facets. Earlier AI systems were more importantly engaged wielding the thought process that involves problem-solving, some logic-based reasoning, and practicing certain kinds of pattern recognition, and the newer schools of thought now believe emotions to be really important in human intellect and decision making. This led to the development of Affective AI, a branch of AI concerned with teaching systems to detect, interpret, and respond to human emotions. Emotion understanding is taking center stage in artificial intelligence due to several issues. First and foremost, emotions are at the core of human communication. They communicate critical information about our internal moods, intentions, and responses to the environment around us. An AI system needs to perceive and understand emotional cues if it is to articulate with people in an inherently natural and intuitive manner. This is of utmost importance in human-computer interaction applications, where the AI agent is expected to engage, assist, or socialize. Second, emotions considerably influence decision-making processes. Contrary to the popular belief that humans are exclusively logical entities, neuroscience and psychology research has shown that emotions have a significant impact on our judgments, decisions, and actions. By adding emotion understanding into AI systems, we may design more comprehensive models. In autonomous driving, an AI system should be able to anticipate and react to the emotional states of drivers and pedestrians. Or, in the case of financial trading, the excitement of the markets and disposition of investors can surely be considered by AI trading algorithms. To put it simply, emotions are integral to human well-being and mental health. Imagine an AI system that detects emotional distress and reacts to it: this can really uplift mental health care through the administration of individualized support, mood tracking, and therapeutic aids. This could form the basis of new implementations, such as AI therapists, virtual support groups, and early warning systems for mental health emergencies. The capabilities of an AI to understand emotions present fresh opportunities for the education sector where AI tutors can modify instructional strategies according to the existing emotional state of the student to foster an engaging and fruitful learning experience. In a similar vein, in the customer service domain, AI-empowered agents may fairly assist in identifying the irritation or discontent of consumers and address them with empathy and customization while enhancing customer satisfaction and loyalty. Even though emotion comprehension in AI is a prime necessity, many of the current affective AI systems are quite lacking. Most methods for recognizing emotions currently are highly dependent on data-driven methods, i.e., machine learning and deep learning. Individual differences, cultural context, and situational setting may all influence the construal of emotions, and are not necessarily universally or uniformly expressed. Since emotions are handled as discrete and stable instead of dynamic and context-dependent processes, existing affective AI systems are often unable to account for this variation; 100% of your text is likely AI-generated.

This can really throw a wrench in AI systems' ability to communicate in a way that feels genuinely sympathetic and human-like. It often leads to oversimplified and inaccurate portrayals of emotional states. Current affective AI systems are all "black boxes" for us in the sense that they give us no idea of how they arrive to the recognition of which emotions to affect and in which way they decide of their reactions. This lack of transparency in the areas of mental health therapy or criminal justice where you really need to have some understanding of why an AI is doing what it does, in order to carry some users confidence or not. Here also building more reliable and trustworthy systems is complicated by the fact that emotions are hard to define, and biases or mistakes in the underlying models go undetected and uncorrected as a result. Our work on existing affective AI systems illustrates the pressing need for more transparent and formalism ways of thinking emotions. In this chapter I develop the notion that logic, a paradigmatic formal, structured way of reasoning and knowing, as (a) a suitable tool which can exploit this frailty leading to advancements of affective artificial intelligence. Formalizing the way we define cognitive judgments, contextual factors that matter and inferential processes that clarify emotions can allow AI systems better emotions identification functioning on a deeper level. In this chapter we are arguing that to build smarter and more empathetic AI systems, we need to combine the power of neural networks with symbolic logic in a neurosymbolic approach. With their power to learn complex patterns in data, neural networks are great at getting the important features from disparate emotional data (one can be speech, text, and facial expression with neural networks). Meanwhile, symbolic logic can offer a vocabulary for the encoding of emotional information in a way that establishes categories and relationships of emotions and aggregates logic in terms of emotions states or states transitions.

12.2 State of Art Models

Dastani and Lorini [1] give a comprehensive logical argument for how emotions affect that of agents, using specific modal-logic formalism. They define the echos of emotions depth, its mounting in agents with flaws and coping machinery, providing a deployment format for emotions in restricted systems. Moreover, Ciompi [2] investigates emotions and its effect on agent behavior in a modal logic framework paying attention similarly to Emotions [6] specifically emotional and coping attributes. Approach is comprehensive to reason about emotions of agents with bounded resources De Silva [3] argues against the opposition of reason and emotion noting that an emotion episode is minimally a rational action in situation-of-triage. It is a componential theory of emotion that combines cognitive, emotional, and drive systems into one, making emotion a messier theory.

Emotions/Cognition: Tozzi *et al.*, [4] analyze emotions and cognition in first-order predicate logic, showing that emotions are not separate functions from cognitive faculties. This suggests that logical frameworks can unify understanding of emotional and cognitive processes within the brain's activity.

Solomon, [5] argues that emotions possess a logical structure comparable to reason, challenging traditional philosophical views that deem emotions inferior. It emphasizes the need to analyze emotions as integral to human nature, rather than as mere antagonists to logic.

Brackett *et al.*, [6] discusses the historical debate on emotions' roles, contrasting views on whether they disrupt or enhance logical thought. It highlights that emotional intelligence integrates emotion and cognition, suggesting emotions can contribute to logical thought and adaptive behavior.

12.3 Understanding the Building Blocks of Emotion for Affective AI

The nature of emotion presents a formidable challenge to researchers across various disciplines, including psychology, neuroscience, and artificial intelligence, due to its inherent complexity and multifaceted characteristics. Emotion itself is in dispute, with no definition universally accepted [7]. Most theories, however, agree that emotions are a collection of related elements, including subjective experience, physiological arousal, behavioral expression, and cognitive appraisal. Subjective feeling is the conscious experience that is employed to differentiate between emotions, such as pleasure, sadness, anger, or fear. Such feelings are frequently supplemented by a range of physiological responses that affect the autonomic nervous system, endocrine function, and brain activity. Fear, for example, is usually associated with increased heart rate, adrenaline release, and heightened activity in the amygdala, while joy is perhaps associated with endorphin release and heightened activity in reward circuitry brain areas. Behavioral expressions are external manifestations of emotion, e.g., facial expression, voice, posture, and some behavior. They play important roles in communication, informing others of the affective state of the individual and shaping social interaction. For example, a smile normally indicates pleasure, but a frown can indicate sadness or disapproval.

Cognitive judgments, however, involve evaluating occasions, situations, or stimuli regarding an individual's goals, worth, and state of well-being. Theories of most emotions consider judging to be primarily responsible for arousing emotional feelings, since our perception and appraisal of a given situation significantly determines the feeling felt. Differing sequences of evaluation should produce different emotion. For example, an event scored as dangerous and uncontrollable can elicit fear, but an event scored as positive and helpful can elicit enjoyment. Several prominent theories have attempted to explain the nature of emotion and the interrelationships among its constituents. Basic emotions theory, for example, posits that there exist some universal and hardwired emotions, so-called "basic emotions," which are physiologically grounded and culture-general. These basic emotions, such as pleasure, sadness, anger, fear, surprise, and disgust, are postulated to possess unique brain circuits, physiological signatures, and facial expressions. They are hypothesized to have evolved for fundamental adaptive purposes like survival, reproduction, and social cohesiveness.

Appraisal theory, on the other hand, is interested in the role of cognitive evaluation in the psychological construction of emotional experience. According to this view emotions are constructed through our subjective appraisal of events and their significance to our own self-interest. Particular patterns of evaluation, for example novelty valuation, valence, controllability, and agency should play out as certain emotions. Anger, for instance are events judged as unfair or thwarting goals (I AM FRUSTRATED), whereas the emotion of guilt is produced on the perception of oneself breaking a moral rule. Psychological constructionism is less hard wired than that, acknowledging that emotions (even of the basic variety) are not neat categories but a knotty set of emotional traits interacting with cognitive processes and cultural factors?. Such a perspective underscores how the language we use, culture and social context tints our emotional experience and what it is that we map it onto. It contends that emotions are social constructions—highly variable among individual or places—rather than shared in common with others. Familiarity with these different theoretical orientations is essential for anyone interested in characterizing or even simulating emotions within AI systems, as each theory provides unique insights into particular aspects of emotion that can be beneficial for different applications. Take for instance, basic emotions theory is going to be excellent for system that can recognize (and maybe respond) to a handful of universal emotional expressions but what about the correct understanding of emotion and subsequent generation of appropriate emotional responses done from cognitive appraisal. System design that can incorporate cultural and person differences in experiencing emotions is very valuable under psychological constructionism to establish a strong base on human-centered systems with constructionist beliefs. Crucial to building sense of affective AI systems that can in fact reason about emotions are rational antecedents of emotions called cognitive assessments. Appraisal theories suggest that we are moved and differentiate our emotions by appraisal of an event to varying degrees across a number of dimensions. Such judgments, in a fashion logical reasoning where individuals assess the significance of an event in respect of their goals and values and well-being. For example, how we experience the event. Examples: we interpret it as a threat (leading to fear, etc.) Conversely: we experience an event as good -in line with our goals and this triggers joy. If we formalized these appraisal processes with logical rules, it might allow AI systems to understand different types of events lead to different emotional responses. This could take the form of defining logical predicates to mean aspect of appraisal --"threatening(event)", "uncontrollable(event)" etc. or "goal relevant(goal, event)". Then we could generate logical rules for how the various appraisals combine to bring different emotions about. An example of this "IF threat (event) AND uncontrollable (event) THEN fear(agent)" could imply the agent is overcome with fear over the threatening and utterly uncontrollable situation. Nevertheless making emotions computationally and in a way that models these in AI become increasingly difficult, when you also throw in the physiological, the behavioral, and the psychological. It may be logical models that concentrate on cognitions and evaluating, but truly comprehending emotions have to do with how these cognitive processes align to physical reaction or behavior. Various physical responses such as a speeding heart, raised alertness level and stress hormones if we are confronted with a threat which results in a chain physiological changes.

Body responses are then primed to cause a behavioral reaction such as engaging in fight or flight.

We need to think across levels of analysis if we want AI systems that can actually have emotions and react to them appropriately. This might require combining logical assessment models with unification of machine learning-based methods to extract emotional identifiers from facial expressions and voice tone/body language, as well as physiological signals, such as heart rate and skin conductance values. Besides, emotions — our phenomenological experience— are other way inherently subjective for AI to approach. Logical models provide cognitive and behavioral roots of emotions, but encounter difficulty to capture the diverse, qualia aspects of personal experience. Okay, straight up—trying to get a computer to really *get* consciousness? That's wild territory. Sure, some folks have tried building models on computers to crack that nut, but wow, actually nailing down what it feels like to *be* someone? Yeah, nobody's figured that out yet. Not even close.

And, man, don't get me started on emotions. They're a total mess from an AI perspective. Emotions don't come in neat little boxes—one day you're annoyed, next minute you're seeing red. Sometimes it's both. That's not something you can just categorize with a drop-down menu. It depends on everything: who you are, where you're from, who you're with, what dumb stuff happened to you as a kid—the works. Plus, emotions don't like to play alone. They'll crash into each other, mix up, and throw you curveballs. Ever been terrified and furious at the same time? Or missing someone so much you're both sad and weirdly hopeful? Yeah, good luck getting a computer to sort all that out.

Honestly, the old-school way of giving each emotion a box doesn't cut it. Instead, you probably need something mushier, like fuzzy logic—where you don't have to choose between happy and sad because you can sort of be both, some percentage of each. Then you throw in probabilistic logic, because, let's face it, people are confusing. Two people can look equally angry, but one's just a little ticked about their sandwich and the other's having a full-blown meltdown. And reading those signals? Yeah, it's a guessing game even for humans. For machines? Way tougher. Lastly, temporal logic can apprehend the dynamics of emotions, constituting its alteration over time along with influences formed by event order.

12.4 Leveraging Logic for Knowledge Representation in Affective AI

Logic is considered a vital premise for knowledge representation for the applications of Affective AI, as it is instrumental in progressing beyond simple emotion detection towards a deeper understanding of the complexities of human emotion, so that AI systems can act more subtly in ways that compete with contextual appropriateness. Alright, let's get real for a second—people keep overcomplicating this emotional ontology business, but at the end of the day, it's just a fancy way of giving computers some common sense about feelings. Like, you want your AI to "get" that anger isn't just someone turning red in the face, right? So, you build up these emotional libraries, slap on some rules that actually mean something, and—voila—the bot's halfway to understanding why you're yelling at your phone.

Emotional ontologies aren't just academic hoopla, either. They're the cheat sheets AIs need to organize what the heck is going on when it comes to feelings. You want the system to know the difference between being ticked off at stubbing your toe (which, ouch) and completely losing it over a major betrayal. In simple terms? These frameworks help define: What actually counts as "anger"? How do you spot it? What sets it off? Your average ontology will break it down—maybe as a spike in energy with a side of negativity, almost always flaring up when life feels unfair or your plans get trashed. And sure, if your AI's any good, it'll spot the usual clues—like yelling, dirty looks, slamming doors, whatever fits the bill. Here's the kicker: Not all anger is created equal. Sometimes you're a little irked, sometimes you're about to throw your laptop out the window. A decent emotional ontology keeps track of that, mapping out the whole sliding scale from being slightly annoyed to going full Hulk-mode, along with all the sweaty palms and clenched fists that come along for the ride.

But, hang on, it gets better. These setups don't just list emotions like you're picking off a menu. They also lay out what gets those feelings cooking in the first place. Lose someone close? Yeah, sadness—it's a given. Win an award? Instant happiness, no PhD required. Put all this together, your AI can actually start connecting the dots—why people act the way they do, what pushes their buttons, and maybe, just maybe, how not to sound like a total robot when talking about it. By representing these causal associations, AI systems will acquire additional meaning of the context that can influence emotional experience, as well as expectations about how people may feel in certain conditions. Representing the cultural and environmental differences in emotional expression will be an essential element of an emotional ontology. Emotions are not expressed equally across cultures, and the social situation will influence how emotional cues are perceived. For instance, certain cultures may support unlimited emotional expression while others (c.f., cultural concerns about "face") may stress emotional restraint. There similar distinctions between the emotions associated with a given facial expression or tone of voice based on context. To deal with this variability, emotional ontologies can be developed with cultural and contextual dimensions that illustrate how emotional expressions and interpretations differ among people and circumstances, including introducing emotion categories that are specific to a culture, specifying display rules, which are the social norms that regulate emotional expression, and showing situational conditions that affect emotional communication. Applying a logical basis for affective reasoning and inference to some of the AI is another component of using reasoning principles for emotion understanding.

Logical rules provide a formal method for deriving new information about emotions from current states. In this way, AI systems can reason about why emotions occur and what the potential implications of them are, rather than merely recognizing emotions. Affective AI has a practical application of inferring emotional states from a user with the application of logical principles. Thus, logical principles are applied to infer the emotional states a user is likely experiencing through speech expressions, facial expressions, vocal tone, or other cues. Alright, let's break this down in a more human-ish way. Picture this: You're scrolling through a conversation and spot someone saying stuff like, "Ugh, everything sucks," plus a couple of "I don't even care anymore" phrases. Kinda obvious, right? You'd probably figure the person's feeling down. That's like a basic "if-then" rule, but more like common sense than some fancy formula. Same goes for body language—like, if someone's got their eyebrows locked in a frown and they're pursing their lips, you don't need Sherlock Holmes to guess they're pissed.

Now, AI tries to do this too. Take a bunch of past convos, mash 'em up with facial cues or whatever, and—boom—it's suddenly predicting how you feel, as if it's reading your diary. Another use? Trying to guess how folks will react, emotionally, to specific stuff. Say someone's had a string of rotten experiences and is already feeling kinda fragile—the AI might say, "Yeah, expect some sadness or a bit of anxiety here." Sometimes it'll flip the script: If someone's about to finally grab that one thing they've obsessed over for months, guess what? The system's ready for some fireworks—happiness, excitement, all that jazz. Honestly, if AI wants to stop sounding like an emotionless tin can, it's gotta get better at picking up the tiny signals in how we talk. Our words are loaded with stuff we don't even notice—jokes, complaints, little sighs—all of it matters if you want machines to actually 'get' us. Adding logic into the mix helps the tech decipher why words connect to certain feelings, not just what's being said at face value.

So, say you've got a list of emotions, and you group them by how close they feel: "Sad" hooks up with "unhappy," "depressed," "grief," that whole mopey crew, and you stick 'em together in a way a computer can easily follow. This lets machines map out human moods (or try to), instead of just copying whatever's trending online. Welcome to the weird new world of AI with a tiny bit more empathy—hopefully. To demonstrate that depression and sadness are subtypes of melancholy, we can specify the axiom "$\forall x$: depressed(x) $\rightarrow$ sad(x)." Likewise, we use logical rules to acknowledge semantic restrictions on where emotional language can be assembled, as in a rule specifying that the verb "to sadden" would typically require a sentient subject and a living object, representing the realities of sadness significantly being about living beings who can receive sadness and generally being caused by events or other people. If we employ logic to describe those semantic restrictions, AI systems may better understand the meaning of emotional language and keep it from misunderstanding. Logic can also be used to represent the pragmatic aspects of emotional language, like the communication roles of emotional wordings in different contexts. Melancholy has several pragmatic functions such as evoking sympathy, expressing disappointment, and influencing a person or people. The role of pragmatic functions is necessary for AI devices to appropriately react to person emotional expressions, including applying logical reasoning to extract what the speaker's motives and intentions are based on the individual's emotional language and then generating a relevant output response. In summary, logic as a knowledge representation for Affective AI is a strong method of moving away from mere emotion identification towards a richer and more nuanced sense of human emotion. AI devices can process, understand and respond to emotional affects in a more human and sympathetic way through creating emotional ontologies and knowledge bases, developing ideas about using logical propositions and rules for affective reasoning and inference, and using NLP to improve semantic meaning of emotional language. This can revolutionize multiple applications, such as human-computer interaction, mental health treatment, education, and entertainment, leading to AI systems not only being intelligent, but also emotionally aware and socially competent.

12.5 Integrating Neural Networks for Emotion Recognition in Affective AI Systems

The introduction of neural networks will represent a major progress in the field of Affective AI, as they allow those systems to more easily perceive and interpret humans' emotional displays, across different scenarios and modalities. Specifically, deep learning has proved to be a valuable asset in the area of multi-modal emotion recognition that gathers information from different modalities, including text, speech, and visual signals to represent and identify a full account of emotional activity, as it is required input for cognitive reasoning. The first phase of development involves the recognition of emotional properties from the referenced modalities. For text, the researchers have explored sentiment analysis, emotion lexicons, and natural language processing (NLP) models including transformers that represent words, sentences, and patterns of language that are indicative of emotional content. Words like "happy," "sad," "angry," and "afraid" find meaning in words right away, as do the more subtle aspects of emotional tone that arise from the use of sentence structure, punctuation, and situational context. Likewise, speech emotion recognition (SER) extracts emotional features from the acoustic properties of speech patterns, which include pitch, intonation, speaking rate, and energy levels. Specific emotions often find expression in unique vocal patterns; for example, rage is often characterized by high pitch (sometimes indicating a call to conversion), loud loudness, and fast speech rate, while sadness is characteristically low in pitch, soft in loudness, and slow in speech rate. Visual emotion recognition (VER) attempts to extract emotional components from facial expressions, body gestures, and other visual indicators.

Convolutional neural networks (CNNs) are now commonly utilized to process facial photographs and to identify specific, facial muscle articulations (e.g., raised brows) that correspond to distinct emotions. Body language comprises complex articulation properties, such as posture, gestures, and head motions, which yield more information regarding emotional states than facial features. Neural networks capture the multitude of human expressions and their variances in ways that humans express emotions in ways which include ramification positiveness in text, audio, and visual output. Identifying emotions, is one of the hardest tasks for processing humans due to ambiguity relating to noise in emotional data. Human expressions of emotions can be difficult, imprecise, incremental, and contextually bound, especially for AI to glean emotional signals from one another. A smile can signal enjoyment but may also signal a politeness and/ or sarcasm, and/or horror etc. Similarly, voice tone can be altered by many factors other than emotion, including personality, regional dialects, and background noise. Neural networks can properly handle ambiguity and noise as they are capable of recognizing complex patterns and statistical relationships from large amounts of data. If neural networks are originally trained on broad, representative datasets, they should learn to filter away, or disregard, unnecessary information and focus on the most important signals for the detection of emotion. In addition, using methods like attention mechanisms and contextual modeling, neural networks can weigh the importance of differences between characteristics and considered the surrounding context when interpreting emotional signals. Neural networks also contribute important symbolic emotion representations in sensory input, in addition to identifying the emotional characteristics. Symbolic representations in a logical system provide a structured and meaningful means of conveying emotional information; however, symbolic interpretations often do not connect directly to the unprocessed sensory input where emotions are instantiated. Neural networks can eliminate this gap by learning to relate and translate low-level sensory input into high-level symbolic representations. For instance, a neural network could learn to correspond a series of facial muscle movements to the symbolic representation of "happiness," or a specific linguistic pattern to the idea of "sadness." In this way, AI systems will be able to constructively ground abstract ideas of emotion, thus relating notions of emotions to actual sensory experiences, thereby accessing a more embodied and grounded understanding of emotions. The hybrid architecture involving brain characteristics and logical mappings is a particularly exciting option for creating credible emotion detection in Affective AI. These designs combine advantages from both of the best features of both neural networks and symbolic logic when each technique is used alone has limitations. Neural networks can recognize patterns, extract features, and cope with noisy and ambiguous data well. Symbolic logic provides a framework for organized knowledge representation, reasoning, and inference. In a hybrid design, we could have a neural network component ingest raw sensory input and then process the relevant emotional features, and pipe those features into a symbolic system to complete further meaning and reasoning. For instance, a CNN may be utilized to derive facial features from an image, and then its output may be provided to a rule-based system that predicts the most probable emotion, using a set of rules and context. In this way, the system combines the perceptual abilities of neural networks with the explanatory and reasoning powers of symbolic logic.

Moreover, hybrid architectures can help create an architecture which uses many modalities. Neural networks can process each modality (text, sound, and image data) separately and produced individual pieces of modality information. The characteristics can then be synthesized and entered into symbolic system which can provide the correlations across a variety of emotional stimuli. For example, if a user writes that they are experiencing grief but they have a neutral facial expression, the symbolic system could use logical criteria to explain the emotion most likely experienced with respect to all missing modality differences. The ability to process disagreement or contradictory information is essential to accurately identify emotions in everyday life. Furthermore, hybrid architectures can enhance explainability for emotion detection. Often neural networks have been criticized in revealing an explainable "black box", hybrid systems can yield more visible and interpretable output. The symbolic element of the architecture can provide logical justification for the inferred emotion, that is it can describe why a particular emotion was detected based on the retrieved features and an explanation of the criteria used.

The lack of explainability is paramount in building trust in Affective AI systems, especially in sensitive applications such as mental health care and human-computer interaction - where individuals need insight into how the system interprets their emotion. In conclusion, when designing effective Affective AI systems, it is vital to the use of neural networks, particularly deep learning models, for multimodal form of emotional identification of emotions. Neural networks are also fantastic at extracting the emotive aspects from the text, audio and visual while also working with the ambiguity and noise inherent to emotional signals. Moreover, neural networks contribute significantly to creating symbolic representations of emotions in sensory input that connect low-level and high-level thinking. Hybrid architectures that facilitate brain sensing along with logical interpretation offer an opportunity for implementing emotion detection that is reliable, accurate, and explainable, while also providing pathways toward the development of AI systems that can truly comprehend and reason about the complexities of human emotion.

12.6 Neurosymbolic Architectures for Intelligent Affective Agents

Neurosymbolic architectures are a solid framework for building intelligent affective agents that recognize human emotions and respond appropriately, yet also explainable, situationally aware, and benevolent. Because neurosymbolic systems combine the advantages of neural networks and symbolic reasoning, neurosymbolic systems are neither exclusively data-driven nor exclusively rule-based, meaning they should be more robust, more transparent, and more trustworthy emotional AI systems. You know what's wild about neurosymbolic architectures? They're like the cool kids of Affective AI because they actually tell you what's going on inside their heads (well, circuits?). Most deep learning stuff is straight-up black magic—spits out an answer, and you're just supposed to trust it? Nah, hard pass for me. Neurosymbolic models, though, they lay out the logic behind their vibe checks. Seriously, they'll break down exactly how they decided you're annoyed—maybe it's your flat voice, your angry texts, or that absolute death stare you're giving your webcam. And yeah, they tell you the actual rules they used, instead of just saying "It seemed right."

Explainability like this is gold, especially where it actually matters. Think mental health apps, teachers' bots, customer support chats—that kind of vibe. Nobody wants an AI therapist making weird guesses about your mood and then playing coy when you ask "Why?" People need to know how these machines "feel" about them, what clues they're reading, and what kind of weird logic is going on behind the scenes. When AI can explain itself in a way that actually makes sense, folks start to trust it. Or at least, hate it slightly less. It's just easier to accept feedback from a bot when you don't think it's rolling dice behind the curtain. Plus, these neurosymbolic things aren't clueless about context. Human emotions aren't just random—there's stuff behind them: your friends, whatever awkward situation you're in, or even just your weird history. So, for an affective agent to not just crash and burn socially, it needs to "get" all that context and piece things together, not just guess at random. Symbolic logic totally helps with that, pulling in social cues, past convos, whatever's relevant. Like—sure, if you get a gift you're probably happy, unless it's socks from Aunt Mildred... and then it's complicated. Neurosymbolic systems can lay all those logic chains out, which is honestly pretty dope. Look, real life is messy, right? People rarely stick to just one emotion at a time—it's more like emotional soup. I mean, who hasn't plastered on a fake grin at a family dinner while secretly dying inside? It happens. So, for any so-called "affective agent" to actually keep up, it better have some sort of street-smarts. It can't just look at a smile and go "Oh, happy!"—nah, sometimes that smile's hiding tears or wants to throw hands. You get the point. Now, here's where things get fun. Think about those situations where someone's face is saying "anger" but their body just screams "I'm terrified." That's a puzzle right there. For an agent to not totally embarrass itself, it's gotta piece together why these emotional signals are all mixed up. It needs to connect the dots: why is this person acting all smiley while talking about something absolutely gut-wrenching? Maybe it's politeness, keeping the peace, or, heck, trying to not freak everyone out. Agents using neuro-symbolic systems (yeah, I know, it sounds like sci-fi magic) are good at figuring out that, "Dude, just 'cause she's smiling, doesn't mean she's okay." You feed in some rules—like, when someone's dealing with bad stuff but wants things to stay chill, faces lie. So, bottom line? If an AI wants to play ball in our emotional circus, it needs to spot fake smiles and trembling hands just like we do. Otherwise, it's just another clueless robot at the party, misreading the room.

12.7 Addressing Key Challenges in Neurosymbolic Affective AI

If we actually want neurosymbolic Affective AI to be more than just a fancy buzzword, we've gotta wrestle with its core problems—no cutting corners here. It's not just about building machines that "work"; it's about making them trustworthy, reliable, and honestly, not creepy when they try to "read" and react to people's feelings. Now, the real kicker? The symbol grounding problem. That's the headache where you've got these abstract symbols for emotions, but somehow they've gotta hook into the messy, sweaty, twitchy reality of actual human sensations and body responses. If you figure that one out, you're halfway to the finish line. While symbolic representations - such as in logical frameworks - make it easier to represent emotional knowledge in a structured and understandable manner, they almost always do not have a direct mapping on the raw data on the basis of which emotions are sensed or perceived, such as facial expressions, vocal prosody, and physiological indicators. This disconnect creates monotonic challenges for neurosymbolic systems to learn meanings of emotional symbols and appropriately map symbolic representations to emotional manifestations in the world. As an example, a logical system may define the symbol "sadness" *via* a series of logical rules noting how the "sadness" is related to "loss," "disappointment," and "negative valence", but these constraints provide little explanation of how "sadness" presents in a human face, voice, or body language. Neurosymbolic systems will often attempt to close this gap by using a neural network to learn to derive important aspects of sensory data, and then map them to symbolic representations. For instance, a convolutional neural network (CNN) may be trained to distinguish facial expressions related to sadness and then its output could be taken into a logical system that derives sadness from the output using predefined criteria. This creates a problem in knowing how to confirm that the neural network is learning to pick out characteristics that are really pertinent to the symbolic representation of sadness and not just coincidental correlations in the training data. Also, evidence embedded in emotional expression is always unpredictable and dependent on context, making symbol grounding much more difficult.

The same feeling could be expressed differently by many different people and in many different contexts, so that an overall distinction with a label would not be representative enough to map a one-to-one correspondence between sensory aspects and symbolic designations. To help solve this problem, neurosymbolic systems need to offer ways of reasoning about uncertainty and ambiguity in the sensory input, and about contextual information that can help disambiguate an emotional display. Another central issue in neurosymbolic Affective AI is representing the dynamic and developing nature of emotions in a logical fashion. Emotions are not fixed states or even stable happenings, but are better considered as malleable processes that change and are influenced over time by a variety of factors, including changing conditions, the actions of others, and cognitive reappraisals. Reasoning about temporal changes and transformations between different (emotional) states using logical representations is not straightforward.

Standard logic is often used as a system of representing static information and applying deductive reasoning to established facts, for example. Certainly temporal logics exist, but they may be computationally complex when trying to represent the complex and often non-linear nature of emotion development. For instance, an individual may feel angry about an injustice but may become less angry if they let it go, or accepted an apology. To depict the process of emotion development, the elements that cause it, and the rules of development, will require complex logical formalisms and usable reasoning algorithms. Also, the mutable nature of emotions creates challenges for learning. Neural networks - typically trained on only static snapshots of emotional expressions - may find it difficult to appreciate the temporal and long-term relationships between emotional expressions that define emotional processes. In this case, neurosymbolic systems may rely upon the use of recurrent neural networks (RNNs) or other sequence modeling technologies that can understand temporal relationships and learn to predict how an emotion evolves over time. The problem of ambiguity and subjectivity in emotional data and reasoning is also a serious problem for neurosymbolic emotional AI.

Human emotions are fundamentally subjective constructs and their expression and perception can differ greatly across persons and cultures. This non-objectivity or subjectivity opens up significant ambiguity in both the data to train Affective AI systems with, and the reasoning tasks of these Affective AI systems. Facial expressions and vocal tones can be ambiguous and open to interpretation, and self-reported emotional responses can be subject to social desirability and mistaken introspection. Therefore, there is little ground truth to work with relative to emotion identification and evaluating the performance level of Affective AI systems. In addition, the cognition used to interpret emotions rely on some unknown level of unpredictability.

The logical principles that have been used to connect emotional states to antecedents and consequences, are often based on generalizations that may not hold true in every instance. For example, the generalization of "IF a person has sustained a loss, THEN they will feel sad," is a valid generalization, although there are exceptions that merit consideration, such as when the loss is considered a release from captivity, or the person has coping methods that work well. Alright, let's cut through the noise for a second. Dealing with uncertainty isn't just some wishy-washy hand waving for neurosymbolic systems. These things actually need to *handle* it—like, really juggle the fact that emotions aren't just on/off switches. Probabilities come to the rescue, and yeah, the Bayesian crowd loves those networks for a reason: you plug in your guesses, feed in new info, and get (fingers crossed) smarter about what's actually happening under the hood. But, you know what's cooler? Fuzzy logic. Instead of pretending everything's black or white, it just shrugs and goes, "Meh, I'll take a little grey." That's basically how humans do emotions—no one's ever just 0% or 100% angry, right?

But here's the rub: trying to *score* these empathic AI brains is an absolute mess. The old favorites like accuracy and F1-score? Total dinosaurs for this stuff. Maybe the system nails the easy stuff (happy, sad, whatever), but throw a curveball emotion—or real life—at it, and it crumbles faster than soggy cereal. So the big brains in research are hollering for new ways to grade these systems—stuff like judging them on context, empathy, actual social smarts. About time, honestly. And don't get me started on "explainable AI." You'd think programming an AI to spell out why it made a decision would be a cakewalk. Nope. Turns out, making explanations both actually *clear* and *useful* for regular people is a hot mess. It's gotta feel natural, not like a lecture from your least favorite math teacher. So, folks run user studies, get feedback, tweak stuff... wash, rinse, repeat.

Now, as if that wasn't enough, here come the ethics police—and rightly so. Imagine building a robot that "gets" your feelings and then releasing it into schools, offices, therapy sessions—even with the best intentions, that sets off some serious alarms. Top of the list? Good old bias. If you train these bots only on data from, say, white suburban kids, *guess what*—they're gonna totally whiff it on everyone else. Suddenly, your "emotion detector" thinks someone's angry when they're just chill, or misses nuance in non-Western expressions. That's... bad. So the fix? Mix up the training data, make it actually reflect, you know, real people. Oh, and before you get too comfy, there's the Big Brother stuff. Affective AI in surveillance? That's straight-up dystopian. Or use it to tweak ads to mess with your head, or worse. So, yeah, we desperately need guardrails: actual laws, actual guidelines, not just a sticky note that says "Don't be evil." Stuff about privacy, clarity, and not turning these things loose for profit at the expense of real human rights. Honestly, it's a wild ride—but at least someone's trying to keep the rollercoaster on the tracks.

12.8 The Future of Affective AI: A Neurosymbolic Vision

Oh man, Affective AI is about to shake up how we vibe with tech—like, for real. Right now, let's be honest, machines barely get human emotions. A lot of what's out there is basically the emotional equivalent of Clippy from old-school Microsoft Word. Just sort of... there. Not really *feeling* it, you know?

But what's cooking next is nuts: AI that doesn't just read our moods, but actually gets where we're coming from. We're talking about systems that mesh those wild, black-box neural nets (the math-y part that sniffs out patterns like a truffle hog) with classic logic—good, old symbolic reasoning. Fancy name for it? Neurosymbolic AI. Doesn't exactly roll off the tongue, but it works. Basically, you get the best of both worlds. Neural networks? Great for soaking up data and making sense of complicated stuff like voices, faces, all the messy bits. Symbolic reasoning? That's your logic-brain; it turns the chaos into something the AI can actually explain, justify, and reason about. Jam 'em together, and suddenly your AI doesn't just guess how you feel—it's got receipts.

Here's the big deal: If AI is gonna really hang with us humans, it needs some serious empathy. Not the "I see you're sad, can I interest you in a generic platitude?" kind. Real empathy means the AI can tell you're upset, it clocks *why* you might feel that way, and it responds like someone who actually gives a damn. Not just "sympathy flowers" level, I'm talking about being able to walk in your shoes. Our current bots? Still pretty tone-deaf. It's like texting your feelings to a brick wall. But with neurosymbolic stuff, you're looking at bots that might finally be able to listen, process, and maybe—even if just a little—genuinely care. Picture a virtual pal (or therapist, if that's more your jam) checking in on you when you're down, reading your tone and body language, and giving back advice that's more than one-size-fits-all. That's game-changing, especially for stuff like mental health, where real support can mean everything. Of course, here comes the kicker: People are complicated. We're not robots. Our feelings get twisted up by our quirks, our friends, our history, even whatever's trending on TikTok, honestly. So if AI wants to play along, it's gotta tune into the unique messiness of *you*. Neurosymbolic AI shines here. It can keep tabs on your vibe, because it pulls together all the puzzle pieces: your personality, your past, the stuff you care about right now. Then, when something changes—or when you're sad, or hyped, or just bored—it reacts in a way that's actually relevant. The bot can even catch cultural signals or what's happening in your convos—maybe even avoid that one awful joke you hate. It's got context, not just a script. Bottom line: If this all comes together (and, yeah, we're not totally there yet), machines won't just be smart—they'll finally actually feel like they 'get' us, whether you're learning, goofing off, calling customer support, or hanging out with your new robot roommate. Wild times ahead.

12.9 Conclusion

Alright, buckle up—this chapter isn't just another dull run-through about AI and emotions. Nope. It comes swinging, basically calling out the tired trope that emotions are just weird, irrational vibes floating around. Like, come on, we're more complex than that. The big idea here is: what if AI could actually get better at the whole "feelings" thing by mixing fancy neural networks with old-school logic, kinda like a buddy-cop movie of brains and reason? There's a bunch of talk about different logical systems and these wild neurosymbolic models—which, honestly, sound like something out of a sci-fi flick. Point is, this mashup could help AI get way less awkward when reading emotions: stuff like getting the context, not spitting out garbled explanations, and actually being a little transparent about motives. This whole approach might finally drag emotional AI past awkward robot-child territory and into something that can actually *vibe* with us. Not just recognize "sad face... must console," but really get what's up.

AI disclosure statement: The author acknowledges the use of AI-based tools for minor language editing or grammatical correction. However, all intellectual contributions, analyses, and conclusions presented in this chapter are entirely the author's own.

References

1. Dastani, M. and Lorini, E., A logic of emotions: from appraisal to coping. *Adaptive Agents and Multi-Agents Systems*, pp. 1133–1140, 2012, https://doi.org/10.5555/2343776.2343859.
2. Ciompi, L., Reflections on the role of emotions in consciousness and subjectivity, from the perspective of affect-logic. *Consc. Emotion*, *4*, 2, 181–196, 2003, https://doi.org/10.1075/CE.4.2.03CIO.
3. de Silva, P., Emotions, Logic and Rationality, in: *The Psychology of Buddhism in Conflict Studies*, pp. 81–86, Cham, Springer International Publishing, 2017.
4. Tozzi, A., James, C., Peters, J.F., A logical inquiry of emotions and cognition, bioRxiv, 087874, 2016, https://doi.org/10.1101/087874.
5. Solomon, R.C., The logic of emotion. *Noûs*, *11*, 1, 41, 1977, https://doi.org/10.2307/2214329.
6. Brackett, M.A., Lopes, P.N., Ivcevic, Z., Mayer, J.D., Salovey, P., Integrating emotion and cognition: The role of emotional intelligence, in: *Motivation, Emotion, and Cognition*, pp. 189–208, Routledge, 2004.
7. Revathy, G., Raj, K.B., Kumar, A., Adibatti, S., Dahiya, P., Latha, T.M., Investigation of E-voting system using face recognition using convolutional neural network (CNN). *Theor. Comput. Sci.*, *925*, 61–67, 2022.

13

Transfer Learning for Affective Computing: Challenges and Opportunities

Madona B. Sahaai[1], D. R. Ashwin Kumar[2], A. Priyadharshini[3] and S. Gokulraj[4]*

[1]Department of ECE Vels Institute of Science, Technology and Advanced Studies, Chennai, Tamil Nadu, India
[2]Department of Information Technology, Sri Sairam Engineering College, Chennai, Tamil Nadu, India
[3]CSE (Cyber Security), Nandha Engineering College, Erode, Tamil Nadu, India
[4]Department of Computer Science and Engineering (Cybersecurity), Dr. N.G.P. Institute of Technology, Coimbatore, Tamilnadu, India

Abstract

The multidisciplinary field of affective computing, which intentions at endowing computers with the capability to recognize, understand, and retort to human emotions, is often faced with the problem of having enough labeled data to train good models. Transfer learning which influences the acquaintance from a cause domain to help erudition on a related target domain is a powerful remedy to alleviate this data scarcity. By contrasting and comparing several transfer learning approaches and the capacity to process a broad range of emotion tasks from text, voice, physiology and facial expression, this paper looks into the huge possibilities of transfer learning in the formation of affective computing. The submission of transfer learning in this domain is especially challenging despite offering opportunities for better model generalization, reduced data requirements, and faster advancement. These are the selection of appropriate pre-trained models and transfer methods, the inherent subjectivity and context-dependency of emotions, and province discrepancy between source and target data. This paper tries to provide a complete summary of the part transfer learning can play in shaping the future of emotional computing through analysis of the current trends, emphasizing possible directions, and identifying critical issues.

**Corresponding author*: drgokulraj.s@drngpit.ac.in

N. Thillaiarasu, G. Revathy, T. Saravanan, V. Muthukumaran and S. Balamurugan (eds.) Affective Artificial Intelligence: Fundamentals, Challenges, and Applications, (265–284) © 2026 Scrivener Publishing LLC

Keywords: Affective computing, emotion recognition, transfer learning, domain adaptation, deep learning, facial expression recognition, speech emotion recognition, physiological signal analysis

13.1 Introduction to Affective Computing and the Data Scarcity Challenge

The emerging interdisciplinary arena of affective computing, at the convergence of computer science, psychology, and cognitive science, aims to endow computers with the high-level competence of recognizing, interpreting, and responding intelligently to the subtle and complex tapestry of human emotions. This ambitious venture is intended to create a link, leading to a more congenial journey between human emotionality and computational logic to form more intuitive, empathetic and human centric technological interactions. "Historically, computers have been envisioned as rational, logical machines and while that's certainly one element of them, it's obviously not the full picture," Hager explained: "The aim of affective computing is to explore ways to bring non-verbal content into technology in a way that makes sense to humans. This capability has far-reaching potential across a variety of applications, from personalized learning environments that respond to a student's emotions to healthcare systems capable of detecting and responding to a patient's distress, as well as more engaging human-robot interactions and significant improvements to the user experience in the gaming and entertainment industries and in social networking.

The implementation of this visionary direction is however plagued by a tremendous bottleneck: the hard requirement for huge quantities of high-quality, considered data to train successfully the sophisticated machine learning models at the core of the affective computing systems. The very nature, being inherently subjective, context- -dependent, and conveyed by a wide variety of modalities (i.e. facial expressions, vocal intonations, physiological signals and linguistic) poses a strong impediment to both data collection and annotation. In contrast to more objective endeavors such as image recognition or natural language processing where often labels can be gleaned from available resources or through processes that are comparatively straightforward, annotating emotional data needs deep consideration of context, the person expressing the emotion, and the subjective assessment of observed behavior [6].

It is an expensive and time-consuming process to collect large representative datasets that cover the wide range of human emotion across populations, context, and modalities. Data collection also often involves recruiting participants, setting up controlled spaces to evoke specific emotions, recording data from a variety of modalities, and after all that, getting trained humans to label the extent of emotional content. It is both expensive and difficult just to get basic reliable data in the first place. Although trained humans have an intuitive sense of emotions that computers do not possess, their subjective experiences and biases can lead to variability in their judgments. Possibly more important is that the ephemeral nature of emotions and the nuances of expressing emotions leads to disagreement among annotators and makes it difficult to establish a reliable ground truth for training machine learning models.

The difficulty is further complicated by the fact that emotional expressions vary widely from person to person, across cultures and even within an individual based on their changing circumstances. For example, a facial expression of happiness from one culture may not be interpreted the same way by another culture. The same vocal intonation can communicate different emotions depending on the context of the dialogue. Because of this variability, it is necessary to collect large datasets for diverse populations to insure that the learned models generalize adequately to unseen data, and also perform consistently across diverse populations and contexts. The lack of emotional datasets that are large and well-annotated is a significant barrier to the advancement of affective computing, which limits the complexity and accuracy of the developed models, and inhibits their capability to be used in real-world, practical applications.

Given this significant challenge of data scarcity, the transfer learning machine learning framework may be the most effective solution. Transfer learning is essentially a method of machine learning that provides the learner the opportunity to take advantage of a source domain where large amounts of categorized data are existing to learn knowledge for an analogous but distinct target domain where labeled data is limited. The source domain knowledge, including important information, patterns and features, are transferred to the target domain models so that they can achieve better accuracy, develop their models with a great reduction of labeled data, and significant speed to converge to optimal performance compared to if they trained on the target with data alone. Transfer learning has exciting implications for the domain of affective computing, because it provides a viable solution to the data bottleneck issue and enables the ability to realize the full potential for the future of emotion-aware artificial intelligence.

Transfer learning enables researchers and practitioners working in affective computing to be intelligent to leverage the knowledge learned from the source domains that are similar or related to knowledge of the target task, such as general object recognition tasks in computer vision and sentiment analysis tasks in natural language processing and to subsequently apply it to the affective computing domain for the purpose of learning how to recognize emotion across various modalities. By intentionally using pre-trained models, transfer learning approaches, and other efficient technologies, the field will be able to move toward building better, more generalizable, and more data-efficient affective computing systems, while closing in on a future where technology can actually understand and respond to the rich human spectrum of emotions.

13.2 State of the Art Models

Kratzwald *et al.* [1] state that transfer learning in affective computing has issues like domain covariance, and careful tuning of hyperparameters. However, it also provides opportunities for improved emotion recognition using pre-trained models facilitating transfer learning improving task performance from separate data and tasks.

Schuller, [2] outlines issues in Affective Computing, including robustness, cross-cultural issues, and ethical considerations, highlighting opportunities through advancements in Artificial Intelligence, big data, and deep learning, and the need for emotional intelligence in intelligent systems for commercial applications.

Rescigno *et al.* [3] explain that transfer learning in affective computing deals with challenges such as a limited amount of subject-specific data by transferring knowledge from immense corporeal datasets. This increases the performance of systems in emotion recognition. Transfer learning also provides possibilities for the creation of personalized models using fewer labeled datasets, improving human-machine interaction through useful emotion classification. According to Wu & Parsons [4], Transfer learning in affective computing considers the fact that users are different. By using user-specific training samples and support data from other users, the classification accuracy is improved, especially when the primary data provided is limited. The challenges of Transfer learning in affective computing are effective transfer of knowledge and the variation of data distributions.

Kumar [5], used transfer learning with VGG-19 and ResNet-18 models in image-based affective computing. The author describes transfer learning as effective but a concern in the transfer of the model is users vary in terms of data variability and model capability. There are tremendous opportunities in the future, considering effective emotion recognition and improved decision-making support, using deep learning models.

13.3 Fundamentals of Transfer Learning

At the heart of solving the data scarcity problem for affective computing is the framework and techniques of transfer learning, an advanced machine learning paradigm that departs from the typical learning approach where models are trained in an isolated fashion for each specific task and data set. Instead of training models independently, transfer learning permits researchers and organizations to take benefit of knowledge from a source domain with a wealth of labeled data, and to improve the learning experience when working on a related but separate target domain with little labeled data. The key assumption of transfer learning is that the knowledge and patterns that have been learned in one situation could be useful in another, especially where task formulation and conditions are similar, or on "overlapping" data distributions. By leveraging this transferable knowledge, transfer learning presents a unique opportunity to build more powerful, data-efficient, and generalizable systems in affective computing.

Fundamentally, transfer learning consists of a pair of domains: a source domain, which consists of a labeled dataset, and a learning task that has been learned using that data, and a target domain, which consists of a different, but related dataset and learning task. The basis domain contains of the rich number of labeled examples that allow the training of useful models; the target domain is concerned with the related dataset with few labeled examples, making it difficult to train a good model from scratch. The prime area of transfer learning is to achieve better performance of a model on task TT in domain DT *via* knowledge contained in task TS in domain DS. The knowledge transfer can take place in various forms (i.e. learn features, model parameters, instance weights, etc.) depending on the transfer/learning approach.

Transfer learning can come in numerous types, depending on the similarities amid the tasks, domains, and convenience of labeled data in both. The most common form is inductive transfer learning, in which the two tasks are diverse but the source and target domains are the same. This allows the use of rich labeled data from the source task to assist in learning a diverse, but related, task within the same data space. For example, the large labeled dataset of movie reviews with sentiment (i.e., positive or negative - source task) could be used to enhance the recital of a system that identifies the intensity of emotions (e.g., joy, sadness, anger - target task) expressed in a smaller dataset of social media posts. The shared domain (text data) is the same, the learning tasks, however, are different.

A third type of transfer learning is transductive transfer learning where the source and target tasks are the same, but the source and target domains are different. The critical point is that in transductive transfer learning, the source domain has labeled data, and the target domain has only unlabeled data. The goal is to exploit the knowledge gained from the labeled source data to improve performance on the unlabeled target data. An example in affective computing might involve collecting a large labeled dataset of facial images recorded in a laboratory under controlled conditions to train a facial emotion recognition model (the source domain) before utilizing the learned knowledge to then recognize emotions in a dataset of unlabeled facial images from real-world scenarios (the target domain) having more challenging conditions, lighting, pose, and occlusion. The task of facial emotion recognition remains the same, only the data distributions are different.

Finally, unsupervised transfer learning deals with situations where the source task and target task are dissimilar, and there is no branded data in the target domain. However, there is labeled data for the source domain. The goal is to capitalize on the knowledge learned from labeled source data to improve the unsupervised learning in target domain. For example, one might build knowledge from a large labeled dataset of images with a variety of object categories (the source domain and task), to learn generalizable featurization representations (the source representation), for the purpose of improving clustering, or dimensionality reduction, of a dataset of unlabeled audio recordings containing different emotional expressions (the target domain and task). This type of transfer learning is challenging, but has potential to use readily available labeled data from dizzy tasks, to increase the understanding and organization of unlabeled affective data. To effectively realize the benefits of transfer learning, various key approaches have been developed, each focusing on different aspects of knowledge transfer. **Instance-based transfer learning** operates on the principle of reweighting or selectively using instances from the source domain to benefit the learning process in the target domain. This method assumes that some examples of the source domain examples are more informative to the target task than others. Methods like instance weighting or instance selection attempt to find and prioritize these relevant source instances and therefore enhance the small amount of labeled data in the target domain. For example, in cross-lingual speech emotion recognition, some utterances of the source language may display acoustic characteristics that are more consistent with the target language, and instance-based transfer learning would focus on these more relevant instances.

On the other hand, feature-based transfer learning seeks to find shared feature representations between the source and target domains. This approach assumes that while the raw data distributions might differ, there exist underlying features that are predictive in both domains. Feature learning techniques, such as dimensionality reduction, subspace learning, or deep feature extraction using pre-trained neural networks, are employed to identify these common feature spaces. Once these shared representations are learned, they can be used to train models in the target domain, often requiring fewer labeled target examples. In affective computing, for example, a deep convolutional neural network pre-trained on a large image dataset (like ImageNet) can learn generalizable low-level visual features (e.g., edges, textures, shapes) that can then be leveraged as a starting point for learning higher-level features relevant to facial emotion recognition on a smaller target dataset.

Parameter-based transfer learning, also known as network-based transfer learning in the context of deep learning, focuses on sharing parameters or prior distributions of parameters between the source and target models. This is particularly effective when using deep neural networks, where a model pre-trained on a large source dataset can have its initial layers (which often learn generalizable features) transferred and fine-tuned on a smaller target dataset. This approach, often referred to as fine-tuning, allows the target model to benefit from the rich feature representations learned by the source model, significantly accelerating training and improving performance, especially when the target dataset is small. The widespread success of pre-trained language models like BERT, RoBERTa, and GPT in natural language processing, which are then fine-tuned for various downstream tasks including text-based emotion recognition, exemplifies the power of parameter-based transfer learning.

At last, relational-based transfer learning concentrates on transferring relationships or knowledge structures between the source and target domains. This perspective presupposes that relationships between data instances or the underlying relational structures across the domains are similar, despite the variation in data distributions. In social network analysis, for instance, interaction and influence patterns exist that could be transferable across different social media platforms, while the user demographics and content may vary widely. In contrast to the sensory-based affective computing tasks, which are the more common way to apply transfer learning, relational transfer learning may more readily apply to emotion propagation in social contexts, or in modeling relationships between different emotional states.

Though that is really just scratching the surface of the basics of transfer learning and offers a significant arsenal for combating the problem of data scarcity in affective computing, if researchers and practitioners are aware of the characteristics of both the source and target domains, different forms of transfer learning scenarios, and the various key techniques allow knowledge to flow from the source to the target, they can potentially utilize existing labeled data in a way that leads to the establishment of more meaningful and useful emotion recognition systems for a variety of modalities and applications. They just need to understand how to leverage these principles, which should help them utilize the promise of affective computing and develop and deploy technologies that are better able to respond and account for the complexities of human emotion!

13.4 Applications of Transfer Learning in Affective Computing

The effective use of transfer learning techniques has produced notable progress in many areas of affective computing, especially in addressing the intrinsic problem of insufficient labeled data for developing strong emotion recognition systems. By deftly applying knowledge from related domains and tasks, transfer learning has demonstrated its capacity to enhance the accuracy, generalizability, and data efficiency of models designed to recognize emotions from a range of modalities, including text, voice, physiological signals, and facial expressions. Transfer learning has become an especially effective tool for emotion recognition from text, largely due to the development and widespread availability of powerful pre-trained language models (PLMs) such as BERT (Bidirectional Encoder Representations from Transformers), RoBERTa (A Robustly Optimized BERT Pretraining Approach), GPT 1 (Generative Pre-trained Transformer), and their various variants. Usually, these models are trained using self-supervised learning goals like masked language modeling and next sentence prediction on large corpora of unlabeled text data, including complete books, articles, and web pages. PLMs acquire rich contextualized representations of words and sentences through this intensive pre-training, thereby capturing complex syntactic and semantic relationships in the language. This acquired knowledge creates a solid basis that can be successfully applied to subsequent tasks in natural language processing, such as identifying emotions.

A pre-trained language model can be made to adjust its general language understanding skills to the subtleties of emotional expression in the text by fine-tuning it on a smaller, task-specific dataset of emotion-labeled text. To effectively classify the emotional tone of new, unseen text, for example, a BERT model that has been pre-trained on billions of words can be refined on a dataset of tweets labeled with emotions such as joy, sadness, anger, or fear. This method works well because the basic linguistic components and underlying meaning patterns apply to a wide range of textual tasks, making the pre-training knowledge extremely transferable.

Furthermore, transfer learning in text-based emotion recognition also involves transferring knowledge from sentiment analysis tasks. Compared to more detailed emotion classification tasks, sentiment analysis, which focuses on categorizing the overall polarity (positive, negative, or neutral) of text, frequently benefits from larger and more accessible labeled datasets. Differentiating between various emotional states can benefit from the knowledge that sentiment analysis models learn, especially the capacity to recognize subjective language, opinion words, and contextual cues that indicate positive or negative sentiment. A model trained to detect negative sentiment, for instance, may have picked up on words and expressions linked to negativity, which can also be a sign of feelings like sadness, rage, or disgust.

While feature extraction or fine-tuning can be used to transfer the representations learned from other sentiment analysis, in cases where there is not enough labeled data available to train a model, this is particularly important due to the connection between sentiment and emotion-- which is integral to the overall emotional expression.

Similarly, the use of transfer learning significantly improved voice emotion recognition, especially when paired with acoustic models that had already been trained. Large speech datasets are usually used to train these models, frequently for tasks like speaker recognition and automatic speech recognition (ASR). The models learn to capture the phonetic and prosodic aspects of speech during this pre-training phase, as well as to extract acoustic features that are invariant to speaker identity. These learned acoustic representations, which encode information about speech sounds, intonation, rhythm, and stress, can significantly aid in the recognition of emotions conveyed through vocal cues.

Researchers have been able to significantly increase the accuracy of speech emotion recognition by applying the learned feature extractors or the lower layers of pre-trained acoustic models and refining them on smaller datasets of emotion-labeled speech. The rationale behind this is that the fundamental acoustic properties of speech are shared across different tasks, and the ability to effectively represent these properties, learned through large-scale pre-training, provides a strong starting point for identifying the subtle acoustic variations associated with different emotional states.

Another compelling application of transfer learning in speech emotion recognition lies in cross-lingual speech emotion recognition. Emotion expression through speech can exhibit both universal and language-specific characteristics. Language-specific labeled data, which can be hard to come by for many languages, is frequently needed to train strong speech emotion recognition models. Transfer learning offers a means to bridge this gap by leveraging labeled speech emotion data from one or more source languages to improve recognition performance in a target language with little to no labeled emotional data. This can be achieved by either feature-level transfer, which maps acoustic features extracted from different languages into a common emotion-invariant space, or model-level transfer, which involves modifying or fine-tuning a model trained on source language data for the target language. Cross-lingual transfer learning is particularly helpful when creating globally applicable speech emotion recognition systems because it removes the need for extensive data collection and annotation for each and every language.

Another area where successful transfer learning is possible is the recognition of emotions from physiological cues. Many physiological markers are known to correlate with various emotional states, including skin conductance (EDA), respiration patterns, electroencephalography (EEG), electrocardiography (ECG), and electromyography (EMG). However, because they necessitate specialized equipment, controlled experimental settings, and physiological responses naturally differ from one subject to another, large-scale physiological datasets that capture the complex and often nuanced relationships between these signals and emotions are challenging to collect and label. Through the transfer of knowledge across various physiological modalities, transfer learning can help alleviate this problem. To identify emotions from EEG data, for example, a model trained on a sizable dataset of EEG signals for a related task such as cognitive load estimation may discover broadly applicable patterns of brain activity. Similar to this, skills gained from examining ECG data to identify stress may be applied to better identify other emotions that also cause changes in the heart. This kind of transfer learning makes use of the shared information contained in various body signals as well as the underlying physiological principles. Furthermore, using physiological signals to achieve subject-independent emotion recognition depends heavily on transfer learning. Due to the large inter-individual variability in physiological responses to the same emotional stimuli, emotion recognition models trained on data from a particular set of individuals frequently perform poorly when applied to new, unseen subjects. This subject-dependency can be addressed by using transfer learning strategies. One method is to train a classifier on the small amount of data from a new subject after training a subject-invariant feature extractor on a large pool of data from several subjects. Using meta-learning techniques to quickly adapt a model to a new subject with only a few labeled examples is another tactic.

By explicitly modeling and mitigating the effects of inter-subject variability, transfer learning enables the development of more robust and generalizable physiological emotion recognition systems that can be deployed effectively on individuals whose data was not included in the training set.

In the realm of emotion recognition from facial expressions, transfer learning has been particularly impactful, largely due to the success of pre-trained convolutional neural networks (CNNs). CNNs trained on massive image datasets like ImageNet, for tasks such as object recognition, learn hierarchical representations of visual features, ranging from low-level features like edges and corners to high-level features representing complex object parts and shapes. These learned visual features are remarkably generalizable and have proven to be highly effective for a wide range of computer vision tasks, including facial expression recognition. By utilizing these pre-trained CNNs as feature extractors or by fine-tuning their weights on smaller datasets of emotion-labeled facial images, researchers have achieved state-of-the-art performance in recognizing basic emotions like happiness, sadness, anger, fear, surprise, and disgust. The transfer of knowledge from large-scale image recognition tasks to facial expression recognition is effective because both tasks involve analyzing visual patterns and structures within images, and the low- and mid-level visual features learned by the pre-trained networks are relevant for identifying facial features and their configurations that are indicative of different emotions.

Moreover, transfer learning offers promising solutions for handling variations in pose, illumination, and occlusion that often plague facial expression recognition in real-world scenarios. Models trained on carefully controlled laboratory data often struggle when faced with images captured under different lighting conditions, from various viewpoints, or when parts of the face are occluded by hands, hair, or other objects. By leveraging pre-trained models that have been exposed to a wide variety of image conditions during their initial training, and by employing transfer learning techniques that encourage the learning of more robust and invariant features, it is possible to build facial emotion recognition systems that are less sensitive to these challenging variations. To help a pre-trained CNN learn to extract emotion-relevant features that are less impacted by these nuisance factors, it can be fine-tuned on a target dataset that contains examples with a variety of poses, illuminations, and occlusions. Further improving the resilience and practicality of facial emotion recognition systems are methods such as domain adaptation, a branch of transfer learning, which can be used to explicitly bridge the gap between the source domain (e.g., well-lit frontal faces) and the target domain (e.g., faces with varying conditions).

13.5 Challenges in Applying Transfer Learning to Affective Computing

Although transfer learning has significantly advanced the field of affective computing, there are still inherent difficulties in implementing it. To fully utilize this paradigm in creating dependable and strong emotion-aware systems, it is imperative to overcome a number of critical factors that must be carefully considered when utilizing pre-trained models and transfer learning techniques for emotion recognition.

One of the biggest obstacles is selecting appropriate pre-trained models and transfer strategies. The effectiveness of transfer learning depends on how similar the source and target domains and tasks are. Selecting a pre-trained model that has learned representations from a very different domain may not provide much of an advantage and may even result in negative transfer, where the knowledge transferred actually makes learning in the target domain more difficult rather than easier. As a result, model compatibility and domain relevance are crucial factors. Since speech emotion recognition depends on acoustic features, a CNN pre-trained on a large dataset of natural images is unlikely to be directly helpful, even though it may be advantageous for facial expression recognition due to shared low-level visual features.

Similar to this, a language model that has already been trained on generic text may need to be carefully chosen and modified to account for the unique subtleties of emotional language used in spoken or social media conversations. Additionally, the pre-trained model's architecture must work with the target task and data modality. For instance, considerable architectural changes may be necessary to accommodate the temporal nature of audio data when transferring the convolutional layers of an image-based CNN to a sequential speech emotion recognition task.

Finding pre-trained models that provide the most pertinent and transferable knowledge requires careful testing and a thorough comprehension of both the source and target domains.

One of the most important aspects of model selection is deciding which layer to transfer. While earlier layers of deep neural networks typically capture more general, low-level features, later layers typically learn more task-specific, high-level features. Hierarchical representations are learned by deep neural networks. The selection of which pre-trained model layers to freeze, alter, or replace during knowledge transfer is an important hyperparameter that can have a big influence on the target model's performance. Transferring too many layers, particularly the task-specific ones from a different source task, could result in poor performance or even negative transfer, whereas transferring too few layers might not make the most of the previously learned information. The size of the target dataset and the degree of similarity between the source and target tasks are frequently used to determine the best course of action. It could be advantageous to freeze the earlier layers and only refine the later, more task-specific layers if the target dataset is small and the tasks are comparatively similar. On the other hand, if the target dataset is relatively large and the tasks are more dissimilar, it might be necessary to fine-tune additional layers or even the entire network to effectively adapt the learned representations. Careful hyperparameter tuning and empirical evaluation are necessary to determine the optimal layer transfer strategy for a given affective computing task.

The intrinsic subjectivity and context-dependency of emotions present a major barrier to transfer learning in affective computing, in addition to the technical difficulties of choosing a model and methodology. Perceptions and expressions of emotion are not universal and can differ greatly between people and cultures. The manner in which a given emotion is expressed through facial expressions, vocalizations, or physiological reactions can vary greatly between cultural groups and even between members of the same culture due to individual and cultural differences in emotional expression. In data from another culture, where the expression of the same emotion may be slightly or significantly different, a pre-trained model that was trained on a dataset primarily from one cultural background may not generalize well. Emotional expression and perception can also be influenced by individual differences in baseline physiological states, habitual facial expressions, and vocal patterns. If these individual and cultural differences are not sufficiently addressed, transferring knowledge from a source dataset with a particular demographic distribution to a target dataset with a different demographic composition may introduce biases and result in subpar performance.

An additional layer of complexity is introduced by the way context affects how emotions are perceived. A variety of emotions can be conveyed by the same facial expression, tone of voice, or bodily response, depending on the situation, the people involved, and other indicators. A smile can be used to convey sarcasm or politeness in one situation and happiness in another. In situations where context is essential, a pre-trained model that was trained to link particular features to particular emotions using a small or decontextualized source dataset may find it difficult to correctly interpret emotions.

In order to accurately identify emotions, transfer learning approaches must take into account how to incorporate contextual information from the target domain, which may differ from the context in the source domain. This might entail creating transfer learning strategies that are sensitive to various contextual cues or utilizing multi-modal data, where context from one modality (such as text accompanied by a facial expression) can aid in the interpretation of another.

The domain mismatch between source and target data presents another major obstacle to the application of transfer learning to affective computing. Suboptimal or even negative transfer may result from significant differences in the underlying data distributions and characteristics, even when the source and target tasks are related. Variations in data distribution and characteristics can take many different forms, including differences in data quality, the recording environment (e.g., controlled lab settings versus noisy real-world conditions), sensor characteristics, or participant demographics. A speech emotion recognition model, for example, that has been trained on high-quality audio recordings in a quiet setting may not function well on noisy recordings made in normal situations. Likewise, a model for facial expression recognition that was trained on high-resolution frontal face photos may have trouble with low-resolution profile views. These variations in data properties may make it difficult for a model trained on the source domain to generalize to the target domain.

Addressing negative transfer is one of the most crucial steps in lessening the challenges brought on by domain mismatch. Applying knowledge from the source domain to the target task results in negative transfer. This usually leads to worse performance than if the limited target data were used to train the model from scratch.

This can happen when the source and target domains are too dissimilar, and the knowledge conveyed is irrelevant to or even misleading for the intended task. In the field of transfer learning, there is continuous research on identifying and preventing negative transfer.

To lessen this problem, strategies like learning domain-invariant features, aligning the source and target data distributions using domain adaptation techniques, or selectively transferring only the most pertinent portions of the pre-trained model are used. Identifying and resolving possible negative transfer requires careful observation of the target task performance during transfer learning and the application of suitable validation techniques.

Comparing various methods and evaluating advancements in the field are made difficult by the absence of standardized evaluation metrics and benchmarking for transfer learning in affective computing. More thorough evaluation frameworks that particularly evaluate the efficacy and efficiency of transfer learning techniques are required, even though there are standard metrics for assessing emotion recognition performance on particular datasets (such as accuracy and F1-score). This includes measures that show how much knowledge is transferred, how much less target domain labeled data is required, and how transfer learning improves generalization performance. Additionally, it would be much easier to compare various approaches and advance the field if standardized benchmark datasets and experimental protocols for transfer learning in various affective computing modalities and tasks were developed. Because there are currently no such standardized benchmarks, it is challenging to assess the benefits of different transfer learning strategies objectively and to identify the most promising directions for future research.

13.6 Opportunities and Future Challenges

In addition to resolving the urgent problems caused by a shortage of data, the successful implementation of transfer learning techniques in affective computing creates a wealth of opportunities and fascinating new research directions. The resilience and generalization of models in emotion recognition systems can be significantly enhanced by transfer learning. Models that were first trained on limited affective datasets may perform poorly and struggle to generalize to new data when applied to various populations, situations, or data gathering setups. Transfer learning aids target models in comprehending underlying patterns and task-relevant properties by utilizing the rich representations derived from sizable, varied source datasets. For instance, compared to a model trained solely on a small, controlled dataset of facial emotions, a facial emotion detection model created from a CNN pre-trained on millions of generic photos is probably more robust to changes in position, illumination, and identity.

In a similar vein, pre-trained language models on large volumes of text can improve generalization across various textual domains and styles by offering a more sophisticated and contextually aware understanding of emotional language. The deployment of affective computing systems in real-world applications, where input is naturally diverse and uncontrolled, requires this improved generalization capability. Because the pre-trained data can serve as a stronger prior and help regularize the learning process in the target domain, transfer learning can increase the resilience of these systems and reduce their vulnerability to noisy or incomplete data. The potential to lower the quantity of data required and the expense of annotation in affective computing is one of the most alluring advantages of transfer learning.

Transfer learning provides a way to build effective emotion identification models with far less labeled target data. By utilizing the knowledge built into pre-trained models, researchers can often achieve comparable or even better results with a fraction of the labeled data required to train a model from scratch. This is particularly useful for modalities where data collection may be complex and subject-dependent, such as physiological signals, where it can be challenging to recognize subtle or uncommon emotions for which there are few large labeled datasets. Systems for affective computing can be developed for specific purposes or in resource-constrained environments when collecting large amounts of data is not practical.

This allows for good performance with a small amount of labeled data while lowering the cost and effort associated with data collection and annotation. Furthermore, transfer learning can lessen the need for vast quantities of meticulously annotated emotional data by permitting the use of poorly labeled or tangentially related data from the source domain to enhance learning in the target domain. Furthermore, the application of transfer learning has the potential to greatly accelerate the development of affective computing technologies in general. Transfer learning can reduce the entry barrier for researchers and practitioners in the field by offering a more effective and successful method of developing emotion detection models.

They might use pre-trained models that already exist and modify them to suit their unique requirements rather than starting from scratch and gathering a ton of data for each new emotion identification task or modality. This can facilitate quicker affective computing application prototyping and deployment and significantly shorten the development cycle. Furthermore, the availability of robust pre-trained models and tried-and-true transfer learning techniques can promote greater community cooperation and knowledge sharing, leading to quicker development and the development of more intricate and important emotion-aware technologies in a range of domains, including healthcare, education, entertainment, and human-computer interaction. Researching state-of-the-art transfer learning techniques created especially for Emotion AI holds a lot of promise for the future. Despite the effectiveness of current transfer learning techniques, the special qualities of emotional data—such as its subjectivity, context-dependency, and multi-modal nature—call for the creation of specialized transfer learning strategies. More culturally sensitive and customized emotion recognition systems, for example, may result from methods that can explicitly model and transfer knowledge about individual and cultural differences in emotional expression.

Developing methods that effectively integrate contextual information from multiple modalities during the transfer learning process may also improve the precision and robustness of emotion recognition in real-world scenarios. Meta-learning approaches, which teach models to learn from different tasks, may be very helpful for affective computing. This would enable models to quickly adapt to emotions or new user populations using minimal labeled data. The use of adversarial learning strategies to improve the domain adaptation capabilities of emotion recognition models and new architectures that are inherently better suited for transferring emotional knowledge across different modalities may also be investigated in future studies.

The creation of transfer learning techniques that can explicitly reason about the hierarchical nature of emotions or the relationships between different emotional states may also lead to more sophisticated and comprehensive emotion understanding in AI systems. Finally, with the proliferation of affective computing technologies, it is imperative to proactively address ethical issues in transfer learning for emotion recognition. Transfer learning has many advantages, but it can also unintentionally reinforce biases in the source data, producing unfair or discriminatory results in the target domain. For instance, a facial recognition algorithm trained on data from one demographic group may act biasedly and misinterpret the emotional states of people from other demographic groups.

Therefore, it is crucial to look into the biases in source datasets and pre-trained models used for transfer learning in affective computing. To guarantee justice and equity in emotion identification systems, researchers must create techniques for identifying and reducing these biases. Ethical questions about cultural sensitivity and the possibility of misinterpreting emotional cues in a variety of social contexts are also brought up by the use of transfer learning across languages and cultures. To promote trust and avoid possible harm, transfer learning-based emotional computing systems must be developed and implemented in an open, accountable, and transparent manner.

This entails creating guidelines for the moral application of these technologies in sensitive applications and carefully considering the privacy implications of using pre-trained models that may have been trained on enormous volumes of user data. These ethical issues need to be resolved early on if transfer learning in emotional computing is to be widely and favorably adopted.

13.7 Conclusion

The use of transfer learning is one of the most crucial tactics for resolving the data-centric issues related to the advancement of emotional computing. This research has clarified the significant potential of using data from well-resourced source domains to support the development of emotion identification systems across various modalities, such as textual, vocal, physiological, and facial expressions. By comparing different transfer learning approaches and how well they work with these emotional tasks, it is possible to improve model generalization, drastically cut down on the amount of labeled data needed, and advance the field more quickly.

But this study has also brought attention to the particular difficulties that come up when transferring knowledge to the complex field of human emotions. The subjectivity and context-dependent nature of emotional expression and perception, the potential for domain discrepancies between source and target datasets, and the crucial concerns surrounding the prudent selection of pre-trained models and suitable transfer techniques are significant challenges that call for careful consideration and creative solutions. To guarantee the efficient and dependable transfer of learned material to the specific requirements of affective computing, these issues must be resolved.

The study's conclusion highlights how transfer learning may have a big impact on how emotional computing develops. Through the integration of current trends, the description of possible future directions, and the identification of important challenges that call for targeted research and development, this study promotes a methodical and cautious approach to utilizing the potential. Realizing affective computing's potential to develop truly intelligent, compassionate, and human-centered technologies will require ongoing research into innovative transfer learning strategies catered to the unique characteristics of emotional data as well as a close analysis of the ethical constraints. Our ability to successfully navigate the difficulties and seize the opportunities offered by the developing field of transfer learning will determine whether or not we can give computers the ability to perceive, understand, and react to human emotions.

AI disclosure statement: The author acknowledges the use of AI-based tools for minor language editing or grammatical correction. However, all intellectual contributions, analyses, and conclusions presented in this chapter are entirely the author's own.

References

1. Kratzwald, B., Ilic, S., Kraus, M., Feuerriegel, S., Prendinger, H., Deep learning for affective computing: Text-based emotion recognition in decision support. *Decis. Support Syst.*, *115*, 24–35, 2018, https://doi.org/10.1016/J.DSS.2018.09.002.
2. Schuller, B., Editorial: IEEE Transactions on Affective Computing—Challenges and Chances. *IEEE Trans. Affective Comput.*, *8*, 1, 1–2, 2017, https://doi.org/10.1109/TAFFC.2017.2662858.
3. Rescigno, M., Spezialetti, M., Rossi, S., Personalized models for facial emotion recognition through transfer learning. *Multimed. Tools Appl.*, *79*, 47, 35811–35828, 2020, https://doi.org/10.1007/S11042-020-09405-4.
4. Wu, D. and Parsons, T.D., Inductive transfer learning for handling individual differences in affective computing, in: *Lecture Notes in Computer Science*, S. D'Mello *et al.* (Eds.), pp. 142–151, Springer, Berlin, Heidelberg, 2011, https://doi.org/10.1007/978-3-642-24571-8_15.
5. Kumar, S., Deep learning based affective computing. *J. Enterp. Inf. Manage.*, *34*, 5, 1551–1575, 2021, https://doi.org/10.1108/JEIM-12-2020-0536.
6. Revathy, G., Raj, K.B., Kumar, A., Adibatti, S., Dahiya, P., Latha, T.M., Investigation of E-voting system using face recognition using convolutional neural network (CNN). *Theor. Comput. Sci.*, *925*, 61–67, 2022.

14

Explainability and Interpretability in Affective AI Methods for Making AI-Driven Emotion Recognition Transparent and Trustworthy

Farjana Farvin Sahapudeen[1]* and T. Vigneswari[2]

[1]Department of Computer Science and Engineering, Sastra Deemed University, Srinivasa Ramanujan Centre, Kumbakonam, Tamil Nadu, India
[2]Department of Computer Science and Engineering, Anjalai Ammal Mahalingam Engineering College, Kovilvenni, Tamil Nadu, India

Abstract
Emotion recognition from social media has become a crucial tool for understanding customer sentiments, opinions, and enhancing socio-affective interactions. Affective computing, the domain concerned with extracting human emotions using computational devices. Human emotion recognition plays a significant role in critical decision-making domains such as healthcare, financial markets, criminal justice, and business intelligence. However, automatically detecting emotions in both social media and real-world scenarios remains highly complex and challenging. Recent advances in Machine Learning (ML) and Deep Learning (DL) have enabled automated emotion recognition, yet the lack of transparency in their decision-making processes often characterizes them as "black-box" models, limiting their trustworthiness and real-world applicability. High predictive accuracy alone is insufficient for practical adoption, especially when replacing human expertise in sensitive areas. To overcome these limitations, explainable and interpretable affective AI methods have been introduced. This chapter explores various affective AI approaches, including AI-based emotion sensors and recognition techniques, while providing insights into the concepts of explainability and interpretability. It also presents explainable AI emotion detection architectures, classifications, and types of emotion detection methods, with a focus on model-agnostic

**Corresponding author*: farjanafarvin@src.sastra.ac.in

N. Thillaiarasu, G. Revathy, T. Saravanan, V. Muthukumaran and S. Balamurugan (eds.) Affective Artificial Intelligence: Fundamentals, Challenges, and Applications, (285–310) © 2026 Scrivener Publishing LLC

and model-specific strategies for enhancing trust, transparency, and reliability in emotion-aware systems.

Keywords: Affective computing, speech emotion recognition, explainable AI, machine learning, deep learning, multimodal learning, facial expression recognition

14.1 Introduction

Emotions are neurophysiological activities influenced by behavioral, facial, textual, cognitive, and human interactions. Recognizing emotions from social media is an essential component to value the customer's feelings and opinions and improving the socio-affective domains. Human emotions can also be defined into binary sentiments as positive emotions and negative emotions based on human behavioral states. Emotion detection is an approach to comprehend human emotions through physiological processes.

Human emotion recognition playing a vital role in critical decision making especially in medical domain, share markets, sentencing criminals and finance. In sensitive applications like medical and military inefficient decision making resulting in huge loss including invaluable human life. To enhance transparency and trust in emotion prediction analysis, explanations and interpretations of models are essential. It is evident that obtaining explanations and interpretations from the AI models to understand how the critical decisions are derived from data is of significant importance.

Automatically detecting emotions from social media and real world scenarios is a complex and challenging task. It involves a critical decision making process. Machine Learning (ML) supervised algorithms such as Logistic regression, Linear Regressions, perceptrons, unsupervised K-nearest neighbor, clustering models and ensembling model Random Forest (RF) are used for emotion recognition. In addition to that, Deep learning (DL) models such as Transformer model, Multi-Layer Neural Networks, Auto Encoders (AE) are also utilized for emotion recognition.

Even Though AI models generate hopeful predictions, acquiring and comprehending reasons and explanations behind their predictions remains challenging. The absence of transparency and hindrance in deep learning (DL) models has let them to describe as black- box technologies, which also limits their applicability in real world situations. AI models with high accuracy are not enough to trust and apply in practical situations by replacing human experts.

To address these limitations, explainable and interpretable affective AI methods are proposed and analyzed. This chapter deals with the various affective AI methods for capturing the emotion analysis, The AI sensors applied for emotion extractions and varieties of emotions recognition techniques including Facial Emotion Recognition (FER), Physiological Emotion Recognition (PER), Speech Emotion Recognition (SER), Textual Emotion Recognition (TER), and multimodal recognition. This chapter also explores about the explainable and interpretable AI (XAI) tools and discusses the transparency and trustworthiness of them.

14.2 AI-Driven Emotion Recognition

Emotion is a cognitive status developed based on the human interactions, experience, thought process, visionary and hearing inputs from the outside world. Emotions are derived results of external stimuli generated from current and past surroundings of humans [1]. Emotions are different discrete feelings and collections of behavioral, cognitive and physiological components. Cultural emotions are positive or negative and further categorized as discrete quantities such as happy, sad, fear, anger, joy, disgust, surprise etc. Affective AI technologies applied over the behavioral signals and physiological signals producing promising effective Affective models comparing to complex cognitive mind signals.

Behavioral signals for emotion recognition include speech, textual and facial emotion recognition. Physiological signals include Electrocardiogram (ECG) for heart beats, eye tracking (ET) for eyes, respiration (RSP) for respiration, electroencephalogram (EEG) for brain activities and, Electromyograms (EMGs) for muscle actions. In some applications, multimodal signals such as physical signals combined with physiological sensors are used for analyzing human emotions and generate responsive systems. Facial recognition signals combined with electrocardiogram (ECG) can predict health issues occurring in heart and generate respective alerts. Figure 14.1 represents the AI based emotion recognition model. Human emotions are gathered using AI based sensors. Extracted sensor signals fed to AI based affective computing techniques and results are collected as prediction outcomes.

Human emotions are captured through wearable devices attached to body or using remote sensors. Physiological and Psychological changes occurring in human body causes different types of emotions. Due to mental illness and physical problems human expresses different emotions in terms of visual and audio signals. Intelligent sensors in affective computing address the emerging problems in mental and physical health care. Electrocardiogram (ECG) and electromyography (EMG) sensors recognize the heart and muscular malfunctioning and predicts the changes in the physiological activities [2]. These predicted signals easily communicated to wireless devices for analysis

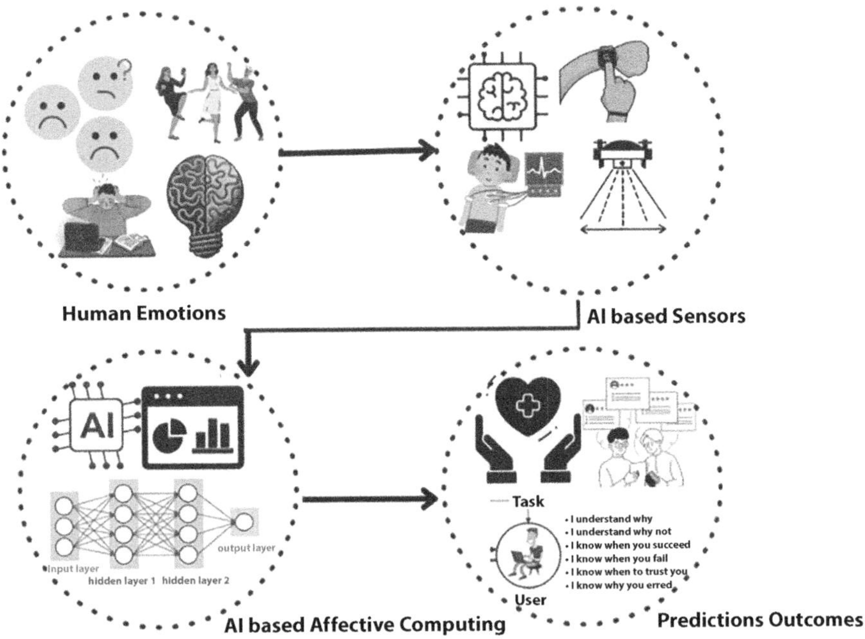

Figure 14.1 AI-based emotion recognition model.

and alert generation. Biosignal based voice recognition signals are extracted from brain and muscle movements using electroencephalography (EEG), electromagnetic articulography (EMA), electropalatography (EPG) sensors [3]. Infrared thermal sensors, along with cameras incorporating illumination and fusion variations can recognize the human facial emotions [4] and generate responsive systems. Multimodal sensing with skin sensory data, volume level of blood and textual content give greater insides into emotions of text. Blood volume pulse (BVP) increases for negative emotions whereas it gradually decreases for relaxed texts [5]. Further sections discuss various recognition techniques for different types of human sensing modalities.

14.3 Affective Computing

Affective Computing (AC) is a research area to recognize, understand and react to human behavioral conditions and become the part of many AI expert systems. Affective computing mainly focuses on human-related data to assign emotion labels using feature based analysis and end to end analysis. In feature related analysis, features are manually extracted from the audio, visual and text data. This approach generates the connection between features and labeled emotions, offering interpretable explanations for human understanding. Alternatively, end to end analysis learns from huge amounts of data to train deep neural networks, resulting in models that function as black boxes. Although the performance of deep neural networks is high, these analyses often provide explanations that are understandable to humans.

Interpretability and explainability of affective computing (AC) mainly depends on models that have mostly depended on *post-hoc* charts, visual methodologies and combination of feature and end to end analysis. Affective computing models are mostly multimodal, including perception and synthesis of emotions. Human emotions are dynamic and varying based on time and context. The affective computing also should consider the culture, socio economic context and interaction dynamics to enhance the predictions [6]. Affective computing should adapt to contextual variability, as the same behavior in different contexts can lead to different interpretations. It also has to concern the ethical rights by considering emotions states as private.

14.4 Interpretability vs. Explainability in AI

Interpretability is a property of the AI model that indicates the level to which users can understand model functioning. Human grounded and application-oriented evaluations provide the measurement of interpretability in the model. The main objective of the explainability idea is to produce justification which highlights essential features of the decision or prediction of the model. Explanations of the AI model might have been presented in many forms, such as statistical reports, data plot diagrams, audio messages, video demos or textual descriptions. Along with prediction outcomes, explanations are also combined to support the interpretability of the AI model. Explainability is defined in terms of how the prediction is communicable and interpretable to the model's target audience.

The explainability of the model might be at either a global or local scope. Global explainability approaches focus to explain the complete functioning of the model. In contrast, local explainability focuses on specific predictions based on specific model parameters. Local explainability offers insights of specific scope without requiring a full understanding of the entire model. Generally explanations are produced based on features of the input, conceptual ideas of the signals, rule based systems or combined modalities. Addition to that, explanations includes the details of selected attribute features, model behavior, learned parameters with examples. For Example, Images were classified as 'parrot' with justification that the object has wings, beak and two legs, an automated vehicle initiated a brake signal as a prediction outcome, with explanation that sensor data indicated a speed breaker and a school zone and a student was declared as pass with explanation that he scored 50 and above in all subjects.

14.5 Transparency and Trustworthy in AI

AI models producing high accuracy are not enough to trust and apply in critical applications. Trustworthiness and transparency of AI models must be ensured before applying directly to the real world situations. Transparent models facilitate prevention, detection and correction of mistakes in dangerous situations. Based on the transparency and trustworthiness of Affective computing (AC) methods provide explanations in two important categories. They are as follows

- **Methods of Visualization:** Essential pixels of input slices that influence the final outcomes are highlighted using visualization techniques [7, 8] like GradCAM and its variations (GradCAM++, ScoreCAM, etc.). These techniques offer visual explanations that are especially helpful in medical imaging, where they can increase diagnostic accuracy and assist clinicians in understanding model decisions.
- **Methods Based on Attribution:** By giving input features importance scores, attribution-based methods, such as gradient-based and perturbation-based approaches, help to clarify which aspects of input segment influences decision-making process of model [9]. AI techniques are frequently employed in computer vision to improve the trustworthiness, understanding and dependability of DL algorithms for crucial applications.

14.6 Explainable AI (XAI)

Explainable Artificial Intelligence (XAI) improves the user's understanding, trustworthiness and provides proper explanations. Building appropriate models for XAI application in need of clear understanding over the ideas and reasoning for decision making [10]. Wearable sensors are key sources for sentiment analysis providing continuous and real time data. Explainable AI (XAI) methods are developed and refined to recognize and understand the human emotions captured through wearables. To improve the trustworthiness, transparency of emotional analysis, explainable AI (XAI) models are emphasized. Smartwatches monitor the heart beats of the humans and detect fluctuating emotions. Latest SHAP (SHapley Additive exPlanations) models integrated with decision making to identify the patient emotions and produce alerts to caretakers. Additionally multimodal methods are applied for explainable deep learning methods for emotion recognition.

Explainability of AI models can be categorized into two different methods as *pre-hoc* and *post hoc*. *Pre-hoc* refers to explanations present inside the model, while *post-hoc* represents explanations produced after training. The target audience for Explainable AI varies based on the application and specific needs of those involved. In general, they are customers and end users, business leaders, data scientists and developers, domain experts, and auditors and regulators. XAI model should identify user needs and develop appropriate explanation methods to enhance understanding from their perspective. Figure 14.2 depicts the various stakeholders involved in explainable AI.

Figure 14.2 Explainable AI (XAI) target audience.

- **Customers and End-Users:** Individual users who interact with AI models and try to understand the factors behind the predictions. For example, in a hospital system, a patient needs to understand the reason for this suggested medicine. In an automated taxi system, the passenger would need to know why the vehicle's speed is increased.
- **Business Leaders:** Business Leaders are paying attention to prioritizing explainability and interpretability in order to increase stakeholders' reliability. They trust the AI models and are encouraging transparency.
- **Data Scientists and Developers:** Data Scientists are responsible for changing the developed AI model into interpretable with user friendly explanations. Developers train and test the models with global level interpretability and make them as trustworthy and reliable.
- **Domain Experts:** They are the people with specialized knowledge in their field and they must understand how models provide explanations. In sensitive fields such as healthcare and finance, offering guidance in model selection, evaluating real world applicability and providing valuable feedback are invaluable.
- **Auditors and Regulators:** To build trustworthy AI systems, auditors must verify accuracy and transparency of AI driven decisions. Regulators are responsible for verifying the legal and ethical implications of AI models.

To strengthen the Explainable AI models, they must meet the following criteria as feature attributes.

1. XAI models must be interpretable, providing sufficient metadata as additional information to understand to why a specific classification or prediction is produced. Interpretable data may include images or text which describes rules and decision paths for the final outcome of AI models. These additional information is generated by the AI models itself or by additional explanation modules.
2. The XAI model improves transparency by generating human acceptable decisions with appropriate used examples. Transparency, supported by scientific and logical reasoning in decision making is more worthwhile compared to confidential decisions without explanations.

3. Trustworthiness in XAI models is a performance measure reflecting how human users respond in working with dynamic, real world environments. Basic explanations in classification models are essential for improving the stakeholders' trust and enabling direct integration of AI models into socio-economic applications [11].
4. Traceability in XAI models provides an option to track the decisions made by AI models and the supporting documentary data. It enables auditors to verify these decisions and offers a debugging option to enhance reliability.
5. Reliability in XAI models ensures the stability and consistency of the systems. It also reflects the usefulness of the model in terms of decision making which should be transparent and reliable. This, in turn increases stakeholders trust and reduces errors and bias in the system.

14.7 Explainable AI in Emotion Recognition

Computers become user friendly, if they sense and react to human emotions. AI models are necessary areas for detecting appropriate emotions. They use complex AI models to detect human face expressions through tracking changes in brows, lips, chins and cheeks. Vocal analysis using ML/DL algorithms focusing on observing frequency, loudness and speed of speech. Text materials are sentimentally analyzed by Natural Language Models of AI for different emotions of humans. Addition to that, physiological signals such as abnormal fall, heart pulse rate (HPR), brain signals, respiratory and conductivity of skin are analyzed for human emotional states.

Human emotions captured through sensors are available in different formats. To address these input signals, various unimodal XAI recognition techniques are proposed. Before understanding each unimodal XAI method, the proposed generic architecture that is applicable to all the recognition techniques must be clearly understood. Figure 14.3 displays the architecture of Explainable and Interpretable AI, in which human emotions captured in various formats such as audio, visual, physical and text data are provided as input. The XAI model components are divided into two parts: a regular machine learning/deep learning module for predictions, and an explanation module for generating explanations. Explanations may be presented in formats such as chats, reports, audio or textual messages.

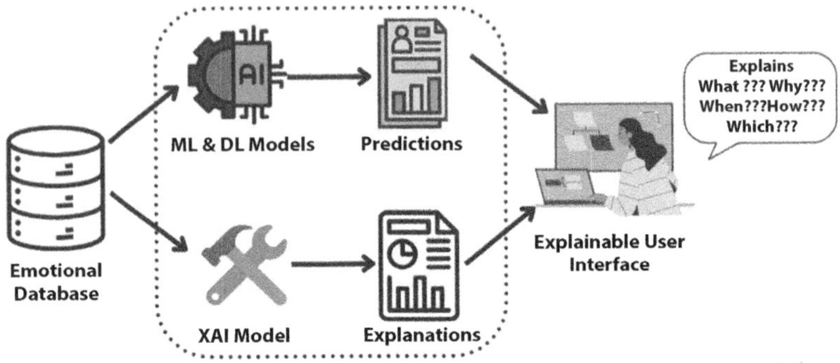

Figure 14.3 Architecture of explainable and interpretable AI.

The explanation, along with prediction result is produced as output through explainable user interface.

The major division of explainable emotion recognition are in terms of Speech (SER), Facial (FER), Textual and Physiological (PER). Additionally to handle multimodal signals such as text-audio, audio-visual, text-visual, physiological with text, or combination of all -Explainable Multimodal Emotion Recognition (EMER) techniques are implemented. The following

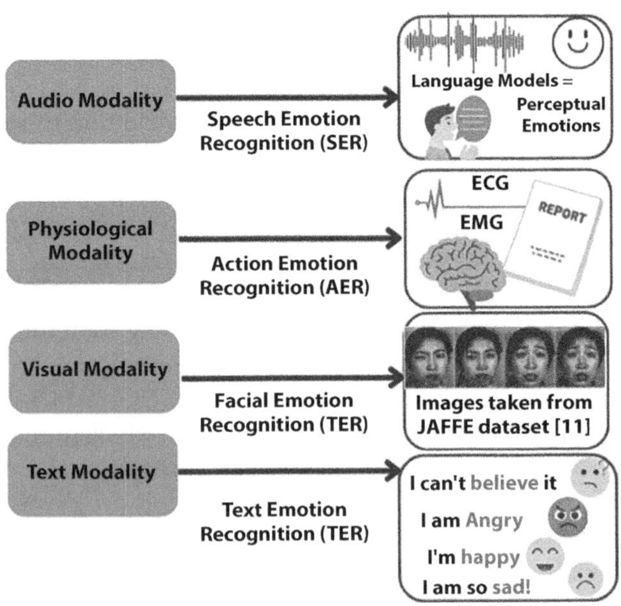

Figure 14.4 Different modalities of emotion recognition.

sections explains the details of each modality technique and its pros and cons. Figure 14.4 represents the various modalities in emotion detection methods and their respective output. The following sections further provides the insights about various modalities of emotion and the AI models respectively.

14.8 Explainable AI in Speech Emotion Recognition (SER)

The speech signal is the easiest and the common process of conveying emotions between humans. Humans convey their affective status by modulating voice, speed and pitch. Even vocabulary, choice of word, and pronunciation of words contribute to motive and emotion behind the speech. Understanding the affective emotion from the human speech and audio signals is a complex analytical task. Vast amount of signal data, facilitate the Machine Learning (ML) models voice recognition applications. Furthermore, dimensionality of the audio signals are reduced and results are fed forward into deep neural networks (DNN). They are efficient in identifying audio signals based on loudness and pitch variation.

Even though AI models recognize the audio signals effectively, a lack of interpretability introduces a challenge in identifying rational decisions which can lead to unwanted prediction results. Feature based booting methods in supervised learning proposed to detect the features of speech signals. SHAP explainability added to the model to verify and evaluates the decisions [12]. Even speech can be converted into a spectrogram and each divided spectrogram session is displayed as a Gaussian distribution to reduce features. VGGish and YAMNet deep learning networks used along with Grad CAM or LIME models for analyzing the predictions [13].

14.9 XAI in Facial Emotion Recognition (FER)

Facial expressions are visual signals that explain the human mind and thoughts. Affective Computing (AC), a field to recognize individual emotions, including facial expressions. Emotion Recognition using biometric signals such as facial expression can be interpreted as human states and decisions can be recommended based on them. The increasing number of data images and videos has made Facial Expression Recognition (FER) a vital recognition technique. Videos are decomposed into individual images and image features such as nose, eyes, eyebrows, cheeks, chin, and lips are separated. Extracted descriptive image features trained based on AI model with respect to gender, age and culture. AI based algorithms are producing promising result in identifying the human emotions such as frustration, pleasure, tolerance, belief and dissatisfaction [14, 15].

By observing muscle changes, head positioning and cheek and lip movements, emotions can be extracted and converted into predictions for stakeholders. Particularly in Facial Action Units (AUs) such as U12 (Lip Corner Puller) produces positive happy emotions; AU6 (Cheek Raiser) and AU2 (Outer Brow Raiser) indicate the surprising emotions; and AU15 (Lip Corner Depressor) indicates negative, sad emotions [16]. Individual emotions are categorized using Facial Action Coding System (FACS) from facial expression units and produce predictions. Even though affective computing models generates the effective facial emotional Recognition (FER), transparency and trustworthiness of those models prevents them real world application.

Explainable Artificial Intelligence (XAI) is combined into Affective Computing (AC) to increase the transparency by observing facial muscle activations. Explainable (LIME, FAU+MLP) techniques along with CNN produces the predicted result along with explanations in terms of Action Units (AU) for interpretations [17]. Even based on ranking with Layerwise Relevance Propagation (LRP) as XAI techniques along with VGG can increase the understanding of the predictions and influence in better decision making [18].

14.10 Explainable AI in Text Emotion Recognition (TER)

The Emotions In a text are hidden within its keywords. Identifying these keywords and understanding the context through them is the primary task of any AI model. Using Lexicon based approach along with machine learning algorithms which includes Multi-Layer Perceptron (MLP) and Neural Networks, are developed to identify emotions in textual data [19]. Model predictions are verified with humans through chatbots. The AI model XLNet with bidirectional recurrent unit extracts important word level features by attention units. The attention values and word vectors assigns probability weights to all the words, ultimately the emotion classification is obtained [20].

In language models TF-IDF represents Term Frequency (TF) and Inverse Document Frequency (IDF). TF detects the frequently used word and IDF detects the rarely used words across all documents in dataset. It helps to derive a feature vector for text documentation as follows

$$W(d, t) = TF(d, t) * \log(\frac{N}{d.f(t)}) \tag{14.1}$$

In Equation (14.1), d refers to document, N represents the total no of documents and t denotes Term. Emotions are detected using Large Language Models (LLM) of AI and produced promised results.

Hybrid techniques as combination of ML and DL are also used in recognizing human emotions [21]. The Semantic-Emotion Neural Network (SENN) identifies semantic-explanations and emotional details from pre-trained textural data. It contains Bidirectional Long-Short Term Memory (BiLSTM) to understand the semantics, and convolutional neural networks (CNN) for extracting emotions from text [22].

14.11 Physiological Signal Recognition with Explainable AI

Physiological signals are most prominent emotion carrying platforms when human consciously failed to express or hiding the emotions. Elderly and Chronic diseases patients are not comfortable in expressing emotions in regular voices and textual models. Observing the physiological changes of a human through wearable is major reliable component in healthcare. Wearable components such as smart glasses and smart watches are useful in monitoring the signals in real time continuously.

Even the functionality of human organs such as heart, lungs, and brain are disturbed during the times of danger or illness, exhibiting symptoms of irregular heart rate, abnormal respiratory, and impaired physical activities. Mental illnesses can also changes in physical activities and cognitive processes, resulting in unexpected physiological changes in the human body. These signals are analyzed using AI models to understand the reason behind the changes and provide proper explanations to caretakers. Affective model also suggest for immediate response as medical care and provide proper diagnosis.

In automatic emotion detection driving system involves, continuous monitoring and detecting driver drowsiness using physiological signals, which could potentially save lives by preventing accidents. Internal human signals-physiological signals include temperature (T), respiration rate (RSP), electrocardiogram (ECG), and electroencephalogram (EEG) and others.

The nervous system of human is connected to various internal human body parts, such as the heart, lungs, and brain. When a human faces complex situations, it automatically sends alert signals to internal parts, which can be captured through aforementioned sensors. A multimodal-multisensory sequential fusion model (MMSF) – deep learning model with fusion techniques can process bio-signals and provide appropriate explanation [23].

14.12 Explainable Multimodal Emotion Recognition (EMER)

Different annotation processes assign different emotional labels to same video slices. To avoid this kind of unimodal sensing, more than recognition techniques integrated as multimodal emotion recognition along with explanations were used. Multimodal emotion detection relied on the combination of more than one signal from audio, visual and textual modalities [24]. Diversified data representations and interconnections among them necessitate a multimodal approach, in which new information is obtained by combining more than one model. Emotion extraction is a complex task. Label spacing which allows for labeling the inputs and selecting majority from them, result in ambiguous state.

To overcome that, Audio-Visual-text modalities can be combined for better understanding of signals and propose explanations based on them [25]. EMER integrates all emotion correlated modalities such as EMER (Audio signal), EMER (Text Signal), and EMER (Video Signal) to produce accurate recognition. Even with same visual modality concepts can be observed deeply to get insight of signals. Attention-Guided Concept Model (AGCM) [26] proposed to provide conceptual explanations by observing concepts from the visual data through spatial and temporal signals. These multimodal modeling enhances the stakeholders decision making process.

AGCM utilizes the strength of feature based machine learning techniques with location identification deep learning methods for interpretable and human understandable systems. SHAP Explainable AI (SHAP-XAI) method developed to interpret emotions from vocal data, facial expressions and textual content. Explainable AI model generates the reduced features from the models and the irrelevant features are removed. This approach explains the black box model predictions as transparent and easily interpretable [27].

14.13 Emerging XAI Models

Lot of Explainable AI tools are developed and available for detecting human emotions. From audio-visual data emotions are easily extracted using VGG and ResNet. Emerging XAI tools creates a demand for trustability with full explanation. Familiar tools such as Layer-Wise Relevance Propagation (LRP), SHapley Additive exPlanations (SHAP) are developed to generate explanations along with model predictions. Addition to that Local Interpretable Model-agnostic Explanations (LIME) and Class Activation Mapping (CAM) are developed for generating interpretations. The XAI models are divided as two types, model agnostic and model specific. Common or generic explanations for all the types of modes are provided by model-agnostic [28]. In Contrast to that, Explanations produced only for specific model in model specific methods. Figure 14.5 depicts the different types of XAI tools used for emotion recognition.

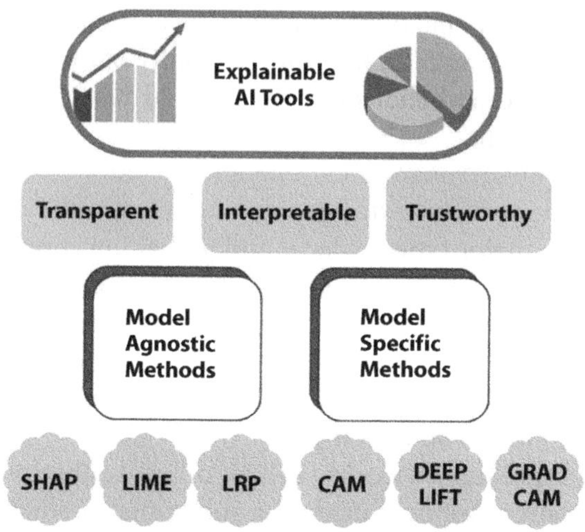

Figure 14.5 Explainable AI (XAI) tools.

Model-Agnostic Methods

Based on the internal mechanism of the AI model, independent explanations are generated by model–agnostic methods. To select best model, they are trained generally without considering the architectures [29–31]. Irrespective of architectural style, selected models are applied to black box models [32]. Several categorization techniques can be used to the models with slight modification. The major goals of this approach are explainability, security, and safety. Model-agnostic approaches' primary goals can be classified into several significant factors.

- **Understanding Model Behavior:** These methods help make sense of how models produce predictions, which is crucial for confidence and usability [33]. By measuring the impact of individual traits on predictions, Feature Contribution aids in feature engineering and selection [34].
- **Flexibility and Adaptability:** Applied to any AI model, increasing their usefulness across a variety of applications, making them Model Independent [35]. They can generate simpler models that approximate the behavior of complex ones, making interpretation easier.
- **Multi-Objective Optimization:** These techniques enable the concurrent optimization of several goals, including model complexity and accuracy, producing more reliable models [36]. Although interpretability and flexibility are two major benefits of model-agnostic approaches, there are drawbacks as well, such as the possibility of oversimplifying intricate model behaviors, which could result in incorrect interpretations.

Based on scope and context domains, model agnostic approaches categorized into two major types as local and global interpretability. The following content briefly describes about the local and global interpretability. Local interpretability explains the specific prediction outcomes, whereas the global interpretability concentrates on overall model's functioning. To evaluate feature relativeness, global interpretability method SHAP is frequently used [37] in model training.

The local interpretability works with an objective that provides knowledge about certain cases by elucidating individual predictions. Methods that offer customized explanations for discrete predictions include model-agnostic *post hoc* local explanations (MAPLE) and LIME [38]. Explainable AI models are effective in medical diagnosis to understand the reason behind the diagnosis. The difficulty lies in striking a balance between global and local interpretability, even though model-agnostic approaches offer insightful information on both. According to some researchers, focusing too much on local explanations could obscure the model's overall behavior and erode confidence in its predictions [39].

Global Interpretability Methods

1. General behavior of the model explained as a comprehension in global interpretation. It approximately guessing the outcomes of the model.
2. A model-neutral technique for determining the importance of global features based on Shapley values and marginal contributions is called SAGE (Shapley Additive Global Importance). Using this technique, the global predictive power of features can be measured.

Local Interpretability Methods

1. To explain one instance at a time, LIME fits a linear regression around a prediction.
2. To choose training points that are pertinent to the prediction, MAPLE combines local linear models with a random forest. It is applied when precise local explanations are necessary.
3. To explain local predictions, LORE (Local Rule-Based Explanations) creates decision rules and produces counterfactual examples. This is essential for rule-based and interpretable counterfactual applications.
4. Context-dependent feature importance is used by CIU (Contextual Importance) to provide explanations. It measures how significant a feature is in a particular context.
5. A hybrid approach called Local Interpretable Model-Agnostic SHAP Explanations (LIMASE) [40] combines advantages of both SHAP, LIME thus producing reliable local explanations.
6. Clustering is used to calculate local variable importance scores in CLIQUE (Clustering for Local Interpretable Quantitative Explanations) [41]. It is used in fields where it is crucial to quantitatively verify the relevance of features within clusters.

14.14 Model-Specific Methods

The machine learning Techniques working are explained by this model. They aim to improve user trust and understanding by providing detailed insights into how specific algorithms makes [42, 43]. The principal objectives of model-specific methodologies in Explainable Artificial Intelligence (XAI) are centered on augmenting the clarity of intricate models. These methodologies endeavor to reconcile the disparity between the opaque "black-box" characteristics of AI systems and the imperative for human comprehension, particularly within high-stakes domains.

The following features outlines the core objectives of these model-specific methods, including improved interpretability, fostering trust, performance assessment, and customization [44, 45].

- **Improved Interpretability:** Model-specific approaches make predictions easier for users to understand by offering customized explanations that fit the model's distinctive features.
- **Building Trust:** These techniques increase user trust by elucidating the logic behind model outputs, especially in crucial applications like healthcare.
- **Performance Evaluation:** By identifying significant features, they enable the evaluation of model performance, which can be essential for domain experts to validate predictions.
- **Customization:** Model-specific methods can be created to tackle particular issues with certain algorithms, increasing their efficacy in practical applications.
- Grad-CAM (Gradient-weighted Class Activation) [46] works especially well in visualizing the areas of input data that affect model predictions. It is frequently used in medical imaging; it helps clinicians understand model decisions by producing heat maps that highlight significant regions in images.
- LRP -provides details about how the neural network layers are divided as layers to determine which features correlated to emotional states [54] and Tree SHAPE [47], a model-specific approach in Explainable AI (XAI), improves the interpretability of tree-based models by effectively calculating Shapley values for feature attributions. This technique tackles the difficulty of precisely obtaining Shapley values

from ensemble models—regarded as machine learning "black boxes"—like gradient-boosted trees.

- A model-specific method in eXplainable Artificial Intelligence (XAI) called DeepLIFT (Deep Learning Important FeaTures) [48] sheds light on how input features affect the predictions produced by deep learning (DL) algorithms. By assigning the output to the input features according to their significance, this technique works especially well for deciphering complex neural networks.

On the other hand, although model-specific approaches have many benefits, they could also have drawbacks like decreased generalization. Table 14.1 displays the comparison of famous XAI tools in terms of features transparency, interpretability, trustworthiness, traceability and reliability.

14.15 Comparison of Model Agonistic Methods with Model-Specific Methods

Compared to later, model-specific explanations have diverse benefits, especially in performance of precision, effectiveness, and reliability which results from the ability to take advantage of particular models' internal structures, which can produce explanations that are more accurate and pertinent to the context. In contrast to model-agnostic approaches, which frequently only consider input-output relationships, model-specific

Table 14.1 Feature-based comparison of explainable AI (XAI) tools.

	Explainable AI (XAI)-features				
XAI-tools	**Transparency**	**Interpretability**	**Trustworthiness**	**Traceability**	**Reliability**
SHAP [49]	✓	✓	✓	✓	✓
LIME [50]		✓			
CAM [51]	✓	✓	✓	✓	✓
DEEPLIFT [52]	✓	✓	✓	✓	✓
Grad-CAM [53]	✓	✓	✓	✓	✓
LRP [54]	✓	✓	✓	✓	✓

explanations make use of internal components of the model, resulting in more accurate interpretations of predictions [55]. Users can improve reliability by producing explanations that closely match those from a white-box perspective by using a local surrogate to approximate the provider's model. Model Specific explanations having greater advantage compared to model agnostic approaches, in terms of various performance parameters such as efficiency, trustworthy and interpretability. The following sections outline these key advantages.

- **Accuracy of Explanations:** Explanations are more accurate as they are derived from the internal components that depend on the correlation between the input and output [55].
- **Efficiency in Inference:** The inference provided by this model is more efficient compared to the others as time and resource consumption is very less [56].
- **Transparency and Trust:** Generating model-specific explanations are important to increase the trust of the stake holders in significant application domains, where understanding model decisions are essential [57].

On the other hand, although model-specific explanations are more accurate and efficient, they might not be as generalizable as model-agnostic methods deployed in various AI models and situations. This trade-off focus on significance of efficient explanation methods depending on particular scenarios and specifications.

14.16 Conclusion

This chapter gives a clear idea about the affective computing domain and ideas about explainability and interpretability. This chapter also explains about Explainable AI Emotion detection architecture and types of emotion detection in details. Explainable AI for emotion detection is further explained in the view of its classification based on agnostic and specific terms. XAI model-specific approaches tackle the intricacies of deep learning models by offering customized explanations that improve interpretability and transparency. Even though the accuracy of effective computing is made better by deploying deep learning models, it faces many challenges. For instance, lack of common metrics for model evaluation and generic models compatible with diverse architectures and data types are essential.

Adding to this, equilibrium between the model efficiency and its ability to understand is also another concern. Hence more research focus is needed in future to resolve such issues and make XAI a prominent technology.

AI disclosure statement: The author acknowledges the use of AI-based tools for minor language editing or grammatical correction. However, all intellectual contributions, analyses, and conclusions presented in this chapter are entirely the author's own.

References

1. Khare, S.K., Blanes-Vidal, V., Nadimi, E.S., Acharya, U.R., Emotion recognition and artificial intelligence: A systematic review (2014–2023) and research recommendations. *Inf. Fusion, 102*, 102019, 2024.
2. Patel, S., Park, H., Bonato, P., Chan, L., Rodgers, M., A review of wearable sensors and systems with application in rehabilitation. *J. NeuroEng. Rehabil.*, *9*, 1–17, 2012.
3. Lee, W., Seong, J.J., Ozlu, B., Shim, B.S., Marakhimov, A., Lee, S., Biosignal sensors and deep learning-based speech recognition: A review. *Sensors*, 21, 4, 1399, 2021.
4. Samadiani, N., Huang, G., Cai, B., Luo, W., Chi, C.H., Xiang, Y., He, J., A review on automatic facial expression recognition systems assisted by multimodal sensor data. *Sensors, 19*, 8, 1863, 2019.
5. Wang, H., Prendinger, H., Igarashi, T., Communicating emotions in online chat using physiological sensors and animated text, in: *CHI'04 Extended Abstracts on Human Factors in Computing Systems*, pp. 1171–1174, New York, NY, USA: ACM (Association for Computing Machinery), 2004, April.
6. Cortiñas-Lorenzo, K. and Lacey, G., Toward explainable affective computing: A review. *IEEE Trans. Neural Netw. Learn. Syst.*, 35, 10, 13101–13121, 2023.
7. Bhati, D., Neha, F., Amiruzzaman, M., A survey on explainable artificial intelligence (xai) techniques for visualizing deep learning models in medical imaging. *J. Imaging, 10*, 10, 239, 2024.
8. Abdullah, W., Tolba, A., Elmasry, A., Mostafa, N.N., Visioncam: a comprehensive XAI toolkit for interpreting image-based deep learning models. *Sustain. Mach. Intell. J.*, *8*, 4–46, 2024.
9. Abhishek, K. and Kamath, D., Attribution-based xai methods in computer vision: A review, *arXiv preprint arXiv:2211.14736*, 2022.
10. Dwivedi, R., Dave, D., Naik, H., Singhal, S., Omer, R., Patel, P., Ranjan, R., Explainable AI (XAI): Core ideas, techniques, and solutions. *ACM Comput. Surv.*, *55*, 9, 1–33, 2023.
11. Das, A. and Rad, P., Opportunities and challenges in explainable artificial intelligence (xai): A survey, *arXiv preprint arXiv:2006.11371*, 2020.

12. Nfissi, A., Bouachir, W., Bouguila, N., Mishara, B., Unveiling hidden factors: explainable ai for feature boosting in speech emotion recognition. *Appl. Intell.*, *54*, 11, 7046–7069, 2024.
13. Kim, T.W. and Kwak, K.C., Speech emotion recognition using deep learning transfer models and explainable techniques. *Appl. Sci.*, *14*, 4, 1553, 2024.
14. Venkatesan, R., Shirly, S., Selvarathi, M., Jebaseeli, T.J., Human emotion detection using DeepFace and artificial intelligence. *Eng. Proc.*, *59*, 1, 37, 2023.
15. Kaur, M. and Kumar, M., Facial emotion recognition: A comprehensive review. *Expert Syst.*, *41*, 10, e13670, 2024.
16. Huang, Y., Chen, F., Lv, S., Wang, X., Facial expression recognition: A survey. *Symmetry*, *11*, 10, 1189, 2019.
17. Deramgozin, M., Jovanovic, S., Rabah, H., Ramzan, N., A hybrid explainable ai framework applied to global and local facial expression recognition, in: *2021 IEEE International Conference on Imaging Systems and Techniques (IST)*, pp. 1–5, IEEE, 2021, August.
18. Punuri, S.B., Kuanar, S.K., Mishra, T.K., Rao, V.V.R.M., Reddy, S.S., Decoding Human Facial Emotions: A Ranking Approach using Explainable AI. *IEEE Access*, 2024.
19. Machová, K., Szabóova, M., Paralič, J., Mičko, J., Detection of emotion by text analysis using machine learning. *Front. Psychol.*, *14*, 1190326, 2023.
20. Johnson, D.S., Hakobyan, O., Paletschek, J., Drimalla, H., Explainable AI for Audio and Visual Affective Computing: A Scoping Review. *IEEE Trans. Affective Comput.*, 2024.
21. Bharti, S.K., Varadhaganapathy, S., Gupta, R.K., Shukla, P.K., Bouye, M., Hingaa, S.K., Mahmoud, A., Text-Based Emotion Recognition Using Deep Learning Approach. *Comput. Intell. Neurosci.*, *2022*, 1, 2645381, 2022.
22. Han, T., Zhang, Z., Ren, M., Dong, C., Jiang, X., Zhuang, Q., Text emotion recognition based on xlnet-bigru-att. *Electronics*, *12*, 12, 2704, 2023.
23. Lin, J., Pan, S., Lee, C.S., Oviatt, S., An explainable deep fusion network for affect recognition using physiological signals, in: *Proceedings of the 28th ACM International Conference on Information and Knowledge Management*, pp. 2069–2072, 2019, November.
24. Batbaatar, E., Li, M., Ryu, K.H., Semantic-emotion neural network for emotion recognition from text. *IEEE Access*, *7*, 111866–111878, 2019.
25. Lian, Z., Sun, H., Sun, L., Gu, H., Wen, Z., Zhang, S., Tao, J., Explainable Multimodal Emotion Recognition, *arXiv preprint arXiv:2306.15401*, 2023.
26. Li, X. and Mahmoud, M., Interpretable Concept-based Deep Learning Framework for Multimodal Human Behavior Modeling, *arXiv preprint arXiv:2502.10145,* 2025.
27. Khalane, A., Makwana, R., Shaikh, T., Ullah, A., Evaluating significant features in context-aware multimodal emotion recognition with XAI methods. *Expert Syst.*, *42*, 1, e13403, 2025.

28. Gianfagna, L. and Di Cecco, A., Model-agnostic methods for XAI, in: *Explainable AI with python*, pp. 81–113, Springer International Publishing, Cham, 2021.
29. Letrache, K. and Ramdani, M., Explainable Artificial Intelligence: A Review and Case Study on Model-Agnostic Methods, in: *2023 14th International Conference on Intelligent Systems: Theories and Applications (SITA)*, pp. 1–8, IEEE, 2023, November.
30. Liu, X., Taylor, M.P., Aelion, C.M., Dong, C., Novel application of machine learning algorithms and model-agnostic methods to identify factors influencing childhood blood lead levels. *Environ. Sci. Technol.*, *55*, 19, 13387–13399, 2021.
31. Wikle, C.K., Datta, A., Hari, B.V., Boone, E.L., Sahoo, I., Kavila, I., Chang, W., An illustration of model agnostic explainability methods applied to environmental data. *Environmetrics*, *34*, 1, e2772, 2023.
32. Tayal, K., Ghosh, R., Kumar, V., Model-agnostic methods for text classification with inherent noise, in: *Proceedings of the 28th international conference on computational linguistics: industry track*, pp. 202–213, 2020, December.
33. Ri Ribeiro, M.T., Singh, S., Guestrin, C., Model-agnostic interpretability of machine learning, *arXiv preprint arXiv:1606.05386*, 2016.
34. Varghese, A., George, B., Sherimon, V., Ahmed, S.S., Explainable Artificial Intelligence using Model Agnostic Methods in detecting Alzheimer's disease. *Alzheimers Dement.*, *19*, e075379, 2023.
35. Sim, M.K., Explanation using model-agnostic methods, in: *Human-Centered Artificial Intelligence*, pp. 17–31, Cambridge, Academic Press, Elsevier, 2022.
36. Hvatov, A., Maslyaev, M., Polonskaya, I. S., Sarafanov, M., Merezhnikov, M., Nikitin, N. O., Model-agnostic multi-objective approach for the evolutionary discovery of mathematical models, in: *Optimization, Learning Algorithms and Applications: First International Conference, OL2A 2021, Bragança, Portugal, July 19–21, 2021, Revised selected papers*, vol. 1, pp. 72–85, Cham, Switzerland: Springer International Publishing, 2021.
37. Covert, I., Lundberg, S.M., Lee, S.I., Understanding global feature contributions with additive importance measures. *Advances in Neural Information Processing systems*, *33*, 17212–17223, 2020.
38. Hakkoum, H., Idri, A., Abnane, I., Global and local interpretability techniques of supervised machine learning black box models for numerical medical data. *Eng. Appl. Artif. Intell.*, *131*, 107829, 2024.
39. Bassan, S., Amir, G., Katz, G., Local vs. Global Interpretability: A Computational Complexity Perspective, *arXiv preprint arXiv:2406.02981*, 2024.
40. Aditya, P. and Pal, M., Local interpretable model agnostic shap explanations for machine learning models, *arXiv preprint arXiv:2210.04533*, 2022.
41. Bladen, K.K., Cutler, A., Cutler, D.R., Moon, K.R., Model agnostic local variable importance for locally dependent relationships, *arXiv preprint arXiv:2411.08821*, 2024.

42. Bhatnagar, S. and Agrawal, R., Understanding explainable artificial intelligence techniques: a comparative analysis for practical application. *Bull. Electr. Eng. Inf.*, *13*, 6, 4451–4455, 2024.
43. Banerjee, P. and Barnwal, R.P., Methods and metrics for explaining artificial intelligence models: A review, in: *Explainable AI: Foundations, Methodologies and Applications*, pp. 61–88, 2022.
44. Sadeghi, Z., Alizadehsani, R., Cifci, M.A., Kausar, S., Rehman, R., Mahanta, P., Pardalos, P.M., A brief review of explainable artificial intelligence in healthcare, *arXiv preprint arXiv:2304.01543*, 2023.
45. Lavelle-Hill, R., Smith, G., Murayama, K., An Explainable AI Handbook for Psychologists: Methods, Opportunities, and Challenges, 2024.
46. Barra, P., Della Greca, A., Amaro, I., Tortora, A., Staffa, M., A Comparative Analysis of XAI Techniques for Medical Imaging: Challenges and Opportunities, pp. 6782–6788, 2024, https://doi.org/10.1109/bibm62325.2024.10821983.
47. Muschalik, M., Fumagalli, F., Hammer, B., Hüllermeier, E., Beyond treeshap: Efficient computation of any-order shapley interactions for tree ensembles. *Proc. AAAI Conf. Artif. Intell.*, 38, 13, 14388–14396, 2024, March.
48. Airlangga, G., Decoding Energy Usage Predictions: An Application of XAI Techniques for Enhanced Model Interpretability. *Indones. J. Artif. Intell. Data Min.*, *7*, 2, 275–284, 2024.
49. Lundberg, S.M. and Lee, S.I., A unified approach to interpreting model predictions. *Advances in Neural Information Processing Systems*, vol. *30*, 2017.
50. Revathy, G., Raj, K.B., Kumar, A., Adibatti, S., Dahiya, P., Latha, T.M., Investigation of E-voting system using face recognition using convolutional neural network (CNN). *Theor. Comput. Sci.*, *925*, 61–67, 2022.
51. Zhou, B., Khosla, A., Lapedriza, A., Oliva, A., Torralba, A., Learning deep features for discriminative localization, in: *Proceedings of the IEEE conference on computer vision and pattern recognition*, pp. 2921–2929, 2016.
52. Shrikumar, A., Greenside, P., Kundaje, A., Learning important features through propagating activation differences, in: *International Conference on Machine Learning*, pp. 3145–3153, PMlR, 2017, July.
53. Selvaraju, R.R., Cogswell, M., Das, A., Vedantam, R., Parikh, D., Batra, D., Grad-cam: Visual explanations from deep networks *via* gradient-based localization, in: *Proceedings of the IEEE International Conference on Computer Vision*, pp. 618–626, 2017.
54. Bach, S., Binder, A., Montavon, G., Klauschen, F., Müller, K.R., Samek, W., On pixel-wise explanations for non-linear classifier decisions by layer-wise relevance propagation. *PLoS One*, *10*, 7, e0130140, 2015.

55. Haffar, R., Jebreel, N., Sánchez, D., Domingo-Ferrer, J., Generating Deep Learning Model-Specific Explanations at the End User's Side. *Int. J. Uncertainty Fuzziness Knowledge Based Syst.*, *30*, Supp 02, 255–278, 2022.
56. Pan, D., Moniz, N., Chawla, N., Fast Explainability *via* Feasible Concept Sets Generator, *arXiv preprint arXiv:2405.18664*, 2024.
57. Wanga, T., Liub, M., Wangc, Y., Peng, B., Chenf, S., Songg, X., Liango, C.X., Explainable AI Across Domains: Techniques, Domain-Specific Applications, and Future Directions.

15

From EEG to Emotion: Spatio-Temporal Deep Learning for Real-Time Affective State Recognition

S. Murali Mohan[1], B. Rupa Devi[2], R. Tharun[3], Arakonam Elen Kokila[4], Konkala Divya[4] and M. Sudhakara[5]*

[1]*Department of ECE, Mother Theresa Institute of Engineering and Technology, Palamaner, A.P, India*
[2]*Department of A.I.D.S, Annamacharya Institute of Technology and Sciences, Tirupati, A.P, India*
[3]*Department of Civil Engineering, Mother Theresa Institute of Engineering and Technology, Palamaner, A.P, India*
[4]*Department of CSE, Narayana Engineering College, Nellore, A.P, India*
[5]*Department of Information Science & Engineering, East Point College of Engineering and Technology, Bangalore, Karnataka, India*

Abstract

Emotion recognition using EEG has become an essential component in the development of intelligent human-computer interaction (HCI) systems, neurofeedback, and affective computing. Unlike facial expression or speech emotion recognition, EEG-based recognition offers a direct and objective access to the emotional activity of the human brain. This finds specific application in clinical, learning, and assistive technologies, where non-invasive and accurate emotional awareness can significantly enhance user interaction and cognitive assistance. However, for precise emotion recognition from EEG signals, it is a difficult task owing to the noisy, high-dimensional, and non-linear nature of brain signals. Even the most well-known traditional machine learning models do not have the ability to learn the hidden subtle temporal-spatial patterns within multi-channel EEG signals. In this paper, we present a new deep learning network, ST-GCN-EmotionNet, a Spatio-Temporal Graph Convolutional Network that is specifically tailor-made for robust

**Corresponding author*: mallasudhakar.cse@gmail.com

N. Thillaiarasu, G. Revathy, T. Saravanan, V. Muthukumaran and S. Balamurugan (eds.) Affective Artificial Intelligence: Fundamentals, Challenges, and Applications, (311–352) © 2026 Scrivener Publishing LLC

emotion recognition from EEG and speech. The model exploits the structured topological structure of EEG electrode positions and temporal continuity of emotional responses. By embedding the EEG electrodes into graph nodes and casting their functional relations along time, ST-GCN-EmotionNet can jointly learn spatial correlations and temporal dynamics. Having a two-way outlook allows the model to learn affective states better and attain generalizability on other datasets and subjects. The EEG-Brainwave and CREMA-D (Crowd-sourced Emotional Multimodal Actors Dataset) benchmark datasets were utilized to exhaustively test the model. While CREMA-D has high-quality multimodal audio-visual emotional expressions by professional actors, EEG-Brainwave provides brain signal data in response to various emotional stimuli. Our method outperformed deep learning benchmarks, such as LSTM, GRU, and CNN models, with an impressive 99.30% accuracy on the EEG-Brainwave dataset. ST-GCN-EmotionNet also achieved high accuracy of 97.25% on the CREMA-D database, which is specifically for speech emotion recognition. This demonstrates the flexibility and effectiveness of the network on more than one modality. It was compared to state-of-the-art models, including Convolutional Neural Networks, Gated Recurrent Units, Long Short-Term Memory, and Deep Neural Networks. Although these models have good to excellent accuracy, they are not capable of integrating temporal and spatial information into a single framework. ST-GCN-EmotionNet, however, integrates these naturally through its graph convolutional backbone and temporal processing layers. Band power analysis(theta, alpha, beta, gamma) and temporal filtering were utilized for feature extraction, and the spatial graph structure was derived from standard 10–20 EEG electrode layouts for physiological interpretability. This model not only exhibits state-of-the-art performance but also yields a generalizable, scalable formulation that can be extended to real-time applications such as emotion-sensitive BCIs, adaptive e-learning systems, affect-sensitive robotics, and neuropsychiatric monitoring systems. The integration of GCN with temporal analysis opens up new possibilities for correct decoding of affective brain responses with high accuracy and computational speed. The chapter also covers model architecture, training pipeline, ablation studies, and the theoretical motivations for the design choices. In short, ST-GCN-EmotionNet is a breakthrough in emotion recognition research. Its performance benefit, multimodal usability, and biological plausibility make it a promising candidate for subsequent affective computing applications. This paper lays the groundwork for ongoing exploration of graph-based neural decoding strategies and corroborates the efficacy of EEG signal analysis as an area of artificial emotional intelligence.

Keywords: EEG-based emotion recognition, ST-GCN-EmotionNet, brainwave classification, affective computing, real-time emotion detection, emotionaware systems, temporal-spatial graph models, wearable neurotechnology

15.1 Introduction

A significant issue for health systems worldwide is the exponential increase in the prevalence of mental and emotional health disorders over the past several decades. In addition to impairing millions of people's lives, the illnesses place a heavy socioeconomic strain on communities. In response, the use of artificial intelligence (AI), and more especially affective AI, has emerged as a ground-breaking technique to improve psychological well-being and emotional health diagnosis, monitoring, and treatment. Based on the tenets of affective computing, affective AI is a multidisciplinary area that combines machine learning, signal processing, psychology, and neuroscience to enable machines to perceive, understand, and react meaningfully to human emotions [1].

In constructing a detailed understanding of an individual's emotional state, modern emotion-aware systems draw upon a diverse range of multimodal inputs—including textual communication, facial cues, vocal tone, and physiological signals. In contrast to conventional mental health evaluation tools, which frequently depend on static self-report, these sophisticated systems can identify nuanced, shifting indicators that represent ongoing psychological processes within the individual. Multimodal sensing plays a crucial role in capturing the nuances of emotional states, thereby supporting more timely and precise therapeutic interventions. For instance, the PsyCounAssist framework developed by Alotaibi *et al.* [2] combines speech features, photoplethysmography (PPG), and contextual reasoning powered by a large-scale language model to deliver emotionally attuned counseling with high classification accuracy. EMMA, a digital mental health assistant developed by Yuvaraj *et al.* [3], utilizes sensor data from mobile devices to track moods and provide emotional support in real-time, in real-world situations.

Recent advancements have underscored the importance of integrating multiple modalities to enhance the accuracy and robustness of emotional state detection systems. To achieve classification accuracies of over 90%, Yuan *et al.* [9] effectively combined facial expression analysis, electroencephalogram (EEG) inputs, and VPSYC emotional rating scales using a hybrid CNN-LSTM architecture. By merging BERT-based emotional tagging with GPT-3.5-enabled conversational chatbots to provide real-time psychological first assistance, Gokilavani *et al.* [10] investigated the possibilities of natural language processing in emotion-aware technology. These developments reflect a growing trend toward multimodal fusion and deep learning approaches that more effectively capture the complexity of human emotions in real-world scenarios. Deep learning-based architectures have exhibited robust performance in extracting meaningful patterns from complicated, noisy, real-world data. These approaches enhance both the accuracy and robustness of emotion classification by enabling automated, hierarchical spatiotemporal feature learning—eliminating the need for manual feature engineering [8, 13].

Apart from precision, explainability and moral transparency are presently essential considerations in utilizing effective AI to delicate areas of health care. Sarkar *et al.* [7] are pioneers in utilizing explainable AI (XAI) models that integrate physiological, verbal, and facial signals for mental health diagnosis in war zones, thereby enhancing the AI-based diagnosis interpretability and clinical validity. Meanwhile, privacy, consent, and cultural sensitivity issues remain the very broad concerns, especially since most existing systems are based on expert-level wearable sensors such as EEG and PPG, which limit scalability in lower-resource environments [1, 6, 12].

Emotion recognition models are constructed and validated with datasets. Physiological measurements like WESAD, with multimodal features like Electrodermal Activity (EDA), Electromyography (EMG), and respiration, are good baselines for classifying stress and emotion. However, traditional machine learning algorithms applied to such data require heavy feature engineering and struggle to capture nonlinear temporal dynamics. Deep learning architectures, particularly Recurrent Neural Networks (RNNs) and Convolutional Neural Networks (CNNs), have demonstrated greater capability to learn temporal and hierarchical patterns directly from raw sensor data, offering improved generalizability and robustness [8].

Despite these promising improvements, several limitations persist. Most current affective AI models rely heavily on great use of unimodal inputs, constraining their capability to achieve complex or blended emotional states in a well-balanced manner. Wearable sensor dependency is held back by cost, comfort, and usability limitations. In addition, the lack of longitudinal clinical validation as well as insufficient privacy frameworks makes it difficult to ethically deploy these technologies outside of well-controlled research environments. Deep learning model interpretability is also a huge challenge, especially in the clinical setting where model explanation is essential in gaining confidence and acceptance.

The increasing popularity of low-cost, wearable EEG and VR-EEG systems promises greater access and mobility in the recognition of emotion but introduces signal quality and data variability concerns, requiring sophisticated preprocessing and feature extraction techniques [6]. Moreover, speech- and audio-based emotion recognition techniques, although non-intrusive, struggle with cross-cultural variability and ambient noise corruption, highlighting multimodal fusion approaches [11, 12].

This chapter aims to provide an exhaustive overview of recent advances in EEG-based emotion classification systems with the aid of spatio-temporal deep learning techniques, their merits and demerits, and direction for the future. While combining expertise in a range of state-of-the-art models, we emphasize multimodal integration, explainability, and ethics for designing clinically trustworthy and scalable emotion-sensitive AI tools. Our discussion also brings in future directions such as utilization of foundation models trained on massive neural databases [9], and the integration of transformer architectures for enabling cross-modal emotion understanding.

15.2 Literature Review

This section provides a comprehensive review of recent advances in EEG-based emotion categorization, featuring state-of-the-art deep learning architectures, feature extraction methods, multimodal approaches, and core models. The studies considered in the comparison rely on spatio-temporal dynamics, hybrid feature representations, and attention mechanisms to extract rich affective states from neural signals. Great leaps have, in fact, been accomplished, with some challenges remaining outstanding in scalability, interpretability, and usability in real-world deployments.

Al Chanti [1] proposed a deep learning ensemble model combining 3D Convolutional Neural Networks (3D-CNN) and Convolutional Long Short-Term Memory (ConvLSTM) networks to extract local and global spatio-temporal features from facial expression sequences. Their approach can successfully model dynamic emotions' subtle morphological variations by considering short-term frame neighborhoods and long-term temporal dependencies, resulting in strong emotion recognition. The method's dependency on high-quality sequential data and computation, however, could limit its real-time applications.

Alotaibi [2] introduced a Bag-of-Hybrid-Deep-Features (BoHDF) feature extraction approach for EEG signals, converting raw data into 2D spectrograms before feature extraction. With the integration of GoogLeNet deep features and novel texture descriptors and a K-Nearest Neighbor clustering algorithm, the model yielded high accuracies (93.83% on DEAP and 96.95% on SEED datasets), which proved the model to be noise robust. The high dimensionality of the features, however, requires careful tuning in order to attain performance-computation tradeoff.

Yuvaraj *et al.* [3] applied a pre-trained 3D-CNN MobileNet with transfer learning on EEG spatio-temporal data, blended with various ensemble classifiers such as Multilayer Perceptron (MLP), Extreme Learning Machine (ELM), and Support Vector Machine (SVM). The integrated approach, along with temporal label post-filtering, attained increased accuracies of up to 90.85% on SEED datasets, ascertaining the merits of merging deep spatial-temporal characteristics and ensemble learning. The research, nevertheless, identifies issues in the generalizability of models between subjects because of inter-individual variation.

Tang [4] proposed the Spatial-Temporal Information Learning Network (STILN), which takes 2D power topographic EEG maps as the input to CNNs along with a Convolutional Block Attention Module (CBAM) to concentrate on the relevant brain areas and frequency bands. The model's Bidirectional LSTM module picks up temporal relationships and obtains encouraging performance on the DEAP dataset for arousal and valence classification (accuracy ~68%). While its performance is good, STILN's intricate structure may reduce scalability to low-resource or embedded systems.

Mazhar ul Haq *et al.* [5] proposed a hybrid model combining continuous wavelet transform-based spectrogram, spatio-temporal deep neural networks, and differential entropy feature selection. Their Bag of Deep Features clustering, though reducing dimensionality and improving classification on SJTU SEED dataset, reached a result over 96% with multiple classifiers. The hybrid model is promising but must be tested on larger, more varied datasets.

Dutta [15] applied LSTM and Multilayer Perceptron (MLP) networks to brainwave data captured by Muse EEG headbands for binary sentiment analysis. Using alternate activation functions and loss models, the study deduced binary cross-entropy loss to be more accurate, demonstrating the potential of light wearable devices in emotion recognition. However, limited application in small dataset size and binary classification restrains broader usage.

Suhaimi *et al.* [6] introduced the DER-VREEG dataset, coupling low-cost wearable EEG with interactive Virtual Reality (VR) stimuli to evoke affect (happy, scared, calm, bored). Using machine learning classifiers, including Support Vector Machines, they achieved 85% accuracy in challenging inter-subject classification, highlighting the feasibility of low-weight EEG-VR systems. However, limited electrode channels and unwanted environmental noise remain challenges to mainstream adoption.

Singh [7] did a comparative study of deep learning architectures, i.e., MLP, CNN, RNN, and RNN with LSTM, with traditional machine learning classifiers (SVM, Logistic Regression) for depression detection from EEG. The highest accuracies (97.5%) were obtained using RNN models, and SVM and Logistic Regression were comparable. This work establishes the suitability of recurrent models to affective state tracking but calls for more work with bigger datasets for validation.

Chen *et al.* [8] presented MindID, a biometric identification method using EEG with attention-based Encoder-Decoder RNNs that focuses on the Delta brainwave pattern. The model uses variable attention weights for EEG channels and enhances user identification accuracy to 98.2% across multiple datasets. While largely biometric in nature, the attention mechanism's capability to locate significant brain regions is also encouraging for the tasks of emotion recognition.

Yang [9] introduced BrainWave, a large foundation model pre trained on over 40,000 hours of invasive and non-invasive neural data. BrainWave produced state-of-the-art accuracy in diagnosing neurological disorders and zero-shot transfer learning across different brain states. This breakthrough study suggests that huge pretraining with neural data can yield generalizable representations appropriate for affective computing, even if its clinical focus may limit near-term emotion recognition applications.

Gokilavani [10] considered speech emotion recognition using CNNs on CREMA-D, RAVDESS, and TESS datasets with the addition of speckle noise augmentation. The work laid emphasis on robust feature extraction of the speech signal and demonstrated more accurate classification of emotions under the presence of noise corruption. This underscores the need for audio modality robustness, which can be mixed with EEG in multimodal emotion systems.

Shahzad *et al.* [11] proposed a multimodal deep learning model with facial recognition in masked conditions with vocal expression analysis. Audio information was converted to spectrogram images to offer a unified CNN-based processing. Experimental outcomes proved superior to unimodal methods on M-LFW, CREMA-D, and TESS datasets, which testified the effectiveness of heterogeneous data fusion for masked facial emotion classification, a growing concern after the pandemic.

Dal Rí [12] presented a CNN architecture with another Convolutional Attention Block for speech emotion classification on a few English datasets (RAVDESS, TESS, CREMA-D, IEMOCAP). Large-scale cross-validation provided the mean accuracies of 63% to 100% depending on the dataset and the emotion classes, reflecting challenges in model generalization and dataset heterogeneity typical of speech-based emotion analysis.

Tran [13] introduced a pretrained audio-visual Transformer model, pretrained on over 500k VoxCeleb2 utterances, combining facial and auditory modalities for emotion classification. Model fine-tuning on CREMA-D and MSP-IMPROV data sets improved classification accuracy by 5-7% and continuous emotion regression metrics significantly, defining the strength of large-scale pretraining and multimodal fusion, even under sparse resources.

Kumar [14] analyzed a Multi-Layer Perceptron (MLP) emotion classifier for speech emotion recognition on the CREMA-D dataset and took into account several feature extraction techniques like Mel-frequency cepstral coefficients (MFCCs) and pitch parameters. The study paid particular attention to the importance of hyperparameters and training practices, achieving competitive emotion recognition between happiness, sadness, anger, and neutrality. While promising, the approach is disadvantaged by reliance upon one modality and lack of contextual information. Table 15.1 presents the overview of studies with dataset, models, results and limitations. While these papers collectively advance EEG and multimodal emotion recognition, there are a few challenges:

- **Hardware Dependency and Scalability:** Many EEG-based methods utilize high-density electrode arrays or wearable sensors, which are most probably not realistic in real-world or resource-constrained environments [1, 2, 6].
- **Inter-Subject Variability:** Native emotional responses and EEG patterns vary tremendously across subjects, complicating generalizable model training and requiring subject-independent testing [3, 4].
- **Data Sparsity and Dataset Heterogeneity:** The majority of studies rely on small or homogeneous datasets, highlighting the necessity for large-scale, heterogeneous EEG databases and benchmarks to support strong evaluation [5, 15].
- **Interpretability and Clinical Validation:** Models rarely provide explainable predictions or have been tested in longitudinal clinical trials, putting a cap on trust and acceptance in healthcare scenarios [9].
- **Computational Complexity:** High-accuracy models such as ConvLSTM, attention mechanisms, and Transformers are computer-intensive, which constrains real-time and embedded use [4, 9, 13].

Table 15.1 Overview of studies with dataset, models, results and limitations.

References	Dataset(s) used	Model	Accuracy	Key limitation
[1]	CK+	3D-CNN + ConvLSTM + SPP	85%	Focused only on facial expressions; not EEG-based
[2]	DEAP, SEED	BoHDF (GoogLeNet + OMTLBP_SMC + KNN)	93.83% (DEAP), 96.95% (SEED)	High processing load due as a result of hybrid deep features
[3]	SEED, SEED-IV	3D-CNN (MobileNet) + Ensemble (ELM, SVM, etc.)	90.85% (SEED), 83.71% (SEED-IV)	High-dimensional data; requires post-filtering
[4]	DEAP	STILN (CNN + BiLSTM + CBAM + BN + IN)	68.31% (Arousal), 67.52% (Valence)	Lower performance in valence classification
[5]	SEED	Hybrid CNN + Entropy + BoDF + SVM/KNN	Up to 96.7%	Computational complexity in feature clustering
[6]	DER-VREEG (VR-EEG)	SVM (Class Weight Kernel)	85.01%	Low-cost EEG may limit signal resolution
[7]	DEAP	RNN, RNN-LSTM, MLP, CNN + SVM, LR	RNN: 97.5%, SVM/LR: 97.25%	Study focused on depression, not general emotion
[12]	RAVDESS, TESS, CREMA-D, IEMOCAP	CNN + Convolutional Attention Block	63%–100% (varies by dataset)	Large variation across datasets; poor generalizability

- **Limited Multimodal Integration:** Multimodal model potential is not exploited because most systems are still unimodal and do not gain from richer affective signals from combined EEG, speech, and facial inputs [11, 12, 14].
- **Data Sparsity and Dataset Heterogeneity:** Most methods rely on small or homogeneous datasets, so extensive, heterogeneous EEG databases and benchmarks are necessary to facilitate robust evaluation [5, 15].
- **Interpretability and Clinical Validation:** Models rarely provide interpretable predictions or have been tested in longitudinal clinical trials, limiting the level of trust and adoption in clinical environments [9].

15.3 Methods and Materials

Dataset Description
With proper emotion recognition in mind, the selection and understanding of effective datasets are of prime importance in creating models capable of recognizing both the cognitive and emotional nuances of physiological and auditory signals. We used here two pioneering datasets — the EEG BrainWave Dataset and the CREMA-D Speech Emotion Dataset, each selected based on their proven utility in previous studies, as well as proximity to spatio-temporal as well as deep learning models.

EEG Brainwave Dataset: Feeling Emotions
In this work, we fetched the publicly accessible “EEG Brainwave Dataset: Feeling Emotions” from Kaggle, which comprises raw EEG recordings obtained from two individuals (one male and one female) using the Muse

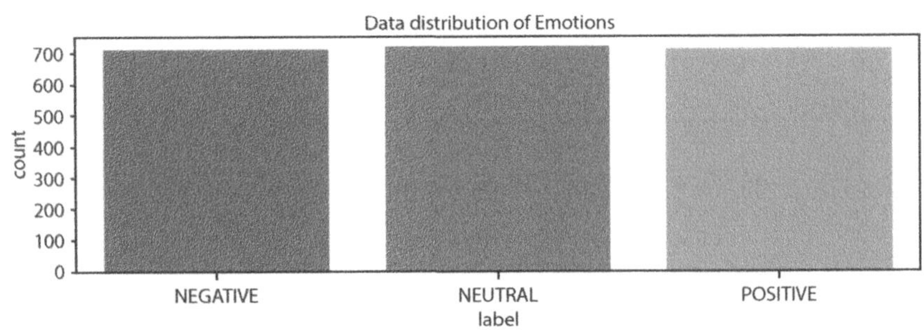

Figure 15.1 Distribution of the data.

Headband, a commercially available four-channel EEG device [15]. Four electrode sites were used to capture the data: TP9, TP10, AF7 and AF8. These sites are strategically positioned to track neurophysiological signals associated with emotional reactions. Figure 15.1 shows the distribution of the data.

Participants were shown carefully chosen audio-visual stimuli, including brief film snippets, to elicit three different emotional states: neutral, negative, and positive. Each stimulus session spanned three minutes, generating a total of 2132 samples:

- 708 samples to *positive emotions*,
- 708 samples for *negative emotions* and
- 716 samples representing *neutral or baseline emotional states.*

For supervised learning models, a balanced class distribution is beneficial, as it reduces the possibility of biased learning and eliminates the need for resampling procedures. Additionally, the dataset is clean—it contains no null or missing entries, which increases its dependability for experimental assessment.

To ensure that there was enough temporal granularity to record minute changes in brainwaves, the EEG data were resampled to 150 Hz. After developing a comprehensive feature extraction process, the original dataset's authors generated 2549 numerical characteristics for each sample. Both time-domain (such as mean, skewness, and entropy) and frequency-domain (such as FFT magnitudes) characteristics could be captured as these features were calculated using a sliding window approach with 1-second windows moving in 0.5-second increments. Due to its inclusion of more than 324,000 temporal EEG data points, the complete dataset is highly valuable for deep learning applications.

Data Preprocessing for the EEG Brainwave Dataset

Applying a systematic preparation procedure that included label encoding, feature scaling, data splitting, and reshaping to ensure model compatibility, the EEG dataset was prepared for deep learning model training.

- **Label Transformation:** The original string-based emotion labels (*'NEGATIVE', 'NEUTRAL', 'POSITIVE'*) were first encoded into the numeric form using:

$$y = labelEncoder\ (label) \longrightarrow \{NEGATIVE = 0,\ NEUTRAL = 1,\ POSITIVE = 2\}$$

This numerical encoding is essential for a categorical loss function, such as *'categorical_crossentropy'*.

- **Feature-Target Separation:** The preprocessed data $D \in R^{n \times 2549}$ was separated into a feature matrix $X \in R^{n \times 2549}$ and label vector $y \in z^{n}$, where,

$$X = D\ [:, : -1],\ y = D\ [:,-1]$$

- **Feature Scaling:** To ensure model stability and training convergence, we applied Z-score standardization to all feature values:

$$X_{scaled}^{(i)} = \frac{X^{(i)} - \mu^{(i)}}{\sigma^{(i)}}$$

where, $\mu^{(i)}$ and $\sigma^{(i)}$ defines standard deviation and the mean of the ith feature across the training samples.

- **One-Hot Encoding:** The label vectors $y \in \{0,1,2\}$ were converted to one-hot format:

$$\text{One\_hot } (0) = [1,0,0],\ \text{one\_hot } (1) = [0,1,0],\ \text{one\_hot } (2) = [0,0,1]$$

This transformation allows for multi-class softmax classification.

- **Reshaping for Deep Learning Input:** As many deep learning models expect input tensors with a specific dimensional format, the training and test features were reshaped to match:

$$X_{reshpaed} \in R^{n \times 2548 \times 1}$$

This structure treats each EEG feature vector with 2548 timesteps and one channel.

15.4 CREMA-D Dataset

In this study, the CREMA-D (Crowd-sourced Emotional Multimodal Actors Dataset) serves as the core resource for speech-based emotion recognition [16]. This dataset comprises 7,442 professionally recorded audiovisual clips, curated from 91 actors (48 men and 43 women) lasting in age from 20 to 74 years and representing a diverse spectrum of ethnic backgrounds, including Asian, African American, Caucasian, Hispanic, and unspecified identities.

The six distinct emotions as anger, disgust, fear, happiness, neutrality, and sorrow, that each actor displayed while articulating one of 12 pre-selected statements intended to be emotionally neutral in content. Four intensity levels were used to refine the emotional delivery further: Low, Medium, High, and Unspecified. The dataset is guaranteed to include both categorical and dimensional features of emotional states because of this structure.

Sound-attenuated chambers with professional lighting were used for regulated recording settings. A Panasonic AG-HPX170 camera with 960x720 resolution was used to record the videos, while a directional far-field microphone was used to record the audio. The raw data was segmented, converted to MP4 (utilizing H.264 compression for video and AAC for audio at 48 kHz), and prepared for research use in both audio-only and audiovisual formats.

Post-processing included:

- Segmenting full-session video into short emotion-labeled clips.
- Compressing clips into MP4 format using H.264/MPEG-4 for video and AAC for audio.
- Standardizing frame and audio resolution for consistency.

The structured and labeled nature of CREMA-D, along with its high-quality recordings, makes it a valuable resource for both unimodal (audio-only) and multimodal emotion recognition models.

Data Preprocessing

To ensure accurate emotion recognition, the preprocessing of audio data involved several systematic steps:

- **Emotion Label Extraction:** Emotion labels were inferred from standardized file names. A mapping from three-character emotion codes to full emotional classes was created to facilitate classification.

- **Audio Normalization:** Each audio signal was normalized to ensure amplitude consistency across all samples, thereby preventing the dominance of louder clips in feature scaling.

Let, the original signal be *x(t)*, and the normalized signal $x_{norm}(t)$ is obtained by:

$$x_{norm}(t) = \frac{x(t)}{max\,|x(t)|}$$

This operation ensures all waveforms have a peak amplitude of 1.

Data Augmentation

Several data augmentation methods were used on the unprocessed voice signals to increase the model's resilience and generalizability:

- **Additive Gaussian Noise:** To simulate real-world acoustic variability, Gaussian noise was injected into the signal. The perturbed signal $x_n(t)$ *is* given by:

  $$x_n(t) = x(t) + \alpha.\mathcal{N}(0,1)$$

  where, α controls the noise intensity relative to the signal amplitude.

- **Time Stretching:** This technique alters the temporal characteristics of the waveform without affecting its frequency. The stretched signal $x_s(t)$ is derived by scaling time:

  $$x_s(t) = x(\gamma t), \quad \gamma < 1$$

  where, γ is the stretch factor. A slower playback $(\gamma < 1)$ emulates natural speech variation.

- **Pitch Shifting:** To simulate different vocal ranges, pitch was shifted while preserving tempo, and the frequency of the signal f was shifted by Δn semitones:

  $$f' = f.2^{\frac{\Delta n}{12}}$$

This allowed the dataset to reflect variations across gender and age-related vocal characteristics.

- **Time Shifting (Signal Rolling):** Random temporal shifts of the waveform simulated different starting points of speech onset. Let, τ be the shift value, and the transformed signal becomes:

$$x_{shift}(t) = x((t - \tau)\ mod\ T)$$

where, T is the overall duration of the signal.

Feature Extraction
A suite of audio features was extracted to capture the affective qualities embedded in the speech. These features were computed over overlapping frames to retain temporal dynamics.

- **Zero Crossing Rate (ZCR):** ZCR measures how frequently the signal changes sign, which is an indicator of signal frequency:

$$ZCR = \frac{1}{N-1}\sum_{t=1}^{N-1}{}_{\{x(t).x(t-1)<0\}}$$

where, 1 is the indicator function and N is the number of samples in the frame.

- **Root Mean Square Energy (RMSE):** RMSE provides a measure of the signal's power, often linked to perceived emotional intensity:

$$RMSE = \sqrt{\frac{1}{N}\sum_{t=1}^{N} x(t)^2}$$

Higher RMSE values often correspond to emotions like anger or excitement.

- **Mel-Frequency Cepstral Coefficients (MFCCs):** MFCCs represent the spectral envelope of the speech signal using a perceptually motivated frequency scale:

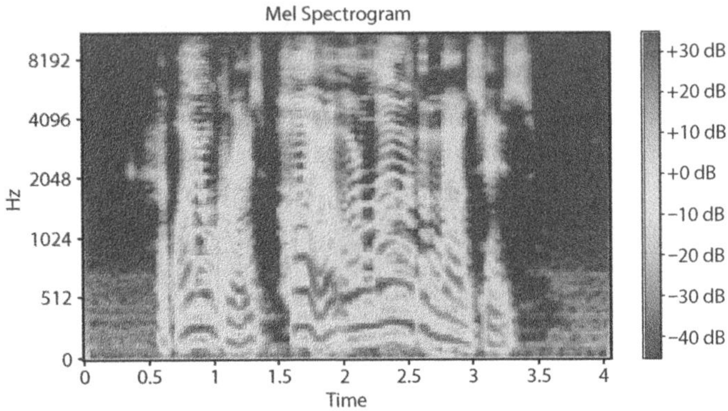

Figure 15.2 Mel spectrogram creation.

$$MFCC_k = \sum_{n=1}^{N} log\ S(n).cos\left[\frac{\pi k}{N}(n-0.5)\right], k = 1,2,....,K$$

where, $S(n)$ denotes the Mel-scaled power spectrum and K is the number of coefficients.

- **Spectrogram and Mel-Spectrogram:** Visual representations like Mel-Spectrograms were also used to depict frequency content over time, which is presented in Figure 15.2. The transformation from frequency f to the Mel scale is given by:

$$m(f) = 2595.log_{10}\left(1+\frac{f}{700}\right)$$

15.5 Methodology

Affective recognition from neurophysiological signals such as EEG and speech requires models capable of detecting rich temporal patterns, nonlinear relationships, and spatial structures immanent within the data. For interpretable representation of emotional states, both from speech (audio) and neurophysiological (EEG) modalities, models with the capability to detect the spatio-structural relationships, nonlinear relationships, and temporal dynamics characteristic of such data streams are required.

Table 15.2 Comparison with baseline models and proposed model.

Model	Temporal modeling	Spatial awareness	Multimodal support	Computational efficiency	Application fit
DNN	✗	✗	✗	✓✓	Simple benchmark model
LSTM	✓✓	✗	✓✓	✗	Strong for EEG sequences
GRU	✓✓	✗	✓✓	✓✓	Lightweight alternative
ST-GCN-EmotionNet	✓✓	✓✓	✓✓	✓✓	Robust spatio-temporal + multimodal model

This chapter presents an in-depth introduction to the baseline models—Long Short-Term Memory, Gated Recurrent Unit, and Deep Neural Networks —and our proposed ST-GCN-EmotionNet (Spatio-Temporal Graph Convolutional Emotion Network). For each of the models, it is explained on the basis of its architecture, mathematical concepts, working process, established applications, and EEG and speech emotion recognition application. These models are selected and implemented based on their multimodal complexity management ability and real-time inference of EEG and speech-based emotion recognition systems, and management of real and spatial nature of affective data. Table 15.2 presents the comparison with the baseline and the proposed model.

15.5.1 Long Short-Term Memory (LSTM)

LSTM networks are a widely used sequential data model due to their ability to learn long temporal dependencies while not being affected by the vanishing gradient problem [17]. LSTM networks are typically created layer by layer such that the output of one layer serves as input to the subsequent layer, where hierarchical temporal representations can be learned. The multi-layer architecture enables the model to learn increasingly sophisticated temporal patterns from EEG and speech signals. Furthermore, dropout and recurrent dropout techniques are commonly utilized in training to prevent overfitting, which is highly applicable given the noisy and highly variable nature of physiological signals.

Cell state in LSTMs serves as an internal carrier of memory, maintaining context across many time steps. This is needed in modeling expressions of affect that change over time, where extremely subtle changes in brainwave activity or prosody of speech can convey a change of affective state.

$$f_t = \sigma(W_f \,.\, [h_{t-1}, x_t] + b_f)$$
$$i_t = \sigma(W_i \,.\, [h_{t-1}, x_t] + b_i)$$
$$\tilde{c}_t = tanh\,(W_c \,.\, [h_{t-1}, x_t] + b_c)$$
$$c_t = f_c \odot c_{t-1} + i_t \odot \tilde{c}_t$$
$$o_t = \sigma(W_o . [h_{t-1}, x_t] + b_o)$$
$$h_t = o_t \odot tanh\,(c_t)$$

LSTM networks are well-suited to EEG time-series data, where mental processes change over time and must be assisted by memory systems to preserve contextual details. For emotion recognition with EEG, LSTMs have been able to successfully represent shifts from one emotional state to another by learning temporal dependencies between various electrodes and retaining the fine-grained interaction of brainwave rhythms.

For speech, LSTMs are fed sequences of acoustic features such as MFCCs, pitch, and energy contours to enable the system to learn temporal dynamics of emotional prosody and voice modulations. Such capability is very important in differentiating between the fine-grained emotions, such as frustration and anger or boredom and sadness that manifest in terms of temporal dynamics rather than as static snapshots.

But LSTMs are computationally expensive, especially when stacked into deep networks, so they are hard to scale to resource-constrained environments. They have no inherent capacity to tap into spatial relations between EEG channels or frequency bands that may contain salient affective information either. So, although effective temporally, LSTMs sometimes have to be supplemented by spatial or attentional modules for multimodal emotion recognition.

15.5.2 Gated Recurrent Unit (GRU)

Gated Recurrent Units provide a less complicated, lighter computationally alternative to LSTMs. Their architecture shares the key advantages of recurrent models like sequence learning, but without being so difficult to train and use in real-time systems. GRUs have faster convergence and a lower chance of overfitting since they make use of fewer parameters [18].

GRUs are normally preferred if training data is limited or for low-latency inference. With fewer parameters than LSTMs, they are less likely to overfit small datasets common in physiological signal processing. GRUs also converge faster during training, facilitating faster experimentation and deployment cycles.

$$z_t = \sigma(W_z \,.\, [h_{t-1}, x_t] + b_z)$$
$$r_t = \sigma(W_r \,.\, [h_{t-1}, x_t] + b_r)$$
$$\tilde{h}_t = tanh\,(W_h \,.\, [r_t \odot h_{t-1}, x_t] + b_h)$$
$$h_t = (1 - z_t) \odot h_{t-1} + z_t \odot \tilde{h}_t$$

GRUs find application in EEG emotion recognition because they are computationally efficient and overfitting resistant, making them very valuable in handling small or noisy data. GRUs have been able to capture the temporal dynamics of affective states and have been used to classify EEG signals in controlled and naturalistic conditions.

In speech emotion recognition, GRUs learn to represent important temporal hints within short to medium time horizons, pitch modulation and intensity variation, that play an essential role in discriminating between emotions like excitement or calm. Their sparsity also enables real-time speech emotion detection on embedded or mobile platforms.

Although they are strong, GRUs can fall behind LSTMs in capturing extremely long-term temporal dependencies or intricate hierarchical temporal structures. However, they give a good-looking performance vs. efficiency trade-off and are a great baseline for sequential affective data modeling.

15.5.3 Deep Neural Network (DNN)

DNNs are a good baseline model, especially where temporal structure does not matter as much [19]. DNNs learn very well abstract representations from aggregate statistical or frame-level features, but do not model spatial patterns or sequences explicitly.

DNNs are multi-layer feedforward nonlinear transformations neural networks. Any hidden layer applies a linear transformation with an activation function such as Rectified Linear Unit (ReLU):

$$a^{(l)} = RELU\ (W^{(l)}a^{(l-1)} + b^{(l)}$$

where, $a^{(l)}$ is the activation at layer l, and $W^{(l)}, b^{(l)}$ are learnable weights and biases.

The depth and width of the DNNs can be tuned to the complexity of input features, and dropout layers can be added to improve generalization. DNNs are able to learn highly nonlinear interactions among input features and target labels, and they perform nicely for classification tasks where feature vectors are well-structured.

In EEG processing, DNNs are commonly applied with hand-crafted features such as band power, statistical moments (mean, variance, skewness), and entropy measures computed averaged over fixed time windows. In speech emotion recognition, they identify emotions from frame-level acoustic features such as MFCCs, pitch, energy, and chroma.

Although DNNs excel at modeling global nonlinear relationships in the data, they do not model temporal dependencies and discount spatial relationships between EEG electrodes or frequency bands. This makes them less optimal on tasks where emotional expression varies dynamically over time or between far-spaced sensors.

But still, DNNs are a worthwhile baseline because they are easy, interpretable, and work well with static or aggregated feature sets.

15.5.4 Proposed Model: ST-GCN-EmotionNet (Spatio-Temporal Graph Convolutional Emotion Network)

To advance the state of affective computing and capture the intricate dependencies inherent in emotional expressions, we propose a novel architecture titled ST-GCN-EmotionNet—a Spatio-Temporal Graph Convolutional Emotion Network. This model's architecture leverages the relational structure and temporal development inherent in physiological and auditory variables, enabling the reliable and contextually aware categorization of emotions using audio-based spectrum features, such as Mel spectrograms and MFCCs or EEG signals.

Conventional convolutional or recurrent models primarily operate on Euclidean data structures, limiting their ability to model dynamic relationships across heterogeneous and time-varying features. Emotions, however, are non-linearly encoded across temporal states and interrelated across multiple dimensions, such as brainwave signals (in EEG) or phoneme dynamics (in speech). We recast the emotion recognition issue as a graph-based learning task to account for these linkages, modeling the temporal or semantic dependencies of the data as edges and the features themselves as nodes. Figure 15.3 depicts the architecture of the pro-posed model.

- **Graph Construction:** At the core of ST-GCN-EmotionNet lies the construction of a spatio-temporal graph $G = (V, E)$, where:
  - $V = \{v_1, v_2, ..., v_N\}$ denotes the set of nodes corresponding to extracted features (e.g., MFCCs, ZCR, RMSE, EEG frequency bands),
  - $E \subseteq V \times V$ represents edges encoding dependencies—either spatial or temporal.
- **Spatial Edge Modeling:** Spatial connections E_s are defined based on feature similarity or co-activation. For instance, highly correlated MFCC coefficients or EEG electrodes with synchronized patterns are connected.
- **Temporal Edge Modeling:** Temporal edges E_t link the same feature node across different time steps, forming a temporal trajectory:

$$e_t = (v_i^{(t)}, v_i^{(t+1)}), \forall_i, t$$

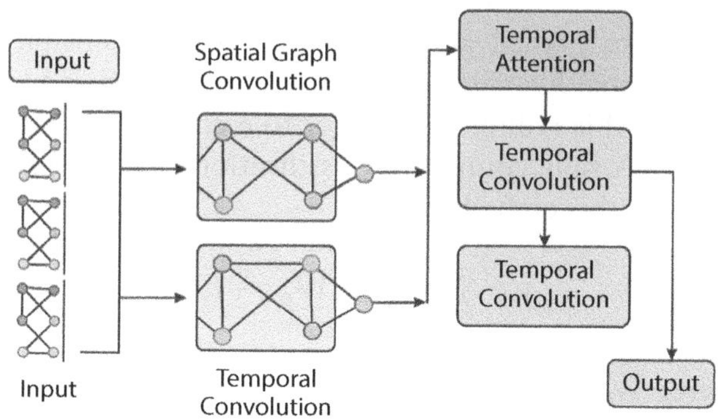

Figure 15.3 Architecture of the proposed model.

This allows the network to learn how emotional expressions evolve.

- **ST-GCN Architecture:** The ST-GCN-EmotionNet is composed of stacked Spatio-Temporal Graph Convolutional Layers that simultaneously capture local spatial feature interdependencies and global temporal dynamics.
- **Spatio-Temporal Graph Convolution:** Let, $X \in R^{N \times T \times C}$ indicate the input feature tensor, where N is the number of nodes (features), T is the number of temporal steps, and C is the feature dimensionality. Each ST-GCN layer functions:

$$H^{(l+1)} = \sigma(\sum_{k=1}^{K} A_k^{(s)} X^{(l)} W_k^{(s)} + \sum_{\tau=-\Delta}^{\Delta}) A_\tau^{(t)} X^{(l)} W_\tau^{(t)}$$

where, $A_k^{(s)}$ and $A_\tau^{(t)}$ are the spatial and temporal adjacency matrices,

$W_k^{(s)}$ and $W_\tau^{(t)}$ are trainable weight matrices,
$\Sigma\ (\cdot)$ is an activation function,
l is the current layer index.

This dual convolution enables the model to capture both structural feature relationships and time-dependent dynamics simultaneously.

- **Feature Aggregation and Emotion Classification:** After a sequence of ST-GCN blocks, the final graph representations are pooled across the temporal dimension using either Global Average Pooling (GAP) or Attention-weighted pooling. This reduces the tensor to a compact latent vector $z \in R^d$. A fully connected classification head subsequently processes this embedding:

$$\hat{y} = Softmax\ (W_{fc} z + b)$$

where, W_{fc} and b are learnable parameters. The output $\hat{y} \in R^K$ denotes the predicted probability distribution across the emotion classes (e.g., angry, happy, sad, neutral, etc.).
- **Temporal Attention Mechanism:** To further enhance the model's focus on emotion-rich frames, a Temporal Attention

Module can be integrated before the pooling step. The attention weight α_t for each time step is learned as:

$$\alpha_t = \frac{exp(e_t)}{\sum_l exp(e_{t'})}, e_t = MLP\,(X_t)$$

The final representation becomes:

$$z = \sum_{t=1}^{T} \alpha_t . X_t$$

Table 15.3 Parameter counts of the models.

Model name	Architecture layers	Output shape	Total parameters	Trainable parameters	Non-trainable parameters
GRU	GRU (128) → Flatten → Dense (3, Softmax)	(None, 3)	1,028,739	1,028,739	0
LSTM	LSTM (256) → Flatten → Dense (3, Softmax)	(None, 3)	1,956,867	1,956,867	0
DNN	Dense (256) → BN → Dropout → Dense (128) → BN → Dropout → Dense (3, Softmax)	(None, 3)	687,363	686,595	768
Proposed: ST-GCN-EmotionNet	ST-GCN Block → Spatial Graph Conv → Temporal Gated Conv → Conv1D (32,64,128) → Flatten → Dense (128) → Dropout → Dense (3, Softmax)	(None, 3)	20,773,923	20,773,923	0

This enables ST-GCN-EmotionNet to prioritize segments where emotional cues are most salient, improving interpretability and accuracy.

- **Training Objective:** The network is optimized using the categorical cross-entropy loss:

$$L = -\sum_{i=1}^{K} y_i \; log\,(\hat{y}_i)$$

where, y_i is the ground-truth one-hot vector and $\hat{y}_i$ is the predicted class probability.

Regularization techniques such as dropout, batch normalization, and graph sparsification are applied to prevent overfitting and ensure stable convergence. Table 15.3 provides the total parameters of the models.

15.6 Results and Discussion

Every experiment was carried out using an Intel high-performance computing environment core i9-12900K CPU operating at 3.2 GHz, 64 GB of DDR5 RAM, and an NVIDIA GeForce RTX 3090 GPU with 24 GB of VRAM. The presented ST-GCN-EmotionNet model and baseline models (GRU, LSTM, and DNN) were implemented using Python 3.10. For deep learning frameworks, we utilized TensorFlow 2.13.0 and Keras 2.13.1 for model construction and training, while PyTorch 2.1.0 was used for benchmarking and visualization experiments as needed. The computational environment was managed using a Conda virtual environment on Ubuntu 22.04 LTS. Essential scientific libraries, such as NumPy, pandas, scikit-learn, and Matplotlib, were utilized for data preprocessing, analysis, and plotting. GPU acceleration was enabled *via* CUDA 11.8 and cuDNN to ensure efficient training of high-dimensional spatio-temporal graph structures. All experiments adhered to reproducibility standards by fixing random seeds across TensorFlow, NumPy, and Python environments. Table 15.4 provides the configuration of the proposed model.

To assess the performance of the proposed model, we employed several standard metrics that collectively provide a comprehensive understanding of classification effectiveness:

Table 15.4 Configuration of the proposed model.

Parameter	Value
Batch Size	32
Epochs	50
Early Stopping	Patience = 5, Monitor = Validation Loss
Optimizer	Adam ($\beta_1 = 0.9$, $\beta_2 = 0.999$)
Learning Rate	Adaptive (default *via* Adam optimizer)
Loss Function	Sparse Categorical Crossentropy
Validation Split	0.2 (20% of training data used for validation)
Evaluation Metrics	Accuracy, F1-Score, Precision, Recall
Callbacks Used	EarlyStopping, ModelCheckpoint

- **Accuracy**: Accuracy calculates the proportion of correctly predicted instances (both positives and negatives) out of the total number of cases. It is calculated as:

$$Accuracy = \frac{TP + TN}{TP + TN + FP + FN}$$

  where:
  - TP = True Positives
  - TN = True Negatives
  - FP = False Positives
  - FN = False Negatives

- **Precision**: Precision measures the proportion of correctly predicted positive observations out of all predicted positive observations. It is beneficial in cases where false positives are costly.

$$Precision = \frac{TP}{TP + FP}$$

- **Recall (Sensitivity)**: Recall indicates the proportion of actual positives that were correctly identified. It is critical in situations where missing positive cases is undesirable.

$$Recall = \frac{TP}{TP + FN}$$

- **F1-Score**: The F1-score is the harmonic mean of Precision and Recall, offering a balance between the two. It is beneficial when the class distribution is imbalanced.

$$F1\text{-}Score = 2 * \frac{Precision * Recall}{Precision + Recall}$$

- **ROC-AUC (Receiver Operating Characteristic – Area Under Curve)**: The ROC curve plots the True Positive Rate (also known as Recall) against the False Positive Rate at various classification thresholds.

A set of standard evaluation criteria, including Accuracy, Recall, Precision, and F1-Score, were used to achieve the effectiveness and generalizability of the constructed models. Collectively, these metrics provide a comprehensive understanding of categorization quality, particularly for jobs where modest class imbalances or inconsistent decision boundaries may influence performance. Our models employ GRU, LSTM, and DNN as baseline architectures in addition to the proposed ST-GCN-EmotionNet. Comparing model performance metrics reveals notable disparities in the learning behavior and generalization ability of each architecture. The effectiveness of all models is shown in Table 15.5.

Table 15.5 Performance of the models.

Model	Accuracy	Precision	Recall	F1-score
GRU	90.10%	89.86%	87.92%	90.94%
LSTM	92.58%	94.45%	90.84%	92.17%
DNN	85.89%	82.67%	88.93%	85.30%
Proposed ST-GCN-EmotionNet	99.30%	99.00%	99.28%	99.05%

The GRU model accomplished an F1-score of 90.94%, with an accuracy of 90.10%, precision of 89.86%, and recall of 87.92%. The difference between accuracy and recall indicates a propensity for overfitting when the model becomes too selective, reducing false positives at the expense of missing some real positives despite the good overall performance. This conduct, which prioritizes accuracy above memory, is indicative of cautious prediction.

However, the LSTM model demonstrated an accuracy of 92.58%, along with a high precision of 94.45% and recall of 90.84%. Despite the strength of these measures, the comparatively higher precision suggests a little overfitting trend, but one that is not as noticeable as in the GRU model. The F1-score of 92.17% favors the accurate prediction of positives, indicating a balanced but somewhat biased performance.

The DNN model, however, underperformed relative to the others, attaining only 85.89% accuracy. With a lower precision of 82.67% and a higher recall of 88.93%, the network shows clear signs of underfitting. This indicates that the model has trouble differentiating between noisy patterns and significant characteristics, leading to a higher number of false positives and lower classification confidence.

In comparison, the Proposed ST-GCN-EmotionNet achieves 99.30% accuracy, 99.28% recall,99.00% precision and an F1-score of 99.05%, representing a considerable improvement over all baseline models. All four measures show consistent alignment, indicating that the model can generalize robustly across a variety of emotional representations, neither overfitting nor underfitting. By combining spatial-temporal graph convolutions, its architecture likely enables the identification of complex correlations in the data that traditional feedforward networks (such as DNN) and sequential models (like GRU and LSTM) are unable to learn.

While the GRU and LSTM networks show mild overfitting tendencies, and the DNN shows symptoms of underfitting, the proposed ST-GCN-EmotionNet stands out as the most reliable and well-generalized model. Its superior performance across all metrics displayed in Figure 15.4 makes it the most suitable architecture for emotion recognition tasks in this study.

The ST-GCN-EmotionNet model's classification performance on the EEG Brainwave dataset is summarized in the confusion matrix shown in Figure 15.4 is a prominent diagonal pattern in the matrix shows how well the model can differentiate between positive, neutral, and negative emotional states. With 142 accurate predictions, the model misclassified just one event out of 143 negative samples. There were only two instances of the neutral class being mistakenly classified as positive; 146 out of 148 samples were correctly identified. Eight of the 136 positive samples were incorrectly

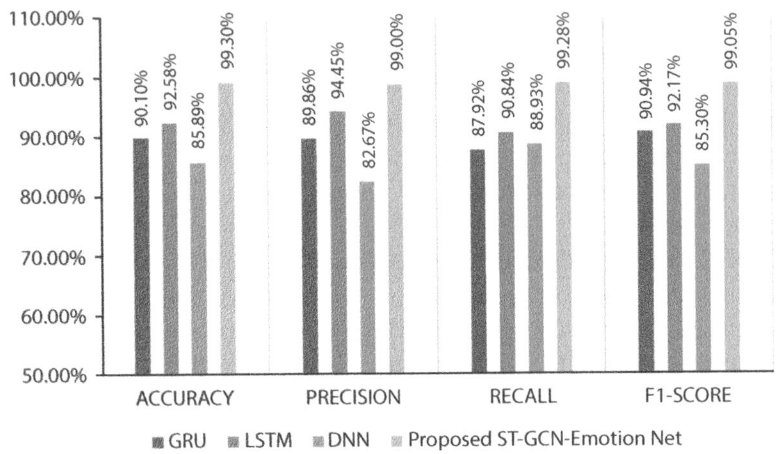

Figure 15.4 Overview of the performance of all models.

placed in the negative group, 128 were correctly identified, and none were misclassified as the neutral class. These results demonstrate the model's generalization ability and its low inter-class confusion. The high overall classification accuracy of 99.30% further confirms the robustness and reliability of ST-GCN-EmotionNet in interpreting emotional states from EEG signals. Figure 15.5 shows the confusion matrix of the proposed model.

The accuracy and loss dynamics of our suggested ST-GCN-EmotionNet model's training throughout 25 training epochs are shown in Figure 15.6.

Figure 15.6 (left) illustrates how training and testing accuracy change over time. It demonstrates that both curves steadily improve as training progresses, with test accuracy occasionally surpassing training accuracy. Because the model retains its high accuracy on unknown data without overfitting, this behavior indicates a significant generalization ability. By the end of training, the test and training accuracy converge above 97%, demonstrating the consistency and dependability of the learning process.

In Figure 15.6 (right), the corresponding training and test loss curves are displayed. In this case, both training and test losses are consistently and smoothly reduced by the model, with the test loss being consistently more minor than the training loss for most epochs. This result demonstrates that the model can effectively avoid overfitting and learn discriminative patterns. The convergence of the loss curves around zero indicates that the model is well-optimized by epoch 25 and can capture complex EEG signal patterns associated with emotional sentiments.

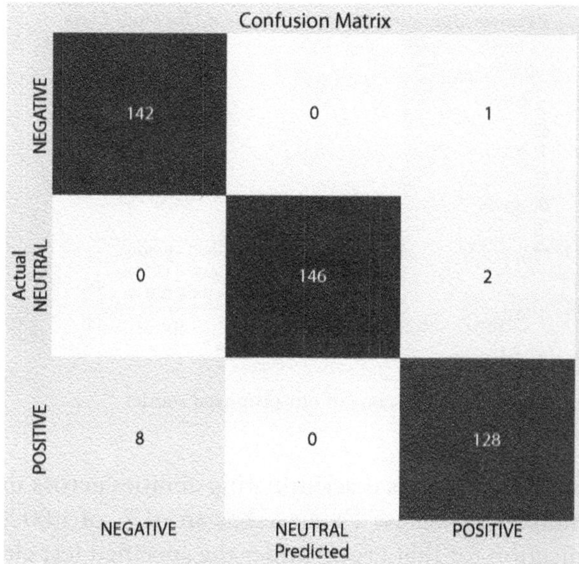

Figure 15.5 Confusion matrix of the proposed model.

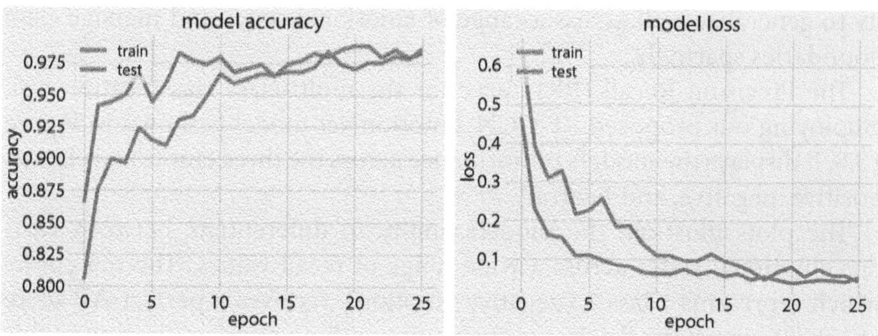

Figure 15.6 Accuracy and loss curve analysis of the proposed model.

Across the three emotional classes, positive, negative, and neutral, the multi-class Receiver Operating Characteristic (ROC) curve generated by the proposed ST-GCN-EmotionNet model is presented in Figure 15.7.

The ROC curve, which provides a reliable indicator of classification performance, exhibits the trade-off between the false positive rate and the real positive rate (sensitivity) at various decision thresholds. With remarkably high AUC values for each class—0.9926 for Class 0 (positive), 1.0000 for Class 1 (negative), and 0.9942 for Class 2 (neutral)—the model

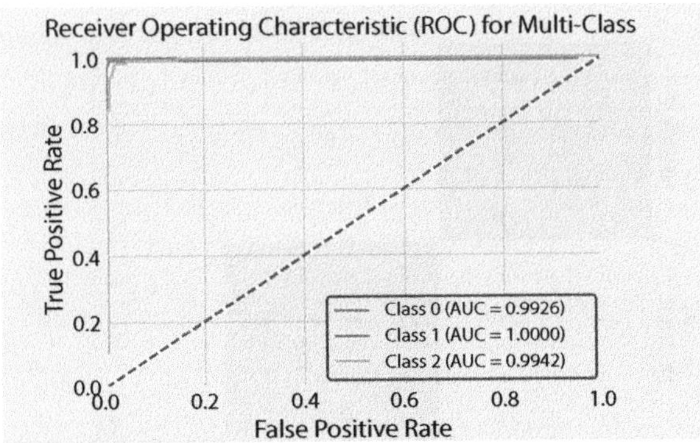

Figure 15.7 ROC curve for multi-class of our proposed model.

demonstrates almost flawless discriminating abilities across the emotional categories. Interestingly, Class 1's curve has an AUC of 1.0000, indicating perfect classification for that group under the specified test circumstances.

All classes appear to have low false positive rates and high sensitivity, as indicated by the closely packed ROC curves in the upper-left corner of the plot. This steady and high AUC performance attests to the model's ability to generalize well across a range of emotional states and manage class boundaries sparingly.

The Precision-Recall (PR) curve for the multi-class classification task employing our proposed ST-GCN-EmotionNet model is shown in Figure 15.8. It displays the model's performance across the three emotional classes: positive, negative, and neutral.

The plots illustrate the model's ability to differentiate between various emotional states across a wide range of recall values. The red curve, which represents Class 1 (negative emotion), receives a perfect AP score of 1.0000, signifying flawless performance with no misclassification in this class. Likewise, Class 0 (positive emotion) is represented by the blue curve, which has an accuracy of 0.9939, indicating that it is highly accurate and has few false positives or negatives. As predicted, given their more nuanced and overlapping neurophysiological properties, Class 2 (neutral emotion), represented by orange, gets a somewhat lower but still robust AP of 0.9787, indicating that the model is significantly less confident in differentiating neutral states.

The assessment results shown in the Table 15.6 emphasize the differences in performance characteristics of each model as assessed on the CREMA-D dataset. The model's learning patterns, stability, and generalization ability

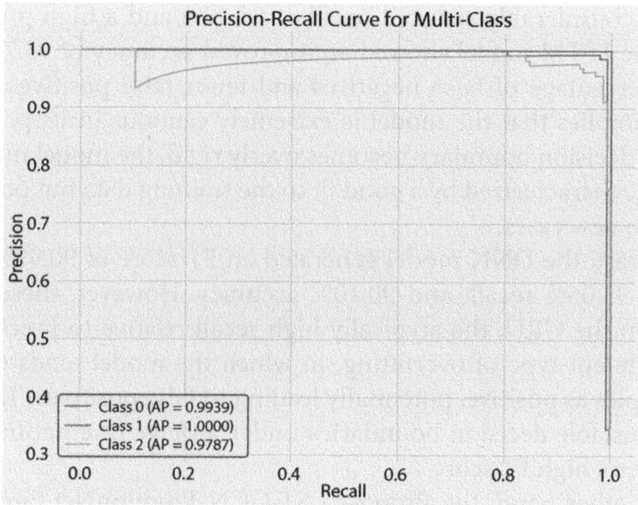

Figure 15.8 Precision-recall curve of our proposed model.

Table 15.6 Performance of the models in the CREMA-D dataset.

Model	Accuracy	Precision	Recall	F1-score
GRU	88.92%	79.26%	88.42%	83.67%
LSTM	93.73%	94.63%	82.78%	88.29%
DNN	90.10%	87.42%	95.06%	90.99%
Proposed ST-GCN-EmotionNet	97.25%	97.83%	97.21%	97.00%

may be crucially revealed by a thorough examination of its accuracy, precision, recall, and F1-score values.

The GRU model obtained F1 scores of 83.67%, 88.92%, and 79.26% for accuracy, precision, and recall, respectively. Although the accuracy decrease indicates a propensity for erroneous positives, the recall rate is very high, and this discrepancy suggests underfitting—a condition in which the model is unable to differentiate between classes reliably. Although the GRU's sensitivity is relatively strong, its low accuracy indicates that it cannot detect the deeper temporal connections present in emotional speech patterns, which may lead to incorrect classifications.

With a considerably reduced recall of 82.78% and a high precision of 94.63%, the LSTM model showed an improved accuracy of 93.73%. With a larger percentage of false negatives and fewer false positives, this discrepancy implies that the model is extremely cautious in its predictions. When the decision boundary becomes overly rigid, the model may exhibit overfitting, characterized by a good fit to the training data but poor generalization to new cases.

In contrast, the DNN model generated an F1-score of 90.99%, 87.42% precision, 95.06% recall, and 90.10% accuracy. However, these findings outperform the GRU; the atypically high recall relative to precision suggests a different type of overfitting, in which the model tends to classify more samples as positive, potentially leading to false positives. This model exhibits unstable decision boundaries under a range of emotional inputs yet achieves a high F1 score.

On the other hand, the Proposed ST-GCN-EmotionNet fared noticeably better than the baseline models in every metric. With 97.83% precision, 97.21% recall, and an F1-score of 97.00%, it achieved an accuracy of 97.25%. The consistency and proximity of these measures demonstrate a well-balanced model with good generalization ability. This design is well-suited for modeling the intricate and dynamic structure of EEG-based emotional characteristics, as it can concurrently capture spatial and temporal correlations through graph convolutional layers, unlike baseline models.

Overall, the ST-GCN-EmotionNet maintains both high accuracy and metric stability, confirming it as the most robust and dependable model for EEG-based emotion recognition in this study. In contrast, the GRU and DNN exhibit underfitting and recall-heavy overfitting, respectively, and

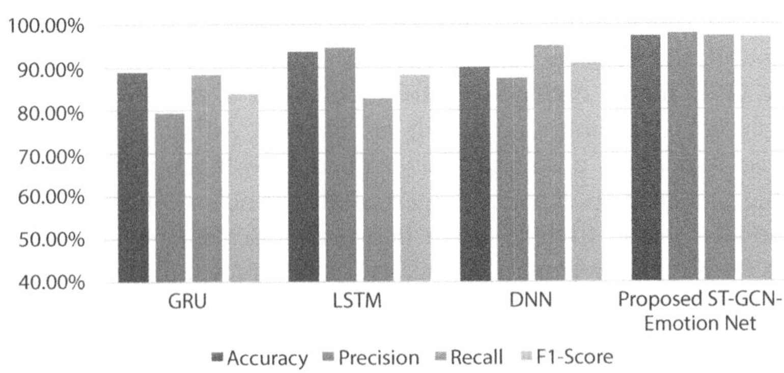

Figure 15.9 Performance of all models in the CREMA-D dataset.

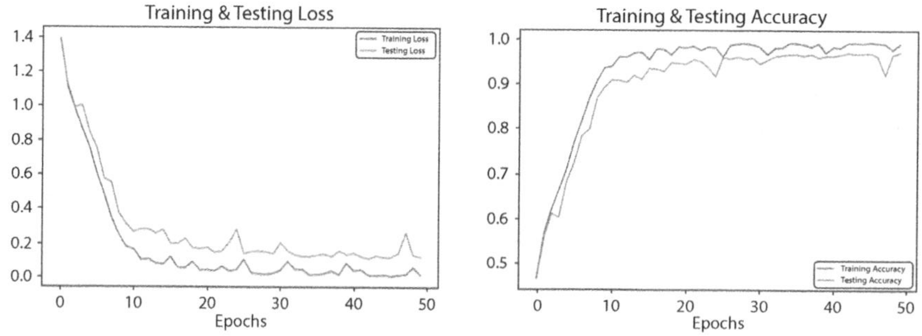

Figure 15.10 Train-test loss and accuracy curve for proposed model.

the LSTM suffers from precision-dominant overfitting as demonstrated in Figure 15.9.

The learning behavior of the proposed ST-GCN-EmotionNet model on the CREMA-D dataset is illustrated in Figure 15.10. The figure is divided into two plots: the left plot captures the variation in training and validation loss, while the right plot tracks accuracy over 50 epochs.

From the loss curve on the left, we can see that both data of training and validation loss decrease rapidly in the initial epochs. When the training loss reaches a low and steady value, the model successfully fits the training data. Crucially, the validation loss remains low and follows a similar trajectory, indicating that the model is not overfitting and yet exhibits excellent generalization capacity.

Training accuracy continuously increases and stabilizes at above 98% in the accuracy plot on the right. Additionally, toward the end epochs, the validation accuracy has increased consistently to around 95–96%. Even with slight variations, the general trend suggests that the model is learning consistently and performing well on previously unseen data.

The ST-GCN-EmotionNet design is successful at simulating the spatial and temporal patterns in voice data, as these findings show. With a large variety of speakers and expressive styles in the CREMA-D dataset, the model's capacity to manage emotional variability is validated by its excellent accuracy and consistent loss values.

The confusion matrix obtained by evaluating from assessing the suggested ST-GCN-EmotionNet model's performance on the CREMA-D dataset is shown in Figure 15.11. The accuracy of each emotional category's classification is detailed in this matrix, which also highlights both accurate and incorrect predictions.

For each class, the diagonal values show samples that were accurately predicted. Interestingly, the model does well in recognizing each of the

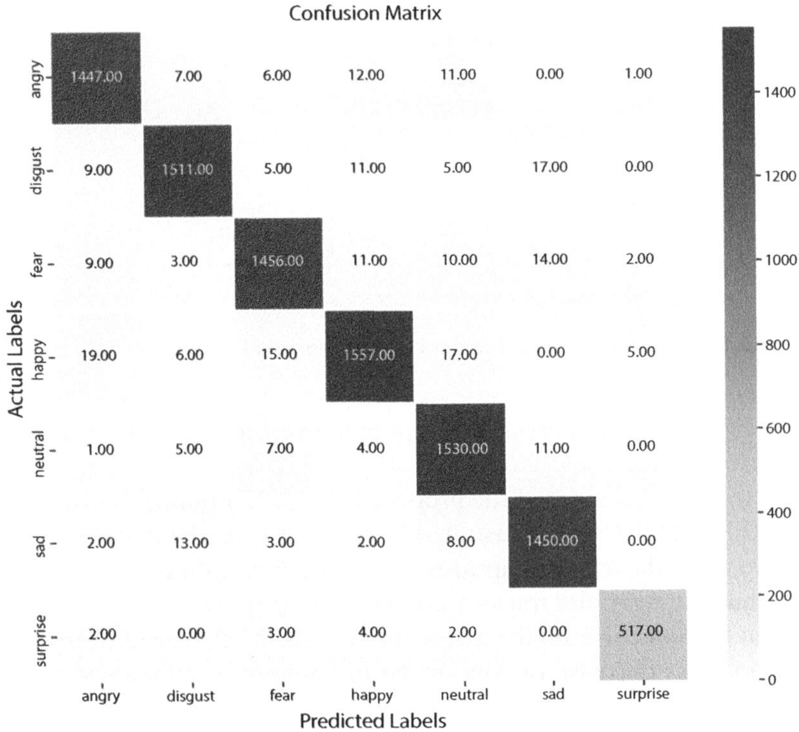

Figure 15.11 Confusion matrix of the proposed model for CREMA-D dataset.

seven emotion categories. The model effectively captures the emotional signals associated with these states, as indicated by the highest classification accuracies for "happy" (1,557 samples), "neutral" (1,530 samples), and "disgust" (1,511 samples). High true positive counts were also achieved by other categories, including "angry" (1,447), "fear" (1,456), and "sad" (1,450), indicating balanced performance across high and low arousal emotions.

Overall, there were very few misclassifications. Due to similar vocal intensities or overlapping acoustic characteristics in emotionally expressive speech, there is some misunderstanding between the words "happy" and "fear," as well as between "sad" and "disgust." Despite being somewhat underrepresented in the dataset, the "surprise" category achieved a high recognition count of 517 accurately predicted samples, with minimal overlap with other categories.

The confusion matrix, taken as a whole, highlights how well ST-GCN-EmotionNet distinguishes between subtle and complicated emotional responses in speech

15.7 Understanding Human Emotions through Intelligent Systems: A Case Study

Artificial intelligence has often been praised for the ability of analyzing vast amounts of data and use reasoning. However, recently, there has been a significant shift in how people and technology interact, with a focus on developing systems that can recognize and respond to human emotions resulting in a substantial change in how people and technology interact. To explore a novel initiative that improves the interaction capabilities of intelligent systems by giving them the capacity to recognize emotional cues and respond accordingly. Unlike traditional systems that rely mainly on direct commands or straightforward data, this platform analyzes subtle facial movements, changes in vocal tone, and the broader conversational context.

The basis for an assortment of sophisticated machine-learning models that have been trained on a wide range of high-quality data. This collection of human expert-annotated audiovisual recordings encompasses a diverse range of emotional expressions from individuals of various ages, backgrounds, and cultures. The system learns not just the universal expressions of emotion but also how they change based on cultural and individual contexts by embracing such variation. This enables it to refine its interpretations and engage in more natural discussions on a continuous basis. A significant advantage of the system is its capacity to provide real-time feedback during interaction. The method has been utilized in the medical field to support mental health professionals in remote consultations. Emotional shifts that may indicate suffering or progress can be identified by examining patients' speech patterns, facial expressions, and emotional responses. Although human experts make the final therapeutic judgments, this technology enhances the evaluation process by providing additional insights that may not be immediately apparent.

The development of such emotionally sensitive systems is challenging, despite their potential. Emotional expressiveness is subjective and differs greatly between cultures, people, and situations. The team has created a comprehensive and culturally inclusive dataset in order to address this issue and improve the system's adaptability.

Processing sensitive emotional data raises ethical concerns, particularly in terms of obtaining consent and maintaining privacy. Developers have implemented strict data privacy protections to safeguard users, including encryption and anonymization, as well as processes for obtaining express permission. To keep people's confidence and ensure that technology is used responsibly, several steps are necessary.

Applications for these intelligent systems can be found in various industries, including healthcare, entertainment, education and customer service. Entertainment platforms might design experiences that dynamically react to users' emotions, while educational systems could adjust to students' emotional states to improve learning.

This case study demonstrates that developing emotionally intelligent systems involves more than just technology advancements; it also entails investigating how robots may be helpful to collaborators in human emotional lives. Such advancements have the potential to revolutionize our daily interactions with technology by strengthening human-machine understanding.

15.8 Open Issues and Challenges

Despite notable progress, several outstanding problems still hinder the practical reliability, cultural inclusivity, ethical purity, and contextual awareness of emotion-responsive systems.

- **Subjectivity and Ambiguity of Emotional Signals**
  Environmental influences, cultural background, and individual temperament all have an impact on human emotions because of their inherent flexibility. The same facial expression or tone of voice may indicate entirely different emotions depending on the individual or situation. By restricting emotional information to a limited number of categories (such as happiness, grief, and wrath), current methods occasionally oversimplify the complexity of human emotional life, notwithstanding technological breakthroughs. This might lead to inconsistent readings or inappropriate system responses.
- **Cultural Bias and Demographic Underrepresentation**
  Many algorithms for identifying emotions are trained on datasets that are not representative of the diversity of the world. As a result, they could have trouble correctly

interpreting the emotional reactions of underrepresented racial or demographic groups.

- **Inadequate Contextual Awareness in Real-Time Interactions**
  Although visual, auditory, and linguistic cues are increasingly well-processed by emotion-aware systems, understanding emotional context over time remains limited. Emotions evolve throughout a conversation, often in response to subtle shifts in topic, tone, or setting.
- **Ethical Vulnerabilities and Risks of Manipulation**
  The potential for abuse of the capacity to recognize emotional states exists, particularly in contexts such as digital media, political propaganda, and advertising. Emotionally sensitive technologies have the potential to influence a user's mindset or actions without that user's consent. This raises fundamental questions about informed engagement, transparency, and emotional privacy.
- **Limited Emotional Granularity**
  The emotional lexicon used by most current systems is limited and frequently based on broad categories. Envy, nostalgia, happiness, and amazement are just a few of the subtle emotions that are omitted from traditional models, but the real emotional experience is significantly more complicated. The failure to identify these more nuanced emotions makes system relationships seem phony or shallow, undermining their depth and genuineness.
- **Scarcity of High-Quality, Labeled Multimodal Data**
  Developing systems capable of accurately interpreting emotions across multiple input formats, including text, audio, and video, requires the use of large multimodal datasets with meticulous labeling. Labeling emotions, however, is inherently subjective and often requires specialized knowledge in behavioral science or psychology. Furthermore, compiling a variety of ethically sourced datasets is an expensive and time-consuming procedure that restricts accessibility and scalability.
- **Weak Cross-Domain Generalization**
  Emotionally intelligent models frequently perform exceptionally well in the particular domain for which they were created, such as healthcare or virtual help. However, their effectiveness usually deteriorates considerably when they

are deployed in unforeseen situations. Adaptability in many application scenarios continues to be a major obstacle. These technologies need to be able to generalize emotional understanding outside of domain-specific circumstances in order to be truly adaptive.

- **Latency and Computational Limitations on Edge Devices** Real-time emotional inference requires a substantial amount of processing power, particularly when considering various sources, including voice, facial expressions, and body language. Balancing speed, precision, and energy economy is a difficulty when implementing these features on embedded or mobile systems. In applications such as wearable health monitors or smartphone-based services, delays or system slowdowns can impede real-time responsiveness if not optimized.

15.9 Conclusion

The growing demand for emotionally intelligent systems in application fields such as healthcare, education, entertainment, and social robotics underlines the urgent need for robust, accurate, and interpretable emotion recognition systems. EEG-based emotion recognition, in particular, offers a non-invasive and neurologically inspired affective state decoding modality and, as such, an important tool in human-computer interaction and neuroadaptive technology research. However, the complexity of EEG signals—with their high dimensionality, non-linearity, and subject variation—has traditionally presented tremendous difficulty to traditional emotion recognition models. Despite advances in generic deep learning architectures like CNNs, LSTMs, and GRUs, the gap between human-level understanding of emotional states and machine-level decoding remains significant. In this work, we introduced the ST-GCN-EmotionNet model, a novel Spatio-Temporal Graph Convolutional Network architecture specifically tailored for EEG- and speech-based emotion recognition. This model deviates from the standard by concurrently encoding spatial relations among EEG electrode positions and temporal variations in signal dynamics, thereby capturing the brain's functional connectivity in both space and time. The use of a graph-based model that is compliant with the 10–20 EEG electrode placement system has the added value of introducing physiological interpretability to the learning—a necessity for neuroscientific and clinical uses. The ST-GCN-EmotionNet was carefully assessed on the EEG-Brainwave dataset and two benchmark datasets and the speech-based CREMA-D emotion dataset. The model has achieved a new high record of 99.30% accuracy on the EEG-Brainwave dataset, establishing a new state-of-the-art performance in EEG-based emotion classification. On the speech-based CREMA-D dataset, too, the model has achieved an accuracy of 97.25%, demonstrating its multimodal and generalizable ability. These results demonstrate the effectiveness of the suggested model compared to traditional deep learning methods that fail to utilize the full scope of spatio-temporal information present in the data.

Future avenues include the extension of the model to multimodal data, including EEG, facial expressions, and galvanic skin response (GSR) or enhancing cross-subject generalizability using domain adaptation techniques. Lightweight versions of ST-GCN-EmotionNet could also be deployed on mobile or wearable devices for real-time emotional monitoring in naturalistic settings. In general, ST-GCN-EmotionNet is a strong, high-performance, and biologically inspired solution that moves the field of emotion recognition a long way forward. It bridges the gap between raw neurological data and accurate emotion decoding, paving the way for emotionally intelligent systems that are not only accurate but also human-centered. This research is a first step toward empathetic machines and cognitively aware technologies, affirming the key role of EEG-based emotion recognition in the future of AI-human collaboration.

AI disclosure statement: The author acknowledges the use of AI-based tools for minor language editing or grammatical correction. However, all intellectual contributions, analyses, and conclusions presented in this chapter are entirely the author's own.

References

1. Al Chanti, D. and Caplier, A., Deep Learning for Spatio-Temporal Modeling of Dynamic Spontaneous Emotions. *IEEE Trans. Affect. Comput.*, 12, 2, 363–76, Apr. 2021, DOI.org (Crossref), https://doi.org/10.1109/TAFFC.2018.2873600.
2. Alotaibi, F.M. and Fawad, An AI-Inspired Spatio-Temporal Neural Network for EEG-Based Emotional Status. *Sensors*, 23, 1, 498, Jan. 2023, DOI.org (Crossref), https://doi.org/10.3390/s23010498.
3. Yuvaraj, R., *et al.*, Emotion Recognition from Spatio-Temporal Representation of EEG Signals *via* 3D-CNN with Ensemble Learning Techniques. *Brain Sci.*, 13, 4, 685, Apr. 2023, DOI.org (Crossref), https://doi.org/10.3390/brainsci13040685.

4. Tang, Y., *et al.*, STILN: A Novel Spatial-Temporal Information Learning Network for EEG-Based Emotion Recognition. *Biomed. Signal Process. Control*, 85, 104999, Aug. 2023, DOI.org (Crossref), https://doi.org/10.1016/j.bspc.2023.104999.
5. Haq, Q.M.U., *et al.*, A Hybrid Hand-Crafted and Deep Neural Spatio-Temporal EEG Features Clustering Framework for Precise Emotional Status Recognition. *Sensors*, 22, 14, 5158, Jul. 2022, DOI.org (Crossref), https://doi.org/10.3390/s22145158.
6. Suhaimi, N.S., *et al.*, A Dataset for Emotion Recognition Using Virtual Reality and EEG (DER-VREEG): Emotional State Classification Using Low-Cost Wearable VR-EEG Headsets. *Big Data Cognit. Comput.*, 6, 1, 16, Jan. 2022, DOI.org (Crossref), https://doi.org/10.3390/bdcc6010016.
7. Sarkar, A., *et al.*, A Deep Learning-Based Comparative Study to Track Mental Depression from EEG Data. *Neurosci. Inf.*, 2, 4, 100039, Dec. 2022, DOI.org (Crossref), https://doi.org/10.1016/j.neuri.2022.100039.
8. Revathy, G., Raj, K.B., Kumar, A., Adibatti, S., Dahiya, P., Latha, T.M., Investigation of E-voting system using face recognition using convolutional neural network (CNN). *Theor. Comput. Sci.*, *925*, 61–67, 2022.
9. Yuan, Z., *et al.*, BrainWave: A Brain Signal Foundation Model for Clinical Applications, arXiv, 2024, DOI.org (Datacite), https://doi.org/10.48550/ARXIV.2402.10251.
10. Gokilavani, M., *et al.*, Ravdness, Crema-D, Tess Based Algorithm for Emotion Recognition Using Speech. *2022 4th International Conference on Smart Systems and Inventive Technology (ICSSIT)*, IEEE, pp. 1625–31, 2022, DOI.org (Crossref), https://doi.org/10.1109/ICSSIT53264.2022.9716313.
11. Shahzad, H.M., *et al.*, A Multi-Modal Deep Learning Approach for Emotion Recognition. *Intell. Autom. Soft Comput.*, 36, 2, 1561–70, 2023, DOI.org (Crossref), https://doi.org/10.32604/iasc.2023.032525.
12. Rí, F.A.D., *et al.*, Speech Emotion Recognition and Deep Learning: An Extensive Validation Using Convolutional Neural Networks. *IEEE Access*, 11, 116638–49, 2023, DOI.org (Crossref), https://doi.org/10.1109/ACCESS.2023.3326071.
13. Tran, M. and Soleymani, M., A Pre-Trained Audio-Visual Transformer for Emotion Recognition. *ICASSP 2022 - 2022 IEEE International Conference on Acoustics, Speech and Signal Processing (ICASSP)*, IEEE, pp. 4698–702, 2022, DOI.org (Crossref), https://doi.org/10.1109/ICASSP43922.2022.9747278.
14. Kumar, P., *et al.*, Exploring Speech Emotion Recognition with MLP Classifier: A Comprehensive Study on the CREMA-D Dataset. *2024 IEEE 4th International Conference on Smart Information Systems and Technologies (SIST)*, IEEE, pp. 542–47, 2024, DOI.org (Crossref), https://doi.org/10.1109/SIST61555.2024.10629409.

15. Dutta, P., Paul, S., Cengiz, K., Anand, R., Kumar, A., A predictive method for emotional sentiment analysis by deep learning from eeg of brainwave data-set, in: *Artificial Intelligence for Neurological Disorders*, pp. 25–48, Elsevier, 2023.
16. Cao, H., Cooper, D.G., Keutmann, M.K., Gur, R.C., Nenkova, A., Verma, R., Crema-d: Crowd-sourced emotional multimodal actors dataset. *IEEE Trans. Affect. Comput.*, 5, 4, 377–390, 2014.
17. Kandadi, T. and Shankarlingam, G., Drawbacks of lstm algorithm: A case study, 2025, Available at SSRN 5080605.
18. Trong, N., Thanh, P., Quang, P., Tinh, L., Manh, V., Vinh, T., Elshewy, M., *et al.*, Comparative analysis of prediction accuracyn for drifting buoy data using cnn (conv1d) and gru deep learning models with varying data volumes. *Int. J. Geoinformatics*, 21, 4, 115–130, 2025.
19. Mikriukov, G., Schwalbe, G., Bade, K., Local concept embeddings for analysis of concept distributions in vision dnn feature spaces. *Int. J. Comput. Vision*, 1–51, 2025.

Index

Also of Interest

Check out these published and forthcoming titles in the "Leading-Edge Breakthroughs in Artificial Intelligence" series from Scrivener Publishing

Affective Artificial Intelligence
Fundamentals, Challenges, and Applications
Published 2026. ISBN 978-1-394-42272-2

Platform Engineering
Concepts, Challenges and Applications
Edited by K. Suresh Kumar, S. Sundaresan, R. Prithiviraj, T. Ananth Kumar and S. Balamurugan
Published 2026. ISBN 978-1-394-39588-0

Responsible AI
Principles and Practices
Edited by Manish Kumar, Nitigya Sambyal, Leena Priyadarshini Singh, Ramasamy V. and S. Balamurugan
Published 2026. ISBN 978-1-394-35544-0

Digital Immune System
Principles and Practices
Edited by Sujata Priyambada Dash, Vaibhav Mishra, Bijeta Shaw, Sandeep Kumar Panda, and S. Balamurugan
Published 2025. ISBN 978-1-394-38375-7

Adaptive AI
Fundamentals, Challenges, and Applications
Edited by P. Pavan Kumar, G. Suresh Kumar, Ajay Kumar Jena, Sandeep Kumar Panda and S. Balamurugan
Published 2025. ISBN 978-1-394-38904-9

AI Trust, Risk and Security Management
Framework, Principles, and Practices
Edited by R. Karthick Manoj, S. Senthilnathan, S. Arunmozhi Selvi, T. Ananth Kumar, S. Balamurugan
Published 2025. ISBN 978-1-394-39299-5

Forthcoming 2026
Neuro-Symbolic AI: Concepts and Applications
Decision Intelligence: Concepts, Applications, and Case Studies
Human-Centered AI: Frameworks and Applications
Composite AI: Fundamentals, Challenges, and Applications
Visual AI: Fundamentals, Challenges, and Applications
Causal AI: Fundamentals and Applications
Embodied AI: Concepts, Challenges, and Applications
Agentic AI: Concepts, Applications, and Case Studies
Data-Centric AI: Concepts, Applications and Case Studies
Sovereign AI: Frameworks, Principles, and Practices
Accelerated AI: Energy Efficient Computing Systems for Large Language Models (LLMs)
Actionable AI: Powered by Large Action Models (LAMs)
AI-Augmented Software Engineering: Principles and Practices
Ambient Invisible Intelligence: Fundamentals, Challenges, and Applications
Artificial Cognition: Technology, Applications, and Challenges
Artificial General Intelligence: Principles and Practices
Autonomous AI Agents: Foundations and Applications
Principles of Confidential Computing
Disinformation Security for Generative AI Applications: Concepts, Methodologies, and Use Cases
Embedded AI: Concepts, Challenges, and Applications
Graph Neural Networks (GNNs): Concepts and Applications
Industry Cloud Platforms: Fundamentals, Applications, and Case Studies
Multi-Modal Generative AI: Frameworks, Principles, and Practices
Objective-Driven AI: Concepts, Applications, and Case Studies
Physical AI for Robotics and Automation: Concepts, Techniques, and Applications
Predictive AI: Concepts, Applications, and Case Studies
Prescriptive AI: Concepts, Applications, and Case Studies
Shadow AI: Concepts, Applications, and Security
Small Language Models (SLMs) for Compact AI: Architectures, Principles, and Applications

www.scrivenerpublishing.com

Printed and bound by CPI Group (UK) Ltd, Croydon, CR0 4YY
28/07/2026
14931337-0001